PUBLIC MANAGEMENT
IN THE STATES

PUBLIC MANAGEMENT IN THE STATES

A Comparative Study of
Administrative Performance
and Politics

RICHARD C. ELLING

PRAEGER

Westport, Connecticut
London

Library of Congress Cataloging-in-Publication Data

Elling, Richard C.
   Public management in the states : a comparative study of
administrative performance and politics / Richard C. Elling.
      p.   cm.
   Includes bibliographical references and index.
   ISBN 0–275–93432–2 (alk. paper)
   1. State governments—United States—Case studies.   I. Title.
JK2408.E43   1992
353.9—dc20   92–15784

British Library Cataloguing in Publication Data is available.

Library of Congress Catalog Card Number: 92–15784
ISBN: 0–275–93432–2

First published in 1992

Praeger Publishers, 88 Post Road West, Westport, CT 06881
An imprint of Greenwood Publishing Group, Inc.

Printed in the United States of America

The paper used in this book complies with the Permanent
Paper Standard issued by the National Information Standards
Organization (Z39.48–1984).

10 9 8 7 6 5 4 3 2 1

In memory of my father, Clement Ernst Elling (1915–63);
and my Wayne State University colleagues
Ann Workman Sheldon (1926–91),
and C. Dale Vinyard (1932–90).

From each I learned so much, and each was gone too soon.

Contents

Figures and Tables

FIGURES

TABLES

Acknowledgments

Anyone who has undertaken a research project that extends over a number of years finds it virtually impossible to acknowledge all who have contributed to bringing such a project to fruition. I thus apologize to anyone whose contributions are ignored in what follows. My greatest debt is to the more than 800 state administrators who took the trouble to carefully respond to my lengthy survey. I hope that at least some of them will find this book to be useful.

The collection of much of the data on which this book is based was facilitated by a Faculty Research Grant from Wayne State University. Two additional smaller grants from the university's Office of Research and Sponsored Programs greatly speeded the preparation of the final manuscript. A former chair of the Wayne State University Department of Political Science, Professor Bryan Jones, along with the department's current chair, Professor Charles Elder, also provided various kinds of support.

The task of coding a substantial portion of the survey data that constitute the basis for Chapters 2, 3, and 4 was executed in splendid fashion by an exceptional Wayne State undergraduate and—now—political science doctoral student, Mark Glenn. Various members of the support staff of the Wayne State University Department of Political Science also made significant contributions. These include Linda Laird, Nancy Kaminski, Patricia Abbott, and, most especially, Sharon Flowers, who ably typed all of the tables for the book.

I also want to acknowledge the helpful suggestions of panel discussants or manuscript reviewers concerning those pieces of this book that were originally presented in other settings. The latter portion of Chapter 3 draws heavily on an article of mine, "Civil Service, Collective Bargaining and Personnel-Related Impediments to Effective State Management," which appeared in Volume 6 (Summer 1986) of the *Review of Public Personnel Administration*. Permission to reprint much of that article is gratefully acknowledged.

Permission to quote from James Svara's article, "Dichotomy and Duality:

Reconceptualizing the Relationship Between Policy and Administration in Council-Manager Cities,'' which appeared in *Public Administration Review* 45 (January–February 1985), pp. 221–232, and to reprint materials from pp. 223 and 228 that constitute the basis for Figures 5.1 and 6.1 in this volume, is also acknowledged. These materials are reprinted with permission from *Public Administration Review* © by the American Society for Public Administration (ASPA), 1120 G Street NW, Suite 700, Washington, DC 20005. All rights reserved.

Drs. Patrick Grasso and Roy E. Green, whom I came to know well at differing points in my life but who both came to work in the same division of the U.S. General Accounting Office in Washington, helped me think through various matters. Roy Flemming and Wilbur Rich, former Wayne State University colleagues, also made a number of helpful suggestions regarding the design of the mail survey and my subsequent analysis of the resulting database. My colleague John Strate, and my late Wayne State colleague, Ann Workman Sheldon, both helped as I wrestled with methodological issues. Two former Wichita State colleagues, James Kuklinski, now at the University of Illinois, and Leonard Robins, now at Roosevelt University, were important sources of advice and encouragement over the years. My friend James Conant, Director of Public Administration Programs at the University of Oklahoma, carefully read the entire manuscript, made numerous suggestions, and raised various concerns. I tried to respond to most of his suggestions and to address many of his concerns. His own work on state public management has been an important stimulus to my own.

James R. Dunton, Editor-in-Chief of Praeger Publishers, was most helpful and displayed patience as unforeseen events forced me to miss several deadlines. I very much appreciate his confidence in the value of this project.

While acknowledging the various contributions of the foregoing individuals, and profiting from them, I do, of course, absolve them of any and all responsibility for the deficiencies in what follows.

Suffering in the shadows of nearly every book project are those nearest and dearest to the author. I hope that my wife, Sandy, who has seen me through three degrees, and followed me to five colleges and universities, is pleased with the book. She is most certainly pleased with its completion, having had to bear a disproportionate share of the responsibility for managing our household for far too long while pursuing her own demanding career. My youngest son, Benjamin, literally can not remember a time when his Dad wasn't at work on ''the book.'' As a six-year old, my son Joshua helped affix stamps to return envelopes. As a high school student, he helped code some of the data. Each of these members of my family sustained me in important ways. I only regret that I will never be able to adequately repay them for their support and patience.

Chapter 1

The Study of State Administration

THE NEGLECT OF STATE ADMINISTRATION

This book examines the dynamics of managing state administrative agencies based upon the views of key administrative officials in 10 American states. One focus is on these officials' perceptions of the problems that they confront as they seek to accomplish the responsibilities of their units. Another is the extent to which these managers have made use of various techniques and strategies for "improving" the operations of their units and how effective they believe these techniques or strategies to be. A third general focus of the book is on managers' views regarding their relationships with various external actors and the consequences of these relationships for administrative performance.

In their book on the politics of state and city administration, Glenn Abney and Thomas Lauth (1986b, p. 11) lament the fact that the study of city and state administration has been largely neglected by public management scholars.

Students of public administration are taught about administration at the national level, but considerably less attention is given to either state or municipal administration. Yet in terms of numbers of employees and in terms of where the bulk of domestic program money is ultimately spent, governmental administration in the United States is primarily state and local (see also Sharkansky, 1971; Fox, 1974).

The neglect of state administration is worrisome because—with responsibilities ranging from A (agriculture, the arts, aviation) to Z (zoos)—state administrative agencies and their more than 3.2 million employees do most of what state governments actually do. For the average citizen, "state government" is as often a state agency and one of its employees as the governor, legislature, or the courts. Modern government is bureaucratic government no less at the state than at any other level.

To be sure, state elected officials, like their counterparts at other levels of

government, are increasingly attracted to "privatization" strategies such as
contracting as a way of implementing state programs. But while many units
with transportation, health, and social services responsibilities may expend half
or more of their budgets in the form of contracts, privatization has made less
headway at the state level (Chi, 1988; Rehfuss, 1989). Moreover, even when
services are provided by private or nonprofit contractors, state administrative
employees have important roles to play in assuring the effectiveness of such
service arrangements.

The neglect of state administration is also unfortunate because state governments have become increasingly important actors in the federal system. Recent
writings trumpet the "resurgence of the states" (Bowman and Kearney, 1986),
the "growing importance of state government" (Conant, 1989), the "reinvigorated states" (Reeves, 1990), and the emergence of "the entrepreneurial states"
(Van Horn, 1989). Van Horn (pp. 209–210) asserts:

No longer passive partners in the federal system, the states are a driving force in American politics. They raise and spend vast sums of money; manage vexing public problems; and seek to conquer new policy frontiers. States aggressively set policy agendas
for the nation and fashion innovative solutions for stimulating the growth of high technology firms, treating the medically indigent, curbing drunken driving, reforming the
schools, and other important matters. . . . The states trailed the federal government in
recognizing and responding to the challenges of the postwar era. But, contemporary
state governments are capable and resourceful; they are strong participants in the design
and implementation of public programs. Constitutions have been amended, political
institutions have been restructured and strengthened, and professional expertise has been
assembled.

The renewed or resurgent role of state governments is the result of numerous
changes, changes that need not be examined in detail here (on the factors that
have contributed to this renewal or resurgence see Bowman and Kearney, 1986,
pp. 10–22; Conant, 1989; and Reeves, 1990). Suffice it to say that there is
today absolutely no justification whatsoever for ignoring the operations of state
administrative agencies.

There is a second problem, however, that goes beyond the paucity of research on state administration. This is that existing research on state administration exhibits a preoccupation with certain issues at the expense of others.
Since the mid-1960s, a number of scholars have explored some of the political
dimensions of state administration in comparative perspective. Most important
are the series of 50-state studies undertaken by Deil Wright and his associates.[1]
Abney and Lauth (1986b) have extended this tradition in their recent 50-state
survey. These comparative studies highlight the importance of the political dimension of state management. State administrative officials are dependent upon
nonadministrative actors for necessary resources, find their operations to be
significantly affected by these actors, and are ultimately expected to discharge
their responsibilities in a manner that is pleasing to the citizens of a state.

In general, however, these studies exhibit limited concern with internal agency management. Little is said about the severity of management problems or how state management might be improved. Those studies that have focused on such questions have tended to examine a narrow range of impediments to more effective state management or strategies for management improvement. Few comparative studies exist. Comparative studies that focus on a single type of management problem or improvement include those by Conant (1988), Garnett and Levine (1980), and Meier (1980) examining executive branch reorganization; by Schick (1971, 1979) examining budget reform; and by Dresang (1978, 1982) and Cohen and Ingersoll (1985) examining personnel practices and reforms.

One of the few exceptions to the lack of focus on agency performance in the comparative literature on state administration is Lee Sigelman's (1976) research on the "quality" of state administration. This research will receive more attention in Chapter 2. Here I simply note that while Sigelman's work has been an important stimulus to my own, it has flaws.

The existing comparative literature on state administration is deficient in another respect. It exhibits a top-level preoccupation. Almost without exception those surveyed are agency or department heads. While such officials play important roles in state administration, they are but the tip of the bureaucratic iceberg. A focus on administrative performance in all its dimensions, and on the factors that impede or enhance managerial effectiveness, requires that one also adopt a "view from the bureaus." It is imperative that one focus on the administrative subunits in which most of the day-to-day work of managing occurs. Moreover, a focus on second- and third-level managers and units is increasingly necessary as more states, as a consequence of reorganization, create a smaller number of large "holding company" departments in which top-level administrators are farther removed from operating levels. Herbert Kaufman (1981) has described federal bureau chiefs as "sparsely studied wielders of power." If this is true at the federal level, it is most certainly true at the state level. It is for this reason that the respondents in this study include managers farther down the administrative chain of command.

THE BOOK'S RESEARCH FOUNDATION

This book represents an attempt to at least partially remedy the deficiencies just noted. It is based on data collected as part of the Comparative State Management Project. This database consists of the responses of agency heads, division and bureau chiefs in 10 American states to a lengthy questionnaire that was mailed to them between August and November 1982. The states focused on were Arizona, California, Delaware, Indiana, Michigan, New York, South Dakota, Tennessee, Texas, and Vermont. The questionnaire explored in depth the nature of the problems facing state managers; their familiarity with, use, and opinions concerning the efficacy of a host of means for "improving" state administrative performance; their involvement in the policymaking process; and their interaction with various administrative and nonadministrative officials, groups, or institutions. Questionnaires were sent to all but the smallest or least significant state administrative units (an example would be boards with purely advisory responsibilities). Managers of both line and staff units were contacted. In smaller agencies, the agency head and all division and bureau chiefs were contacted. In larger departments, selected division and bureau chiefs were contacted along with the department head.[2]

A total of 847 administrators returned the questionnaire for a response rate of 40%. Across the states, response rates varied from 34% to 50%.[3] The number of respondents ranged from 34 in Vermont to 149 in California. Since more than 2,100 administrators were initially contacted, the size of the resulting sample was sufficient to permit detailed analysis.

Comparison of respondents with nonrespondents in several of the states did not indicate that respondents were atypical in terms of the functional responsibilities of their units or their rank in the administrative hierarchy. The characteristics of those who responded in one state were also compared with those who responded in another. Data on interstate variation in the characteristics of respondents are contained in Appendix 1. In general, such variation was limited.[4]

I would not claim that the 10 states in the study constitute a representative sample. Indeed, to some extent they were selected with an eye to capturing variation in characteristics thought to have theoretical relevance. These include factors such as the size and complexity of their bureaucratic establishments, extent of civil service coverage and collective bargaining, legislative professionalism, gubernatorial power, and the relative strength of interest groups, to name a few. But these 10 states are a diverse lot. They vary in population demographics, size, and growth rate, in economic base, in political culture, in partisan complexion, and in geographical location. Such heterogeneity at least suggests this set of states is not atypical.

The diversity of the states included in this study, as well as differences in the circumstances of individual agencies within any state, suggest, on the one hand, that considerable variation is likely to exist with respect to management problems, views on management improvement, or the impact of particular nonagency actors. On the other hand, the realities of contemporary public management, commonalities in career experiences, and the continued erosion of state differences as a result of numerous developments may mean that it matters little that some of these managers practice their craft in Albany, New York, or Sacramento, California, while others do so in Pierre, South Dakota, or Nashville, Tennessee.

In concluding, let me address two concerns that readers may have about the data that serve as the basis for the book. The first involves when the survey was conducted. The data were collected in the summer and fall of 1982. It might be argued that various findings reported in this book would be different if the survey were conducted today. Since no single period of time is ever representative, this is undoubtedly true to some extent.

Like the early 1990s, the early 1980s were a challenging time for state agencies. The nation was suffering through its worst economic downturn in 50 years. Combined with the effects of the "tax revolt" that erupted in California—one of the study states—a few years earlier, the effect of the early 1980s recession on state revenues was substantial. Between 1978 and 1986, state government employment for all functions grew much more slowly than in the preceding eight years, with employment growth typically not keeping pace with increases in state population (Elling, 1990). Layoffs occurred in 44 states during fiscal 1981 and 1982 (Lewin, 1983). Although often concerned about what they considered to be excessive levels of taxation, pressures from citizens for state services continued unabated. Hence, state agencies were often forced to try to do more with less in the early 1980s.

State agencies were forced to do more with less for another reason. Scarcely 18 months before the survey was conducted, the most conservative national administration since Herbert Hoover came to power. Although President Reagan was committed to an enhanced role for the states in the federal scheme, he was disinclined to fund it. The real dollar reductions in federal aid that had begun during the last years of the Carter administration expanded in scope and magnitude in the early years of the Reagan presidency.

In short, the period of time focused on in this study was one of considerable turbulence for states and their administrative agencies. This certainly affected the responses of the managers I surveyed. We would expect, for example, that fiscal problems would rank high among those cited as impediments to effective management. At the same time, if the data reveal reasonably adequate levels of administrative performance despite the environmental turbulence to which state agencies were subjected during this period—if state agencies "managed to manage" during the early 1980s—we can conclude that in better times such performance may be even higher.

A second concern that some may have about this research is that it is based on the judgments and perceptions of state managers. It is possible that the administrators I surveyed dissembled or misperceived reality. Certainly neither of these possibilities can be ruled out. But I would defend the study's methodology on several grounds. First, the perceptions of administrators have served as the basis for most of the comparative studies of state management conducted over the course of the past 25 years. Second, to the extent that my findings are consistent with those of other scholars based on survey data or collected in other ways, confidence in the validity of the data is increased. In the chapters that follow I continually seek to place my findings in the broader context of existing research on state management. Finally, it is sensible and useful to ask those centrally involved in the administration of state programs about the problems they face, what the sources of those problems may be, how those problems might be ameliorated, and how much influence various external actors have on their administrative units.

While the administrative perspective is not the only one to which attention must be paid, administrators are certainly knowledgeable informants and their perspective is an extremely important one. In a recent examination of the environment of state agencies that relies on agency heads' judgments of the influence of various actors, Brudney and Hebert (1987, p. 189) point out that the "importance of perceptions of the environment is well established in the organizational literature." They go on to cite Karl Weick's (1979, p. 135) argument that members of an organization determine the "'enacted environment' in which they function. Through processes of enactment, selection and retention, 'people create the environments which then impose on them.' " Perhaps more to the point is Rosenbloom's (1983, p. 225) assertion—in the context of his discussion of the three distinctive approaches contained in American public administrative theory—that

attention must be paid to the practical wisdom of the public administrative practitioners whose action is circumscribed by internal considerations of checks, balances, and administrative and political pressures generally. Individual administrators are often called upon to integrate the three approaches to public administration [which Rosenbloom discusses] and much can be learned from their experience.

Hence, I would argue that neither the timing of this study, nor the fact that it is based on administrators' perceptions, reduces the relevance or significance of the findings reported in this book. At the same time, one must be sensitive to how either the time frame of the study or its reliance on administrators' judgments may have influenced the findings. Ultimately, of course, such bias can only be detected with the completion of similar studies at other points in time or based on other kinds of data.

THE PLAN OF THE BOOK

The first half of the book focuses on state administrative problems and possible solutions to those problems. Chapter 2 explores the nature and severity of the problems facing state managers, while Chapter 3 seeks to identify some of the correlates of variation in the severity of those problems. Chapter 4 concludes the first part of the book. It examines the extent to which state managers use, or have been subject to the application of, various means to "improve" administrative performance. It also explores managers' assessments of the effectiveness of various management "improvements."

The second half of the book, consisting of Chapters 5 through 8, shifts the focus to "macroadministration." The role of state administrative units and managers in the policy process and the interaction between these agencies and managers and various nonagency actors is explored in depth. Chapter 5 focuses on the "policyshaping" role of state administrators. Chapter 6 sketches the broad outlines of the "influence matrix" of state administration, while Chapter 7 explores administrative interaction with governors and the state legislature in depth. Patterns and consequences of administrative interaction with interest groups and clients are investigated in Chapter 8. Chapter 9 summarizes major findings and presents some conclusions about the condition of state management and the sources of state management problems. This chapter ends with a discussion of the implications of the book's findings for efforts to improve state administrative performance.

NOTES

1. See Deil Wright, "Executive Leadership in State Administration," *Midwest Journal of Political Science, 11* (1967), 1–26; Deil Wright, Mary Wagner, and Richard Mc-Anaw, "State Administrators: Their Changing Characteristics," *State Government, 50* (1977), 152–159; Deil Wright and Alfred Light, "State Administrators in the Policy Process," paper presented at the 1977 annual meeting of the Southern Political Science Association; F. Ted Hebert and Deil Wright, "State Administrators: How Representative? How Professional?" *State Government, 55* (1982), 22–28; Nelson Dometrius, "Some Consequences of State Reform," *State Government 54* (1981), 93–98; F. Ted Hebert, Jeffrey Brudney, and Deil S. Wright, "Gubernatorial Influence and State Bureaucracy," *American Politics Quarterly, 11* (1983), 243–264; Jeffrey Brudney and F. Ted Hebert, "State Agencies and Their Environments: Examining the Influence of Important External Actors," *The Journal of Politics, 49* (1987), 186–206; Peter J. Haas and Deil S. Wright, "The Changing Profile of State Administrators," *The Journal of State Government, 60* (1987), 270–278; Cheryl Miller, "State Administrators' Perceptions of the Policy Influence of Other Actors: Is Less Better?" *Public Administration Review, 47* (1987), 239–245; and F. Ted Hebert and Jeffrey Brudney, "Controlling Administrative Agencies in a Changing Federal System: Avenues of Gubernatorial Influence," *American Review of Public Administration, 18* (1988), 135–147.

2. Because the survey focused on second- and third-level administrators in addition to agency heads, a source such as the Council of State Government's *State Administrative Officials Classified by Function* (Lexington, KY:1981–82) was inadequate in identifying managers to be surveyed. Following discussions with officials in various states, and based on my experience in identifying state administrators for personal interviews, in previous research, it was decided that the state government telephone directory in each state was the single best source of information. In some states supplementary sources were also used. An example is the use of the *Texas State Directory,* 25th ed. (Austin: Texas State Directory, 1982).

3. Leege and Francis (1974) suggest that response rates of 25% to 40% may typically be expected in mail surveys while Goyder (1985) reports response rates that vary from 30% to 70%. My response rate is slightly better than the 38% rate in the 1984 American State Administrators Project conducted by Deil Wright and his associates (Miller, 1987).

4. Save for units with health-related functions in Vermont, and those with economic development responsibilities in South Dakota, no functional area is totally unrepresented among the responses for any state. Some differences in the proportion of respondents

from agencies with certain functions are readily explicable. Thus, the higher proportion of respondents from units with natural resources management responsibilities in Arizona and California reflects the existence of large water resources management units in these two "thirst belt" states. Differences in the proportion of respondents holding top level positions in states such as California, Michigan, New York, and South Dakota are a reflection of their having reorganized bureaucracies composed of relatively fewer agencies, each of which has very extensive functional responsibilities. In these states administrators who might be agency heads in other states are second- or even third-level administrators.

Chapter 2

The Problematic World of State Management

INTRODUCTION

The crucial role played by administrative agencies in the accomplishment of public purposes is a major reason why concerns about their performance abound. In the 1970s and 1980s, bureaucracy-bashing (Gormley, 1989b) became increasingly common not only among conservatives—who have traditionally harbored antibureaucratic sentiments—but among political moderates and liberals as well. While the "grand assault" on public bureaucracy (Goodsell, 1985) has focused on the federal level, state bureaucracies have also increasingly come under fire. Because the rate of growth of state (and local) bureaucracies has outstripped that at the federal level, state (and local) bureaucracies are also tempting targets for those exercised about "bloated" government such as elected officials, the media, and candidates for office. Because a very substantial share of any state's budget is spent by administrative agencies in pursuit of their responsibilities, and to pay their employees, concern over state taxes and spending readily translates into animosity toward those agencies. Concern over the role of administrative agencies in policy implementation, as well as other aspects of the policy process, also stems from the fact that those who staff these agencies are typically appointed rather than elected.

The purpose of this chapter is to provide some comparative perspective on state administrative performance. I begin by examining various standards of administrative performance. Difficulties in assessing agency performance with respect to particular standards are then discussed. This is followed by an examination of impediments to effective management of state agencies as viewed by state administrators themselves. The chapter concludes with a discussion of whether an "if-only" style of management exists in the 10 states focused on in this book.

STANDARDS OF STATE ADMINISTRATIVE PERFORMANCE

Despite their importance, and despite concerns about their performance, systematic evidence on the performance of state administrative agencies is sparse. One reason for this is the multidimensional character of the concept of administrative/bureaucratic performance or effectiveness. Mark Emmert (1986, p. 82) laments how the "formless nature of organizational effectiveness as a construct has left many an otherwise confident social scientist frustrated and diffident." Campbell et al. (1974) consider organizational effectiveness to be "an extremely untidy construct."

At the most general level one can identify at least three standards of public bureaucratic performance: efficiency, effectiveness, and political or public accountability. The first two standards can, of course, be applied to administrative organizations of all types—public, private, or "third sector." Indeed, it has been typical to want public agencies to attain levels of efficiency and effectiveness that are at least thought to typify private enterprises.

An efficient organization gets the most out of a given amount of resources. This standard is concerned with the relationship between inputs and outputs. It asks, for instance, if a greater volume of litter along a highway right-of-way can be collected at a comparable or lower cost. Effectiveness is goal-oriented. An effective organization gets the job done. It also asks the question, "So what?" For example, however efficiently it is done, does vocational training for incarcerated felons improve their chances of securing jobs on release and reduce the likelihood that they will engage in future criminal activity?

In what was one of the first, and remains one of the few, efforts to assess state administrative performance in comparative perspective, Lee Sigelman (1976) argued that administrative "quality" consisted of at least seven standards or dimensions. Four of these—expertise, information-processing capacity, innovativeness, and efficiency—were said to be standards of the "professional" quality of administration that together "represent 'good government' standards of operation which could be applied to all organizations, public or private" (p. 110). Sigelman also identified a broad "political" standard that included representativeness, partisan neutrality, and integrity as elements. James Q. Wilson (1967) suggests that appropriate standards of administrative performance include accountability, equity, efficiency, responsiveness, and fiscal integrity.

Even if agreement can be reached on standards of administrative performance or effectiveness, simultaneous maximization of each of them is unusual. Because various standards often conflict, difficult trade-offs abound. While often uttered in the same breath, this is so even for efficiency and effectiveness as standards. A relatively inefficient organization may still be relatively effective. On the other hand, while efficiency may enhance effectiveness, it can not assure it, as the following story illustrates.

In the late 1960s, Governor Ronald Reagan of California curtailed the amount of money going to the state university system. He was concerned that state university campuses, particularly Berkeley, were indoctrinating students in radical, left-wing ideas. In response to these political pressures and to forestall further budget cuts, the administrators attempted to demonstrate that they were educating students at an ever lower cost per student. Not surprisingly, this argument had little impact on the governor; indeed it missed the point of his criticism. Producing revolutionaries at lower cost was not what the governor wanted; rather, he questioned whether the universities produced anything that justified giving them state funds (Pfeffer and Salancik, 1978, p. 12).

While one might disagree with Governor Reagan's characterization of the products of the California public university system, the difference between the concepts of efficiency and effectiveness is neatly captured by this story.

In the public sector, a very common trade-off is between efficiency or effectiveness on the one hand, and political accountability on the other. Accountability as a performance standard has at least two dimensions. A *process* dimension is concerned with the constitutionality or legality of administrative actions, with honesty, observance of due process, impartiality, and decency in dealing with the public. More demanding expectations concerning the meeting of this standard is one fact that distinguishes public from private management. Efforts to assure process accountability can, and often do, increase costs and erode efficiency or effectiveness. The mandating of detailed procedures to be followed in service delivery so as to prevent arbitrary actions tends to generate much despised "red tape" (Kaufman, 1977; Goodsell, 1985, pp. 61–67; Baldwin, 1990).

A second dimension of accountability is *responsiveness*—whose goals do bureaucracies attempt to achieve? In Chapter 5 the difficult issue of to what, or to whom, public bureaucracies ought to be responsive is more directly addressed. Here it is sufficient to note that expecting public agencies to be answerable to one or another nonbureaucratic actor may hamper efforts to achieve efficient or effective administration of the people's business.

Often we act as if administrative accountability matters more than either efficiency or effectiveness. Perhaps this is as it should be in a democracy. Nonetheless, clear thinking about administrative performance requires awareness of the tensions between these performance standards.

OPERATIONALIZING STANDARDS OF ADMINISTRATIVE PERFORMANCE

Even when we can agree on the standards of administrative performance that are to be applied, difficulties loom in appropriately operationalizing them. Public agencies primarily provide services rather than tangible products. Some state government programs lend themselves to more precise measurement, but most do not. While organizations such as the U.S. General Accounting Office, the Bureau of Labor Statistics, and the Urban Institute (Holzer, 1984; Hatry, 1989) have made progress in devising valid indicators of administrative efficiency and effectiveness, other efforts have foundered on the shoals of measurement (Downs and Larkey, 1986; National Association of State Budget Officers, 1975; Washnis, 1980). Sigelman's (1976, pp. 136–137) observation of 15 years ago remains substantially true today. "Although some progress has been made in quantifying governmental priorities . . . and in developing quantitative indicators of nonmonetary government policy outputs, . . . techniques for measuring efficiency are still quite primitive and exploratory."

Nor are difficulties in determining efficiency or effectiveness stemming from the absence of convenient, public-sector "bottom line" indicators the only or even the major problem. Indicators of administrative accountability are even more difficult to specify. Accountability is very much in the eye of the beholder, as Kaufman (1981, p. 170) has noted in addressing the issue of administrative responsiveness to Congress: "Autonomous . . . does not mean 'independent' in this context; it means under the control of someone other than the accuser. That is a far cry from being a free agent."

EXISTING STUDIES OF STATE ADMINISTRATIVE PERFORMANCE

Difficulties in conceptualizing and assessing administrative performance are among the reasons that there is little systematic evidence on the performance of state bureaucracies. Research comparing the performance of one state's bureaucracy to another is virtually nonexistent.

Faced with various difficulties, those interested in the subject of administrative performance have adopted one of several research strategies. One is to ask citizens or agency clients about their experiences with public agencies. Here one is seeking to assess administrative performance in terms of several of the "strategic constituencies" that Emmert (1986) has identified.[1]

Despite much antibureaucratic rhetoric, American citizens express relative satisfaction with their bureaucratic encounters at all levels of government (Katz et al., 1975; Goodsell, 1985). According to a 1973 national survey, 65% of those who had gone to a state agency to "get them to do something," not related simply to routine matters such as paying taxes or applying for a license, were "highly" or "somewhat" satisfied with how their problem was handled (U.S. Congress, Senate Committee on Government Operations, 1973). Half of the Michiganians surveyed in 1980 and 1987 felt state employees did at least an "average job." The proportion saying state bureaucrats did a good job was two to three times larger than the proportion who felt they did a poor one (Michigan Department of Civil Service, 1987). A study of 1,700 clients of the Maine Bureau of Social Welfare found that 90% felt their social worker had treated them with respect and had "explained things so they (the clients) could understand" (Goodsell, 1985, p. 19). More than 80% of the 6,000 Wisconsin residents surveyed about their contacts with state transportation employees (highway patrolmen and driver's license examiners among them) characterized those contacts as either "good" or "excellent" so far as "courtesy of treatment" and "helpfulness" were concerned (Goodsell, 1985, p. 20).

Recorded statistics on agency operations also suggest adequate state administrative performance. The administration of welfare programs is often criticized. But a study of the administration of the Aid to Families with Dependent Children program found that incorrect eligibility decisions occurred in just 5 percent of cases across the states. Erroneous payment decisions were made in 18% of the cases—with caseworkers erring on both the low and high sides (Campbell & Bendick, 1977). Considering the difficulties involved in determining client resources, and the ambiguity of regulations on the subject, an error rate of less than 20% is impressive. Finally, a study of state unemployment compensation operations found that 90% of unemployment claims across the states were paid within three weeks (Goodsell, 1985, p. 34).

Unfortunately, data of the sort discussed in the two preceding paragraphs have usually been collected for only a few states, agencies, or programs. Although both state and local governments have made increasing use of surveys of citizen/clientele perceptions of program or administrative performance, data from such surveys may be flawed in various ways and are difficult to interpret (Daneke and Kolbus-Edwards, 1979; Stipak, 1980a; Rochefort and Boyer, 1988). The link between perceptions and more objective indicators of performance may be highly tenuous even when respondents have actually been clients of a given agency or program (Stipak, 1979; Brown and Coulter, 1983).[2] Methodological problems aside, the fact remains that studies that would permit one to compare citizen or client satisfaction with state agencies or programs across a number of states are nonexistent.

An alternative strategy for securing comparative data on state administrative performance is represented by the work of Lee Sigelman (1976). As noted earlier in the chapter, Sigelman identified seven standards of what he termed state administrative "quality": efficiency, expertise, information-processing capacity, innovativeness, partisan neutrality, integrity, and representativeness. Sigelman developed measures of five of these standards of state administrative quality and ranked the states on each of them. His study included indicators of neither administrative integrity nor efficiency, however.

Some of the indicators he developed were essentially prerequisites for higher quality administration. These included indicators of expertise, such as the proportion of professionally trained managers in a state and administrative salary levels; of partisan neutrality, such as the proportion of state government employees covered by a comprehensive merit civil service system; and indicators of information processing capacity, such as the number of computers available for state government use. Other indicators of state administrative quality developed by Sigelman were more output-oriented. These included the number of publications issued by each state government, as an indicator of information processing capacity; and whether a state made use of various types of performance data in its budget documents, as evidence of administrative innovativeness.

Barrilleaux, Feiock, and Crew (1990) have recently updated and extended Sigelman's work. In contrast to his effort, they developed indicators of administrative integrity and efficiency. They also utilized operational indicators of dimensions such as information processing capacity and innovativeness that seem, on their face, to be more valid.

The measures of state administrative quality utilized by Sigelman and Barrilleaux et al. have the important virtue of being fairly readily available. But the approach represented by these two studies has serious flaws. Elsewhere I have explored the adequacy of Sigelman's approach in greater detail (Elling, 1987). Suffice it to say that accepting Sigelman's measures, or those of Barrilleaux et al., as valid indicators of state administrative quality requires several leaps of faith. In both studies the focus is on the *potential* for administrative performance, given their heavy emphasis on administrative resources as inputs. Alas, the relationships between administrative inputs and outputs, to say nothing of the relationships between outputs and outcomes, are often tenuous.

State bureaucracies face administrative tasks of varying scope and difficulty. A larger state, one with a more complex administrative apparatus, one in which administration must be conducted in a more conflictual sociopolitical setting, may require the application of more or higher "quality" resources simply to achieve as much as can be achieved with fewer or lower "quality" resources in another. More police are associated with more crime. This is so not because police cause crime but because hiring more police is a response to rising crime. Similarly, the presence of higher quality administrative resources may be a response to more severe administrative difficulties. The problematic nature of state administration is some function of administrative resources of a certain type, quantity, or quality, on the one hand, and the character and magnitude of the demands confronting a given state's administrative apparatus, on the other.

While the approach to assessing state administrative performance represented by the work of Sigelman and Barrilleaux et al. deserves to be refined, my study approaches the issue of state administrative performance quite differently. It adopts a problem- and manager-centered perspective. In exploring the quality of state management it seems sensible and useful to ask those centrally involved in the administration of state programs not only how well they believe their units are doing but what prevents them from doing better. Connolly, Conlon, and Deutsch (1980), as well as Emmert (1986), have argued that meaningful assessment of the performance of an organization requires that one identify and take into account the perspectives and criteria embraced by a number of different constituencies. Some of these constituencies may be internal to the organization while others—particularly in the case of public agencies—are external. This study focuses on a key internal constituency of state administrative agencies—middle and upper level management.

The state managers surveyed were asked to respond to closed-ended, Likert-scale questions concerning the severity of 52 conditions, circumstances, practices, and such that might exist in their administrative units and that might hinder the "efficient and effective administration of the programmatic responsibilities" of those units. For each, the administrators were asked to indicate whether it was "not a problem," a "minor problem," a "serious problem," or a "very serious problem."[3] These estimates of the severity of various impediments to effective management provide important insight into the problematic world of state administration.

STATE MANAGERS VIEW MANAGEMENT PROBLEMS

In addition to asking state managers about the severity of specific administrative practices or conditions, they were asked to indicate how successful, overall, their particular units had been in achieving their programmatic goals. Responses to this query provide some context for the more detailed analysis to follow. Overall, two-thirds felt that their unit had been "very successful," with majorities ranging from 58% in South Dakota to 76% in Texas reporting such success. Only in Indiana did less than a majority (45%) report that their unit had been very successful in achieving its goals. At the other extreme, only in Vermont did more than 1 percent say that their unit had been "less than successful."

That managers are highly sanguine about the overall performance of their units is perhaps not surprising. Even when guaranteed anonymity, it must be hard for managers to admit to failure, especially when such failure will surely be partially laid at their feet.[4] Given that a positive assessment is encouraged, what seems significant is that substantial proportions of managers—more than 33% overall and more than 40% in Delaware, Indiana, and South Dakota—admitted that their unit's performance left something to be desired. The responses to this question suggest that state management is often problematic.

Examination of the severity of specific potential impediments to effective management tells us more about why state administrative performance is problematic. To facilitate examination of the severity of the large number of potential impediments, the set of problems was trichotomized on the basis of perceived severity. Table 2.1 presents data on the 11 most serious problems.

Of the six problems considered to be serious impediments by one-third or more of the managers, four concerned personnel matters while the remaining two related to the actions of the state legislature. Excessive restrictions on expenditures—a problem that may be substantially of legislative origin—ranked as the tenth most serious impediment.[5] Problems relating to either the adequacy or the utilization of human and fiscal resources comprise 8 of the 11 most serious constraints on achievement of organizational objectives.[6]

Table 2.1
Most Serious State Management Problems in 10 Study States

Problem or Problem Source[1]	Mean Problem Severity[2]	Percent Managers Reporting as "Serious"[3]	Interstate Range in Percent Serious	Number of States in Which Problem Ranked Among 10 Most Serious[4]
Adequately rewarding outstanding employees	1.5**(1)	51%	35-67%	10
Insufficient appropriations	1.4**(4)	45	20-60	10
Legislative program expansion without additional funding	1.3*(1)	40	27-62	10
Disciplining/dismissing employees	1.2*	34	17-41	9
Civil service procedures for recruiting/selecting staff	1.1*(15)	34	3-56	7
Filling key vacancies/Retaining key staff	1.1*(3)	33	18-55	8
Complexity of process for promulgating rules	1.1*	30	17-44	6
Paperwork and clearance requirements on decisions	1.1	28	15-40	6
Organizational resistance to change	1.1	24	17-30	4
Excessive restrictions on appropriations	1.0	23	18-29	4
Unpredictability of federal grant funding	0.9	30	23-36	9

1. Problems with a mean severity of 1.0 or greater and/or 25% or more of administrators reported them to be "serious" or "very serious" impediments to the effective management of their unit.

2. Column entry is the average severity, across all of the administrators surveyed in the 10 states, of a given problem. It was calculated from responses to a question on the Comparative State Management Survey in which, for each of 52 problems, administrators indicated how seriously a problem impeded the "efficient and effective administration of the programmatic responsibilities" of their unit.

    Responses were coded as follows: "No Problem" = 0, "Minor Problem" = 1, "Serious Problem" = 2, "Very Serious Problem" = 3. Mean severity could range between 0.0 and 3.0. The total number of respondents was 847. The number of responses regarding the severity of particular problems ranged between 794 and 845. An asterisk indicates that interstate variation in mean severity was statistically significant (F-test .01 significance level). The parenthetical figures in this table, as well as in Tables 2.2 and 2.3, indicate the number of pairs of states between which significant differences (.05 level) in mean problem severity existed. The multiple comparison of means test used was the Scheffe Test.

3. Column entry is the overall percentage of responding administrators reporting a given problem to be "serious" or "very serious."

4. Column entry is the number of states in which the proportion of administrators reporting a given problem to be "serious" or "very serious" ranked in the top 10 for problem severity in that state.

Approximately half of the problems were moderately severe (see Table 2.2). Only one of the problems in this larger group—ineffective organizational planning—was considered to be serious by more than one manager in five. Still, a fair number of managers were concerned about difficulties in assessing organizational performance, a lack of time for making decisions, inadequate facilities, supervisors lacking necessary management skills, having either too little or too much information, and interest group opposition to their efforts. On the other hand, structural complexity, legislative "meddling" in purely administrative matters, vague legislative intent, legislative casework inquiries, and controlling subordinates were not seen as terribly serious problems.

Finally, approximately one-third of the problems were rarely seen to seriously impede effective management. This disparate group, summarized in Table 2.3, includes the impact of collective bargaining, gubernatorial interaction with agencies, patronage practices, racial or sexual discrimination, and aspects of agency relationships with the federal government and with local governments.

The data just presented suggest that the world of state managers is less problematic than might be supposed given the rhetoric of critics of public bureaucracies. Half of the potential impediments have a mean severity of 0.7 or less. For 20 of the 52 problems only 1 administrator in 10 reported them to be serious. An aggregate measure of the severity of the entire set of problems (see Table 2.4) also suggests only small to moderate difficulties in most administrative units.[7] It is noteworthy that certain problems that have preoccupied many public management scholars are of little concern to these managers. These include inadequate information for decisionmaking, program coordination, monitoring subordinates' actions, communicating with superiors or subordinates, and organization complexity. Still, a substantial number of managers do consider a handful of problems to be serious impediments to effective organizational performance. These tend to be problems that involve the nature and utilization of fiscal and human resources.

Deciding if the patterns that emerge indicate state bureaucracies that are functioning in an adequate or an inadequate fashion is complicated by the general absence of a benchmark data. The findings from a study of federal managers by Lynch and Gabris (1981) are, however, generally consistent with those of this study. Thus, 72% of their federal respondents felt that administrative support systems made it difficult to hire employees while 67% complained that such systems failed to provide them with a pool of qualified professional, technical, or managerial talent that was adequate to meet their needs. Such systems were seen as making it difficult to fire low-performing subordinates by 78% of the federal managers surveyed and only 32% said that the systems allowed them to readily sanction poorly performing employees. More than 50% stated that administrative arrangements made it difficult for them to reward competent employees. In reviewing their findings, Lynch and Gabris conclude that many

Table 2.2
Moderately Severe State Management Problems

Problem or Problem Source[1]	Mean Problem Severity	Percent Managers Reporting as "Serious"	Interstate Range in Percent Serious
Ineffective organizational planning	0.9	22%	18-30%
Assessing organizational or program effectiveness	0.9	19	15-23
Insufficient time to make decisions	0.9	18	6-27
Inadequate facilities	0.8*(1)	20	13-27
Supervisors lack management skills	0.8*	18	6-24
Information "overload"	0.8	17	12-23
Interest groups opposition to unit programs	0.8*	17	6-23
Decisionmaking with inadequate information	0.8	15	8-23
Administrative superiors provide inadequate direction/support	0.7	19	7-27
Legislature creates hard-to-implement programs	0.7	17	6-25
Coordinating programs with other units	0.7	12	6-21
Legislative limits on unit's discretion	0.7	12	6-17
Assessing subordinates' performance	0.7	11	6-16
Ineffective communication with subordinates	0.7	11	6-16
Insufficiently motivated/diligent employees	0.7*(1)	10	5-20
Lack of legislative interest in unit	0.6*(6)	16	5-36
Paperwork/delay in federal grant programs	0.6	14	9-22
Conditions attached to federal grants	0.6	13	8-22
Complexity of organizational structure	0.6	11	6-19
Media hostility to unit and its program	0.6	11	5-22
Legislative "meddling" in purely administrative matters	0.6*	11	7-17
Vague/ambiguous legislative intent	0.6	10	5-16
Inadequate publicity on unit's programs/ Eligibility criteria for programs	0.6*	10	6-17
Monitoring/Controlling subordinates' actions actions	0.6	8	3-12
Handling legislative "casework" inquiries	0.6*	5	0-18

1. Problems with a mean severity less than 1.0 but greater than 0.5 and/or 11% to 24% of managers report them to be "serious" or "very serious." See Table 2.1., notes 2 and 3 for meaning of other entries.

Table 2.3
Least Serious State Management Problems

Problem or Problem Source[1]	Mean Problem Severity	Percent Managers Reporting as "Serious"	Interstate Range in Percent "Serious"	Number of States in Which Problem Ranked Among Ten Least "Serious"
Lack of gubernatorial interest in unit and its programs	0.5	13%	5-20%	1
Communication with superiors	0.5	10	3-17	3
Security-oriented employees	0.5	6	0-8	9
Employees treating clients badly	0.5*(1)	4	0-8	9
Federal grant-matching requirements	0.4	10	5-13	2
Courts mandating service levels	0.4	10	3-13	1
Lack of clarity in unit's objectives	0.4	7	4-10	5
Collective bargaining limits managerial authority	0.4*(22)	7	0-17	5
Existence of collective bargaining for unit employees	0.4*(17)	7	0-21	6
Relations with federal agencies	0.4	6	0-9	7
Relations with local government officials	0.4	3	1-7	10
Gubernatorial "meddling" in purely administrative matters	0.3*(9)	5	2-17	7
Patronage practices	0.3*	5	2-10	8
Broad span of control	0.3	5	0-8	8
Collective bargaining on inappropriate matters	0.2*(8)	4	0-9	7
Racial/sexual discrimination	0.2*(2)	3	0-5	10

1. Mean severity below 0.6 and/or 10% or fewer managers reported problem to be "serious" or "very serious." See Table 2.1, footnotes 2 and 3, for meaning of other table entries.

Table 2.4
Aggregate Severity of Management Problems, Overall and by State

State	Aggregate Severity[1]		Coefficient of Variation[2]	Range
	Mean	Median		
Arizona (54) [3]	24.54	21.48	.433	4.49-50.6
California (127)	23.68	21.80	.439	3.21-54.4
Delaware (63)	24.85	23.08	.503	1.28-53.2
Indiana (52)	23.23	22.76	.553	0.00-71.5
Michigan (104)	24.21	24.68	.391	4.49-55.1
New York (90)	24.89	23.72	.404	2.56-51.2
South Dakota (54)	20.06	18.59	.537	1.28-49.3
Tennessee (49)	21.90	20.51	.424	0.00-44.2
Texas (70)	18.54	16.67	.539	1.92-46.8
Vermont (31)	19.67	18.59	.601	3.85-62.8
Overall (693)	22.95	21.80	.468	0.00-71.5

$F=3.103$; 9/684 d.f.; $p=.001$
eta$=.198$

1.   Aggregate problem severity was calculated by first summing each manager's responses across all 52 potential management impediments where "not a problem" = 0, "minor problem" = 1, "serious problem" = 2, and "very serious problem" = 3. The resulting sum was then multiplied by a constant (.64103) so that aggregate severity could range between 0.00 and 100.00.

2.   The coefficient of variation (C.V.) is the standard deviation divided by the mean. A rule of thumb is that a C.V. greater than .30 indicates substantial variation.

3.   The number of respondents is reduced because aggregate severity was only calculated for those cases in which there was a response to all 52 problems.

federal managers feel they "have their hands tied and can not make effective use of organizational resources" (p. 10).

Lynch and Gabris also report that senior federal managers perceived a "pervasiveness of red tape." Procedures and requirements imposed by the president and the Office of Management and Budget, the Congress, the Office of Personnel Management, and the General Services Administration were considered to be needlessly complex "nearly all of the time" or "rather often" by more than 40% of these managers. Federal managers' complaints about the consequences of these external constraints are mirrored in those of state managers about complex rulemaking processes, restrictions on expenditures, paperwork and clearance requirements on decisions, and various personnel system requirements. Several other studies of federal management reach similar conclusions (Hyde, 1991; Pfiffner, 1981-82, 1983; Lau, Newman, and Broedling, 1980; National Academy of Public Administration, 1983).

The significance of personnel-related problems as constraints on effective management is highlighted in Rainey's (1979) study comparing middle managers in four state agencies and a federal unit in one state with those in four business organizations. The public managers perceived considerably less flexibility in personnel procedures so far as rewarding high performers or punishing low performers was concerned. A study by Norman Baldwin (1990) of more than 1,000 managers from all levels of government as well as in private organizations found that the public managers were very likely to feel that personnel "red tape" was a problem. They were also significantly more likely than private managers to see this as a problem.

In short, many of the problems that those state managers I surveyed considered to be important obstacles to effective management emerge as concerns in other studies. This suggests that the survey has accurately tapped sources of management difficulty in the states.

VARIATION IN STATE MANAGEMENT PROBLEM SEVERITY

In their analyses of state administrative quality, Sigelman (1976) and Barrilleaux et al. (1990) found that much interstate variation existed. State managers' assessments of the severity of particular problems similarly exhibit variation both across states and within any one of them. Reexamination of Tables 2.1, 2.2, and 2.3 discloses that interstate variation in state managers' estimates of severity exists for 24 of the 52 potential impediments to effective management (F-test, .01 level or better). The number of problems cited as serious by a quarter or more of the administrators in a particular state varies from 4 in South Dakota, and 6 in Texas and Vermont, to 8 or 9 in California, Delaware, and Michigan, and 10 or 11 in Arizona, Indiana, New York, and Tennessee. The indicator of the severity of the entire set of problems suggests (see Table 2.4) that the most troubled state bureaucracies are those in New York, Delaware, Arizona, Michigan, and California. Those in South Dakota, Vermont, and Texas are least troubled.

These findings indicate the difficulty in generalizing about administrative performance across a number of states. For various reasons, some of which will be explored in subsequent chapters, certain problems are more serious in some states than others. But evidence of interstate variation must be kept in perspective. The large sample size means that small differences in average severity may be statistically significant. Even though this is so, statistically significant interstate differences existed in the case of less than half of the problems (see Tables 2.1, 2.2., and 2.3). In terms of aggregate problem severity, the range in mean severity was only five or six scale units (see Table 2.4).

A statistically significant difference in problem severity may also result if the response patterns in but one or two states differ substantially from those in the remaining states. This possibility was assessed using a multiple comparison of means test.[8] As the parenthetical figures in the first columns of Tables 2.1, 2.2, and 2.3 make clear, significant interstate differences in mean problem severity are often due to the distinctiveness of the responses of managers in one or two states. Thus, while a significant interstate difference exists in mean severity regarding the problem of rewarding outstanding employees, a significant difference exists *between a pair of states in only one instance*. Problems exhibiting a similar pattern include those that are quite severe overall, such as insufficient appropriations, legislative expansion of programs with no additional funding, filling vacancies and retaining key staff, as well as those that are not, such as insufficiently hard-working employees and staff who treat clients badly. On occasion, a statistically significant F-score exists despite the fact that *none* of the differences in mean severity between pairs of states are statistically significant. This is true of problems disciplining and dismissing low performers, the complexity of the rulemaking process, supervisors lacking management skills, legislative meddling in a unit's affairs, communication with superiors, and patronage practices. Nor were there any significant differences between pairs of states in aggregate problem severity (see Table 2.4).

Additional perspectives on interstate variation can be gained by examination of the rightmost columns of Tables 2.1 and 2.3. Although the *proportion* of managers in various states reporting a problem to be severe may sometimes vary substantially, the severity of that problem *relative to others in that state* may not. While the percentage of respondents in differing states reporting that adequately rewarding outstanding employees was a serious problem ranged from 35% to 67%, this impediment ranked among the 10 most serious in every state. Similar agreement existed for most of the dozen or so problems that were most serious overall. Table 2.3 indicates that interstate consensus also existed regarding the problems that were least severe overall.

Interstate differences in problem severity are not significant because *intrastate* variation in severity is often so great. If we focus on the 20 most serious problems overall, it is the case that intrastate variation is high for most of them. Coefficients of variation of .40 or greater exist in 129 of 200 cases (variation in each of 20 problems in each of 10 states) while coefficients below .30 occur in just five instances. Table 2.4 indicates that similarly substantial intrastate variation in aggregate problem severity exists as well.

Greatest consensus within states exists on the difficulty in rewarding employee performance, the adequacy of appropriations, organizational resistance to change, about assessment of organizational performance, about the adequacy of time for decision making; and excessive paperwork and clearances required in making decisions. The next section of the chapter discusses one reason why there should be greater intrastate consensus on the severity of some problems as opposed to others.

STATE MANAGEMENT PROBLEMS AND "IF-ONLY" MANAGEMENT

Many discussions of public management managers stress the complex environment in which such management occurs (Rainey, 1989). In part this complexity reflects the diversity of expectations for administrative performance discussed earlier in the chapter. It also reflects the fact that—to use Emmert's

(1986) phrase again—various "strategic constituencies" are interested in public agency performance, may place demands upon these agencies, or may control resources that these agencies need.

One implication of this situation is that public managers find it more difficult to manage their time because they have to respond to a wide range of external demands. One study of middle-level municipal managers (Porter and Van Maanen, 1983) found that they were much more likely than middle managers in industrial organizations to cite the needs and demands of those outside their organization as an important variable affecting how they allocated their time.

Other consequences of the unique environment in which public managers must function are highlighted in a 1981 article by Joseph Whorton and John Worthley, which takes note of the "paradoxical environment" of American public administration. On the one hand, they argue, American society "gives its public bureaucracy enormous power and expects public managers to energetically provide desired public services" (p. 357). On the other hand, there is also "distrust and disdain evident in the public view of the governmental bureaucracy" (p. 357). Hence, while public managers possess substantial resources for and discretion over the administration of programs, they are also subjected to an array of laws, procedures, and norms designed to constrain their use of these resources or discretionary authority. Or, as Lewis Mainzer (1973, p. 15) puts it, the administration of public programs occurs in the context of a "constraining web of statutes and rules."

Whorton and Worthley go on to argue that the paradoxical environment in which public managers must function encourages the development of a distinctive organizational culture. This is a culture that

develops, reinforces and maintains attitudes and behavioral norms that form what we call the "if-only" approach to management. The work environment of public administrators, replete with its myriad of constraints, is viewed in the "if-only" approach as exacerbating the difficulty of getting the job done. . . . Obstructions are seen as relentlessly impeding the public manager's efforts to get on with the job (p. 359).

The central feature of this "if-only" management style is the palpable presence of various "thems." "Thems" are

creatures that lurk "out there" and whose major purpose is to torment public managers and obstruct efforts to do what needs to be done. They spend a lot of time plotting the downfall of administrators. Sometimes they attack directly, sometimes they are totally indifferent to management. There are many thems. Some of the more prominent are the politicians, the press, the civil service system, the consumer groups, and the budget analysts. They are viewed as causes of inaction and inefficiency (p. 359).

Whorton and Worthley argue that an "if-only" orientation negatively affects the performance of public managers and agencies in two ways. First, it provides a convenient justification for managerial inaction. While various "thems" may complicate the job of managing, this is not to say that they make effective management impossible. But some managers may throw up their hands in dismay at the constraints they face and despair of the chances of working around them. These constraints may be used as excuses justifying a policy of managerial drift.

A second negative consequence of the adoption of if-only management views stems, ironically, from the fact that, as Whorton and Worthley observe, "public managers often do manage—'despite' the legislature, 'despite' the budget office, 'despite' the press leak" (p. 360). But an if-only view of the administrative world supposedly causes public managers to discount their own accomplishments:

So complete is the job of reinforcement through the organizational culture that many managers can not or will not acknowledge their own successes. . . . Like the inferior personality, the public manager discounts performance and holds to a limited view of the possible and these feelings persist even when by objective standards the individual may be performing well and achieving all that might be expected. In such cases, the message of actual performance does not get through to organization members and, perhaps most important, to the public (pp. 360–361).

To the extent, then, that an if-only management view is widespread, managerial passivity as well as a failure to recognize real achievements may result.

Both the causes of, and the remedies for, certain impediments to effective state management are largely outside the control of state administrators or administrative agencies. But granted that administrators may have little ability to ameliorate certain impediments to effective management, is it the case that they are inclined to see impediments of this sort as especially serious? Some may feel that to the extent that this orientation is common it constitutes a rational response to the contradictory expectations and pressures that American public managers confront. But it may also be that most public managers are able to cope with an American tradition that emphasizes administrative economy, efficiency, and effectiveness, as well as due process, accountability, and responsiveness, without seeing themselves and their agencies as under siege by a host of hostile "thems." An if-only orientation may characterize only a small minority of public managers who are either psychologically insecure or deficient in professional skills.

Whorton and Worthley's insights into the origins, dynamics, and consequences of if-only management are intriguing, but they provide no evidence on how common such orientation is among public managers. Other research provides mixed support for the existence of such an orientation. Earlier in the chapter the findings of Lynch and Gabris concerning the views of senior federal managers on obstacles to effective management were discussed. Certainly problems stemming from the actions of various actors external to their agency itself were frequently cited. A study of high-level civilian managers in the Department of the Navy disclosed similar frustration with either a lack of adequate resources whose provision is in the hands of others, or with limits on administrative autonomy resulting from various external checks (Lau, Newman, and Broedling, 1980). Many of these same managers cited "pressure from organizations external to the Navy" as a major source of job stress.

A report by the National Academy of Public Administration (1983) concluded that overhead management controls had become "so burdensome and constraining that they reduce rather than enhance management effectiveness," and, thus, tend to "choke off the kind of individual innovation and initiatives which are crucial to real management effectiveness" (p. 1). A survey by the U.S. Office of Personnel Management of 200 members of the Senior Executive Service uncovered much concern over "administrative overburden" with a majority of those surveyed believing that the "plethora of rules, regulations, and reporting requirements to which they were subjected significantly inhibited their ability to manage" (Pfiffner, 1983, p. 171). According to this study, " 'Let managers manage' would be the most effective way to promote productivity and efficiency in the Federal Government . . ." (Pfiffner, 1981–82, p. 13).

Over against the conclusions of these studies, there is a recent discussion of efforts to improve productivity and quality of work and service to the public on the part of the U.S. Forest Service to consider (Robertson, 1988–89). Relatively few of the impediments to more effective management in that agency were found to be related to the actions of nonagency actors:

We found that 50 percent of the things that our employees viewed as stifling to innovation and creativity or as causing them to do low priority, nonproductive work were within the control of the local line officer. . . . When you added it all up, 70–80 percent of the problem was within the discretion of the Forest Service. . . . That surprised us! The natural tendency is to walk around with the false assumption that we are the innocent victims of circumstances beyond our control. We are big on blaming others. People tend to blame things on the Congress, "the system," or on regulations from "higher up" (pp. 42–43).

Do state managers generally feel they could manage more effectively if only various "thems" would provide them with necessary tools or resources but otherwise leave them alone? If such an orientation exists at all, is it found in an extreme or more moderate form? In this section managers' views of the severity of various potential impediments to effective management are reexamined with an eye to identifying the extent to which an if-only management orientation is common among them.

Operationalizing the Concept of If-Only Management

As is true for many psychological constructs, developing an operational definition of the concept of if-only management is not easy. Whorton and Worthley treat the concept as if it were a dichotomy. Their discussion of various lurking "thems" implies a distinction between "them-problems" and "us-problems." Using slightly different terminology, a distinction might be drawn between "external" and "internal," or between "exogenous" and "endogenous" sources of management difficulties.

It is likely that seeing the source of one's problems in things that one can not control is a matter of degree as much as kind. But, following Whorton and Worthley, we treat the concept of if-only management as a dichotomous variable. Exogenous or "them" problems were defined as those:

1. caused by the actions of institutions or officials outside of the administrative apparatus, and/or

2. resulting from the existence of requirements or processes that administrative units themselves can not generally evade or ignore, and/or

3. whose elimination or amelioration is largely, if not totally, beyond the control of line managers.

Problems stemming from the action or inaction of nonadministrative, usually political, actors are defined as exogenous. But not all exogenous problems are political problems. Those stemming from the actions of—or state administrative interaction with—other levels of government were also defined as exogenous. In contrast, an endogenous or "us problem" is one that fails to satisfy the conditions outlined above.

The 52 problems were initially coded as exogenous or endogenous by the author. Two other public administration scholars then coded the set. Unanimity existed on the classification of 43 of the 52 problems. Of these, 27 were exogenous and 16 were endogenous. Rather than creating a third indeterminate category, the remaining 9 problems were classified according to the judgments of two of the three coders. This resulted in an exogenous set containing 31 problems and an endogenous set containing 21 problems. I would be the first to admit that for some of the problems differences of degree are being treated as differences in kind. But the extent of intercoder agreement suggests that the essence of Whorton and Worthley's distinction has been captured. In Tables 2.5 and 2.6, the problems concerning whose classification only two of the three coders concurred will be noted.

It is important to point out that the respondents themselves were not asked whether a given problem was an exogenous or an endogenous one. One could argue that a more valid measure of the extent of if-only management would emerge if the managers themselves had indicated which were them-problems and which were us-problems. It is conceivable that a manager bent on avoiding responsibility for administrative ineffectiveness would see all problems as exogenously determined. On the other hand, my approach to operationalizing the concept of if-only management is similar to that used by other social scientists who may, for example, classify individuals as more or less authoritarian based on their responses to various questions.

Another caveat is in order. I argue that an if-only management orientation exists if managers generally see exogenous problems as more serious impediments to effective management than endogenous ones. But the data do not permit us to distinguish between two differing *causes* of that orientation. Various "thems" may indeed be out to "get" particular administrators or administrative units, albeit for reasons that these "thems" genuinely believe to be valid. Alternatively, particular external actors may not be out to get managers or agencies, but managers may think that they are. That is, an if-only view reflects certain managers' peculiar psychological orientations to the challenges of administration.

One response to this issue is that, in its absence, empirical evidence on the existence of a phenomenon is valuable even if data on possible causes of the phenomenon are not. Moreover, it is important to determine the extent or intensity of the if-only management orientation because of the supposedly negative effects for administrative performance that result because managers hold such a view. Whether such a view is objectively rather than subjectively true is largely irrelevant so far as the consequences of holding such a view are concerned. Obviously, if such a managerial world view is found to be common, and if it is determined that effective administration requires that this situation be modified, then efforts to reduce its frequency would require that we ascertain whether the roots of this orientation lie in the real world of administration. If they do not, then solutions ranging from psychotherapy to retirement for rabid if-only managers might be in order. But at this point, determining if such a view is widespread, without specifying whether its basis lies in real as opposed to imagined circumstances, has value. Should it be uncommon, there is less need to identify possible causes.

The Prevalence of If-Only Management in the States

What, then, can be said about the relative frequency or intensity of if-only management perspectives among the sample of state managers? Table 2.5 details the severity of the elements of the endogenous problem set, while Table 2.6 focuses on the severity of exogenous "them" problems. None of the endogenous problems were considered to be serious impediments to effective management by more than 25% of the respondents across the 10 states. In the case of more than a third of these problems, 10% or less of the managers viewed them as serious impediments.

In contrast, nearly-one third of the problems in the exogenous set were viewed as serious impediments to effective management by 25% or more of the managers and six problems were considered to be serious by at least 33% of the respondents (see Table 2.6). These include the personnel and fiscal problems that were earlier cited as among the most serious impediments to effective

Table 2.5
Severity of Endogenous Management Problems

"Endogenous" Problems Viewed as "Serious" or "Very Serious" by 10% or Fewer Managers[1]

Racial/gender discrimination (3%) [2]	Monitoring/controlling subordinates' actions(8)
Lower level employees treat clients badly (4)	Inadequate publicity on unit's programs/Eligibility criteria(10)
Broad span of control (5)	Insufficiently motivated/diligent employees (10)
Security-oriented employees (6)	Communication with superiors (10)
Lack of clarity in unit's objectives (7)*	

"Endogenous" Problems Viewed as "Serious" or "Very Serious" by 11% to 25% of Managers

Complexity of organizational Structure (11)*	Supervisors lack management skills (18)
Assessing employee performance (11)	Insufficient time to make decisions (18)*
Communication with subordinates (11)	Assessing organizational performance/program impact (19)
Coordinating programs with other units (12)*	Admin. superiors provide inadequate direction (19)*
Decision making with inadequate information (15)	Ineffective organizational planning (22)
Information "overload": More information than can be effectively assimilated (17)	Organizational resistance to change (24)

"Endogenous" Problems Viewed as "Serious" or "Very Serious" by 26% to 40% of Managers

None

"Endogenous" Problems Viewed as "Serious" or "Very Serious" by More than 40% of Managers

None

1. See text for operational definition of "endogenous" problem.

2. Figure in parentheses is percent of managers reporting problem to be "serious" or "very serious". An asterisk indicates a problem that was coded as endogenous by only two of three coders.

management. On the other hand, another one-third of the problems in this set were not terribly serious, being considered so by 10% or less of the managers. Still, if one focuses on the 13 problems regardless of type that were considered to be serious impediments by 20% or more of the respondents, 11 are exogenous, them-problems.

The aggregate severity of all of the problems comprising either the endogenous or the exogenous set was also calculated in a manner similar to that used for the entire set and described in Table 2.4.[9] On a scale from 0 to 100, the mean severity of endogenous problems was 21.87 while the mean severity of exogenous problems was only slightly greater, 24.97. As a group, exogenous problems were also more severe than endogenous problems in each of the states, although the differences are significant (.025 level, one-tailed T-Test) for only six.

Differences in the aggregate severity of the two types of problems are not large in absolute terms for either the entire sample or for most of the individual states, however.[10] Although exogenous problems may indeed predominate among those viewed as most serious, a manager who considers one particular exogenous problem to be severe may not consider another to be so. That most managers do not view all exogenous problems as severe and all endogenous ones as inconsequential is made clear by the correlations that exist between managers' scores on each. The correlation between the aggregate exogenous and endogenous severity scores is a substantial $+.66$ (Pearson's r). The relationship is also positive for each of the states, ranging from .54 in New York to .80 in South Dakota. While blaming others for some of their difficulties, most managers consider various problems about which they ought to be able to do something also to seriously impede effective management of their units.

Earlier in the chapter it was noted that statistically significant differences in problem severity existed in the case of 31 of the 52 management problems. On the other hand, the strength of the association between "state" and problem severity was weak, save for roughly one-fourth of the set of potential impediments. When the problem set is broken down into exogenous and endogenous types, however, it is the case that there is greater interstate variation in the severity of them-problems. Significant interstate variation existed in the severity of 21 of the 31 exogenous problems but for only 6 of the 21 endogenous problems. "State" is a more powerful predictor of differences in aggregate exogenous than endogenous problem severity with the eta statistic for the former being .21 and that for the latter being .14.

One way to account for greater interstate variation in the severity of exogenous problems is to assume that the sources of these problems typically have broad impact across agencies. For example, civil service provisions, if comprehensive, affect virtually all administrative units in state government. To the extent that such arrangements are perceived by managers to have certain negative effects, these perceptions should vary little across agencies. Moreover, the average severity of civil-service-related problems in that state should differ sub-

Table 2.6
Severity of Exogenous Management Problems

"Exogenous" Problems Viewed as "Serious" by 10% or Less of Managers[1]

Relationships with local officials (3%) [2]
Collective bargaining on inappropriate matters(4)
Legislative "casework" inquiries(5)
Patronage practice (5)
Gubernatorial "meddling" in unit's operations (5)
Relations with federal agencies (6)

Collective bargaining with unit's employees (7)
Collective bargaining limits managerial authority (7)
Vague or ambiguous legislative intent (10)
Courts mandating service levels (10)
Federal grant matching fund requirements (10)

"Exogenous" Problems Viewed as "Serious" or "Very Serious" by 11% to 25% of Managers

Legislative "meddling" in administrative matters (11)
Media hostility to agency and its programs (11)
Legislative limits on unit's discretion (12)
Conditions attached to federal grants (13)
Lack of gubernatorial interest in unit/unit's programs (17)
Paperwork and delays in federal grant programs (14)

Lack of legislative interest in unit/unit's programs (16)
Interest group opposition to unit programs (17)
Legislature creates hard-to-implement programs (17)
Inadequate facilities (20)
Restrictions on expanding appropriations (23)

"Exogenous" Problems Viewed as "Serious" or "Very Serious" by 26% to 40% of Managers

Paperwork and clearance requirements on decisions (28)*
Complex process for promulgating rules/regs. (30)*
Unpredictability of federal grant funding levels (30)

Inability to fill key staff positions or retain staff (33)
Disciplining/dismissing employees (34)*
Civil service procedures for recruiting/selecting (34)

"Exogenous" Problems Viewed as "Serious" or "Very Serious" by More than 40% of Managers

Legislative expansion of programs without commensurate appropriations increase (40)
Inability to reward outstanding employee performance (51)*

Insufficient appropriations (45)

1. See text for operational definition of "exogenous" management problem.

2. Figure in parentheses is percent of managers seeing problem as "serious" or "very serious." An asterisk indicates a problems that was coded as exogenous by only two of three coders.

stantially as compared to the severity of these problems in a state without civil service. Note, in this regard, that the number of pairs of states in which significant differences in severity exist are often greatest in the case of various personnel-related problems that are quite severe overall (see Table 2.1).

The impact of provisions authorizing collective bargaining by state employees is likely to be similar to that of civil service provisions. While collective bargaining-related problems are not seen as serious overall (see Table 2.3), these three problems are among those for which significant differences among pairs of states are most common. Another example might be problems stemming from the penuriousness of the state legislature. Certain agencies may do relatively better than others in such a setting. But, overall, managers in a state with a less generous legislature could be expected to complain more about inadequate appropriations than would those in a state with a more generous one. Indeed, significant differences in the severity of complaints about insufficient appropriations emerge for a number of pairs of states (Table 2.1, first column).

Put differently, exogenous problems constitute contextual variables while endogenous problems more often result from agency-specific causes. The circumstances giving rise to endogenous problems are not unique to particular states, although such circumstances may be more common among agencies of one state than another due to differences in agency size, organizational structures, and many other factors. Support for this line of reasoning is also provided by differences in *intrastate* variation in the severity of endogenous and exogenous problems. In a given state, perceptions of the severity of endogenous problems—which we argue tend to be agency-specific—ought to vary more across agency administrators than do estimates of the severity of various exogenous problems. The logic is, again, that most exogenous problems reflect the imposition of certain requirements or practices on all or nearly all agencies in a state. The coefficients of variation for aggregate endogenous problem severity do indeed exceed those for aggregate exogenous problem severity in 7 of the 10 states.

A final bit of evidence supports this line of argument. Although significant interstate differences in severity occurred much more often for exogenous problems, what of the nine exogenous problems whose severity did not vary significantly across the states? As it turns out, five of these problems relate to the federal grants system. In other words, the source of these problem is not—like most other exogenous problems—state-unique. Another problem in this group of nine involves state administrative interaction with local governments. The exogenous factor is, again, not state-unique. Finally, problems stemming from the courts mandating service levels do not vary significantly across the 10 states. To the extent that the federal courts have been most likely to exhibit such activism, this may be yet another example of a non-state-specific "them" whose actions have relatively the same impact across states.

CONCLUSION

This chapter has examined the severity of a host of potential impediments to effective state management as viewed by state managers themselves in 10 American states. So far as the adequacy of state administrative performance is concerned, the findings are of the "glass is half empty, the glass is half full" variety. Certain state managers face serious hurdles as they seek to do what their state's citizens want done. But few seem overwhelmed by their problems. It is significant that relatively few managers reported that their unit had not been successful in achieving its goals. Only one-quarter of the specific problems were viewed as serious impediments to management by as many as one manager in five. The data suggest that most state managers and agencies "manage to manage."

A judgment about the quality of administration in these 10 states is complicated by several factors, however. One has already been noted: managers may be misperceiving reality or putting the best face on matters. It may be particularly difficult for managers to be honest with respect to certain problems. These managers likely downplayed the severity of race and gender discrimination if for no other reason than engaging in such discrimination is illegal. Surely this problem would be more severe if rank and file state employees had been surveyed instead. A five-state study that did precisely this (Hopkins, 1980) found that about 20% of female state employees felt they had been discriminated against on their jobs because of their gender while more than 40% of nonwhite state employees perceived discrimination based on their race. Similarly, the problem of agency employees treating clients badly would appear more serious if I had data from the clients of particular units as well as their managers.

Nevertheless, I believe that asking managers what ails their units yields valuable information. Managers in each of the 10 states complained most about the adequacy of the financial and human resources at their disposal as they sought to achieve their programmatic objectives. Elected officials or citizens may believe that the quality of public management can be enhanced in other ways, but those actually in the trenches assert that it is limits on the financial resources at their disposal, and how such financial resources can be used, as well as the systems used to secure and utilize human resources, that most seriously constrain their ability to achieve the goals of their administrative units. The involvement of the managers I have surveyed in the day-to-day implementation of state policies suggests that considerable weight be accorded their views.

Moreover, while it would be desirable to have data on perceptions of agency performance not only from managers but also from strategic agency constituents such as clients, legislators, governors, and others, what data are available suggest that managerial judgments are not grossly in error. Thus, there is evidence suggesting that most citizens dealing with state bureaucracies, including the poor who are most vulnerable to bureaucratic abuse, experience generally satisfactory bureaucratic encounters.

The absence of benchmark data even on managers' views of problems is a second factor. How problematic is public management in these 10 states as compared to the remaining 40? How do the problems that the managers I surveyed consider to be severe compare to those that federal or local government managers confront? The 10 states in this study are a diverse lot, but perhaps the 10 best or the 10 worst just happen to have been selected. While I believe the fact that only one-quarter of the management impediments were considered to be serious by even 20% of the respondents is a sign that most agencies are performing adequately, perhaps in other public jurisdictions even fewer managers would view these same problems as serious. Are particular management problems even less severe in private organizations?[11] On the other hand, as discussed above, what little comparable data exists is consistent with the 10 state findings.

Reaching a conclusion about the quality of administration in these 10 states is most fundamentally complicated by the fact that we hold public bureaucracies to diverse standards that include efficiency, effectiveness, and accountability. The lack of consensus about what constitutes "good" public management makes it difficult to decide if what managers define as a serious problem is "really" a problem. Should excessive paperwork and clearances required in making decisions be minimized? The positive side of red tape may be due process and accountability (Kaufman, 1977). That many managers complained about this as a serious impediment may be good rather than bad news because it indicates that procedures designed to prevent unilateral or undocumented decisions by individual bureaucrats are working. Similarly, if one believes, as many public administration practitioners and scholars do, that administrative effectiveness is enhanced to the extent that the involvement of elected officials in daily administrative operations is minimized, the fact that relatively few managers see legislative or gubernatorial "meddling in purely administrative matters" to be a serious problem is good news. Legislators or governors may be forgiven, however, if they wish this was more of a "problem" for managers than it is.

In this chapter I have also sought to determine the extent to which these state managers adopt an if-only style of management that sees those problems whose cause or solution lies largely outside strictly administrative realms as more serious impediments to the effective operation of their administrative unit than are those problems of an endogenous origin. While there is some tendency for managers to consider "them" problems to be more serious impediments than "us" problems, it is not accurate to conclude that the managerial perspectives of most of our respondents exemplify an if-only management orientation.

Managers certainly did not attribute all of their problems to the actions or failings of nonadministrative "thems." On the one hand, a significant number of exogenous problems were seen as serious by only a few managers. These include state legislative casework-handling, gubernatorial "meddling" in agency operations, and relationships with both local governments and federal agencies.

On the other hand, a number of endogenous problems are considered to be quite serious by a significant proportion of state managers. Recall in this regard the high and positive correlations that existed between respondents' aggregate exogenous severity scores and their aggregate endogenous severity scores. Administrators consider various exogenous problems to be severe. But they also report that various endogenous problems seriously impede their unit's ability to achieve its goals.

It is also significant that several of the most serious problems that we classified as exogenous were those on which only two of the three coders agreed. This suggests that these problems originate from the actions or failings of an agency or its employees as well as various thems and that the extent of if-only orientations is overstated. Thus, problems adequately rewarding outstanding performers may be due to the general constraints of state personnel rules or collective bargaining. But they may also reflect the unwillingness of supervisors to distinguish among subordinates who are performing at differing levels. Problems disciplining or dismissing employees may stem in part from the existence of general protections against dismissal other than for cause, and the impact of either civil service or union-negotiated appeal and grievance arrangements. But such difficulties may also reflect the unwillingness of managers to persist in dismissal or discipline proceedings in the face of any complicating procedural requirements. Hence, while placing blame on various other actors, the managers in these 10 states were often willing to admit that they "have met the enemy and it is us."

Disagreement on what constitutes good management is a major reason that managers may come to view their world in if-only terms. Although such an orientation in its extreme form is rare among the state managers, what does one think of managers who may manifest this orientation to even a moderate degree? Are we to conclude that these are managers irrationally using various shadowy "thems" as scapegoats for what are really their own shortcomings? Hardly; thinking someone is out to get you doesn't mean you are irrationally paranoid. The "paradoxical" environment of public administration of which Whorton and Worthley speak is a challenging one. At its worst it may be an impossible one. Legislators, chief executives, interest groups, and other strategic constituencies—sometimes with malign intent, but more often motivated by views as to what will improve public management that they believe to be valid—do seek to influence public management processes. There are also the attitudes of the media and the general populace to consider. Neither gives most administrators the benefit of the doubt. Definitions of what constitutes good public management that move far beyond efficiency and effectiveness narrowly construed, and the actions that they prompt, definitely complicate sincere efforts by administrators to execute their responsibilities.

Despite disagreement on what constitutes good public management, and the complex environment for public managers that results from this disagreement, the fact remains that extreme if-only management views are rare among the managers in these 10 states. Public managers may be better able to cope with the consequences of conflicting approaches to good public administration than we realize.[12]

Most of these state administrators seemed reasonably clear-eyed and clear-headed about what ails their own administrative units. They appeared to strike a realistic balance between blaming certain circumstances or actions beyond their control for their problems and looking closer to home for causes of, and solutions to, the difficulties that daily confront them as they seek to go about their jobs. Such a balanced perspective is certainly more consistent with the realities of the world of public management than an extreme ''if-only'' perspective that views public administrators as relentlessly set upon by a host of hostile ''thems.''

Managers' views of impediments to effective management suggest reasonably adequate levels of state administrative performance. Still, problems exist. A few are quite severe. Moreover, variation existed in the severity of a number of problems both across states and, especially, across agencies within particular states. In Chapter 3 I seek to identify some of the correlates of variation in state management difficulties.

NOTES

1. The other ''strategic'' constituencies of administrative organizations identified by Emmert are the ''executive-management'' constituency, consisting of the chief executive and his staff and budget and personnel agencies; the ''regulators,'' comprised of the judiciary as well as administrative units such as the Environmental Protection Agency of the Occupational Safety and Health Administration; and ''legislative sponsors,'' specifically, the legislature-at-large as well as legislative committees and staff.

2. But see Hatry (1989) for a much more sanguine view of the utility of citizen/client surveys.

3. The list of management problems was a catholic one. It was constructed after perusing the literature on management in general, and public management in particular. Several public management scholars reviewed the initial list and suggested changes.

4. Upward bias in estimates of organizational or program performance may not be limited to managers. It appears that client evaluations of programs also exhibit a positive bias (Scheirer, 1978; Stipak, 1980b).

5. Hereafter in the chapter, when the proportion of managers considering a problem to be ''serious'' or ''severe'' is reported, this is the sum of the proportion who responded that a given impediment was ''serious'' or ''very serious.''

6. The fact that the survey was conducted between the summer of 1982 and the winter of 1983 partially explains the saliency of fiscal concerns. The nation was mired in the most severe economic downturn since the end of World War II and many states faced revenue shortfalls that forced severe budget cuts.

7. Devising this summary measure of problem severity required that I make several assumptions. Chief among these is that each of the 52 potential impediments has equally significant consequences for administrative performance. Clearly, some problems matter

more than others. But being in no position to specify relative impact, each problem was weighted equally in constructing the indicator.

8. Several multiple comparison of means techniques exist. The Scheffe Test is used here.

9. Aggregate endogenous or exogenous problem severity for each respondent was calculated as follows. Each manager's responses were summed across all of the potential problems in either the endogenous or the exogenous set. These sums were then multiplied by a constant (1.587 in the case of the endogenous set; 1.075 in the case of the exogenous set) so that aggregate endogenous or exogenous severity could range between 0.00 and 100.0.

10. Save for the difference of seven scale units between the mean severity of the two types of problems in Arizona, in no other state is the aggregate severity of the exogenous problems more than four units greater than the aggregate severity of the endogenous problems.

11. An even more fundamental issue is how small a percentage of managers must view a problem as serious before it can be concluded that it is not a serious impediment to effective management. I argue that the fact that nearly all potential problems are considered to be serious by no more than one manager in five is evidence of reasonably adequate performance. Such a standard may be too lenient, however. Perhaps only problems that are seen as serious by no more than one manager in ten can be dismissed as inconsequential for administrative functioning. If a 10% standard is used, two-thirds of the 52 problems are severe, and the overall judgment on the adequacy of state administrative performance would change.

12. This conclusion is consistent with the findings that emerged from Porter and Van Maanen's (1983) examination of how city administrators managed their time in comparison to managers in industrial organizations. Municipal managers perceived many more pressures and intrusions on their time from external actors than did industrial managers. But they also found that the most effective city administrators (as rated by their organizational superiors) were those that " 'rolled with the time punches' as it were. Task accomplishment in this type of organizational environment seemed to be related to abilities to accommodate to demands not under one's own control and perhaps not of one's choosing (p. 222)."

Chapter 3

Sources of State Management Problems

INTRODUCTION

Various problems that might hamper the effective administration of state programs were explored in Chapter 2. Certain problems were viewed as much more serious impediments to effective management than others overall. But substantial variation in the severity of a number of problems was also evident. Interstate variation was especially great for "exogenous" problems—those whose amelioration is largely outside the control of state agencies or managers themselves. Substantial variability also exists in the severity of management problems across agencies within states. In this chapter an effort is made to account for some of the variation in state management problem severity.

Variation in the severity of specific impediments to effective state management may be due to many factors. Potentially relevant ones on which the survey provides information include the size of an administrative unit, its place in a state's administrative hierarchy, the number of subordinates that a responding manager supervises, and the functional responsibility of a unit. The first part of the chapter explores the impact of these factors on problem severity. Since these variables prove to have limited explanatory power, I then consider more "problem-specific" correlates of the severity of a subset of the management problems. Subsequent sections of the chapter examine correlates of the severity of personnel and federal government-related impediments to effective state management. In later chapters, most especially Chapters 6, 7, and 8, I attempt to explain variation in other problems using additional predictors.

ACCOUNTING FOR VARIATION IN THE SEVERITY OF IMPEDIMENTS TO EFFECTIVE STATE MANAGEMENT

Organizational Size and Management Difficulties

The size of an administrative unit may complicate management. Larger units may be organizationally more complex. Combined with the existence of more employees, such complexity may create problems in monitoring or controlling subordinates and generate complaints about too wide a span of control. In larger units decisions may take longer to make, paperwork burdens may be greater, communication both upward and downward may be more problematic, and change may be more difficult to achieve. Since they consume more of the state budget, larger units may attract more attention from strategic constituents such as the governor, legislature, and interest groups. Hence, problems stemming from the involvement of these actors in agency affairs may be more common in larger units. At the same time, a lack of gubernatorial or legislative interest should be less of a problem in the case of larger units. Units with larger budgets may fare differently in budgetary decisionmaking than do smaller units.

Beyond its implications for organizational complexity, having more employees may result in more serious personnel-related problems, such as insufficiently diligent employees. Having to monitor the activities of a larger number of employees may complicate employee performance appraisal. This may, in turn, make it more difficult to discipline low performers. Any deficiencies of civil service arrangements may be magnified in a unit with a larger work force.

Although the relationship of organizational size to various dimensions of organizational functioning has been of great interest to analysts, the large body of research on size and organizational performance is characterized by contradictory findings. Various reviews of the size-performance link have been unable to substantiate an unambiguous relationship. Dalton et al. (1980) reported that little research had uncovered any significant size-performance relationship at the organizationwide level. These same authors concluded, however, that a majority of the subunit studies had found negative relationships to exist between various indexes of size and organizational performance. Gooding and Wagner (1985) reach a similar conclusion in their excellent metaanalysis of the literature.

Gooding and Wagner also stress the need to be sensitive to factors that may condition the size-performance relationship. One such factor is how "size" has been operationalized. While size is a multidimensional construct, most research uses measures that capture only one of these dimensions (Kimberly, 1976).

The 10-state survey provides two indicators of organizational size: the size of a unit's budget and the number of persons employed in that unit. Most of the studies of the relationship between size and the performance of public organizations—such as colleges and their academic divisions, school districts, county governments, human service agencies, and mental hospitals—have operationalized size as number of employees. To control for the distorting effects of a few extremely large units in a sample, many studies of both public and private organizations have used the log of number of employees. Size of budget has less often been used as an indicator of organizational size, although a number of studies of private organizations have used indicators such as assets, annual sales, or invested capital (Gooding & Wagner, 1985).[1]

The indicators of organizational performance used in my analysis—the severity of various possible impediments to effective agency performance—differ from those typically used in analyses of the relationship between size and organizational functioning. Dependent variables used in previous studies of public agencies have included nonacademic achievements per college student (Baird, 1969); reading/mathematics achievement (Bidwell & Kasarda, 1975); quality of service ratings (Christenson & Sachs, 1980); key-informant performance ratings of academic divisions (Fiedler & Gillo, 1974); the number of persons served per unit of input in human services agencies (Glisson & Martin, 1980); and units processed per operator in post offices (Smyth, 1982). Given the diversity in operational definitions of the dependent variable of organizational performance, use of yet another indicator seems defensible. If size affects organizational performance, it ought to be related to the severity of at least some of the managerial difficulties of interest in this study.

Organizational "Place" and Management Problems

The location of an administrative unit within a state's administrative hierarchy may also be related to variation in problem severity. Units and managers nearer the top may be exposed to greater external scrutiny. Hence, interest group and media hostility, or legislative or gubernatorial "meddling," may be more of a problem for these units. On the other hand, respondents and units farther down in the administrative hierarchy may suffer from a lack of gubernatorial or legislative attention. Lower level managers may perceive communication with superiors and inadequate direction by these same superiors to be more serious problems. Since lower level units are more likely to be directly involved in the delivery of services, managers in these units may perceive client treatment to be more of a problem.

To explore these and other relationships with problem severity, a measure of the *organizational place* of each respondent—and by extension his or her particular subunit—in the administrative hierarchy of a state was devised. A higher score on this variable indicates a manager is higher up in a state's administrative hierarchy.[2]

Supervisory Burden and Management Problems

Scholars of public administration have long been concerned about how the number of subordinates that managers supervise affects administrative performance. Other things being equal, the larger the number of subordinates supervised, the more likely it is that a manager will report "span of control" difficulties. Monitoring subordinates should be more of a problem when more subordinates report to a supervisor. Managers who supervise a smaller number of subordinates may report fewer problems with employee motivation and diligence, since they may be able to keep closer tabs on them or can more readily appraise their performance. Communicating with subordinates may be easier if there are fewer of them with whom to communicate. To test for these and other relationships with management problems, a measure of *supervisory burden* was developed. This was simply the number of subordinates that managers said reported directly to them.[3]

Functional Responsibilities and Management Problems

The *functional responsibility* of an administrative unit may also be related to the severity of state management problems. Any number of potential relationships suggest themselves. Units with regulatory responsibilities may be especially sensitive to the complexity of the process for promulgating rules and regulations. Those with more highly technical and, hence, less visible functions may be more likely to complain about inadequate publicity, while those that discharge administratively more visible or politically charged functions may complain about excessive legislative or gubernatorial meddling. The relative salience of particular functions may affect budgetary fortunes. Those units with custodial responsibilities, such as corrections agencies or those operating state hospitals, may complain more about the adequacy of facilities. Agencies with criminal justice and certain other responsibilities may be more likely to complain about how the courts affect their operations. Managers of units that provide services to disadvantaged citizens may report that staff treatment of clients is more of a problem.

The classification scheme for functional responsibilities used here is that used by Wright in his surveys of state agency heads.[4] With the exception of a few units that were excluded because they had unique functions, the remaining units were classified into one of 11 functional categories. These categories include staff units with fiscal or nonfiscal responsibilities, as well as line units with criminal justice, economic development, education, environmental, health, income security, natural resources, regulatory, and transportation responsibilities.

MODELING DETERMINANTS OF VARIATION IN STATE MANAGEMENT PROBLEM SEVERITY

Multiple regression techniques were used to sort out the relative impact of the four independent variables just discussed on the severity of each of the 52 potential impediments to effective state management.[5] The functional responsibility of a unit was represented using dummy variables. Since the logs of budget and staff size are closely related, each was entered separately with the other variables. Given their high intercorrelation, each typically explains a comparable amount of variation. Results are reported for one or the other depending upon which linkage made more sense on theoretical grounds and/or which indicator of organizational size explained more of the variation in the severity of a problem.

Table 3.1 summarizes some of the results of the regression analysis. It includes information on those regressions in which the overall model was significant (probability of F = .05 or better) and could account for at least 5% of the variation in problem severity. Information is also provided on the significant predictors that accounted for at least 1% of variation in problem severity in each of the models.

The explanatory power of organizational size and place, functional responsibilities of units, and the supervisory burdens of managers is not great. These four variables can account for even 5% of the variation in the severity of just 11 of the 52 problems. Four of these are problems relating to federal grants-in-aid, while two are related to collective bargaining by unit employees. The functional responsibility of a unit most often predicts variation in grants-related problems, while ''union'' problems are reported to be more severe by managers of units with larger budgets.

Furthermore, some of the stronger relationships between these variables and various problems that do emerge may be spurious. Size of budget is linked to ''union'' problems largely because those states in the sample in which collective bargaining is most extensive—such as California, Michigan, and New York—are among the most populous and, hence, have more state employees and larger budgets. The units in which our respondents are located in these states tend to have larger budgets than does the typical unit in most of the other states.[6] Later in the chapter the models of ''union'' problems are reestimated using a variable that measures extent of collective bargaining by the employees of particular states. Furthermore, the substantial amount of variation in the severity of union problems within particular states that is accounted for by the functional responsibility of a unit is very likely because the proportion of employees who collectively bargain varies by type of agency.[7] It may also be that units with regulatory, staff, criminal justice, and certain other functions see federal grant-related problems as less severe because they are less dependent on federal grant funding than are income security, health, and education units. This possibility is also examined later in the chapter.

MANAGEMENT PROBLEMS AND PROBLEM-SPECIFIC PREDICTORS

A major reason that little of the variation in managers' estimates of the severity of the set of management problems can be accounted for using the independent variables of unit size, organizational place, supervisory burden, and

Table 3.1

Summary of Most Powerful Models of State Management Problem Severity (Stepwise Regression Using Organizational Size, Organizational "Place," Supervisory Burden, and Functional Responsibility of Unit as Predictors)

Management Problem[1]	Explained Variance (Adjusted R^2)	Predictors Accounting for at least One Percent of Variance[2]	B	Beta	Variance Explained by Predictor
Unpredictability of Federal Grant Funding	.177	Fiscal Staff Func.	-.804	-.201	.050
		Regulatory Func.	-.641	-.198	.050
		Income Security Func.	.465	.152	.025
		Education Func.	.414	.124	.021
		Health Func.	.352	.103	.016
Courts Mandating Service Levels	.144	Unit Size (Staff)	.174	.199	.059
		Income Security Func.	.531	.248	.036
		Crim. Justice Func.	.544	.217	.035
Requirements Attached to Federal Grant Programs	.126	Income Security Func.	.219	.092	.040
		Regulatory Func.	-.535	-.216	.027
		Fiscal Staff Func.	-.580	-.187	.021
		Nonfiscal Staff Func.	-.485	-.137	.014
		Criminal Justice Func.	-.384	-.146	.014
		Unit Size (Budget)	.083	.103	.011
Paperwork/Delay in Federal Grant Programs	.125	Regulatory Func.	-.551	-.217	.035
		Fiscal Staff Func.	-.638	-.202	.035
		Nonfiscal Staff Func.	-.516	-.141	.018
		Criminal Justice Func.	-.326	-.122	.016
		Nat. Resources Func.	-.164	-.068	.010
Collective Bargaining by Unit Employees	.106	Unit Size (Budget)	.216	.317	.078
		Organizational Place	-.077	-.115	.015

Problem		Significant Predictors	B	β	Variance
Inadequate Direction/Support from Superiors	.088	Organizational Place	-.194	-.215	.060
		Unit Size (Staff)	-.175	-.162	.022
Organizational Complexity	.079	Organizational Place	-.183	0.235	.063
Managerial Authority Limited by Collective Bargaining	.068	Unit Size (Budget)	.155	.205	.042
		Organizational Place	-.075	-.117	.013
Paperwork and Requirements for Clearance on Decisions	.062	Education Func.	.374	.132	.018
		Unit Size (Staff)	.172	.173	.014
		Organizational Place	-.096	-.116	.016
		Health Func.	.242	.084	.010
Matching Fund Requirement on Federal Grants	.055	Regulatory Func.	-.423	-.183	.020
		Fiscal Staff Func.	-.463	-.160	.019
		Nonfiscal Staff Func.	-.388	-.119	.011
Communication with Superiors	.050	Organizational Place	-.123	-.165	.036
		Unit Size (Staff)	-.114	-.129	.016

1.   The problems included in this table are those for which at least 5% of the variation in severity could be accounted for in a stepwise regression into which were entered measures of organizational size, organizational "place," the number of subordinates reporting directly to a responding manager, and the functional responsibility of the unit. Size of budget and staff were logarithmically transformed to reduce the distorting impact of extreme cases. Since the resulting values for budget and staff size are highly correlated, the regressions for each of the 52 problems were estimated twice, once using budget size with other independent variables and a second time using staff size in place of budget size. When unit size is a significant predictor, the specific indicator used is indicated in parentheses. Organizational place was calculated from a question that asked each manager how many levels of his or her agency were above his or her unit. Since for an agency head, numbers of levels is 0, 1 was added to the number of levels reported. This sum was then subtracted from 10. Hence, the higher a manager and his or her unit is in the administrative hierarchy, the higher the score on the organizational place variable. Scores on this variable ranged from 2 to 9.

2.   This column lists only those significant predictors (F value of B significant at .05 level or better) that could also explain a minimum of 1% of the variation in the severity of the indicated problem. The final column of the table indicates the precise amount of variance accounted for by each of these predictors.

3.   This is the unstandardized regression coefficient.

4.   This is the standardized regression coefficient.

43

functional responsibility is that there is often little variation in problem severity to explain. This is especially true for the large number of problems that were not seen as very serious overall.[8] Lack of success in accounting for variation may also be due to measurement error in the independent variables. In their review of the research on organizational size and performance, Wagner and Gooding (1985) conclude that the strength and consistency of this relationship was affected by how size was operationalized. If we had measured unit size differently it might have displayed greater explanatory power, although a logarithmic transformation of budget and work-force data did not enhance explanatory power greatly.[9] A more complex scheme for classifying units in terms of their functional responsibilities might have resulted in stronger relationships between this variable and the severity of various problems.

Measurement error affecting the dependent variable may also have attenuated relationships. Wagner and Gooding (1985) observe that differences in how organizational performance has been operationalized have conditioned the relationships between it and organizational size. Managerial perceptions of problem severity may be inconsistent with objective reality. While the possibility that serious measurement error exists in one or more of the independent variables, or the possibility that managers' estimates of problem severity are invalid, can not be rejected out of hand, I believe that the explanation for lack of success in accounting for much variation in problem severity lies elsewhere.

The set of management problems is a diverse one. This diversity suggests that each problem has a rather unique set of correlates. Accounting for variation in the severity of particular problems demands the use of highly problem-specific predictors. Unfortunately, I possess data on only a handful of the many potential problem-specific sources of variation in the severity of the set of management problems. But some of the findings on the impact of the four predictors I have used provide support for this line of argument.

The organizational location of a manager was significantly related to only six problems, with those lower down in the organizational hierarchy seeing each as being more severe than did those located at higher levels. Two of the six were "union" problems. But the other four—adequacy of direction by superiors, paperwork and required clearances, organizational complexity, and communication with superiors—are all problems that could be expected to be of more serious concern to those in the bowels of the bureaucracy. Some 34% of the managers who were located four levels below the top of their state's administrative hierarchy considered inadequate direction and support from superiors to be a serious impediment to effective management as compared to 25% of those three levels down and just 12% of those two levels down. Similarly, 22% of those managers located four levels down saw communications with superiors to be a serious problem as compared to less than 10% of those located at the top two levels. Of the managers located four levels below the top, 29% complained about the effects of excessively complex organizational structure as opposed to just 5% of agency heads.

The explanatory payoff associated with a closer match between particular predictors and specific problems is also evident in the finding that managers of units with criminal justice responsibilities complain more about inadequate facilities and about the effects of judicial mandates. State agencies in the criminal justice system include those that operate correctional institutions. In most states the capacity of existing facilities has been strained due to an increase in crime, an increased propensity to incarcerate those who commit crimes, and longer sentences for those convicted of particular offenses. Capacities have regularly been exceeded even as states have built more facilities. It is the inadequacy of these facilities, combined with "double bunking" and other strategies for coping with an increased number of inmates, that have often prompted the suits that have resulted in court orders mandating changes in correctional practices.

The remainder of this chapter provides additional support for the argument that the variables that can best account for the severity of a particular management problem are likely to be quite different from those that can account for variation in the severity of another problem. The next section focuses on variation in the severity of those problems that reflect the capabilities of state administrative personnel themselves or that involve personnel practices and systems. This is followed by a similar effort to account for variation in the severity of federal-government-related problems.

CIVIL SERVICE, COLLECTIVE BARGAINING, AND PERSONNEL-RELATED IMPEDIMENTS TO EFFECTIVE STATE MANAGEMENT

The quality of public employees and the methods used to recruit, select, compensate, promote, discipline, or dismiss them are generally considered to be crucial to organizational performance.[10] The widespread belief that this is so is one reason that many states have undertaken to reform their personnel systems over the past 15 years (Dresang, 1978, 1982; Elling, 1990). As with other potential impediments to effective management, however, there is little comparative data on the severity of personnel-related problems. There is also little systematic evidence on how characteristics of a state's personnel system may be related to the severity of personnel-related problems. Civil service advocates have traditionally pointed to patronage practices as the source of various personnel maladies. Others, however, consider civil service practices to be a major part of the problem (Savas & Ginsberg, 1973; Shafritz, 1975). The development of collective bargaining among public employees has been seen by many, including various defenders of traditional "merit" civil service arrangements, as being a bad idea whose time, alas, has come (Wellington & Winter, 1971; Stahl, 1983, Chs. 23–25).

Among the few relevant studies is one by Marsh (1977) exploring how public personnel administrators in a single state appraised the effects of their state's personnel system.[11] More recently, Elliot (1985) has compared the views of personnel professionals with those of state employees on the consequences of Alabama's civil service system. While both groups had generally positive views of the system's consequences, nearly a quarter of the Alabama employees felt merit system rules were "a greater hindrance than help" in running state government (p. 23). But a 50-state survey of those administering state hazardous waste clean-up programs found that an overwhelming majority did not believe that civil service rules hindered their ability to do so (Cohen & Ingersoll, 1985). As discussed in Chapter 2, Lynch and Gabris (1981) found that many federal managers considered personnel problems to seriously impede effective management.

In this section of the chapter the findings on the severity of various personnel-related problems first presented as part of the more general discussion in Chapter 2 are considered in greater depth. Variation in the severity of these problems is then related to variation in the proportion of a state's work force covered by civil service or that collectively bargains. This analysis provides support for the argument that variation in state management problem severity can be accounted for when appropriate, problem-specific variables are identified.

Patterns of Severity of Personnel Problems

Among the 52 possible impediments to state management, 12 are related to the quality or characteristics of state employees or to various personnel practices. The severity of these 12 problems, overall and by state, is detailed in Table 3.2. Personnel problems are among the most and the least serious impediments. One-third or more of the administrators considered adequately rewarding outstanding employee performance, civil service procedures for selecting and hiring personnel, effectively disciplining employees, and difficulties in filling key vacancies and retaining key staff to be serious problems. As noted in Chapter 2, a perceived inability to reward outstanding employee performance ranked as the most serious impediment among all 52 problems. Civil service hiring procedures, problems disciplining employees, and recruiting and retaining staff ranked third, fourth, and fifth in severity.

At the other extreme, no more than 10% of the managers considered the following to be serious impediments to their unit's performance: (1) lazy employees, (2) the existence of collective bargaining, (3) patronage practices, (4) collective bargaining on "inappropriate" matters such as program planning, (5) limits on managerial authority due to collective bargaining, (6) employees excessively concerned about job security, or (7) racial or gender discrimination. None of these seven problems ranked higher than 40th in severity among the entire set of problems.

Table 3.2 also indicates that considerable interstate variation exists in the severity of most personnel-related problems. Variation was statistically signifi-

Table 3.2
Comparison of Severity of Personnel-Related Management Problems in 10 States

Problem or Problem Source	Percentage of Administrators Reporting a Problem to be "Serious" or "Very Serious"										
	All States (847)[1]	Ariz. (68)	Cal. (149)	Del. (72)	Ind. (73)	Mich. (125)	N.Y. (113)	S.D. (64)	Tenn. (60)	Tex. (89)	Vt. (34)
Adequately rewarding outstanding employees	51%(1)[2]	55%	46%	59%	63%	45%	45%	67%	67%	43%	35%
Civil service procedures for recruiting/ selecting personnel	34(4.5)	44	40	32	18	56	39	18	39	7	3
Disciplining/dismissing incompetent employees	34(4.5)	37	41	31	32	39	41	17	40	21	27
Filling key vacancies/retaining key staff	33(6)	30	33	22	55	45	37	25	33	18	21
Assessing employee performance	21(14.5)	21	16	18	17	21	23	16	20	15	15
Insufficiently motivated/hardworking employees	10(35.5)	9	9	20	18	6	8	14	15	5	6
Collective bargaining by employees of unit	7(41)	9	12	10	0	21	5	2	2	1	6
Limits on managerial authority due to collective bargaining	7(41)	0	13	6	0	17	9	3	2	0	6
Security-preoccupied employees	6(43.5)	5	7	7	6	7	7	8	5	5	0
Use of patronage in filling positions	5(46.5)	3	4	6	10	2	7	6	5	3	3
Bargaining on inappropriate matters like program planning	4(49.5)	0	9	4	0	9	5	3	0	0	6
Race or gender discrimination	3(51.5)	2	4	1	3	5	5	0	0	1	0

1. Parenthetical figure is number of responding administrators. Number responding to questions on severity of particular problems may vary downward somewhat due to missing data.

2. Number in parentheses is the rank in severity for the entire sample among the entire set of 52 managerial impediments.

cant for all but four of the problems: assessing employee performance, security-preoccupied employees, patronage practices, and race/gender discrimination. In contrast to the pattern for other management problems, interstate variation in personnel problem severity is often evident even when overall severity is low.

As was pointed out in Chapter 2, significant interstate differences (F-test) in the mean severity of a particular problem may exist if only one or two states stand out from the remaining eight or nine. Across all 52 problems (see Tables 2.1 to 2.3), multiple comparison of means tests disclosed that significant differences between pairs of states emerged 91 times. The 12 personnel problems account for 69 of these. A half dozen or more pairs of states differed significantly in the case of four of the problems. These are problems hiring staff due to civil service procedures and the three labor relations problems. Significant interstate differences overall usually emerged because of the distinctive responses of administrators in one or two states. Thus, of the 69 instances of significant differences among pairs of states across the 12 problems, 26 involved Michigan administrative responses versus those of some other state. Differences between the pattern of California responses and other states account for 19 cases and between New York responses and others for another 10.

Interstate variation is greatest for problems stemming from civil service hiring procedures or those related to collective bargaining. The responses of Michigan, California, and New York managers tend to be most distinctive. All are states with well-developed civil service systems as well as states in which collective bargaining is widespread. This suggests that differences between these states and others in the severity of certain personnel problems stem from differences in the extent of civil service coverage or the extent of collective bargaining. These possibilities will be examined soon.

Configurations of Personnel Problems: A Factor Analysis

State administrators view some personnel-related problems as more troublesome than others. Certain problems are also more serious in some states than in others. A related question is whether certain personnel problems exist in conjunction with others. Do administrators who report that collective bargaining on "inappropriate" matters poses problems also report that collective bargaining undercuts managerial authority? Is difficulty hiring employees associated with difficulty in firing them? Are either of these associated with complaints about the quality of employees?

The zero-order correlations between the 12 personnel problems indicate numerous significant positive relationships. Of 66 possible correlations, 22 were of the magnitude of .25 or greater, 12 coefficients were .30 or greater, and 5 were .40 or greater.

Factor analysis is a more powerful way to sort out the interrelationships among these problems. It can also help us determine whether certain problems have a common source. If critics of civil service are correct, then complex hiring processes, difficulty disciplining low-performing employees, adequately rewarding superior performance, and the presence of lazy or security-obsessed employees should constitute a cluster of problems. On the other hand, civil service practices should minimize patronage as a problem, as Elliot's (1985) findings for Alabama suggest. Conversely, while administrators functioning within a patronage system might be expected to complain about it, they should be less seriously afflicted by problems that supposedly result from civil service arrangements.

Problems stemming from collective bargaining should load on a common factor. Whether other personnel difficulties would load on the same factor is unclear. Despite assertions about the incompatibility of civil service principles and practices with those that underlie the union movement, there is evidence that the two can coexist (Nigro & Nigro, 1977; Lewin & Horton, 1975). Public unions are often strongest where there is also a long history of support for civil service. In our study, California, New York, Michigan, and Vermont are examples. Unions join civil service advocates in opposition to patronage practices and support protections from dismissal for non-job-related reasons. They also oppose excessive use of provisional or temporary appointments, a practice common to patronage systems. If a "union" factor emerges it should be negatively related to any "patronage" factor that emerges. Texas and Indiana are states in the sample in which little or no collective bargaining occurs but which have reputations for robust patronage politics. It is unclear whether difficulty adequately rewarding superior performance is a civil service or a collective bargaining problem. In practice, the consequences of union preferences for across-the-board salary increases may differ little from those that result from how so-called merit increases are actually awarded under civil service arrangements.

Still, a factor analysis of state personnel problems should result in the emergence of at least three major factors with one identifiable as a "union" factor, another as a "patronage" factor, and a third as a "civil service" factor. Because it was anticipated that these factors would overlap to some extent, an oblique rotation was used to obtain a final factor solution.

The results of the factor analysis, summarized in Table 3.3, only partially conform to expectations. Two primary factors emerged that together accounted for more than 40% of the variance. A third factor could explain an additional 8% of variance.

The factor structure is relatively simple. Each of the 12 personnel problems typically loads on a single factor. The major exceptions are disciplining or dismissing incompetent employees—which loads substantially on both Factors 1 and 3—and rewarding outstanding employee performance—which loads quite substantially on Factor 3 and nearly as substantially on Factor 1. Only racial or sexual discrimination as an impediment to effective management fails to load substantially on any of the factors. This occurs because so few managers indicated this to be a serious problem that there was scant variation to explain.

The meaning of Factor 2 is easiest to infer. All of the collective bargaining-related problems—and only these problems—load heavily on this factor.

Factor 3 explains relatively little variance, but two problems—filling key

Table 3.3
Oblique Factor Structure of Personnel-Related Problems in State Management

Problem or Problem Source	FACTORS		
	1	2	3
Rewarding outstanding employee performances	.415[1]	-.013	.555
Civil service procedures for recruiting/selecting staff	-.289	-.392	.723
Difficulties disciplining/dismissing employees	.648	.315	.492
Filling key vacancies/retaining key staff	.190	-.102	.807
Assessing employee performance	.726	-.168	.208
Insufficiently motivated/diligent employees	.742	-.142	.363
Collective bargaining by employees of unit	.190	-.876	.152
Managerial authority limited by collective bargaining	.290	.864	.202
Security-preoccupied employees	.598	-.396	.166
Use of patronage in filling positions	.474	-.125	.131
Bargaining on inappropriate matters such as program planning	.217	-.823	.117
Race or gender discrimination	.244	-.305	.208
Eigenvalues [2]	3.535	1.697	1.012
Percent of Variance Explained	29.5%	14.1%	8.4%
Cumulative Variance Explained	29.5%	43.6%	52.0%

Factor Correlation Matrix:

	FACTORS		
	1	2	3
Factors 1			
2	-.278		
3	.355	-.188	

1. Table entries are loadings of each problem on a given factor. Loadings greater than .400 are underscored.

2. From unrotated factor solution.

positions/retaining staff, and civil service procedures for recruiting and selecting personnel—load heavily on this factor and only on this factor. Since problems associated with civil service hiring practices load heavily on this factor while patronage practices do not, and since problems filling key positions may stem from the complexity of civil service procedures, this factor might be considered a "civil service problems" factor.

But difficulty disciplining low-performing employees, an often-alleged consequence of civil service, does not load very heavily on Factor 3. Nor does it load as heavily on this factor as on Factor 1. Problems with lazy or security-obsessed employees also fail to load heavily on Factor 3. For these reasons, as well as others to be discussed later, Factor 3 might better be defined as a "staff recruitment/retention" factor. That difficulty rewarding good employees also loads more heavily on this factor than any other reinforces this conclusion. An inability to reward outstanding performers may hamper recruitment and retention of key staff at least as much as the complexity of the hiring process.

Six problems load substantially on Factor 1. The fact that a problem with patronage loads most heavily on Factor 1 may justify a conclusion that patronage-oriented personnel practices underlie this factor. The fact that civil service procedures for recruiting and selecting employees failed to load at all heavily on this factor reinforces such a conclusion. Alternatively, Factor 1 might be labeled an "employee quality" factor. The most substantial loads for lazy employees and for security-obsessed employees are on this factor. A problem rewarding outstanding employees loads nearly as heavily on this factor as on Factor 3. Effectively assessing employee performance loads far more substantially on this factor than on the other two. Finally, difficulty either disciplining or dismissing incompetent employees also loads most heavily on Factor 1.

Civil Service, Collective Bargaining, and Personnel Problems

As discussed earlier in the chapter, efforts to use the size of an administrative unit, its place in the organizational hierarchy, the number of subordinates a particular manager supervises, and the functional responsibilities of a unit to explain variation in the severity of specific impediments to effective state management were not notably successful. I argued that one must identify highly problem-specific variables if one hopes to be able to explain very much of the variation in the severity of particular problems. Evidence in support of this argument was provided in the case of certain of the management problems.

Detailed examination of the severity of the dozen personnel-related problems provides a better opportunity to demonstrate the utility of problem-specific predictors. Unit size, organizational place, supervisory burden and functional responsibility could account for even as much as 5% of the variation in the severity of just two of the personnel-related problems—the general effects of collective bargaining by a unit's employees and limits on managerial authority stemming from its existence. The size of a unit's budget could account for 2% of the variation in these two "union" problems, and in the extent of problems with racial or gender discrimination, with units with larger budgets seeing these problems as more severe. The existence of security-obsessed employees was seen to be a more severe impediment to effective management in the case of managers of units with more employees.

In the case of the three union problems at least, it was argued that the relationship between unit size and problem severity was due to the fact that differences in size often masked differences in the extent of collective bargaining in particular units.

The severity of these and other personnel-related problems may reflect not only the impact of differences in the extent of collective bargaining but also in the extent to which a state embraces merit civil service principles and practices. Unfortunately, information on these two personnel problem-specific predictors was not initially collected as part of the survey. Subsequent to the administration of the survey, information on the proportion of state employees covered under civil service or authorized to engage in collective bargaining was obtained from various published sources as well as from telephone conversations with personnel and labor relations officials in each of the states.[12] Hence, data on the proportion of the employees in individual units that are covered by civil service or that collectively bargain is unavailable. At the same time, the other independent variables that have been used to account for variation in management problem severity are measured at the individual unit level. In the absence of unit-level data on civil service coverage or extent of collective bargaining, a decision was made to assign each case a value on the civil service and collective bargaining variables that corresponds to the aggregate figure for the state bureaucracy in which a unit was located.

As for extent of collective bargaining, this presents little problem in the case of the four states in which no employees bargained, or in South Dakota where just 10% did so. Nor does it present too much of a problem in the case of Michigan, California, New York, and Vermont samples where 70% or more of state employees collectively bargain. It is most distorting in the case of Delaware where 40% of state employees collectively bargained. This methodological compromise also had little distorting effect in the case of the seven states in which 80% or more of state employees are covered by civil service, or in Texas where only 20% are covered. It is most distorting in Arizona and Indiana where the proportions of state employees covered by civil service were 40% and 60%, respectively. Still, given the limits of the data on extent of collective bargaining and civil service, this approach seems preferable.[13]

In the eyes of defenders, merit principles and practices assure a neutrally competent corps of public employees. Others contend that the costs of civil service frequently outweigh its benefits. The introduction of collective bargaining to the public sector has prompted even more spirited debate among scholars, public personnel professionals, and managers. Some see it as fundamentally incompatible with "merit" principles while others are more sanguine about the possibilities for coexistence. The validity of these views will be assessed as the data to be discussed here bear on them. Empirically, extensive merit system coverage often coexists with extensive collective bargaining. In the sample, the correlation between the proportion of a state's employees covered under merit system provisions and the proportion collectively bargaining is .74.

Is civil service as much bane as blessing? Correlational analysis suggests that "merit" systems may entail some costs for effective management (see Table 3.4). A moderate positive correlation exists between extent of civil service coverage and complications in selecting employees stemming from civil service hiring procedures. Smaller positive correlations exist between extent of civil service coverage and several other personnel problems including difficulties disciplining or dismissing employees and the presence of employees who do not work hard. These relationships are consistent with charges often leveled at civil service systems.

Among the strongest correlations with extent of civil service are those for

Table 3.4

Zero-Order Correlations Between Severity of Various Personnel-Related Problems and Extent of Civil Service or Collective Bargaining

Problem or Problem Source	Civil Service	Collective Bargaining
Filling key positions/retaining key staff	.08**[1]	.03*
Civil service procedures for recruiting/ selecting staff	.27***	.24***
Use of patronage in filling positions	.00	.04
Rewarding outstanding employee performance	.00	-.12**
Insufficiently motivated/diligent employees	.08*	.00
Assessing employee performance	.03	.02
Difficulties disciplining/dismissing employees	.09**	.10**
Racial or gender discrimination	.09**	.13***
Security-obsessed employees	.09**	.08*
Collective bargaining by employees of unit	.33***	.40***
Bargaining on inappropriate matters such as program planning	.23***	.26***
Managerial authority limited by collective bargaining	.34***	.42***

1. Table entry is Pearson's r. *= significant at .05 level, two-tailed test; **= significant at .01 level, two-tailed test; ***= significant at .001 level, two-tailed test.

problems relating to collective bargaining. This reflects the linkage between civil service coverage and collective bargaining noted above. More extensive civil service is not significantly related to greater difficulties in rewarding employee performance or assessing employee performance, however, and only modest positive correlations exist between it and difficulties disciplining or dismissing low-performing employees and the presence of unmotivated, lazy, or security-obsessed employees—problems often said to result from the job protections that civil service systems provide for public employees. Some of these problems are not seen as serious in any of the states. Others, such as rewarding exceptional performance, are persistent problems in all states. Thus, 43% of the administrators in largely non-civil-service Texas saw this as a serious problem as did roughly 45% of the administrators in Michigan, New York, and California—states with nearly universal civil service coverage.

The absence of any correlation between civil service coverage and the existence of patronage practices is interesting in light of the fact that civil service is the remedy typically prescribed to cure the ills of spoils politics. One explanation for the lack of a relationship lies in the fact that few managers in any state saw patronage practices to be a problem. A glance back at Table 3.2 indicates that even in Indiana, with its limited civil service coverage, only 10% of the responding managers considered patronage practices in filling positions to be a serious impediment to effective management, a proportion that was only slightly higher than among managers in California and New York, states with much more extensive coverage.

The absence of a relationship between civil service and the severity of patronage practices may be due to several other factors. Since the 1970s, a number of court decisions have placed limits on politically based removals of employees even when the positions held by those employees are not covered by civil service provisions (Freedman, 1988; Meier, 1981; Rosenbloom, 1990, pp. 45–46). The increasing need for persons with technical skills to fill many state government positions, and the difficulty in recruiting career-oriented professionals for these positions without providing some protection against arbitrary dismissal, have resulted in de facto civil service arrangements in certain segments of state bureaucracies even when a comprehensive system is absent. At the same time, even in those states with substantial civil service coverage, patronage problems may exist because civil service procedures are "fudged" for private, administrative, and, especially, partisan reasons to varying degrees in every jurisdiction (See Shafritz, Hyde, and Rosenbloom, 1981, Ch. 4; Shafritz, 1975, Ch. 7).

As for the impact of collective bargaining, the substantial correlation between it and extent of civil service, at least in the sample, means that the correlations between collective bargaining and the severity of personnel problems are similar to those with civil service coverage. The correlation between collective bargaining and difficulties disciplining incompetent employees is nearly identical to that between civil service and this problem. Given the concern of employee organizations about protecting their members from what they often consider to be unjustified adverse actions, a positive relationship between collective bargaining and difficulty disciplining employees is not surprising.

In contrast to the relationship with civil service, a significant, albeit modest, *negative* correlation exists between extent of collective bargaining and problems rewarding employee performance. At least in the eyes of these state managers, giving adequate recognition to outstanding performance doesn't appear to be more difficult in a collective bargaining context. Why this should be so—given a union penchant for across-the-board salary increases and antipathy to vesting discretionary authority over salaries in management's hands—is unclear. Perhaps managers in most states, collective bargaining or no, have little control over the allocation of financial rewards. Another plausible explanation is that collective bargaining generally serves to increase the salaries of public employees—sometimes quite significantly in the short run if not nearly so much in the long run. Hence, hardworking state employees who were especially undervalued in salary terms prior to the commencement of collective bargaining are significantly less so after its institutionalization. For our sample at least, yet another explanation may be that some of the states in which collective bargaining is most extensive—notably California, Michigan, and New York—are among those that traditionally have paid state employees better.

The significant, if modest, positive correlation between collective bargaining and perceptions of the severity of race or gender-based discrimination is less encouraging. Unions' preference for seniority may hamper the efforts of minorities or women to advance within state bureaucracies and erode those gains when reductions-in-force occur. But one must put this correlation in context. Few managers believed, or were willing to admit, that race or sex discrimination was a serious problem in their units. Even in those states with extensive collective bargaining, only about 5% of the respondents reported such discrimination to be a serious problem.

The least surprising figures in Table 3.4 are the strong correlations between extent of state government collective bargaining and administrators' perceptions of the severity of problems that may flow from the process. Managers in heavily unionized state bureaucracies are more likely to complain about the general effects of collective bargaining as well as about more specific effects such as too broad a scope of negotiations or an erosion in the authority that they can exercise over their organized subordinates.

But again some perspective is necessary. Even in states with extensive collective bargaining, only small proportions of managers see union-related problems as serious. In New York only 5% of the respondents saw an "inappropriately" broad scope of negotiations as posing serious difficulties. In both California and Michigan the figure is only 9%. Collective bargaining seems to entail certain problems, but these problems seem not nearly so severe as might be expected given the rhetoric of many critics of public-sector unionization.

When the severity of each of the 12 personnel problems was regressed on the extent of civil service or collective bargaining in models that also included indicators of unit size, organizational place, supervisory burden, and functional responsibility, the results generally confirm the thrust of the correlational analysis. Initial efforts to account for variation in the severity of the 52 potential impediments to effective state management using just unit size, organizational place, supervisory burden, and functional responsibility resulted in models for 11 problems that could account for at least 5% of the variance. Of these, only two—the impact of the existence of collective bargaining by unit employees generally, and a reduction in managerial authority as a result of collective bargaining—were personnel-related problems.

When, however, extent of collective bargaining was used as a predictor along with the four other independent variables, the amount of explained variation in the severity of the three "union" problems increased substantially. In the case of problems associated generally with collective bargaining, explained variance doubled from 11% to 22% with extent of collective bargaining accounting for 17% alone. Staff size was the only other predictor that could account for at least 1% of the variance in the severity of this problem. It accounted for nearly 5%. Extent of collective bargaining and size of unit staff were also the only two factors that accounted for more than 1% of the variation in the severity of scope of bargaining and an erosion of managerial clout due to collective bargaining as impediments to effective management. Extent of collective bargaining is positively associated with an increase in the proportion of managers who see the erosion of managerial authority resulting from collective bargaining to be a serious impediment. It accounts for 17% of the 19% of explained variance in the severity of this problem while the size of a unit's staff is also positively related and accounts for about 2% of explained variance. Extent of collective bargaining is also associated with too broad a scope of negotiations as an impediment. It accounts for 7% of the total of 10% of explained variance in the severity of this problem with staff size accounting for 2% of the total.

The existence of only modest positive correlations between civil service coverage and the severity of certain personnel problems is reflected in the fact that, when the three union-related personnel problems are set aside, using extent of civil service as a predictor increases total explained variance to at least 5% only for problems associated with civil service procedures for recruiting and selecting employees. Extent of civil service is positively associated with the severity of this problem and accounts for 7% of the 9% of explained variance. Because of the high correlation between civil service coverage and extent of collective bargaining, civil service is also a positive predictor of the severity of the three union-related personnel problems when it is entered in the place of extent of collective bargaining. But it has less explanatory power than does collective bargaining. Otherwise, extent of civil service can account for even as little as 1% of the variation only in the severity of problems associated with difficulties recruiting and retaining key staff.

In addition to being a strong positive predictor of the severity of the three unionization-related personnel problems, in the five variable regression models collective bargaining was also directly related to the severity of race or gender bias as an impediment. It could account for only about 1% of the variance in the severity of this problem, slightly less than was explained by unit size. As was evident from the correlational analysis, extent of collective bargaining continues to be negatively associated with difficulties rewarding outstanding employees. While it can account for less than 2% of the variance in the severity of this problem, this is more variance than is explained by any other predictor.

Regression analysis was also used to account for variation in each respondent's scores on the three personnel-problem factors. I argued that Factor 1 might best be considered an "employee quality" factor. If this is so, then the regression analysis suggests that neither extent of civil service coverage nor extent of collective bargaining are associated with management problems resulting from poor-quality state employees. The only significant predictor of variation in the severity of this factor is size of unit and it can account for less than 3% of the variance.

Characterization of Factor 2 as a "union-problems" factor is supported by the fact that extent of collective bargaining is positively associated with higher scores on this factor and can account for almost 20% of the total of 25% of explained variance, while size of a unit's staff can account for another 4%.

The model can account for only about 7% of the variation in scores on Factor 3. That civil service coverage accounts for barely 3% of variation suggests that my hesitancy in characterizing Factor 3 as a "civil service problems" factor is justified. A unit having nonfiscal staff responsibilities is negatively associated with scores on this factor—as it is with the severity of problems stemming from civil service procedures for recruitment and selection of staff, and those related to securing and retaining key staff. Units in this category often have central personnel management responsibilities. Managers in such units may be more highly committed to the concept of civil service and may be reluctant to accept the fact that procedural manifestations of the concept may have negative consequences.

To summarize, analysis of the relationship between civil service coverage and collective bargaining on the one hand, and the severity of various personnel problems on the other, indicates that certain personnel-related problems are more severe in states with either more extensive civil service coverage or collective bargaining activity. The relationship between certain union problems and extent of collective bargaining was especially strong. When factor analysis was used to identify interrelationships among the personnel problems, a "union problems" factor clearly emerged and the extent of collective bargaining was significantly and positively related to scores on this factor. Even in states with extensive collective bargaining, however, unionization problems did not rank in the top half of all sources of management difficulties. That collective bargaining does not seem to pose terribly serious problems for managers even in those states where it is common argues for a temperate view of its consequences for state administration.

Proponents of collective bargaining tend to see it as solving many problems with few costs. Opponents tend to see it as having serious costs and few benefits. Since state managers were only asked if collective bargaining posed certain problems for them and not about any of its benefits, little can be said about the cost-benefit balance. These benefits may, however, include enhanced employee morale, reduced turnover due to improved salaries, and greater employee commitment to agency programs because work methods and programmatic issues are subject to collective negotiations. At the least, the findings are consistent with those of other scholars who conclude that the consequences of collective bargaining in the public sector are mixed, and the mix of consequences often varies across jurisdictions (see, among others, Horton, Lewin, and Kuhn, 1976; Loney, 1989; Methe and Perry, 1980; Reese and Ohren, 1987).

Analysis indicates that managers consider various civil service procedures for recruiting or selecting employees seriously impede effective management and that this is especially so in states with more comprehensive civil service systems. A distinctive "civil service problems" factor did not emerge from the factor analysis, however, and extent of civil service coverage was not strongly associated with the severity of this problem factor.

A number of problems sometimes attributed to the failings of civil service, including lazy, unmotivated, or security-obsessed employees, or difficulties in rewarding outstanding employees, either loaded much more heavily on Factor 1—the factor on which patronage-related problems also loaded—or loaded about as heavily on that factor as on Factor 3. These patterns of factor loadings, along with the fact that various personnel problems commonly ascribed to civil service by critics were also serious in states with more limited civil service coverage, suggest it would be wrong to conclude that civil service practices are the primary cause of various personnel problems.

The findings also suggest skepticism that more "flexible," patronage-infused personnel practices will ameliorate personnel problems. Certain problems may exist under either type of system, although the cause of the problems may differ. Consider the case of a manager seeking to discipline an inadequately performing subordinate. The usual conclusion is that seeking to discipline a low performer protected by civil service is difficult if not impossible. Since managers in states with extensive civil service coverage often complain about difficulties in disciplining employees, this conclusion may be valid.

But in a patronage system the job performance of a politically well-connected employee is largely irrelevant. Moreover, if on-the-job performance is largely irrelevant to one's advancement or continued tenure, patronage employees may not be especially hardworking. In extreme cases they may not be expected to show up for work at all, but will instead devote their time to political tasks. Nor is it surprising that anxiety about job security arises when job performance is not the primary basis for termination. This may explain the substantial loading of this problem on the same factor on which the "patronage problem" loads. Put differently, employees in a civil service system need not be personally obsessed with job security because the system itself is so obsessed.

In the absence of more detailed data on the personnel systems of the states examined in this study, this line of argument ought not be pushed too far. But the data at hand certainly provide some support for it. At least some contemporary apologists for patronage systems hold idealized views of how such systems work. By downplaying the less positive face of such arrangements, these civil service critics risk throwing the baby out with the bath water. My findings suggest that modest civil service reforms are preferable. Fortunately, state personnel reform efforts over the past 15 years have generally pursued a more moderate course.

At the same time, believers in the superiority of civil service ought not to feel too smug. More extensive civil service coverage was not strongly and positively related to more serious personnel problems. But neither did states with more extensive civil service coverage have *less serious* problems. These findings provide some comfort for defenders of civil service, but it is rather cold comfort.

FEDERAL DOLLARS AND FEDERAL GOVERNMENT-RELATED PROBLEMS

Variation in the severity of management problems arising from the relationships between state administrative units and federal government actors further illustrates the explanatory power of problem-specific predictors. Of the 52 problems, 6 are federal government-related. In addition to relationships with federal agencies generally, there are four problems that are specifically related to federal grant funding for an agency. These are matching fund requirements in grant programs, other requirements attached to these grants, paperwork and delay in these programs, and the unpredictability of grant funding. Managers were also asked whether state or federal courts' mandating service levels was a problem.

The severity of these problems ranged across the spectrum. Unpredictability of federal grant funding ranked as the 11th most serious impediment, with 30% of the managers citing it as such. Paperwork and delay, and the "strings" attached to federal grants, were seen as serious by about 15% of the managers, while matching requirements were seen as serious by 10%. Court mandating of services and general relations with federal agencies were seen as serious impediments by 10% and 6% of the managers, respectively.

The four grant problems constitute a complex. The intercorrelations among problems associated with matching fund requirements, other requirements attached to grants, paperwork and delays in such programs, and unpredictable funding levels were of the magnitude of .40 to .65. The general tenor of federal government-state agency relations as a problem was less strongly related to the four grant-related problems, however. The correlations between the quality of federal relations and problems stemming from matching requirements, other requirements attached to grants, and the predictability of grant funding were .26, .37, and .34, respectively. But the correlation between quality of federal relations and problems associated with paperwork and delay in grant programs was .50. The correlations between these five problems and court-mandating were weak, with the strongest of these being a correlation of .25 between judicial mandates and the impact of the strings attached to federal dollars.

Substantial variation in the severity of these problems was evident. Coefficients of variation were all above .40, and were .50 or greater in the case of federal matching requirements, paperwork and delay, unpredictability of funding, and court mandating. Within states, coefficients of variation were similarly great with few of them falling below .45.

The existence of great variation across agencies within states suggests that such variation is not the product of state-specific causes. While the nature and quality of state agency interaction with federal actors might be affected by numerous factors, the most obvious is its relative dependence on federal funding. The relationship of federal funding with federal problems might also be conditioned by the nature of the vehicle used to provide those funds. Dependence on federal funding should be more strongly related to federal problems when that funding is in the form of categorical grants. One of the supposed virtues of block grants is that recipients have much greater freedom in how they can expend federal dollars. In 1981 a number of categorical grants were combined to create several new block grants in areas such as health, social services, and community development (Elling, 1988). At the time the study was conducted, state agencies had just begun to experience the effects of this change. Unfortunately, while possessing data on the share of a unit's budget comprised of federal funds, I do not know what proportion came via categorical as opposed to block grants. Knowing these proportions would help us to better specify the nature of an agency's relationships with federal actors. On the other hand, since block grants still comprise a relatively small proportion of total federal grant funding, overall levels of federal funding may have substantial explanatory power.

For the entire sample, the proportion of federal funds in the budgets of responding units averaged 23%. But substantial variation is evidenced by a coefficient of variation of 1.39. Five percent or less of the budgets for units with fiscal staff, nonfiscal staff, criminal justice, and regulatory functions consisted of federal funds. Units with natural resources responsibilities depended on the federal government for slightly more than 10% of their budgets, while those with health, environmental, economic development, and transportation responsibilities received between 20% and 30% of their budgets from federal sources. Most dependent on federal support were education units, who received 38% of their total resources from federal sources, and income security units, who depended on federal sources for more than 67% of their funding.

The zero-order correlations between managers' perceptions of the severity of these six federal government-related problems and the extent to which a respondent's unit is dependent on federal dollars indicate that federal aid exacts some price so far as agency performance is concerned. The correlations between the proportion of a unit's budget coming from federal sources and the severity of matching requirements and other strings attached to federal grants were .23 and .41, respectively (Pearson's r, significant at .000 level, one-tailed test). Those between federal funding and problems stemming from paperwork and delay in grant programs and unpredictable funding were .36 and .49, respectively. These relationships persist within individual states as well. Those units that are more dependent on federal dollars are particularly likely to view the strings attached to those dollars, the unpredictability of grant funding, and delays and paperwork associated with federal grant programs as serious impediments to the management of their units.

The relatively modest correlation between extent of federal funding and complaints about matching fund requirements appears to be consistent with some of the conclusions of scholars of intergovernmental relations. Deil Wright (1988) cites the conclusions of the U.S. General Accounting Office regarding the limited impact of matching requirements:

Matching requirements usually do not satisfy their Federal fiscal and managerial objectives. They do not limit Federal grant outlays at the national level except in those few programs that are not controlled by appropriations ceilings. In the majority of other programs the objectives are not met because all levels of government want the greatest participation in Federal programs with the least financial burden. Thus, *non-Federal matching requirements are typically low and can often be met with existing resources.* As a result, matching requirements usually . . . do not stimulate additional State and local resources for grant programs (U.S. General Accounting Office, 1980; quoted in Wright, 1988, p. 261, emphasis added).

Few state managers may view matching requirements as a problem for another reason. State dollars for matching have a "leveraging" effect. They generate more funds by the multiple of the matching ratio. Moreover, the existence of state matching dollars

tends to lock in dollars for the program or purpose that is federally assisted. When circumstances force an actual cutback in state or local funds, it is highly rational from a financial standpoint to resist cutting programs where leveraging is greatest and to cut the programs where the state or local dollar gains no supplementary resources (Wright, 1988, p. 261).

Especially in an era of fiscal retrenchment such as existed at the time the survey was conducted, state program managers may consider this to be an important virtue of matching funds requirements.

The substantial correlation between extent of federal funding and concerns about the "strings" attached to the receipt and use of those dollars is not surprising. In 1984, more than two-thirds of a national sample of state administrators indicated dissatisfaction with those strings and indicated that they would use federal funds differently if federal restrictions on their use were reduced (Wright, 1988, pp. 268–269). Still, the correlation between extent of federal funding and complaints about the impeding effects of grant requirements on agency management is far from perfect. One reason is that state managers may not necessarily disagree with stipulations as to how the funds associated with a particular federal grant program can be expended. These strings may provide a convenient rationale for pursuing programmatic priorities that the state managers fully support. But the responsibility or blame for the setting of those priorities can be shifted to federal government actors (See Derthick, 1970, especially Ch. 8).

As hypothesized, the general tenor of federal relations, and the mandating of service levels by the courts, are less clearly related to dependence on federal funding. While the overall correlations were significant ($r = .16$ and $.15$, respectively), within individual states they often were not. In the case of problems associated with court-mandating, had managers been asked specifically whether *federal* court mandating of service levels was a problem, the link with extent of federal funding might have been stronger. But, while the existence of fiscal links between the federal government and state agencies may make federal judicial intervention more likely, judicial intervention is not limited to agencies that receive federal dollars. Analysis of federal court impact to be reported in Chapter 6 will make this clear.

The relationship between the severity of grant-related problems and dependence on federal funding is not strictly linear, however. The severity of grant-related problems is quite great even when the proportion of federal dollars in a unit's budget is modest. Thus, more than one quarter of the managers of units that depended on the federal government for 10% or less of their budget saw the uncertainty of federal funding to be a significant problem. Of the managers of units that received four-fifths or more of their budget from federal coffers, 27% considered paperwork and delay associated with federal grant programs to be a serious problem; but so did 26% of the managers in units that depended on federal sources for only between one-tenth and one-fifth of their funding. Particularly when budgets are tight—as they undoubtedly were when the survey was conducted—even relatively small amounts of dollars may be important. Factors that limit an agency's ability to secure those dollars, or that impede the flow of those dollars, may loom large.[14]

Earlier in the chapter I suggested that certain relationships between federal government-related problems and variables such as functional responsibility or budget size might be spurious because both variables might be related to differences in agency dependence on federal funds. Extent of federal funding does vary substantially across units with differing functional responsibilities and is often strongly correlated with the severity of the federal government-related problems. Hence, it is hardly surprising that when federal funding is included in a regression analysis of the determinants of the severity of these problems, the total amount of variance explained increases and federal funding is a significant predictor of the severity of each of them. Indeed, as Table 3.5 makes clear, extent of federal funding is the most powerful predictor of the severity of each of the problems save for court mandating of service levels. It is a particularly powerful predictor of the severity of the grant-related problems where it accounts for between 5% and 25% of the variance. A model that includes extent of federal funding can explain relatively little of the variance in the general tone of state-federal agency relations. But when federal funding is excluded, the amount of explained variance is only about half as great.

It is surprising that less variation in complaints about court mandating of services can be explained by a model that includes federal funding than by one that does not, even allowing for the fact that the question asked about state as well as federal court actions. Moreover, when federal funding is added to the model, the fact that a unit has income security or criminal justice responsibilities no longer appears to influence the severity of this problem. This is inconsistent with the findings of Hale (1979) that administrators of state agencies with criminal justice/corrections and human services responsibilities, along with those with education responsibilities, are among those most likely to report that federal court decisions had forced their agencies to alter existing programs or initiate new programs.

This anomaly is resolved if unit size is operationalized as number of employees rather than size of budget. In the case of the other federal government-

Table 3.5

Summary of Most Powerful Models of Severity of Federal Government-Related Management Problems (Stepwise Regression Using Organizational Size, Organizational Place, Supervisory Burden, Functional Responsibility of Unit, and Extent of Federal Funding as Predictors)

Federal Government-Related Problems	Explained Variance (Adjusted R^2)	Predictors Accounting for at Least One Percent of Variance [1]	B[2]	Beta[3]	Variance Explained by Predictor
Relations with federal agencies	.058	Federal funding unit size (budget)	.003 .074	.138 .111	.029 .015
Paperwork/delay in federal grant programs	.213	Federal funding	.010	.397	.139
		Income security func.	-.453	-.189	.023
		Regulatory func.	-.408	-.160	.017
		Fiscal staff func.	-.420	-.134	.014
		Nonfiscal staff func.	-.373	-.102	.010
Matching fund requirements for federal grants	.076	Federal funding	.005	.212	.056
		Nat. resources func.	.177	.083	.012
Unpredictable federal grant funding levels	.294	Federal funding	.014	.435	.250
		Regulatory func.	-.413	-.129	.018
		Fiscal staff func.	-.494	-.125	.017
Requirements attached to federal grant programs	.225	Federal funding	.010	.400	.189
		Unit size (budget)	.124	.154	.018
Courts mandating service levels	.062	Unit size (budget)	.167	.217	.053
		Federal funding	.003	.110	.012

1. This column lists only those significant predictors (F value of B significant at .05 level or better) that could explain a minimum of 1% of the variation in the severity of a particular problem. The precise amount of variance accounted for by each of these predictors is indicated in the final column of the table. In many instances there were other predictors that were statistically significant and contributed to the total amount of explained variance but could account for less than 1% of the variance.

2. This is the unstandardized regression coefficient.

3. This is the standardized regression coefficient.

related problems, the substitution of staff size for budget size slightly reduced the amount of explained variance. But when number of employees rather than size of budget is entered into the model for the severity of complaints about court mandating, several important changes occurred. First, the amount of explained variance increased sharply to nearly 16%, an amount that is slightly greater than in the earlier model outlined in Table 3.1. Second, although unit size remains the most significant predictor, it is slightly more powerful when operationalized as number of employees, accounting for 6% of the variance. Third, extent of federal funding drops out of the model while, consistent with past research, units with income security, criminal justice, health, or education responsibilities all complain more about court mandating of services. This suggests that court impact is shaped less by the fiscal links forged by federal aid than by the unique nature of the functions of certain agencies. This, in turn, is related to the ability of those seeking to use the courts to accomplish policy change to frame questions in such a way as to engage the interest of the courts.

In short, as was the case for personnel-related problems, a substantial amount of variance in the severity of various federal government-related problems can be explained when a problem-specific predictor is utilized. If more were known about the forms that federal aid to these state agencies take—that is, formula versus project categorical grants, or categorical versus block grants—it might be possible to account for an even larger proportion of variation in the severity of these impediments to effective state management.

CONCLUSION

Chapter 2 outlined the contours of the problematic world of state managers. In this chapter I have sought to account for some of the variation in problem severity that was noted only in passing in Chapter 2. Explanatory models based on indicators of the size of a unit, its functional responsibility, its location within a state's administrative hierarchy, and the supervisory burden of a manager were developed. In general, however, these factors were of limited utility in accounting for variation in the severity of most of the 52 potential impediments to effective management.

One reason for this is the great diversity in the types of problems focused upon and the consequent need to use more highly problem-specific predictors. Support for this position was provided by various other findings. While unit size, functional responsibility, organizational place, and supervisory burden could explain little variation across a number of problems, one or another of these independent variables was a significant predictor of a few problems—problems that knowledge of administrative dynamics suggest should be most strongly correlated with that particular predictor. Additional support was provided by a detailed analysis of the severity of the subset of personnel-related and federal government-related impediments to effective management. Variation in the severity of personnel problems was often related to variation in the extent to which the employees of a state's bureaucracy were covered by civil service provisions or engaged in collective negotiations. Thus, in the case of certain union-related personnel problems, between 10% and 20% of the variation in severity could be accounted for by knowing the proportion of state employees who collectively bargained. The extent to which a state administrative unit depends upon the federal government for its funding was similarly shown to be positively related to managers' perceptions of the severity of various federal grant and other federal government-related problems.

The other reason that efforts to account for variation in the severity of particular management problems were not more successful is simply that there often is little variation to explain. As discussed in Chapter 2, interstate variation was the exception rather than the rule. When significant interstate variation existed it often was because the managers in but one or two states differed substantially in their estimates of the severity of a given problem, while those in the remaining eight or nine states tended toward consensus. Moreover, even when the proportion of managers considering a particular problem to be serious varied substantially across states, the severity of that problem relative to others tended to be quite similar within one state as opposed to another.

Chapters 2 and 3 have focused on the difficulties that confront state managers as they seek to discharge their responsibilities in a reasonably efficient and effective fashion. The fact that most potential impediments to effective management were not seen to be terribly serious in the eyes of most managers leads to the conclusion that most state managers "manage to manage." But certain impediments were rather severe overall while others were serious in at least some states or agencies. Various solutions to the problems that beset state agencies exist. Chapter 4 examines the extent to which managers and units in the 10 states under consideration here have utilized, or have been affected by, a host of potential "solutions" to various administrative difficulties. It also explores the efficacy of these remedies for managerial maladies.

NOTES

1. The number of persons employed in an organizational unit and the size of its budget are usually positively related, since governments are labor-intensive entities. In the sample, the correlation between the size of a unit's budget and the number of persons employed in that unit is .24 (Pearson's r). Given uncertainty as how best to conceptualize organizational size, both size of budget and size of work force were used in the analysis.

2. Respondents were asked to indicate "how many levels of organization in your agency are above you?" Since for an agency head the answer is none, one was added to the number of levels that respondents indicated were above them. This sum was then subtracted from 10 so that a higher score denotes a higher level position. Hence, the organizational place score for an agency head would be nine while someone three levels down in the agency hierarchy would have a score of six. Organizational place scores ranged between two and nine, although 97% of the managers had scores in the range of six to nine. Specifically, 11% had a place score of six, 32% a place score of seven, 40% a place score of eight, and 14% a place score of nine.

3. While the supervisory burden of the managers in the study varied from a single subordinate to more than 50, 80% of them had 10 or fewer direct subordinates.

4. Wright's elected officials category was not used, because there were few elected administrative officials in my sample. Detail on his functional categories was provided to me by Professor Wright and is contained in his 1990 "Information and Introductory Materials on ASAP" (see also Wright and Light, 1977; and Brudney and Hebert, 1987).

5. Various of the independent variables just discussed are interrelated. Although the correlation between the size of a unit's budget and its work force is only + .24, when these data are logarithmically transformed so as to eliminate the distorting impact of extreme cases, the correlation between budget and work force rises to + .84. In contrast, the intercorrelations among organizational place, supervisory burden, staff and budget size are modest. The correlations between budget size and a manager's organi-

zational location and the number of subordinates a manager supervises are .16 and .20, respectively. Correlations of a similar magnitude exist between staff and organizational location and staff and supervisory burden. The correlation between organizational place and number of subordinates supervised is only + .07. Agencies with particular functional responsibilities differed significantly in the mean size of their budgets and work forces as well as in the organizational rank of respondents (F-test, p = .000). Units with transportation, income security, health, and criminal justice had larger budgets and work forces, on average, than did those with regulatory, nonfiscal staff, economic development, education, and environmental responsibilities. The average organizational rank of managers in fiscal staff, economic development, and regulatory responsibilities was 7.9 as opposed to 7.2 for those in units with environmental responsibilities. Number of subordinates supervised did not differ significantly across units with particular functional responsibilities, however.

6. The mean size of the budgets of responding units in each of the states, in millions of dollars, was: Arizona, $36.7; California, $110.7; Delaware, $13.3; Indiana, $43.9; Michigan, $48.5; New York, $167.2; South Dakota, $8.7; Tennessee, $138.4; Texas, $123.7; Vermont, $7.3.

7. The relationship between the size of a unit's budget and complaints about racial/gender discrimination may also be spurious. As noted, the average budget for a unit in one of the larger states in the sample is higher than the average unit budget in one of the smaller states. Larger states such as Michigan, New York, California, and Texas have larger minority populations than most other states and employ many more minorities in state government than do states such as Vermont or South Dakota (Elling, 1983). Greater minority employment may be associated with more incidents of discrimination. In her survey of state employees' perceptions of discrimination in five states, Anne Hopkins (1980) partially attributes the virtual absence of perceptions of racial discrimination by Nebraska and Oregon state employees to the very small proportion of nonwhites in the populations of these states.

8. Supervisory burden failed to emerge as a significant predictor of any management problem. One explanation for this is that there is limited variation in the severity of those problems that can be most plausibly linked to supervisory burden. Monitoring or controlling subordinates' actions, having too many subordinates to supervise, and difficulties assessing subordinates' performance were among those problems that were least severe overall and for which the range in estimates of severity was limited. Nor is there much variation in supervisory burden. Half of the managers reported that they supervised between four and seven subordinates and more than 80% percent supervised 10 or fewer subordinates.

When the perceptions regarding the severity of problems of those managers with relatively few subordinates (14 or less) were contrasted with those of managers having relatively more subordinates (15 or more), it was the case that twice as many managers in the latter group said that having too many subordinates to supervise was a serious impediment to effective management. But this was only a difference between the 4% of managers with 14 or fewer subordinates who said this was a serious problem and the 8% of managers with 15 or more subordinates who reported this to be a serious impediment. These state managers seem confident of their ability to direct their subordinates regardless of the number that report to them.

9. Although the survey asked respondents to indicate the approximate size of *their unit's* annual budget, it appears that some managers responded with the total budget for

the larger agency in which their unit was located. This is, of course, another source of measurement error in one of the indicators of organizational size.

10. The following discussion of personnel-related management problems draws heavily on Elling (1986).

11. In a discussion of personnel reform in New Jersey, DeNicholas and Lutz (1979) report that state department and agency heads were surveyed to ascertain their "attitudes and experiences with civil service in a wide range of personnel functions." They do not, however, report any of the findings of this survey.

12. The proportion of state employees covered under civil service for each of the 10 states is as follows. Arizona: 40%; California: 93%; Delaware: 85%; Indiana: 60%; Michigan: 97%; New York: 98%; South Dakota: 83%; Tennessee: 90%; Texas: 20%; Vermont: 94%. The proportion of state employees that collectively bargain in these states exhibits even greater variation. In Arizona, Indiana, Tennessee, and Texas, no state employees collectively bargained at the time the survey was conducted in 1982–83. In the remaining six states the proportion of state employees who collectively bargained was 10% in South Dakota, 40% in Delaware, 70% in Michigan, 85% in both California and Vermont, and 95% in New York. Some sources suggest that a small number of state employees in states such as Arizona and Indiana collectively bargain. But for Arizona, Indiana, Tennessee, and Texas I rely on Tanimoto and Inaba (1985, p. 53) who report that there were no state employees in bargaining units as of 1983.

13. Alternatively, the state-level data could be used to explain variation in the average severity of each of the problems across states. There are several problems with this methodological approach. The most serious is that one commits the ecological fallacy—one is correlating a dependent variable measured at the individual level with an independent variable measured at the state level. Such an approach typically inflates the correlation between the two variables. At the same time, since the sample size is reduced from the 847 responses of individual managers to mean figures for just 10 states, even the larger correlations that result may not achieve statistical significance. Such an approach would also not permit us to conduct multiple regression analysis using the other independent variables such as unit size, organizational location, or supervisory burden that were measured at the level of individual units unless we were also willing to work with state means for these variables.

14. A few managers in units with no federal funds complained of grant-related problems. One explanation for this might be that they received a small amount of federal aid but did not indicate this in response to the survey question on the proportion of their budget that was comprised of federal dollars. Perhaps it is the case that some of these units *would have received* some federal funding were it not for matching and other requirements. That is, perhaps the legislature is unwilling to provide them with necessary matching funds. Hence, matching requirements are a problem in that they make it difficult to exploit federal funding opportunities.

Chapter 4

Crusades, Conversions, and Apostasies: "Improving" State Management

INTRODUCTION

The development in the United States of what Dwight Waldo (1980) has called "self-aware" public administration has been inextricably intertwined with efforts to improve the quality of the administration of the public's business. The history of American public administration over the last century is studded with the emergence, flowering, and, as often as not, the withering of various management practices or "reforms."

What is troubling about this history of administrative reform is the extent to which the literature of public administration is comprised of either prescriptions for or descriptions of management innovations rather than systematic efforts to evaluate their consequences. Indeed it is difficult not to see elements of the religious in all this. The perceived problems of public agencies create circumstances in which new administrative prophets and theologies are quickly able to attract a sizable number of disciples.

Continuing with the metaphors of religion, since faith is the essence of religiosity, dispassionate appraisal of the ultimate rightness of a given administrative practice or technique seems somehow out of place. Existing evaluative materials are often case studies written by those involved in the development or application of a new technique (i.e., planning-programming budgeting, zero-base budgeting, management-by-objectives, sunset laws, etc.). While participants may have faced difficulties in implementing a reform, they are typically sanguine about the effects of the technique under discussion. "Evaluations" of this sort are similar to the testimonials offered by those who have been "saved" or "born again." Indeed, an argument that runs along these lines has been put forth by March and Olson (1983) with regard to one of the commonly trod roads to administrative salvation: organizational redesign. Focusing upon such efforts at the federal level, they note, as have others, that there are few attempts

by the initiators of reorganization to discover what really happened as a consequence of their efforts. This is disturbing since the handful of more systematic efforts to assess the consequences of reorganization tend to find its benefits
to be substantially less than proponents assert (see, for example, Meier, 1980;
but compare Meier to Conant, 1986).

In explaining the paucity of evaluative work on reorganization, and the fact
that future reorganizers sally forth like latter-day crusaders to slay the infidels
despite little evidence that previous crusades and crusaders have made much
difference, March and Olson (1983, p. 289) observe that

persistence in the face of apparent failure and indifference to careful evaluation of the
consequences of action are, of course, often observed in human behavior—particularly
in domains of strong beliefs and ambiguous experience. If a favorite social reform fails
to achieve its promised success, we may conclude that the problem lies not in the
reform, but in our failure to push it hard enough, far enough, or long enough. In such
cases it is not only that our interpretation of the outcomes of action are confounded by
our ideologies, but also that our actions have symbolic meaning that is independent of
their instrumental consequences. Action is an affirmation of belief and an assertion of
virtue.

Later in their analysis, March and Olson conclude that

the preponderant evidence is that the symbols of administrative reform are important to
politicians, not only as ways to fool the voters, but also as reflections of their own
beliefs. Incoming administrations, like their supporters, believe in the possibility of
making a difference, and the recurrence of major reorganization efforts is tied to that
belief (p. 291).

Although commitment to administrative improvement may often constitute
an act of faith, this does not mean that administrative problems are not real.
Because they are real, if certain management practices or techniques hold promise
of modifying conditions in a way favorable to goal attainment, adopting them
may make good sense. But it is naive to assume that a given technique will
always achieve what its proponents claim it will under any and all circumstances. Nor should the possibility that a proposed change may have dysfunctional effects be ignored. It is prudent to approach the subject of administrative
reform in general, and the question of the consequences of a specific reform in
particular, with a skeptical "I'm from Missouri, show me" attitude.

Even if one adopts such a stance, assessing the desirability of a particular
reform is complicated by the absence of consensus on what constitutes "good"
administration. The diversity of standards against which administration can be
judged was discussed in Chapter 2. Reflecting this diversity, a number of those
who have written about efforts to improve administrative performance in the
United States have highlighted the differences and contradictions in our approaches to administrative "improvement"—in our administrative "theolo-

gies,'' if you will. Nearly four decades ago, Herbert Kaufman (1956) captured this conflict in terms of three competing "quests"—for representative bureaucracy, for neutral competence, and for executive leadership. Each of these embraces differing administrative forms and practices.

More recently, David Rosenbloom (1983, p. 219) has argued that

the central problem of public administration theory is that it is derived from three disparate approaches to the basic question of what public administration is. Each of these approaches has a respected intellectual tradition, emphasizes difference values, promotes different types of organizational structure, and views individuals in markedly distinct terms.

Rosenbloom labels these approaches the "managerial," the "political," and the "legal." Although it blurs some differences between them, the political and legal approaches are similar to one another, while each is distinct from the managerial approach, in that the first two are preoccupied with assuring the accountability of administrative institutions to external actors or norms.

Judgments as to whether an administrative problem exists will vary depending upon the standard of administrative performance that is emphasized. Since any given administrative reform is more consistent with the values implied by one particular approach or model than another, judgments regarding the effectiveness of particular management techniques or practices must also vary.

Chapters 2 and 3 have examined state administrators' views of the problems that undermine the performance of their units. One issue addressed in Chapter 2 was whether managers were inclined to identify as serious impediments to effective management problems whose source or resolution lies largely outside their control or those that were related to the efforts of nonadministrative actors to influence the course of events in their units. The presumption was that administrators prefer as much autonomy as possible in carrying out their responsibilities and that actions by others to limit that autonomy were likely to be perceived as complicating their lives.

Administrators should exhibit a similar bias when it comes to proposals for "improving" state management. In the language of Kaufman, we would expect them to most strongly embrace the value of neutral competence. In the language of Rosenbloom, they should exhibit a preference for management improvements consistent with a managerial as opposed to a political or legal approach. Put more simply, the respondents should prefer management improvements that increase their autonomy or that insulate them from external control by nonadministrative actors.

At the same time, this argument should not be pushed too far. Administrators are socialized into the same political system as the rest of us. Indeed, to the extent that their career choices reflect more intense interest in political affairs, they may be more imbued with sentiments of democratic accountability, rule of law, and the like than is the average citizen. The managers I surveyed did not blame most of their problems on various nonadministrative "thems." It may also be that they are reasonably tolerant of management "improvements" that strengthen the ability of nonadministrative actors to affect the affairs of their units.

Given my earlier observations about the paucity of systematic efforts to assess the consequences of public management reforms in general, it should come as no surprise to the reader that comparative assessments of management reform in the states are scarce. Indeed, no such assessments of the use or efficacy of a range of management improvements appear to exist. Even multistate assessments of only one or a small number of reforms are rare. Included here would be Meier's (1980) study of the consequences of state executive branch reorganization, and Allen Schick's investigations of the use of planning-programming budgeting (PPB) (1971) and zero-base budgeting (ZBB) (1979) in the states.

Single-state case studies of management improvement efforts are more common. But the absence of any explicitly comparative framework, combined with the fact that such assessments tend to be ideographic or anecdotal in nature, greatly limits their usefulness. It is likely that several biases creep into this literature. One may be the tendency to more readily report success than failure. Another might be for the extremes of experience—the real success stories or the real horror stories—to be overrepresented. What likely gets underplayed is the predominant reality—the fact that a technique or practice has fewer benefits than supporters might hope or assert, but fewer negative consequences than opponents fear.

Studies by the International City Management Association (ICMA) (Fukuhara, 1977), Poister and McGowan (1984), and Poister and Streib (1989) most closely approximate my approach to assessing management improvement in the states. The 1976 ICMA survey of all cities of more than 25,000 found that 40% or more of them were using techniques such as management information systems, management-by-objectives, cost accounting, "reformed" budgeting systems such as PPB or ZBB, program evaluation, and productivity improvement programs. Poister and Streib examined the use of a similar set of management systems or strategies based on the responses of 460 city managers, mayors, and chief administrative or finance officers surveyed in late 1982 and early 1983. A municipal government employing a mix of these tools was "considered to have greater management capacity than one which does not" (p. 217). The techniques focused upon included program/zero-base budgeting, management-by-objectives, management information systems, performance monitoring systems, productivity improvement programs, strategies for improving employee morale and performance through the use of incentives, and productivity bargaining. In comparison to the findings of the 1976 ICMA study, Poister and McGowan found that there had been a substantial increase in the use of these management tools.

In a follow up based on a similar sample, Poister and Streib (1989) assessed the use of a dozen management tools. In addition to those that were the focus of the 1982–83 survey, information was sought on the use of financial trend monitoring, revenue and expense forecasting, strategic planning, and quality circles. The 1987 survey, in addition to determining the extent to which these various techniques were used in particular cities, also asked respondents to indicate how effective a given tool was "as an aid to administration and decision making."

My survey explored state administrator familiarity with and utilization of a much wider variety of techniques, practices, approaches, or strategies than was true of the studies just discussed. Judgments were also sought on the efficacy of these management tools. In recognition of the absence of consensus on what constitutes "good" management or a management "improvement," a catholic approach was adopted in compiling the list of management techniques. The resulting set of 53 techniques consisted of those that at least some important actors in the administrative process, including but certainly not limited to administrators themselves, as well as public administration scholars, have touted as solutions to particular management difficulties that they believe to exist. The list includes various techniques or strategies that administrators themselves are unlikely to consider to be "improvements," or that may be intended to solve administrative "problems" that they do not consider to be problems.

The diversity of techniques on which administrative views were sought permits me to address a question of central interest. To what extent are techniques that embody competing values regarding American public administration used in state administration and what do administrators think about them? William Gormley (1989a) underscores the competition among nonadministrative actors to influence the course of administrative affairs in the 1970s and 1980s that has often resulted in bitter battles for "custody" of state bureaucracies. In this chapter the insights of Kaufman, Rosenbloom, Gormley, and others are drawn upon in seeking to determine the extent to which management practices or strategies that reduce administrative autonomy consistent with political or legal approaches are used in state administration. Differences in administrators' attributions of positive as opposed to negative impacts for techniques that are consistent with varying approaches to management "improvement" are also of interest.

STATE ADMINISTRATORS' FAMILIARITY WITH MANAGEMENT "IMPROVEMENTS"

Examination of management improvement efforts in the 10 study states begins with an exploration of the extent to which various management techniques have penetrated the consciousness of state managers. Administrators in the 10 states were asked to indicate their degree of familiarity with each of the 53 management techniques or practices. The response options were: "unfamiliar with technique and its effects," "familiar with but no experience with/no direct knowledge of technique and its effects," "used in my unit or affects my unit," and "used or exists elsewhere in state government in my state." Any response other than "unfamiliar with" was taken as evidence of familiarity.[1]

Table 4.1 indicates that at least 80% of the managers were familiar with 22 of the 53 techniques. These include practices such as "flextime" arrangements, management-by-objectives, freedom of information requirements, and professional training with which nearly all managers were familiar. Also included are administrative warhorses such as reorganization and the appointment of agency heads by the governor, as well as newer arrivals on the scene such as sunset provisions, sunshine laws, and zero-base budgeting.

At the other extreme was a group of 11 practices with which 60% or less of the managers were familiar. This group includes some of the more sophisticated or esoteric management tools such as operations research, Delphi methods, and organizational development, as well as collective bargaining practices such as compulsory arbitration and productivity bargaining. Finally, there was a third group of 20 or so techniques with which 20% to 40% of the respondents were unfamiliar.

An aggregate "familiarity" score was calculated as a way to assess awareness of the entire set of management techniques. This score was calculated by dividing the number of techniques with which a respondent was unfamiliar by the total number of techniques. This figure was subtracted from 100 so that a higher score indicated greater familiarity.[2] The resulting familiarity score of 73.7% indicates that these state managers were familiar with nearly three out of four management techniques. Variance in familiarity was substantial, however, with the coefficient of variation for this measure being a very large .71. On the one hand, 25% of the respondents were familiar with 9 out of 10 techniques. On the other hand, 25% of the respondents were familiar with less than 40% of them.[3]

"Autonomy Effects" and Familiarity with Management Techniques

Rosenbloom's analysis of three disparate traditions in public administration was reviewed earlier in the chapter. One way to view the thrusts of both the political and legal approaches is that they seek to narrow, albeit in different ways, the scope of administrative autonomy or discretion possessed by administrative agencies. Each represents an effort to increase the influence of particular nonadministrative actors in the administrative process or to force administrators to consider different values, and reflects the belief that the conduct of public administration is too important to leave solely in the hands of administrators. On the other hand, the managerial approach, or what Kaufman (1956) terms the "quest for neutral competence," emphasizes the virtues of isolating administrative processes from more direct political manipulation or control.

Whether individuals are familiar with something may depend on whether

Table 4.1
State Administrator Familiarity with Management Techniques or Reforms

Percentage of Managers Familiar With a Given Technique or Reform [1]

More Than 80% Familiar

Freedom of information requirements (96%)
Flextime (95%)
Management by objectives (95%)
Professional training (94%)
Reorganization (93%)
"Sunset" laws (92%)
Contracting out for services (92%)
Administrative Procedure Act requirements
  for promulgating rules/regulations (92%)
Zero-base budgeting (92%)
Performance indicators (91%)
Sunshine (open meeting) laws (90%)
Program evaluation (90%)

Citizen advisory committees (90%)
Cost-benefit analysis (88%)
Gubernatorial appointment of all agency
  heads, serve at governor's pleasure (87%)
Management information systems (86%)
Ethics laws for state employees (85%)
"Whistleblowing" by employees (83%)
Technological changes enhancing
  performance (83%)
User fees for agency services (82%)
Higher salaries for employees (82%)
Reduce number of agencies (81%)

60% - 80% Familiar

Participative management (79%)
Block grants (79%)
Increased supervisory power to discipline
  subordinates (79%)
Legislative review/veto of agency rules (79%)
PERT (78%)
Surveys of clientele satisfaction (78%)
Administrative requirements in federal grant
  programs (single state agency etc.) (77%)
Delegation of classification/recruitment/
  selection personnel functions to line
  agencies (75%)
Eliminate civil service coverage for many
  middle/upper level managers (74%)

Planning-programming budgeting (73%)
Ombudsman office (71%)
Lump-sum appropriations (70%)
Job enlargement/enrichment (69%)
Agency authority to reprogram appropriated
  funds (69%)
General revenue sharing (69%)
Legislative postaudit (66%)
Career executive systems (64%)
Evening/saturday hours (63%)
"Inspector-general" units in agencies to
  assess performance (63%)
"T-Groups" (61%)

Less Than 60% Familiar

Compulsory arbitration (57%)
Expand civil service coverage (55%)
Performance-based compensation (55%)
Productivity improvement programs (53%)
Organizational development (OD) (52%)
Project/matrix-style organization (50%)

Operations research methods (48%)
Assessment centers (36%)
Gubernatorial authority to initiate
  reorganization with legislative veto (33%)
"Delphi" methods (33%)
Productivity bargaining (27%)

1. The response options were "unfamiliar with," "familiar with but no direct experience/knowledge of technique and its effects," "used in my unit/affects my unit," and "used or exists elsewhere in state government in my state." The table entries are the proportion of managers who responded in any other way than "unfamiliar with" a given technique, change, or development. The Ns for particular techniques varied between 795 for familiarity with expanding civil service coverage to 835 for familiarity with "flextime." For the 53 items the median number of respondents was 817.

they are compelled to become familiar with it. Techniques or practices consistent with political or legal approaches are typically imposed on administrative units by the legislature, the courts, or elected chief executives. Hence, it is likely that managers will be more familiar with those techniques that reduce autonomy than with those that either expand autonomy or have no impact on it.

In order to test this hypothesis, the set of management techniques was partitioned into three subsets. One subset included those techniques deemed likely to reduce administrative autonomy; a second consisted of those that expanded autonomy; while a third included those techniques that seemed relatively neutral in their effects on the scope of administrative autonomy. This partitioning is displayed in Table 4.2. Clearly, these are not entirely crisp sets. It might be argued that the thrust of neither PPB nor ZBB is primarily to reduce administrative autonomy. But certainly some advocates of both saw them as ways of enhancing either gubernatorial or legislative influence in the budgetary process. Reorganization has traditionally been justified on economy and efficiency grounds. But often its real purpose is to enhance or reduce gubernatorial, legislative, or interest group influence over administrative units or programs (Salamon, 1981; Conant, 1988). Others might object to the inclusion of citizen advisory groups in the autonomy-reducing set on the grounds that such groups do not really have much impact on administrative actions. Even if this is so, the point is that such groups are established in the belief that they will make administrative units more conscious of the needs and wishes of clients and other citizens. In short, the partitioning seems to possess considerable face validity.

If Table 4.1 is now reexamined, we can see that those practices or "improvements" that constrain administrative autonomy are overrepresented among those that state managers know best. Practices that constrain autonomy comprise nearly one-half of those in this category, although they constitute less than one-third of the techniques. Only one of the autonomy-constraining practices—gubernatorial authority to undertake reorganization subject to possible legislative veto—ranks among the techniques with which state administrators are least familiar. In contrast, none of the four autonomy-enlarging practices are among those with which the managers are most familiar. Finally, although techniques that are relatively neutral in their consequences for agency autonomy constitute barely 60% of all techniques, they comprise 90% of those with which administrators are least familiar.[4]

Other Sources of Variation in Familiarity with Management Techniques

The considerable interstate and intrastate variation in familiarity with various management improvements that exists suggests that factors other than the impact that these improvements may have on managerial autonomy are at work. Among these factors might be characteristics of individual administrators. More

Table 4.2

Classification of Management Techniques or Reforms in Terms of Their Likely Impact on the Autonomy of State Administrative Agencies

---

Set 1
Autonomy-Reducing
(N = 17)

Administrative procedure act requirements	Legislative postaudit
Citizen advisory committees	Legislative review/veto of rules or
Ethics laws for state employees	regulations
Freedom of information requirements	Ombudsman office
Gubernatorial appointment of all agency	Open meeting ("sunshine") laws
heads	Planning-programming budgeting
Gubernatorial authority to undertake reorgani-	Reorganization
zation subject to legislative veto within	"Sunset" laws
specified time	"Whistleblowing" by employees
Elimination of civil service coverage for many	Zero-base budgeting
middle/upper level managers	Inspector-general units in agencies

---

Set 2
Autonomy-expanding
(N = 4)

Expand civil service coverage	Lump-sum appropriations to agencies
Delegate more authority for classification,	Agency authority to reprogram
recruitment, selection of personnel to line	appropriated funds
agencies	

Set 3
Techniques neutral as to administrative autonomy
(N = 32)

All techniques not included in either Set 1 or Set 2

---

experienced administrators might be more knowledgeable. Administrators in staff agencies with budget, personnel, planning, or other central management responsibilities may be better informed than are managers with line responsibilities. It has been argued that public managers who are better educated and "more professional" are more likely to innovate (Bozeman and Straussman, 1990, Ch. 8; see also Perry and Kraemer, 1980, and Bingham et al., 1978). Hence, better-educated managers—and especially those with graduate education in public management—may exhibit greater awareness of management improvement techniques. Finally, higher level managers with more general management responsibilities may be better informed about management techniques.

Bivariate analysis indicates that the educational background of a manager is positively associated with awareness of management techniques. Cross-tabulations of the relationships between familiarity with management techniques and categories of education disclosed significant differences (Chi Square statistics, p = .05 or better) in the case of 31 of the 53 techniques. Less-well-educated managers reported lower levels of familiarity. Managers without a college degree displayed the lowest level of familiarity with 30 of the 31 techniques. The relationship between education and familiarity is not strictly linear, however.

Managers with Master of Public Administration (M.P.A.) degrees consistently exhibited greatest familiarity. This was so for 49 of the 53 techniques, and 29 of the 31 techniques where significant differences existed. The greater awareness of M.P.A.s was especially pronounced in the case of more esoteric techniques such as PERT, operations research, matrix organization, Delphi methods, T-Group methods, and the like. These are among the techniques with which state managers are generally least familiar.

Across the entire set of techniques, managers without a college degree were familiar with an average of 67% of the techniques while those holding a B.A. or a B.S. were familiar with 72%. Those holding graduate degrees other than the M.P.A. were familiar with 76% of the techniques on average, while the small number of managers in the sample holding the M.P.A. (34) were familiar with an average of 86% of the techniques.

The impact of education on familiarity was also evident when I treated the proportions of a state's managers with various levels or types of education as separate indicators of education and correlated these with the familiarity score for each state's sample of managers. The correlation between aggregate state familiarity and the proportion of managers in a state lacking a college degree was −.64 and was significant at the .05 level despite an N of only 10. The correlations between familiarity and the proportion of a state's managers holding the M.P.A. (.41) or other master's degrees (.38), although not significant at even the .10 level, do have the expected positive signs.

The location of a manager in his or her state's administrative hierarchy is also related to familiarity with management techniques. Higher level managers exhibited greater familiarity with management techniques, as evidenced by a correlation of .19 (Pearson's r, p = .000, two-tailed test) between organizational place and the aggregate technique familiarity measure. Significant positive correlations between organizational location and aggregate familiarity emerged in 7 of the 10 states. In the case of 29 of the techniques, those familiar with a technique have a significantly higher organizational rank than do those who are unfamiliar with it.

We have seen that managers' familiarity with a technique varies as a function of the likely consequence of that technique for administrative autonomy. Across the three categories of techniques, managers holding M.P.A. degrees are the best informed while those lacking a college degree are least informed. But the differences are most pronounced for autonomy-neutral techniques. Managers holding an M.P.A. are familiar with an average of 86% percent of the 32 techniques in this group as opposed to 64% for managers lacking a degree. The correlations between the proportion of managers in a state with differing levels of education and familiarity are significant for three categories of education only in the case of those techniques whose impact on administrative autonomy is relatively neutral. The correlation between the proportion of a state's managers with no degree and familiarity with autonomy-neutral techniques is −.73. Those between the proportion of managers with an M.P.A., or those holding other master's degrees, and familiarity with autonomy-neutral techniques are .47 and .57, respectively. The best explanation as to why level of education matters less for familiarity with techniques that either reduce or expand administrative autonomy is that such practices tend to be mandated by governors, legislatures, or other nonadministrative actors. Thus, managers are more often "forced" to become aware of such techniques as compared to those that comprise the autonomy-neutral set.

The correlation between the organizational location of a manager is weakest in the case of techniques whose impact on administrative autonomy is relatively neutral (r = .15) while the correlations between place and familiarity with techniques that either expand autonomy or that constrain it are .20 and .22, respectively. Higher level managers may be more familiar with techniques that either limit or expand autonomy because they are more likely to engage in goal setting and more broadly political activities. Techniques that limit or expand autonomy may especially affect such activities.

Significant differences also exist between managers of units with varying functional responsibilities and familiarity with techniques, but the differences are small. Aggregate familiarity ranges from a high of about 80% for managers of units with health or criminal justice responsibilities to a low of about 70% for those in units with economic development, natural resources, or regulatory responsibilities.

Since level of education, organizational rank, and functional responsibility may be interrelated, multiple regression analysis was used to assess the relative impact of these factors on familiarity with management techniques. In combination, these three variables can account for about 9% of the variance in managerial familiarity with the entire set of techniques. A manager's organizational location accounts for about 4% of the variance, with higher level managers more knowledgeable than lower level managers. The fact that a manager holds an M.P.A. accounts for another percent or so of variance. Consistent with the analysis of variance, managers of units with regulatory, natural resources, and economic development responsibilities are somewhat less knowledgeable while those with health responsibilities are somewhat more knowledgeable.

When these variables are regressed on familiarity with techniques with varying effects on agency autonomy, it is the case that they can account for only 6% of the variance in familiarity with autonomy-reducing techniques. Although higher level managers are again more knowledgeable—organizational location accounting for about 4% of variance—level of education is not a significant predictor. A similar model exists in the case of familiarity with the small number of autonomy-enhancing techniques. Some 9% of the variation in familiarity with techniques whose effects on agency autonomy are relatively neutral can be accounted for. The most powerful predictor of familiarity with these techniques—explaining about 3% of the variation—is whether or not a manager holds the M.P.A. degree. The organizational location of a manager can account for only about 1% of the variation.[5]

In short, higher level managers and those with more education, particularly specialized training in public management, are somewhat more knowledgeable about a wide range of management techniques. The differences are not especially sharp, however. Moreover, the impact of education is limited primarily to those techniques with which managers are not "forced" to become familiar; that is, those whose effects on agency autonomy are relatively neutral.

THE UTILIZATION OF MANAGEMENT IMPROVEMENT TECHNIQUES IN THE STATES

Managers may know about particular management techniques but not use them. Conversely, what they know little about may still affect them as practices with which they are relatively unfamiliar are, nonetheless, imposed on their units by others. This section of the chapter explores the extent to which state administrators report that they either use, or that their units are affected by, various managerial techniques, practices, or "improvements." The relationship between familiarity and utilization will be explored along with the impact of a manager's organizational location, the severity of problems confronting a manager's unit, and its functional responsibilities on utilization.

Table 4.3 classifies the 53 management techniques in terms of their utilization as reported by the managers in the 10 study states. One-third of the techniques are used or affect one quarter of the administrators at best, while a group of 20 techniques are used in or affect between one-quarter and one-half of the administrative units. A third group of 15 techniques includes those that are used in or affect more than half of the units. When an aggregate utilization score was calculated, it was the case that an average of 37% of the 53 techniques are used in or affect the administrative units of the respondents (see Table 4.4). Across the states, the use of these management techniques was greatest in California and least in Indiana.

Poister and Streib's (1989) findings on the use of a small number of management tools in municipal government were noted earlier. My findings on the use of these tools in state administration mirror theirs. They found that program evaluation, program or zero-base budgeting, and management information systems were used by at least 70% of the responding jurisdictions, while approximately 60% of the jurisdictions reported the use of management-by-objectives (MBO), performance monitoring, and management incentive programs. Among the techniques most often used by the administrative units in my study were program evaluation (72%), performance indicators (72%), management-by-objectives (66%), and management information systems (60%). Use of zero-base budgeting was reported by 46% of the state managers, while 41% reported the use of planning-programming budgeting methods. If we cumulate the use of one or the other budget method, as did Poister and Streib, state utilization of these methods is comparable to that which exists in the municipalities they surveyed. The least-used management technique in the cities surveyed by Pois-

Table 4.3

Utilization of Management Techniques or Reforms

Low Utilization (Less Than 25%) [1]

Productivity bargaining (3%)
Gubernatorial authority to reorganize
  subject to legislative veto (7%)
Delphi method (8%)
General revenue sharing (8%)
Performance-based compensation (8%)
Assessment centers (9%)
Expand civil service coverage (9%)
Ombudsman office (13%)

Evening/Saturday hours (14%)
Operations research (15%)
Project/matrix-style organization (17%)
Productivity improvement programs(17%)
Reducing number of agencies (18%)
Block grants (20%)
Career executive systems (20%)
Inspector-general units in agencies (23%)

Moderate Utilization (25% to 50%)

Lump-sum appropriations (25%)
Organizational development (26%)
Elimination of civil service coverage for
  middle/upper level managers (26%)
"Whistleblowing" (28%)
Authority to reprogram funds (29%)
Job enlargement/enrichment (30%)
Increase employee salaries (32%)
Increase supervisory power to discipline
  subordinate (37%)
PERT (37%)
Surveys of clientele (37%)

Sunset laws (41%)
Planning-programming budgeting (41%)
Legislative veto of agency rules (42%)
User fees (43%)
Delegation of personnel functions to line
  agencies (44%)
Legislative postaudit (45%)
Zero-base budgeting (46%)
Appointment of agency heads by
  governor (49%)
Cost-benefit analysis (50%)
Administrative provisions of federal
  grants (50%)

High Utilization (Greater Than 50%)

Participative management (54%)
Technological changes enhancing
  performance (57%)
Flextime (58%)
Citizen advisory committees (58%)
Management information systems (60%)
Ethics laws for state employees (60%)
Reorganization (61%)
Open meeting ("sunshine") laws (62%)

Contracting for services (64%)
Management by objectives (66%)
Performance indicators (72%)
Program evaluation (72%)
Professional training (74%)
Administrative procedure act
  requirements (77%)
Freedom of information provisions (79%)

---

1. Percentage of administrators indicating that a particular technique or reform was used in their unit or affected their unit. See footnote 1 to Table 4.1 for information on the Ns for particular items in this table.

ter and Streib as well as in my 10 states was productivity bargaining. The fact that 15% of the responding municipalities reported the use of this management tool while just 3% of the state administrative units did surely is a reflection of more extensive collective bargaining in these cities than in the study states.

Table 4.4 indicates that substantial variation exists in the use of management techniques both across states and within them. Sometimes a technique-specific stimulus for utilization may exist in one or two states but not others. Table 4.5 examines interstate differences in the use of selected management techniques. Some of these are extensively utilized overall, others are only moderately used

Table 4.4

Aggregate Utilization of Management Techniques, Overall and by Impact of Techniques on Administrative Autonomy, for Entire Sample and by State

	Aggregate Utilization Score			
	All Management Techniques	Techniques Reducing Administrative Autonomy	Techniques Expanding Administrative Autonomy	Autonomy-Neutral Techniques
All States	37% (.41) [1]	45% (.41) [3]	26% (.93)	35% (.46)
Arizona	38 (.41) [2]	44 (.45)	26 (.98)	37 (.45)
California	44 (.33)	53 (.35)	31 (.79)	41 (.37)
Delaware	34 (.46)	40 (.46)	27 (.93)	32 (.52)
Indiana	30 (.53)	38 (.52)	21 (1.08)	26 (.61)
Michigan	39 (.37)	50 (.36)	19 (1.25)	36 (.45)
New York	37 (.44)	42 (.47)	31 (.91)	36 (.47)
South Dakota	34 (.41)	42 (.46)	23 (.93)	30 (.50)
Tennessee	35 (.39)	45 (.40)	27 (1.07)	32 (.48)
Texas	37 (.34)	45 (.31)	30 (.70)	34 (.46)
Vermont	33 (.45)	34 (.51)	25 (1.00)	34 (.46)
	F = 6.80	F = 7.67	F = 2.46	F = 6.27
	p = .001	p = .000	p = .009	p = .000
	9,755 d.f.	9,800 d.f.	9,749 d.f.	9,776 d.f.
	Eta = .27	Eta = .28	Eta = .17	Eta = .26

1. Column entry is the aggregate utilization of all 53 management techniques. It was constructed as follows: If a respondent indicated that a particular technique was used in or affected his or her particular unit, it was scored as 1, if not it was scored as 0. The number of techniques used in or affecting a given manager's unit was then divided by the total number of techniques. This would be 53 for a manager who responded to all items. Hence, an administrator who indicated that 30 of the 53 techniques were used in or affected his or her unit would have a utilization score of 56.6 %. Because of the nature of the computer procedure used to calculate this score, the denominator varied slightly. The procedure would normally exclude any case in for which there was missing data for any of the 53 items. To avoid a sizable reduction in the number of cases, so long as a manager responded to at least 50 items he or she was included in the analysis. Thus, the denominator used to calculate aggregate utilization varies between 50 and 53. An example of the bias that this decision introduced follows. An administrator who responded in some way regarding the use of all 53 of the techniques, and who indicated that 30 of the techniques were used in or affected his or her agency would, as indicated above, have an aggregate utilization score of 56.6 %. If this manager failed to respond regarding three of the management techniques, his or her aggregate utilization score would increase to 60% (30/50). The effect of this calculation rule is, thus, to inflate aggregate utilization scores slightly. This rule of tolerating up to three missing responses in computing the utilization score reduced the total number of cases by approximately 10% to 765.

2. The figure in parentheses is the coefficient of variation, that is, the standard deviation divided by the mean.

3. The aggregate utilization scores reported in the three rightmost columns are calculated only for the subset of techniques that have the indicated impact on administrative autonomy. This is 17 for the autonomy-reducing set, 4 for the set of techniques expanding autonomy, and 32 for the set of techniques neither expanding nor constraining autonomy. An aggregate score for use of autonomy-reducing techniques was calculated if valid responses existed from a manager on at least 14 techniques. In the case of autonomy-neutral techniques, an aggregate score was calculated for any manager who had valid responses on at least 29 of the 32 techniques in this subset. The figure in parentheses is, again, the coefficient of variation.

overall, and still others are little used overall. In the case of techniques such as productivity bargaining, reorganization, or MBO, variation is relatively limited. For others, there is comparable utilization in most of the states with one or two of them using a technique significantly more. Examples of such a pattern exist in the case of the substantially greater use of assessment centers and the impact of the legislative veto in Michigan. Michigan was one of the pioneers in the use of assessment centers for selecting employees for promotion and also of provisions that provide for legislative review and possible disapproval of proposed agency rules and regulations. Other examples include greater use of gubernatorially initiated reorganization subject only to legislative veto in South Dakota and of matrix organizational forms in California, Arizona, and New York. Some states are conspicuously low in the use of certain management improvements. One example is the limited use of gubernatorial appointment and removal of agency heads in Michigan and Texas. Finally, the mean utilization of certain techniques is simply the point around which extremes of state utilization fluctuate. An example is the use of zero-base budgeting.

The use of a management technique ought to be positively related to familiarity with it. Indeed, this is the case. A correlation of .63 (Pearson's r) exists between the aggregate familiarity score for a manager and his or her aggregate utilization score. Managers do not have complete freedom to adopt any and all management techniques, however. Their freedom is greatest with respect to techniques whose effects on agency autonomy are generally neutral. Hence, it is not surprising that a strong positive correlation (r = .62) exists between aggregate familiarity with this subset of techniques and their use. State managers tended to be most familiar with techniques that constrained agency autonomy. This was so, I argued, largely because such techniques are imposed on particular agencies by others. Managers are forced to become familiar with such techniques. Thus, while a positive correlation of .54 exists between aggregate familiarity with autonomy-constraining techniques and utilization, the direction of causality may as often be from utilization to familiarity as from familiarity to use. The correlation between familiarity and use is weakest (r = .32) in the case of the small number of techniques that expand agency autonomy. This is so because, however familiar managers may be with such techniques and however much they may wish those processes were in place, the decision to adopt these techniques is typically in the hands of nonadministrative actors. These same actors are generally less interested in expanding agency autonomy than in limiting it.

The utilization of autonomy-constraining techniques is affected not only by the fact that they are typically imposed upon agencies by significant nonadministrative others, but also by the fact that, when adopted, they typically apply to most if not all of the administrative units in a given jurisdiction. The result may be a reduction in *intrastate* variation in utilization and an increase in *interstate* variation—at least as long as not all states have adopted a technique. It is relevant that interstate variation in utilization is greatest for autonomy-

Public Management in the States

Table 4.5
Utilization of Selected Management Techniques Across States

Technique[1]	AZ	CA	DE	IN	MI	NY	SD	TN	TX	VT	ALL
Productivity bargaining	0%	3%	6%	3%	3%	6%	3%	2%	5%	3%	3%
Gubernatorial authority to reorganize subject to legislative veto	2	11	4	5	8	1	31	0	0	12	7
Assessment center	6	8	1	0	26	12	7	5	8	3	9
T-Group methods	19	23	10	13	16	9	10	5	10	3	12
Matrix organization	27	29	6	10	16	23	3	9	11	12	17
Organizational development	23	37	21	27	27	22	13	30	23	31	26
Job enlargement	30	38	35	13	31	30	24	24	35	36	30
PERT	37	45	40	29	47	42	21	23	34	19	37
Legislative veto of rules	31	39	36	18	77	28	59	53	24	59	42
User fees	45	5	33	39	45	47	40	48	31	33	43
Zero-base budgeting	44	44	83	10	40	28	37	59	86	18	46
Gubernatorial appointment/ removal of agency heads	44	68	60	59	25	59	58	51	17	52	49
Participative management	68	68	46	43	63	40	41	60	45	55	54
Reorganization	72	77	57	58	73	74	67	69	67	58	61
MBO	77	75	61	56	69	64	57	47	74	57	66
Freedom of information requirements	65	88	80	67	93	90	38	68	91	64	79

1. Table entry is the percentage of responding administrators in a state indicating that a given technique, practice, or "improvement" was used in their administrative unit or affected their unit.

constraining techniques such as legislative veto of rules or ZBB (see Table 4.5). A single agency or unit may decide to experiment with an autonomy-neutral technique such as PERT or job enlargement even as others do not. But freedom of information requirements, other overhead controls, open meetings requirements, and the like tend to be applied in an across-the-board manner.

This fact, combined with the growing concerns of nonadministrative actors about administrative accountability, explains some of the differences in utilization among types of management techniques. Greater use of autonomy-reducing techniques is testimony to the intense battles for custody over state administrative units that exist in many states (Gormley, 1989a). Overall, and in every state except Vermont, the most frequently applied techniques for "improving" state management are those whose effects are generally to constrain administrative autonomy or to enhance the impact of nonadministrative actors upon the affairs of state agencies. Overall, and in nine of the states, the next most used set of techniques are those relatively neutral in their effects on administrative autonomy. The small number of practices that expand administrative autonomy are least frequently utilized. In short, state administrators are most likely to use, or be subjected to, those techniques that not they but others are wont to adopt.

Managerial Education, Problem Severity, Functional Responsibility, Organizational Location, and the Utilization of Management Techniques

We have seen that higher level managers as well as those with more formal education, particularly graduate training in public management, are more familiar with various management techniques. Since, regardless of its effects on agency autonomy, familiarity with a technique is positively associated with the use of that technique, the organizational location of managers and their educational background should also predict utilization. On the other hand, to the extent that decisions to use certain techniques are not in the hands of individual administrators, we might expect a manager's organizational place and educational background to be less clearly related to use than to familiarity.

Managers holding the M.P.A. degree report highest utilization of the entire range of management techniques, while those lacking a degree report the lowest levels of utilization. But these differences are not statistically significant (F-test, $p = .05$ or better; 4,476 d.f.). When the proportion of a state's managers with a particular educational background is correlated with a state's average aggregate utilization only the negative correlation of $-.68$ between the proportion of managers lacking a college degree and aggregate utilization is statistically significant. Although it might be expected that education would be positively associated with the use of autonomy-neutral techniques whose use is more often up to individual managers or agencies, this is not the case. No significant differences in aggregate utilization of such techniques are evident across categories of education.

The location of a manager in the administrative hierarchy appears to influence utilization more than his or her educational background with higher level managers reporting higher levels of utilization. The correlation (Pearson's r, one-tailed test, $p = .000$) between the rank of a manager and use is .18. Significant positive correlations—ranging from .16 in California to .47 in Delaware—between organizational location and aggregate utilization existed in seven states. The correlations between organizational location and utilization of autonomy-reducing and autonomy-expanding techniques were .18 and .17, respectively. The correlation between rank and those techniques with neutral effects on agency autonomy is only .11 ($p = .01$), however.

Since the management techniques of interest here are presumably designed to remedy particular administrative difficulties, managers of units with more serious administrative difficulties should be more likely to adopt various management techniques or have them imposed on their units by others. A significant positive correlation of .14 does exist between the aggregate management problem severity scores for each unit and the score for a manager's unit on utilization of the entire set of management techniques. Moreover, positive correlations (significant at .10 level or better, one-tailed test) existed in 6 of the 10 states.

One reason that the relationship between management difficulties and the use of management techniques is not stronger is because the aggregate measures lump diverse problems or solutions together. A second reason is that particular improvements, and especially those that constrain autonomy, are frequently imposed on all or nearly all of the administrative units in a state. Another possibility is that certain "improvements" ameliorate one problem while exacerbating another. The provisions of administrative procedure acts that structure the processes by which agencies promulgate rules and regulations, that seek to facilitate citizen access to information in the hands of state agencies, or that permit legislative review of proposed agency rules and regulations, represent a response to concerns about agency due process, openness, or responsiveness to legislative direction. But a side effect is greater complexity in the rules promulgation process. Thus, 92% of the managers who consider the complexity and length of the process for promulgating rules and regulations to be a serious impediment to effective agency management reported that they were subject to notice and hearing requirements in state administrative procedure acts, 86% were affected by freedom of information provisions, and 62% were subject to provisions that provide for legislative review or veto of the regulations that they propose. The comparable percentages in units that did not consider the complexity of the rule promulgation process to be a serious impediment to effective management are 80%, 80%, and 50%, respectively.

Finally, although the severity of a particular problem may suggest the need for certain management improvements, a severe problem may exist precisely because particular techniques are *not* used. That is, a problem exists but has not been addressed. A case in point is the relationship between difficulties communicating with administrative superiors and the use of participative management and organizational development (OD) techniques. Only 41% of those who report that difficulties communicating with superiors seriously impede effective management report the use of participative management techniques. But such techniques are used by 70% of the units in which communication with superiors is not a serious impediment to effective management. Similarly, only one-third of those who report that communicating with superiors is a serious problem also report the use of OD techniques. This compares to 52% of the units in which communication with superiors is not a serious problem.

The functional responsibilities of administrative units may also influence the utilization of particular management techniques or the imposition of various "improvements" on them. Units with regulatory responsibilities may be especially likely targets for sunset review or legislative review or veto of proposed regulations. Agencies whose efforts produce more tangible outcomes—such as miles of roads constructed—may find cost-benefit analysis or project evaluation and review techniques to be more useful than do managers of units whose achievements are less easily quantified.

Analysis of variance indicates that significant differences do exist in the utilization of the entire set of management improvements depending upon the functional responsibility of a unit. The mean utilization scores for units with income security, health, transportation, and criminal justice responsibilities are .43, .42, .41, and .41, respectively. Comparable scores for units with nonfiscal staff, education, and regulatory responsibilities are .34, .32, and .31, respectively. The eta statistic is .28.

Use of techniques that either restrict or expand agency autonomy is also significantly related to functional responsibility, although differences are not pronounced. The eta statistic for the relationship between functional responsibilities and the use of the set of techniques that constrain agency autonomy is .17, while that for the relationship between functional responsibilities and use of the set of techniques that enhance autonomy is .20. Techniques that constrain autonomy most often affect units with health, income security, transportation, and criminal justice responsibilities. The aggregate indicator of the use of the four techniques that enhance administrative autonomy ranges from a low of .21 for those with education, environmental, and regulatory concerns, to .36 for units with transportation responsibilities. Variation as a consequence of functional responsibility is greatest in the case of those techniques that have relatively neutral effects on agency autonomy (eta = .30). Units with income security, criminal justice, health, and transportation responsibilities exhibit greatest mean utilization, while those with education, environmental, or regulatory responsibilities are least likely to report using these techniques.

Units with differing functional responsibilities do not utilize all types of management techniques equally, however. Those with income security obligations rank first in the use of the entire set of techniques, and in the use of the set of autonomy-neutral techniques. They rank sixth in the use of the techniques that expand autonomy, however. Health units rank first in the use of those techniques that constrain autonomy but only eighth in the utilization of those techniques that expand autonomy. On the other hand, the proportion of managers in nonfiscal staff units who report that they use or are affected by autonomy-expanding techniques ranks second among the 11 functional categories while the proportion reporting the use of techniques in the autonomy-neutral set ranks eighth. These differences suggest that the sovereigns of administrative agencies are more likely to constrain the autonomy of agencies with certain types of responsibilities than others.

The impact of functional responsibility on the likelihood that a unit will use or be subject to the effects of particular management techniques is also apparent if we look at the use of specific techniques. Functional differences were significantly related (Chi square test, p = .05 or better) to the utilization of 34 of the 53 techniques. Differences in utilization often appear to reflect the appropriateness of particular techniques in light of the mission of a unit. Hence, while 70% of the managers of units with natural resources responsibilities reported the use of user fees (fishing and hunting licenses, state park admission charges, etc.), this was true of only 33% of those units with criminal justice responsibilities. While 82% of health units reported that they contracted for services, this was true of only 54% of units with regulatory responsibilities. More than 80% of transportation units reported the use of cost-benefit analysis as compared to only 47% of regulatory units and 31% of education units. Management information systems were much more common in transportation and criminal justice units, as was the use of operations research methods. Approximately one-third of units with either income security or transportation responsibilities reported the use of T-Group methods as opposed to less than one-tenth of nonfiscal staff or education units.

A Multivariate Model of the Utilization of State Management Improvement Techniques

A multiple regression model incorporating the organizational location of a manager's unit, a manager's educational background, the functional responsibility of a manager's unit, and the aggregate severity of the administrative difficulties confronting a unit can account for about 13% of the variation in utilization of the entire set of 53 management techniques. Organizational place and aggregate problem severity are positively associated with using or being subject to the effects of the entire set of techniques, with each predictor accounting for about 3% of variance. Units that had either income security, transportation, criminal justice, health, or environmental responsibilities were also more likely to report that they used or were subject to the set of management techniques. A manager's educational background was not, however, a significant predictor of utilization.[6]

Multiple regression models were also estimated for the use of techniques with differential effects on agency autonomy.[7] The model for the use of those techniques whose effects on agency autonomy are relatively neutral accounted for roughly 11% of the variance. However, those for the use of techniques whose effects are either to expand or constrain autonomy could explain only 5% of the variance in utilization. Earlier I argued that those nearer the top of the administrative hierarchy may be impacted most by techniques that affect agency autonomy. This is so because efforts to expand or limit such autonomy have their greatest impact on the sorts of political and policy development activities in which higher level managers engage. Regression analysis indicates that the most important predictor of using or being affected by techniques that potentially constrain a unit's autonomy, and of using or being affected by techniques that expand that autonomy, is the organizational location of a manager.

However, this variable can account for only about 3% of variance. In contrast, in the case of autonomy-neutral techniques, organizational location trails the functional responsibility of a unit in predictive power.[8]

To summarize, bivariate and multivariate analysis suggests that using or being subject to the effects of various management techniques is conditioned by several factors. These include where a manager's unit is located in the state administrative hierarchy, the severity of the problems confronting that unit, and the functional or programmatic responsibilities that it must discharge. In general, higher level managers—those whose units confront more serious problems, and that implement income security, transportation, health, and criminal justice programs—report that their units use or are at least subject to a larger number of management techniques or practices. The predictive power of these factors varies to some extent depending upon the effects that particular techniques have on the autonomy of a unit. While better educated managers exhibited greater familiarity with various management techniques, the educational background of a manager was not independently related to utilization. One reason that education does not affect utilization is that managers are not equally free to adopt each and every potential management improvement. At the same time, certain "improvements" favored by external actors are imposed on administrative units despite the wishes of those who head them.

THE EFFICACY OF STATE MANAGEMENT "IMPROVEMENTS"

The management techniques whose use by state administrators has just been explored are presumably intended to improve the operation of state bureaucracies in some way. But do they? What do state administrators think about the efficacy of various management techniques? To determine this, those managers who had indicated that they were familiar with a technique were asked to assess its effects or consequences for "the quality of agency management and the effective implementation" of their unit's programs. To simplify discussion, the "very positive effect" and "slightly positive effect" categories were combined, as were the "very negative effect" and "slightly negative" effect response categories. The other response option was "no effect."

Table 4.6 indicates that a majority of the respondents attributed positive effects to all but four of the techniques. For roughly half of the techniques, three-fourths or more of the administrators saw the effects as positive. Administrators were most positive about the effects of management information systems, operations research, professional training for staff, program evaluation, job enlargement or enrichment, "participative" management, and technological changes. They were least positive about "improvements" such as the legislative veto of agency rules, "whistleblowing" by agency subordinates, elimination of civil service coverage for higher level administrators, compulsory arbitration of labor disputes, and zero-base budgeting systems. Even in the case of

Table 4.6

State Managers' Judgments on Impact of Management Techniques or Reforms

Percentage of Managers Familiar with a Technique Attributing Positive Impact to It [1]

Less Than 50% Positive Effects

Legislative veto of rules (34%)	Elimination of civil service coverage for middle/upper level managers (43%)
Whistleblowing (38%)	
Compulsory arbitration (38%)	

50% - 75% Positive Effects

Expand civil service coverage (50%)	User fees (64%)
Admin. requirements in federal grants (52%)	Evening/Saturday hours (64%)
Freedom of information requirements (53%)	Inspector-general units (67%)
Sunset laws (55%)	Open meeting laws (68%)
Block grants (56%)	Performance-based compensation (71%)
Productivity bargaining (57%)	General revenue sharing (72%)
Gubernatorial power to initiate reorganization subject to legislative veto (57%)	Administrative procedure laws (72%)
Gov. appointment of all agency heads (58%)	Matrix organization (72%)
T-Groups (59%)	PPB (74%)
Reducing number of separate agencies (60%)	Delphi techniques (74%)
Legislative postaudit (62%)	

these four, however, at least one-third of the managers viewed the technique as having positive effects on agency management.[9]

Efficacy and the Impact of Techniques on Administrative Autonomy

Both familiarity with and utilization of particular management techniques varied as a function of the likely impact of those techniques on the autonomy of state administrative units. Reexamination of Table 4.6 indicates that judgments as to the efficacy of particular techniques are similarly tied to the likely consequences that these techniques have on administrative autonomy. The five practices that managers viewed least positively include four that are autonomy-constraining: the legislative veto, whistleblowing, reduction in the scope of civil service coverage, and zero-base budgeting. Moreover, of the 20 techniques about which administrators were least enthusiastic, 11 reduce administrative autonomy. At the other extreme, none of the 20 techniques concerning

Table 4.6 (Continued)

75% or More Positive Effects	
Ombudsman (75%)	Performance indicators (85%)
Reorganization (75%)	Cost-benefit analysis (86%)
Contracting out (76%)	Agency authority to reprogram funds (86%)
Career executive systems (77%)	Organizational development (88%)
Ethics laws (79%)	Surveys of clients (88%)
Lump-sum appropriations (80%)	Increase employee salaries (89%)
Citizen advisory committees (81%)	MIS (89%)
Flextime (82%)	Operations research (90%)
Productivity improvement programs (82%)	Professional evaluation (93%)
Increased supervisory power to discipline subordinates (83%)	Job enlargement (93%)
Delegation of major personnel functions to line agencies	Participative management (95%)
Assessment centers (84%)	Technological changes (96%)
PERT (84%)	

1. Percentages are based on the responses of those managers who indicated some sort of familiarity with a given technique or reform. It was felt that those who had at least some familiarity with a technique, even if they had not used it or been directly affected by it, did have some basis for assessing its potential impact. For the 53 techniques, Ns ranged from 221 managers who were familiar with productivity bargaining to the 795 managers who were familiar with freedom of information provisions. The percentages are those who believed a particular technique or practice did or would have "very positive" or "slightly positive" effects on "the quality of agency management and the effective implementation" of their unit's programs.

which administrators were most positive constrain autonomy, while two of the four autonomy-enhancing practices—delegating personnel functions to line administrators, and the authority to reprogram appropriated funds—ranked among the 20 techniques viewed most positively by managers.[10]

In his recent assessment of efforts to "tame" government bureaucracies, Gormley (1989b) identifies three types of control strategies. At one extreme are coercive controls. Such controls are "solution forcing" and severely limit bureaucratic discretion. They involve the "flexing of muscles" by nonadministrative actors. Coercive controls are "legally and politically irresistible because they are tightly worded and unambiguous" (p. 12). At the other extreme are what Gormley labels "catalytic controls." Such controls are intended to stimulate or help a bureaucracy to act and define a problem, but they "do not predetermine the nature of the bureaucracy's response" (p. 12). Instead, catalytic controls are "attention-grabbing, action-forcing, and energizing. They seek to raise the bureaucracy's consciousness by forcing bureaucrats to take certain ideas, problems and interests seriously" (p. 12). A third category of controls—

those that Gormley labels "hortatory"—fall somewhere between coercive and catalytic controls. They are "catalytic controls with 'bite,' coercive controls with an 'escape hatch' "(pp. 12–13).

Gormley argues that nonadministrative actors concerned about what they perceive to be unresponsive bureaucracies have been too quick to embrace coercive controls and too quick to dismiss catalytic controls. Or, rather, legislators, chief executives, and others have been insufficiently sensitive to the conditions that call for the imposition of one type of control rather than another. In Gormley's eyes, the result of inappropriate or excessive reliance on coercive controls has often been the replacing of one set of bureaucratic ills by another. Overreliance on coercive controls can result in a rigid or hamstrung bureaucracy, whereas the use of catalytic controls to encourage bureaucratic responsiveness is more likely to produce a "well-tempered" bureaucracy. While such a bureaucracy is "forced to respond in some fashion to important problems," it is "free to respond sensibly and creatively" (Gormley, 1986a, p. 6).

The state managers in this study are generally unenthusiastic about management "improvements" that constrain their freedom of action. Given this fact, it is not surprising that they also tend to share Gormley's doubts about the efficacy of coercive as compared to catalytic methods of enhancing bureaucratic performance. Gormley cites legislative vetoes of proposed agency rules, sweeping court injunctions, nondiscretionary executive orders, and technology-forcing statutes as examples of coercive controls. It could be argued that another coercive method is the removal of particular administrative positions from the classified civil service. Across all 53 techniques, state managers were least positive about the consequences of permitting legislatures to review and/or veto proposed agency rules or regulations, with only 34% saying that these arrangements had a positive effect on the effective implementation of their units' programs. Nearly as unpopular was the elimination of civil service coverage for middle and upper level administrators (see Table 4.6).

Examples of catalytic controls cited by Gormley include ombudsman offices, required public hearings, open meeting laws, "proxy" advocacy arrangements, freedom of information statutes, requirements that agencies complete environmental or economic impact statements, and "agenda-setting statutes, such as the Public Utility Regulatory Policies Act (PURPA) which required state public utility commissions to 'consider and determine' the merits of various rate structure reforms" (1989b, p. 12). The state administrators in my study are a good deal more sanguine about the benefits of these catalytic strategies for improving bureaucratic performance. Although only slightly more than one-half saw freedom of information requirements as having positive consequences for agency performance, more than two-thirds considered open meeting requirements to have beneficial effects, while more than three out of four believed that ombudsmen and citizen advisory committees had positive effects.

One example of a hortatory control cited by Gormley is legislative auditing. It might be argued that the existence of inspector-general units within agencies or requirements for sunset review of agencies by the state legislature are other examples of this type of control. Standing as they do between coercive controls at one extreme and catalytic controls at the other, it is not surprising that these instances of hortatory controls occupy a middle ground in administrative judgments of efficacy. While sunset provisions are seen as having positive effects by just 55% of the respondents, legislative postaudit requirements are seen as having positive effects by 62% of the managers and the existence of an inspector-general in an agency is seen by 67% to have positive effects on agency performance.

Utilization of Management Improvements and Managers' Estimates of Efficacy

To this point discussion of the benefits or costs of management techniques has been based on the views of those administrators who said they were familiar with particular techniques, regardless of whether or not they had used or been directly affected by them. But what do those who have actually used or been directly affected by specific techniques think of them? Does utilization breed contempt or does it make a manager's heart grow fonder? Management innovations are sometimes oversold in order to secure their adoption. Hence, disillusionment with them may be common among users. Alternatively, opponents may make the worst case for a reform so that those actually using it or affected by it may be pleasantly surprised.

When whether or not administrators had actually used or been affected by a given techinique was cross-tabulated with administrative assessments of the efficacy of that technique, utilizers were found to be more sanguine than nonutilizers in the case of 45 of the 53 techniques. These differences were statistically significant (Chi square test, $p = .05$ or better) in the case of 34 techniques. In most cases, however, the differences were small. Using an asymmetric uncertainty coefficient to measure the strength of the relationships with the efficacy judgment as the dependent variable, I found coefficients of .21 for participative management, .20 for professional training, .11 for organization development, .08 for cost benefit analysis, and .07 for job enlargement. Much more common, however, for those relationships significant at the .01 level, were uncertainty coefficients in the range of .02 to .05.

What of the eight exceptions to the rule that utilizers were more positive than nonutilizers? Three of the exceptions—compulsory arbitration, productivity bargaining, and performance pay systems—are techniques with which relatively few administrators were familiar and that even fewer had used. Although the differences are not statistically significant, it is interesting that four of the techniques that utilizers appraised less positively than did nonusers were sunset laws, freedom of information requirements, administrative procedure provisions, and whistleblowing. Each of these is a management "improvement" that constrains managerial actions or opens up administrative operations to greater outside scrutiny. Managers take a fairly dim view of these "improvements" and experience with them does little to moderate those views. The techniques for which no significant differences existed in attributions of efficacy as between utilizers and nonutilizers also included seven that were autonomy-constraining or accountability-enhancing. These are legislative veto of agency rules, the governor possessing the power to initiate reorganization, open meeting requirements, inspector-general units, legislative postauditing, and reducing civil service coverage. Both those managers who are familiar with these techniques but have no direct experience with them and those who have had direct experience with them are unconvinced of the merits of these methods.

I have been arguing that utilization breeds a more positive view of the effects of a particular management technique. But the causal arrow may run in the other direction: those who believe that certain techniques will improve the quality of management may be more likely to adopt them. At least this ought to be true for those techniques whose adoption is largely at the discretion of individual administrators or units. Support for this line of reasoning is provided by the finding that techniques likely to constrain administrative autonomy bulk large among the handful of techniques that users view as less efficacious than do nonusers. Additional support is provided by the fact that such techniques are disproportionately found to be among those in which the relationship between use and efficacy is not statistically significant. Adoption of these autonomy-constraining techniques is typically not left to the discretion of particular administrators or administrative units. Hence, the tendency for users to be more positive about the effects of certain techniques, or for the linkage of use and efficacy to occur because those who think well of a technique are more likely to adopt it, primarily exist for those techniques whose use is discretionary.

The overall rankings with respect to utilization and efficacy for techniques that comprise each of the three sets of techniques classified in terms of impact upon administrative autonomy also suggests that this is the case.[11] The rank-order correlation (Spearman's Rho) between utilization and efficacy for the 17 autonomy-constraining techniques is −.73. All but three of these techniques had a higher rank for utilization than efficacy. The situation is reversed in the case of the four autonomy-enhancing techniques. The rank-order correlation is +.80. In the case of the 32 techniques whose effects on administrative autonomy are relatively neutral, the pattern is more mixed although a positive relationship of +.46 existed between utilization and efficacy. Among the techniques in this group, efficacy rank exceeded utilization rank in 60% of the cases.

To summarize, the contention that a positive relationship between utilization and a judgment of efficacy exists because those more positively disposed to a technique are more likely to adopt it, is generally valid only for techniques that do not reduce the autonomy of administrative actors or institutions. Save for a small number of autonomy-enhancing techniques, these are the "autonomy-neutral" techniques that administrators can adopt most freely. In contrast, the use of autonomy-constraining practices is high not because administrators like such techniques but because significant nonadministrative actors are fond of them.

The positive relationship between the use of certain management techniques and attributions of efficacy may account for some of the interstate differences in efficacy ascribed to techniques that were noted above. Since utilization is often positively related to judgments of efficacy, and since interstate differences in utilization of various techniques also exist, it is necessary to control for these interstate differences in utilization. It will be recalled that significant interstate differences in utilization existed in the case of 17 of the techniques. When attributions of efficacy were assessed separately for those familiar with a technique but lacking direct experience with it, and for those who have actually used a technique or been subject to its effects, few significant interstate differences in attributions of efficacy emerged. For those with no direct experience with a technique, significant interstate differences in judgments of efficacy (F-test, $p = .05$ level or better) existed for only seven techniques. These are flextime, assessment centers, lump-sum appropriations, gubernatorial appointment of all agency heads, gubernatorial authority to initiative reorganization, whistleblowing, and PERT.

In the case of those managers who have actually used or been directly affected by a technique or practice, significant interstate differences exist for only five techniques. Interestingly, these include four autonomy-constraining practices: rolling back civil service coverage, reorganization, the legislative veto of agency rules, and administrative procedure provisions. Interstate differences may persist among those subject to these four practices because the content in which each is applied differs. Thus, an effort to reduce civil service coverage may be perceived differently in a state in which current coverage is extensive as opposed to one in which it is already limited. The explanation in the case of differences in attributions of efficacy regarding gubernatorial appointment of agency heads lies partly in the fact that the analysis indicates that those who are at present appointed by the governor like this method of selection, and that the proportion of managers who have reached their current positions via gubernatorial appointment varies across the states. However one accounts for deviant cases, it ought not obscure the fact that—while interstate differences in familiarity and utilization exist with regard to the broad range of management techniques and practices—judgments regarding the positive or negative effects of these techniques do not generally differ significantly among those with comparable degrees of exposure to particular techniques.

CONCLUSION

The examination of impediments to effective management in Chapter 2 suggested that, although state agencies confronted a number of serious difficulti most were performing in a reasonably effective fashion. The picture that e from this chapter is one of state managers who are reasonably well-informed about, and likely to have used, various techniques that promise to remedy one or another administrative difficulty. This was true despite some differences in familiarity or utilization related to the educational backgrounds of managers, their organizational location, the tasks of their units, as well as other factors.

Thus, administrative familiarity with MBO methods was nearly universal and more than two-thirds of those surveyed claimed to have used these methods in their units. Managers were equally familiar with "participative management" approaches and approximately three quarters of them said they had used such methods. More than half of those we surveyed were familiar with OD efforts and one-quarter said they had used such methods. Nearly two-thirds of the respondents were familiar with PERT, and more than two-fifths reported using it, while half were familiar with matrix forms of organization and about one-fifth of them reported using such forms. So, while not all administrators are as au courant as others, most were familiar with a substantial proportion of the techniques. Moreover, a fair number of them had used, or been affected by, these techniques. Certainly there is some upward bias in these administrative responses. Admitting that one is unfamiliar with something that one presumably ought to be familiar with is difficult. Moreover, no penalties for untruthfulness existed. Still, for those concerned about the managerial capabilities of state administrators and administrative agencies, the levels of familiarity with and use of the more than 50 techniques focused on in this chapter are impressive.

The second important point to stress in concluding this chapter concerns the efficacy ascribed to various management techniques by the managers I surveyed. Although variation in attributions of efficacy existed, most administrators felt that most of the techniques with which they were familiar had, or gave promise of having, a positive impact on the operation of their units. Nor were these relatively positive views a function of the fact that managers lacked direct experience with particular techniques. Managers who had used, or been affected by particular techniques, and were in the best position to make judgments on their efficacy, were typically more positive in their assessments than were those who had some knowledge of particular techniques but had had no "hands on" experience with them. In short, while most of the techniques, practices, or "improvements" were not seen as being panaceas, neither were they placebos. The majority were seen as making a positive contribution ministrators and administrative units to do their jobs. e fairly widespread use of many of these techniques, y should be heartening to those concerned about the nt and interested in improving that quality. on this conclusion involves the differential effects of edom of action of state administrative agencies. The s were generally most familiar with, and were most ing subject to, techniques that constrained their autonomy in some fashion, or those that increased the influence of particular nonadministrative actors on the affairs of their units. They were much less likely to be familiar with, or to have used or been affected by, the 30 or so techniques whose effects on agency autonomy were relatively neutral. They were least familiar with, or likely to have used or been affected by, the handful of techniques that expanded their autonomy. These patterns of utilization might lead one to conclude that the major deficiency of state agencies is their lack of accountability to various external political sovereigns.

Administrators' judgments on the efficacy of techniques that had varying effects on agency autonomy tend to be the reverse of those for familiarity or utilization. Managers were most positive about the effects of those techniques that presumably expanded their operational freedom and were least enthusiastic about those that constrained it. The explanation for this pattern of findings is that autonomy-constraining techniques are usually imposed on agencies by political sovereigns and, particularly in an era of "bureau-bashing" (Gormley, 1989b), these sovereigns are especially fond of such vehicles for "improving" public management. Hence, state agencies tend to use or, more accurately, have been made subject to, techniques or practices that do not—in their eyes at least—have positive consequences for unit performance.

This point brings us back to the discussion of differing approaches to public administration that was featured at the beginning of the chapter. In the language of Herbert Kaufman (1956), the state administrators surveyed tend to view techniques consistent with the "quest for neutral competence" as having the most promise for improving administrative performance. Using David Rosenbloom's (1983) terminology, state managers tend to embrace the "managerial" approach to improving agency performance while they are, at best, ambivalent toward techniques or practices generally consistent with "political" or "legal" approaches. However styled, these state managers tend to prefer management "improvements" that enhance administrative autonomy or at least do not reduce it. To a substantial degree, they continue to believe that extensive involvement of nonadministrative actors in the affairs of their agencies hampers what they define to be effective administration. Put another way, these state administrators continue to believe that maintaining some sort of politics-administration separation is a good way to assure efficient and effective administration of the public's business.

The problem for these state managers, as for other public managers, is that practices consistent with "executive leadership," "representative bureaucracy," "political," or "legal perspectives can be imposed on them by a variety of nonadministrative actors. These actors are often enamored of particular practices consistent with these perspectives. My previous work on state legislative oversight (Elling, 1984), for instance, indicates considerable legislative enthusiasm for legislative review/veto of agency rules or regulations and sunset laws, practices that administrators are relatively unenthusiastic about.

In Chapter 2 it was suggested that public managers might see many of their problems as due to the actions and decisions of various nonadministrative "thems," with the result that they adopt what Whorton and Worthley (1981) term an "if-only" management orientation. The evidence presented in this chapter on the use of management techniques and their perceived efficacy might seem to provide further support for the existence of such a management orientation. Those autonomy-reducing techniques that state administrators frequently report being subject to, and which they are less than enthusiastic about, are nearly always products of views of the administrative process held by various nonadministrative "thems." The data depict state administrators who believe that if such constraints were either fewer in number or less rigid in nature, they could do a better job of managing their units. Indeed, various of the exogenous or "them" problems that managers indicate are quite serious likely stem from the application of particular autonomy-constraining strategies to their operations.

But, just as I do not believe it is appropriate to conclude that state managers blame most of their problems on various "thems," so am I not prepared to conclude that their preferences for management "improvements" indicate an if-only orientation to their administrative world. While the managers surveyed tended to view autonomy-constraining techniques in a less favorable light relative to most other techniques, a substantial proportion thought that such techniques had positive effects. With the exception of four autonomy-constraining techniques—legislative veto of rules and regulations, whistleblowing, civil service rollback, and zero-base budgeting—at least half of those familiar with particular autonomy-constraining techniques attributed positive effects to them.

The other reason for rejecting the argument that managers' more jaundiced views of autonomy-constraining techniques is evidence of an if-only management orientation is that they object most strongly to only a certain type of autonomy-constraining strategy. These tend to be what Gormley classifies as "coercive controls," controls that he argues often have dysfunctional consequences for the ability of an administrative agency to effectively discharge its responsibilities. In contrast, those techniques that constrain or channel the exercise of agency discretion, but do so in a "catalytic" fashion, tend to be viewed more positively by the managers in these 10 states. Important examples include the office of ombudsman, open meeting laws, and citizen advisory committees. Examples of "hortatory controls"—those that fall between coercive and catalytic controls—concerning which state administrators were relatively sanguine include legislative postaudit efforts and inspector-generals within agencies.

The views of state managers concerning which techniques and strategies are most likely to improve the operation of their agencies constitute but one perspective on a complicated process subject to diverse definitions. But it is an extremely relevant perspective. Their relatively positive views of the likely or actual effects of many commonly applied strategies for improving agency performance is heartening, as is evidence that many of these techniques are widely used. Their relatively negative views of the effects of certain techniques that constrain their operational freedom—especially those of a highly "coercive" nature—suggest caution in the use of such techniques if our goal is a well-tempered state administrative process rather than one that is hamstrung.

NOTES

1. In a few instances, administrators responded to the question in terms of more than one category. Some responded in terms of a combination of the "familiar but no experience or direct knowledge of effects" category and the "used elsewhere in state government in my state" category. Others responded in terms of the "used in or affects my unit" category and the "used elsewhere in state government" category. The latter combination of responses was recoded as equivalent to the "used in or affects my unit" responses. In a very few cases, administrators asserted that they had no direct knowledge or experiences with a technique and also that a technique was used in or affected their unit. This combination was also coded as indicative of use (and, hence, familiarity with) a technique or being affected by a technique or practice.

2. The denominator in the fraction that comprises the second term of the formula for calculating aggregate familiarity is 53 for a manager who responded to all items. This denominator was less than 53 in some cases, however. This was so because the computer procedure used to calculate the ratio normally handled missing data by excluding any case for which there was missing data for *any* of the 53 techniques. To prevent a sizable reduction in the number of cases, all cases where a manager had responded to a minimum of 50 items were included. Using this rule reduces the total N by about 10%. Had such a rule not been used, however, more than 40% of the cases would have been excluded in calculating the aggregate score. This calculating rule results in a lower familiarity score for the administrator who did not respond to all items, although the effect is minor. For an administrator unfamiliar with 27 items, the familiarity score when all items were responded to was 49.1 [1.00 − (27/53)]. When only 50 items were responded to the familiarity score was 46.0 [1.00 − (27/50)].

3. Aggregate familiarity ranged from a low of 65% in Indiana and roughly 70% in Delaware, South Dakota, Tennessee, and Texas, to a high of 78% in New York and 80% in California. These interstate differences were statistically significant (F-test, p = .000). Within each state, however, variation in familiarity was great with no state coefficient of variation being smaller than .50.

4. A familiarity score was calculated for the techniques in each of the three sets. The score for the autonomy-constraining set was 80%, while that for the techniques that presumably expand administrative autonomy was 67%, and that for the autonomy neutral techniques was 71%. In each of the 10 states managers were most familiar with those techniques that constrained autonomy. In only three states were managers more familiar with autonomy-expanding techniques than with those that were autonomy-neutral.

5. Because the state samples differ in the educational backgrounds of their managers and the rank of those managers, familiarity with management techniques was regressed on these variables, as well as on the functional responsibility of a unit, within each state. (In this analysis the probability of F required for a predictor to enter the regression was increased to .10 from .05). For the entire set of techniques, organizational location was a significant positive predictor of familiarity in seven states while education was a

significant positive predictor in only two. Location similarly outperformed education as a predictor of familiarity in the case of techniques that either constrain or expand autonomy. For familiarity with autonomy-neutral techniques, however, and consistent with the overall model, while place was a significant positive predictor in six states, education was a significant predictor in four.

6. The aggregate utilization model was also estimated separately for each of the state samples. Ten percent or more of the variation in techniques utilization could be accounted for in eight states, with one-third or more of the variance accounted for in Arizona, Indiana, Michigan, Tennessee, and Texas. Aggregate management problem severity was a significant predictor of utilization only in New York and Indiana. The organizational location of a manager was a significant positive predictor of utilization in Arizona, California, Delaware, Indiana, Michigan, South Dakota, and Texas, however, where it could account for between 3% and 10% of the variance. The limited relevance of educational background for utilization is evidenced by the fact that possession of the M.P.A. degree was a significant positive predictor of utilization only in California. The predictive power of unit function generally persists in individual states. Having income security responsibilities was a positive predictor of utilization in Arizona, Indiana, Michigan, and Texas; having transportation responsibilities was a positive predictor in Arizona, Indiana, Michigan, and Tennessee; and having health responsibilities was a positive predictor of utilization in Delaware, Michigan, Tennessee, and Texas.

7. Since subsets of techniques were being focused on, it was inappropriate to include the aggregate management problem severity indicator as a predictor in these models.

8. These patterns are generally evident in individual states as well. Organizational location is a significant positive predictor of using or being subjected to techniques that constrain autonomy in all but two states. In five states it accounted for more than 10% of the variance. It is the most powerful predictor in five states. Organizational location is also a significant positive predictor of using or being subject to techniques that expand administrative autonomy in five states and can account for 5% or more of the variance in four. In six states organizational location is also a significant positive predictor of the use of those techniques whose effects on agency autonomy are relatively neutral, although it is the most powerful predictor in only one state.

9. Although interstate variation exists, the overall patterns for the efficacy of particular management techniques are mirrored in individual states. For two-thirds of the techniques, no statistically significant interstate differences in efficacy existed. Statistically significant interstate differences ($p = .05$ or better) exist in the case of judgments of the efficacy of compulsory arbitration, flextime, Delphi techniques, delegating responsibility for various personnel matters to line administrators, reducing the extent of civil service coverage, the governor possessing the right to undertake reorganization subject only to legislative action disapproving a plan, lump sum agency appropriations, gubernatorial authority to appoint most agency heads, the existence of an ombudsman, matrix-style organization, citizen advisory groups, the legislative veto, administrative procedure act provisions, legislative postauditing, whistleblowing, and PERT.

If we examine interstate differences in how particular techniques rank on attributed efficacy, we find that there is considerable interstate consensus on about one-fourth of the techniques. Five techniques—job enlargement, participative management, professional training, program evaluation, and technological changes—are ranked among the 10 most efficacious by administrators in at least eight states. Another group of nine techniques—including clientele surveys, cost-benefit analysis, management information systems, operations research, organizational development, and performance indicators—are ranked in the top 20 by administrators in eight or more states. There is considerable unanimity of judgment as well in the case of 15 techniques that have relatively negative effects. Seven techniques—reducing civil service coverage, expanding civil service, compulsory arbitration, freedom of information requirements, legislative veto, whistle-blowing, and zero-base budgeting—rank 40th or lower in efficacy in eight or more states. Eight techniques—including federal grant administrative requirements, reducing the number of agencies, gubernatorial appointment of all agency heads, gubernatorial authority to initiate reorganization, Saturday or evening hours, sunset provisions, T-Group methods, and user fees—ranked 30th or lower in efficacy in at least eight of the states.

10. The jaundiced administrative view of the effects of autonomy-constraining management practices is consistent across the states. Autonomy-constraining techniques are significantly overrepresented among the 20 techniques or practices that are viewed least positively in every state, while those whose impact on autonomy is relatively neutral are consistently underrepresented among those to whom lowest efficacy is attributed. In seven states the few techniques that presumably expand administrative autonomy are significantly underrepresented among the 20 techniques that are least positively viewed. The autonomy-constraining techniques that ranked among the "bad 20" in all 10 states were gubernatorial appointment of all agency heads, freedom of information requirements, whistleblowing, and provisions for zero-base budgeting. In nine of the states the reduction of civil service coverage, sunset provisions, and the legislative veto ranked among the 20 least positive practices in their consequences. Legislative postaudit efforts, and governors empowered to undertake administrative reorganization subject only to the legislature taking action to disapprove such reorganization within a specified period of time, were highly unpopular in eight of the states. Ranked among the "bad 20" in no more than five states were open-meeting requirements, inspector-general units, administrative procedure requirements, PPB, ethics laws, and an ombudsman.

11. A utilization and efficacy rank was calculated for each technique with respect to the entire set of 53 techniques. Thus, freedom of information requirements ranked 1st in usage and 28th in efficacy. After ranks were calculated in this fashion for all 53 techniques, the correlational analysis was conducted separately for the set of techniques that comprise each of three subsets based on impact on administrative autonomy.

Chapter 5

State Bureaucracies as Policyshapers

INTRODUCTION

A central purpose of the first half of the book was to examine the challenging nature of state management as reflected in state managers' judgments as to the severity of various potential impediments to effective agency management. A number of the more serious impediments involved actions taken by various nonadministrative "thems." While the argument that most state managers adopt an "if-only" style of management was rejected, many of the managers surveyed in this study do see governors, legislatures, the courts, interest groups, budget offices, the federal government, and others as hampering the effective discharge of the responsibilities of their units. Analysis of administrators' views of the efficacy of various efforts to "improve" state administration disclosed that many expressed doubts about the efficacy of those techniques and strategies—often favored by particular nonadministrative actors—that tended to constrain their discretion or limit the autonomy of their agencies.

As has previously been pointed out, these findings reflect the continuing tension in our thinking on what "good" public management entails. While state agencies are expected to operate in an efficient and effective manner, administrative performance also involves accountability. Efficiency and effectiveness may be affected in various ways by efforts to enhance accountability. Often these efforts entail a reduction in administrative efficiency or effectiveness.

A key element of administrative accountability is responsiveness—whose goals do state agencies seek to achieve? Since few state administrators are elected, their role in policy implementation as well as in other aspects of the policy-making process troubles many. Specifying to whom or to what administrators are or should be responsive is difficult, however. Should they simply comply with the wishes of their administrative superiors? Is primary accountability owed to the governor or to the legislature? What about responsiveness to those groups served by an agency's programs?[1]

Even when agreement is possible regarding the agents to whom administrators ought to be accountable, disagreement may exist on how to assure such accountability. How can various political sovereigns best "manage the managers"? The degree of influence various nonadministrative actors ought to have over the administration of public programs, and what form such influence should take, is a central issue in the study of contemporary public management.

THEORETICAL PERSPECTIVES ON THE INTERACTION OF ADMINISTRATORS AND SIGNIFICANT OTHERS

The classic politics-administration dichotomy held that effective administration resulted if day-to-day administration was largely the province of professionals with considerable security of tenure. This could be justified because administration was largely a technical process that did not require those carrying out programs to make important value choices. These value choices—the marching orders of administrators—were to be made by elected officials. It was they who established the basic organizational framework of agencies, authorized the programs to to be carried out by each, and determined the levels of financial and other resources to be made available to them. In this formulation administrative responsiveness was defined as responsiveness to elected officials.

Even in its heyday, it is unclear if those who embraced the politics-administration dichotomy as a normative standard believed that it ought to proscribe *administrative involvement* in the making of policy. The dichotomy emerged in a historical context in which excessive partisan political influence in administration seemed at the heart of problems of governmental performance. Even then, the intent may have been only to limit political intrusion with respect to certain aspects of administration, such as the staffing of agencies (Fry, 1989, esp. pp. 1036–1039).

The complexity of modern state policymaking, and the fact that nonadministrators control resources crucial to administrative performance, mean administrators often consider policymaking to be too important to leave solely to elected officials. Elected officials are often ill-prepared to determine and define the broad, programmatic goals that, according to the tenets of the politics-administration dichotomy, they are supposed to determine. Their frequent adoption of a short time frame, however understandable given political realities, may mean that they—in the eyes of administrators at least—ignore important, longer term dimensions of problems and policy choices. Administrative agencies have become important actors in the formulation and adoption as well as the implementation of public policies. The highly fragmented or pluralistic nature of the American political system demands that administrators seek to build political support for their agencies and the efforts of those agencies.

From the point of view of nonadministrative actors, administration is too important to leave solely to administrators. The activities of administrative agencies make too much difference in the lives of their constituents for elected officials to be content with leaving these agencies in splendid isolation. On the one hand, state governments, as well as their local governments, were more likely than the federal government to adopt practices designed to limit "political meddling" in the administrative process. Many, for instance, opted for the commission form of administrative organization, which limited the capacity of the governors to provide direction to many of the agencies that comprised the executive branch they nominally headed. On the other hand, states were notably slow to establish the sort of civil service arrangements seen as central to assuring that administrative affairs are discharged by technically competent state employees protected from dismissal for reasons of politics. Patronage practices continue to flourish in a number of states—including several focused on in this study.

Alas, the literature exploring political-administrative interaction has often displayed a tendency to throw the baby out with the bath water. Showing that politicians have sporadic influence in daily administration, or that administrators play a role in the developing of solutions to public problems, is not to say that elected officials are now administrators or that administrators are functioning as elected policymakers. Sensible thinking about the reality and the normative desirability of patterns of administrative and nonadministrative influence requires several things.

First, there is a need for more complex conceptualizations of the relationships between administrative and nonadministrative actors and their relative roles in administration and policymaking. Based upon his review of the existing literature on the relationships of elected officials and administrators in policy and administration, Svara (1985) has identified four models.

The *policy* (or politics)/*administration dichotomy* has already been discussed. Svara notes, however, that it is the only model that is fully developed in the literature. A second model, the *mixture in policy* model, "emerged from the postwar behavioral revolution in political science" and "depends heavily on the redefinition of key terms and the shift in research on policymaking that accompanied the transformation of the discipline" (p. 222). It models a politico-administrative world in which administrators possess extensive opportunities to set policy while "through implementation they shape policy formulated by elected officials" (p. 222). It is a policy *mixture* model because, while insulation of administration is carried over from the dichotomy model, policy is viewed as a "mixture of efforts by elected officials and administrators with the latter sometimes dominant" (p. 222).

The *mixture in administration* model is the logical antithesis of the mixture in policy model. It suggests a passive administrative role in policymaking while elected officials aggressively "insert" themselves into the "depths of administration" (p. 222). Such a model might describe the situation after the Civil

Figure 5.1
Models of Relationships Between Elected Officials and Administrators in Governmental Process

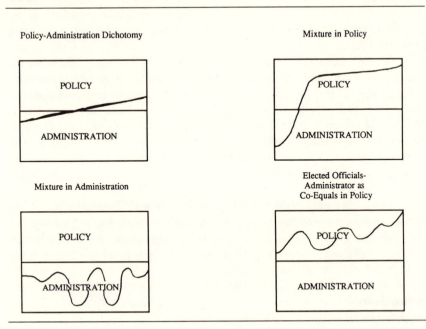

Policy-Administration Dichotomy

POLICY

ADMINISTRATION

Mixture in Policy

POLICY

ADMINISTRATION

Mixture in Administration

POLICY

ADMINISTRATION

Elected Officials-
Administrator as
Co-Equals in Policy

POLICY

ADMINISTRATION

In each figure, the heavy line marks the boundary between the spheres of elected and appointed officials. All of the area above this line is the responsibility of elected officials while all of the area below the line is the responsibility of administrators.

Source: Svara (1985, p. 223).

War and prior to the era of civil service reform. Svara indicates that the logic of the model, but not the extreme interference, is "reflected in the recent reassertion of legislative prerogatives and increased activity in administration through measures such as oversight and legislative vetoes designed to curb the presumed excesses of an 'uncontrolled bureaucracy' " (pp. 222–223).

A fourth model identified by Svara is the *elected official-administrator as coequals in policy* model. It shares many of the characteristics of the policy mixture model but adds a normative dimension. It reflects the arguments of the "new public administration" (Marini, 1971; Frederickson, 1980) that administrators have an ethical obligation to promote social equity and public participation and to oppose actions by elected officials that would be damaging to the interests of the politically disadvantaged. In this model

not only is administrative insulation expected, but also administrators are urged to construct mechanisms for policymaking and administration which bypass elected officials and establish direct linkages between governmental staff and the public. . . . [This model] therefore features administrative intrusion in policy but no reciprocal control by elected officials (p. 224).

None of these models is totally consistent with existing empirical evidence. Nor does any given model satisfactorily address all of the normative issues concerning the proper division of authority between elected officials and administrators. In combination these four models more adequately capture the dynamics of political-administrative interaction. But each emphasizes the interaction of administrators and agencies with elected officials while saying little about administrative interaction with a host of other potentially significant nonadministrative actors.

Using the concepts of stratified systems theory, Burke (1989) argues that organizations be analyzed in terms of *work strata*. She suggests that such a perspective helps us to "reconceptualize and clarify issues of politics and administration" (p. 63). Involvement in politics, and an important role in shaping policy, is largely reserved for those administrative employees in upper strata. On the other hand, "at the lower levels of work (Strata I, II, III) managers will set policy for their subordinates within constraints of higher management . . . policy, but activities of most employees at these levels involve carrying out tasks with virtually no content which may ordinarily be described as political" (p. 66).

Burke argues that early formulations of the politics-administration dichotomy used "administration" to refer "largely to the work of stratum I and II employees and their Stratum III managers" while "politics" referred to "partisan activities of elected representatives and, perhaps, to the activities of higher-level officials they appointed" (p. 66). Initially, civil service arrangements primarily embraced lower level, Stratum I and II employees. As civil service coverage in governments at all levels expanded, however, it came to include higher strata employees whose work included "many tasks commonly defined as political" (p. 67).

The post-World War II scholarly rejection of the validity of the politics-administration dichotomy was at least partly a product of the employment of many scholars in wartime federal agencies. Many observed the political work carried on by higher strata "administrators" and concluded that the politics-administration dichotomy "did not correspond with reality as they observed it" (p. 67). But various postwar assertions of the inextricable intermixing of politics and administration often "did not square . . . with experiences of practicing administrators working at lower organizational levels who rarely were involved in anything they thought of as political" (p. 67). As Burke concludes:

If early formulations of the dichotomy refer to the lower work strata, while later formulations of the unity of politics and administration refer to the higher work strata, both may be seen as true and useful, *each within its own context*. Without such context, neither is particularly useful in helping administrators discuss the realities of their work—largely nonpolitical in lower work strata but highly political in the higher strata, though in ways that are quite different from political activities of elected representatives (p. 67).

Any effort to accurately model administrative-political interaction must identify specific foci or arenas of influence. With respect to what kinds of actions or decisions affecting the administrative process is the role of the administrative agency itself, or that of the governor, or legislature, or interest groups, greater or less? Svara (1985) suggests the need to replace the simple distinction between "policy" and "administration" with a continuum from "pure" policy to "pure" management. *Mission* might be said to encompass "high policy." It involves "determination of what government should or should not address at the broadest level"; that is, "the broad goals it sets for itself, and the things it chooses not to do" (p. 224). In the context of local government, Svara suggests, aspects of mission include "the scope of services provided, philosophy of taxation and spending, policy orientation, e.g. growth versus amenities, and constitutional issues . . . and relations with other local governments" (p. 224). *Policy,* in contrast to mission, refers to "middle-range policy decisions, e.g. how to spend government revenues, whether to initiate new programs or create new offices and how to distribute services at what levels within the existing range of services provided" (p. 225). In Svara's scheme, *administration* refers to the "specific decisions, regulations and practices employed to achieve policy objectives" (p. 226). Finally, *management* refers to

the actions taken to support the policy and administrative functions. It includes controlling and utilizing the human, material and informational resources of the organization to best advantage. It also encompasses the specific techniques used in generating services. Management is largely devoid of policy, even though management systems are not neutral in their effect on internal distribution of resources in the organization (p. 227).

Svara goes on to argue for a *dichotomy-duality* model characterized by a "separation of responsibility for mission and management, with sharing of policy and administration" (p. 230).

Somewhat more concretely, one might inquire—as I do below—as to the relative impact of various actors upon (1) major policy decisions affecting an agency; (2) the determination of the overall budget levels for an agency as well as for specific agency programs; (3) shaping the content of rules and regulations; (4) establishing of administrative practices and processes; and (5) the conduct of daily administrative operations. The first two of these would appear to fall roughly into Svara's policy category, the third and fourth into his administration category, and the last into his management function.

In assessing the role of particular actors in the making and execution of policy, one must also be sensitive to the number of rivals for influence that exist in a given arena or across arenas. Svara's work, while valuable, focuses on elected officials and administrators and, in particular, on city councils and city managers. Power and influence are relational. The situation facing a governor seeking to determine spending levels for administrative agencies differs as between a situation where he or she has few as opposed to numerous rivals. Even a governor who appears to possess weak formal powers, as compared to governors in other states, may still dominate if potential rivals for influence are even weaker. As additional actors come to play a role, all actors become relatively less powerful. The "sum" of power or influence increases as the complexity of the influence context grows while a given actor's "share" becomes smaller.

Finally, whatever general statements may hold about the absolute or relative power of given actors, there is the question of how much variability exists. One source of variability has already been noted: the specific arena of influence. But administrative influence in policymaking, or gubernatorial influence in determining agency procedures, may vary across jurisdictions. Using his more complex model of the influence of city councils and managers in various dimensions of the governmental process, Svara found marked variation among the five cities he studied. Variation within the same government may also exist, reflecting the nature of an administrative agency's functional responsibilities, its size or complexity, and numerous other factors.

The next several chapters of the book explore various elements of the "influence matrix" of state management. The remainder of this chapter focuses on the role and impact of state administrative agencies in various arenas of decision or action of relevance to their operations. Of particular interest is the impact of state agencies and managers as "policyshapers." Chapter 6 seeks to specify the impact of a number of nonadministrative actors—official and unofficial—in these same arenas. In both chapters an effort is made to identify correlates of variability in the impact of various actors across states and agencies. Chapter 7 focuses on the dynamics of the relationships between state agencies and two of the most important external actors in their environments: the governor and the state legislature. Chapter 8 examines the impact of organized groups and the clientele of state agencies on the activities of those agencies.

STATE AGENCIES, ADMINISTRATION, AND POLICYSHAPING

Each of the state managers was asked to indicate how much impact they, their staff, or their unit had with respect to the following:

• the total budget level for their agency/unit
• budget levels for specific programs/policies

- major agency policy/program changes
- the content of agency rules and regulations
- establishing administrative procedures/structures
- day-to-day operations/service delivery

   The pattern of responses, broken down by state, is summarized in Table 5.1. Nearly all of the administrators believed that their units importantly impacted in more narrowly administrative realms such as daily operations and the establishment of administrative procedures and structures. In nearly every state 90% or more felt that their unit had "great" or "very great" impact. The consensus both within and across states is reflected in the modest coefficients of variation and the small values of eta, although differences in impact across states are statistically significant in the case of the establishing of administrative procedures.

   The task priorities of these state administrators underscore the centrality of managerial activities. When asked to rank how much time or emphasis they gave to each of four tasks, two-thirds ranked "internal management of my administrative unit and the direction of subordinates" as of greatest importance. Table 5.2 shows that nearly 90% considered this task to be first or second in importance. Across the states the proportion giving internal management first priority ranged from 56% in South Dakota and Vermont to 73% in Arizona and Delaware. But interstate variation in terms of first and second rank is much smaller. With the exception of South Dakota managers—where 75% ranked internal management first or second—at least 80% of the managers in each of the other states placed first or second emphasis on internal management.

   These findings are consistent with those of Abney and Lauth (1986b). Although they defined the tasks of the agency heads they surveyed somewhat differently, they found that 55% considered "management" to be their most important function so far as "accomplishing agency objectives" was concerned, while 23% ranked it second. Periodic surveys of agency heads in all 50 states since 1964 by Deil Wright and his associates suggest that agency heads devote between 50% and 55% of their time to internal management tasks (Haas and Wright, 1987).

   When the managers in my study were asked how much emphasis they *ideally* would like to place on various job dimensions, a somewhat different picture emerged, however. Less than half ranked internal management as a top priority. Across the 10 states, this proportion varied from 32% in Vermont to 59% in Tennessee. In each of the states the proportion ranking internal management as a preferred first priority was lower than the proportion who reported that they in fact devoted most attention to it.

   These state administrators believed that their units exerted considerable influence in less narrowly administrative realms as well. Nearly three-quarters of the managers surveyed believed that their units had great or very great impact

Table 5.1

Administrators' Estimates of the Impact of Their Agency/Unit in Administrative Decision or Action Arenas, by State

	Decision or Action Arena								
	Determination of Overall Agency Budget Level			Budget Levels for Specific Agency Programs			Major Policy/ Program Changes		
State[1]	Mean Impact[2]	Percent Great Impact[3]	C.V.[4]	Mean Impact	Percent Great Impact	C.V.	Mean Impact	Percent Great Impact	C.V.
Overall	2.8	64%	.275	2.9	68%	.260	3.1	72%	.23
Arizona	2.8	67	.258	2.5	66	.351	3.1	77	.20
California	2.9	62	.254	2.9	62	.246	3.1	73	.24
Delaware	2.5	57	.301	2.6	64	.327	2.9	75	.28
Indiana	2.8	66	.282	2.8	60	.282	3.1	77	.25
Michigan	2.8	66	.256	2.8	74	.265	3.1	79	.23
New York	2.7	59	.301	2.9	63	.247	3.1	77	.21
South Dakota	2.5	53	.350	2.6	59	.304	2.9	71	.25
Tennessee	2.8	64	.256	2.8	68	.261	3.1	80	.25
Texas	3.0	74	.279	3.0	73	.244	3.2	81	.22
Vermont	3.0	74	.226	3.0	74	.222	3.1	82	.20
Eta [5]	.13			.11			.09		

	Content of Rules and Regulations			Establish Administrative Procedures			Daily Administrative Operations		
State	Mean Impact	Percent Great Impact	C.V.	Mean Impact	Percent Great Impact	C.V.	Mean Impact	Percent Great Impact	C.V.
Overall	3.3	85%	.210	3.5	90%	.171	3.7	95%	.13
Arizona	3.2	85	.205	3.4	87	.190	3.6	97	.11
California	3.2	82	.237	3.5	90	.160	3.6	93	.15
Delaware	3.3	84	.214	3.4	88	.159	3.7	96	.14
Indiana	3.2	80	.248	3.7	99	.106	3.7	94	.14
Michigan	3.3	87	.213	3.5	92	.178	3.7	95	.14
New York	3.4	88	.169	3.6	93	.168	3.7	97	.13
South Dakota	3.1	81	.219	3.2	79	.203	3.6	98	.11
Tennessee	3.2	85	.215	3.5	88	.190	3.6	95	.14
Texas	3.4	90	.175	3.5	93	.163	3.7	94	.12
Vermont	3.2	82	.179	3.4	85	.210	3.8	97	.10
Eta	.10			.15*			.07		

1. Variation in number of responding administrators across decision or action arenas is as follows: Overall: 793-820; Arizona: 61-64; California: 143-148; Delaware: 67-69; Indiana: 69-70; Michigan: 117-123; New York: 103-109; South Dakota: 61-63; Tennessee: 54-56; Texas: 82-85; Vermont: 33-34.

2. Mean impact attributed by responding administrator to his or her own agency or unit in a given decision or action arena. Response options were (0) no impact, (1) some impact, (2) moderate impact, (3) great impact, (4) very great impact.

3. This is the percentage of respondents responding "great" or "very great" impact.

4. The coefficient of variation is the standard deviation divided by the mean. A rough rule of thumb is that a C.V. of .30 or greater indicates fairly substantial variation, while one close to or greater that 1.00 reflects very substantial variation.

5. Eta is a measure of the strength of association between two variables. When squared it indicates the proportion of total variability in the dependent variable (the impact of the agency or unit in a particular decision or action arena) that is explained by knowing the values of the independent variable (in this case, the respondent's state). Asterisk indicates mean difference across states significant at .05 level.

Table 5.2

State Administrators' Ranking of Actual and Ideal Amount of Time Spent/Emphasis Given to Various Tasks or Responsibilities

Responsibility	Ranking in Terms of Actual Time Spent or Emphasis Placed on Responsibility				
	First	Second	Third	Fourth	Average Rank
Internal management/direction of subordinates	67%(1)	17%	10%	4%	1.5
Working with fellow administrators or political officials in development of broader agency policy	17	36	27	19	2.5
Keeping abreast of technical developments in my program area/ enlarging professional capacities	3	27	35	38	3.1
Working with clientele or other nongovernmental groups to identify their needs and explaining, promoting and implementing programs	13	23	29	35	2.9

	Ranking in Terms of Preferred Emphasis				
	First	Second	Third	Fourth	Average Rank
Internal Management	45%	18%	19%	18%	2.1
Program Development	30	30	24	16	2.3
Professional Development	9	40	32	28	2.8
Clientele/External Relations	20	27	23	30	2.6

1. Percent of administrators giving responsibility this rank. $\underline{N}$ varies between 828 and 835 depending upon responsibility being ranked.

in the determination of major policy or program changes affecting them, while more than four-fifths reported that they exerted great impact on the content of rules and regulations. The degree of consensus within and across states is again striking, although differences in impact on both broader policy and the content of rules and regulations are statistically significant when administrative responses are broken down by the functional obligations of respondents' units.

Administrators felt they exerted least influence in budgetary decisionmaking. But even here it was not uncommon for two-thirds of them to report that their unit had great impact upon decisions regarding the overall budget level for their unit or the budgets for specific programs. This level of impact may reflect, in turn, the fact that one-third of the managers reported frequent or very frequent communication with legislative budget committees while over half reported at least occasional communication.

The findings on agency impact upon budget decisions are consistent with other research. Sharkansky's (1968) analysis of budgetary dynamics in the states highlighted the impact of agency requests in shaping budgetary choices. A recent 18-state update of this study (Thompson, 1987) suggests that the role of agency personnel in budgetary decisionmaking has grown over the past two decades. "Agencies are more acquisitive and more successful, getting more support on the average from the governor and a greater percentage of their requests appropriated by the legislature" (p. 762). A study of five Western states found that executive and legislative budget staff considered "agency credibility, reputation and legislative relationships" to be fourth most important among more than a dozen major factors affecting appropriations (Duncombe and Kinney, 1986).

So far as agency impact in making major policy decisions affecting agencies is concerned, based on a 50 state survey of agency heads, Miller (1987) found that they considered their influence to exceed that of any other actor involved in the policymaking process. The role of state agencies in "shaping" state policy reflects several factors. Of central importance is the fact that career administrators often know best—in a technical sense—how to deal with problems and implement programs. Public health officials, for instance, typically know more than anyone else in state government about a state's health problems and its public health programs. State administrative expertise is evidenced by the fact that nearly half of all state agency heads are licensed professionals (Haas and Wright, 1987). Their career status reinforces their professional expertise as they give sustained attention to particular problems and policies. Administrative influence in policymaking also reflects the fact that the beneficiaries of the programs that agencies administer often become supporters of those programs and the agencies themselves. Agencies may develop constituencies.

State agencies sometimes shape policy as they draw the attention of elected officials to the existence of a problem or deficiencies in existing problems that have become evident to them as they deal daily with those problems or policies. They help determine the policy agenda. The state policy agenda may contain matters drawn from the larger list of societal concerns (the *systemic* agenda), or items on that agenda may derive from the ideas and the standard procedures of government itself (the *routine* agenda) (Cobb and Elder, 1983). The role of administrators is most significant with respect to shaping the content of the routine agenda. As O'Toole (1989, pp. 227–228) observes:

More routine processes of policy initiation, which consume significant amounts of time, deal with complicated technical matters, and focus especially on the development of feasible alternatives for policymakers, are more likely to involve administrators in important roles. . . . Administrative agencies are often at their most efficient in dealing with the manifold routines of government, and many administrative routines provide the triggers that can move items to the policy agenda. (See also Kingdon, 1984; Nelson, 1984; and Polsby, 1984.)

The influence of state administrative agencies is also evident as they fashion policy responses to issues that achieve agenda status. Of the managers surveyed, 39% reported that half or more of the legislation affecting their unit, (other than minor housekeeping bills) originated in or was initiated by their unit. This compares to just 6% who reported that half or more of agency-relevant legislation originated with the governor or staff. Comparable figures for the legislature and for organized interest groups were only 24% and 17%, respectively. The mean proportion of legislation affecting a unit that originated with it was 37%. The mean proportion originated with the governor was only 12%. Comparable averages for the legislature and interest groups as sources were 28% and 22%, respectively. These findings are consistent with those of Friedman et al. (1966), who reported that 80% percent of the administrators in 11 state, local, and federal agencies considered agency officials to be among the major sources of policy, while interest groups and other governmental actors, including legislative bodies, were listed only half as frequently.

Nor do state administrators sit idly by while others deliberate on policy affecting their operations. Abney and Lauth (1986b) found that two-thirds of state agencies in their 50-state study actively lobbied the legislature, while just 3% did not do so at all. Haas and Wright (1987) found that 45% of agency heads in all 50 states had daily or weekly contact with the governor's staff, with individual legislators, and with legislative staff. Some 35% of the administrators I surveyed reported frequent or very frequent communication with those legislative committees having responsibility for their unit's programs. Slightly more than 50% reported at least occasional communication.

The extent of administrative involvement in the policy process is also apparent if we again look at how state administrators rank various aspects of their jobs. While only 17% ranked "working with fellow administrators or political officials in the development of broader agency policy and new programs" as the responsibility to which they devoted the most time or on which they placed the most emphasis, more than 50% ranked this responsibility first or second. Statistically significant interstate variation is evident here, however, with the proportion ranking program development as a first priority ranging from 10% in Indiana and 11% in Texas to 23% in California and 26% in Michigan. The fact that more than one-third reported that working with clientele and other nongovernmental groups was of first or second priority may be taken as further evidence of the interest these administrators have in "policyshaping."

The priorities that emerge when administrators were asked how much emphasis they would *prefer* or felt they *ought* to place on each function are also revealing. Table 5.2 indicates that the proportion ranking program development activities highest increased from 17% to 30% and the proportion ranking this job dimension first or second increased from 43% to 60%. In every state the proportion placing ideal first emphasis on program development exceeds the emphasis that administrators reported actually placing on this activity. The proportion who would ideally devote either first or second most attention to program development equals or exceeds comparable ideal emphasis on internal management in five states. The proportion ranking working with clientele first or second also increased as between actual and preferred emphasis.

ACCOUNTING FOR VARIATION IN AGENCY IMPACT

We have seen that state agency managers not only considered their units to be highly influential in more narrowly administrative realms but that they also believed they wielded considerable influence in arenas that permitted them to "shape" policy. Moreover, variation across agencies in these perceptions was relatively limited. Nevertheless, some variation was evident. In concluding this chapter, some of the factors that might account for such variation are examined.

Analysis of variance indicated that managers of agencies with differing functional responsibilities also differed in the impact they ascribed to their units. Significant differences across functional responsibilities existed for impact on budgets for specific agency programs, broader policymaking, content of rules and regulations, and establishing of administrative structures and processes. Managers of units with environmental, nonfiscal staff, criminal justice, and transportation responsibilities tended to see their impact in various arenas as greater than was true of managers of units with other obligations.

Functional differences in impact may exist for various reasons. While not enough is known about the specific political environments of agencies in particular states at the time the survey was conducted to be able to completely account for the impact of "function," some possibilities suggest themselves. Variation may be due in part to differences in the clientele that agencies serve. Note, for instance, that units with income security/social services responsibilities ranked relatively low in impact. Variation in the impact of interest groups and agency clientele as a function of the responsibilities of an agency will be explored in greater depth in Chapter 8.

Functional differences may also reflect the saliency of particular problems at the time the survey was conducted. Environmental and criminal justice managers generally saw their units as having greater impact in various arenas than did managers of units with other responsibilities. This may reflect public concern with both environmental and crime issues in the 1980s. But saliency may also undercut agency impact. Units with education responsibilities are relatively less influential than almost any other type of agency. Throughout the 1980s, concerns about the adequacy of elementary and secondary education and prescriptions for reform—albeit often conflicting—were widespread. Combined with the power of local school boards and teachers' organizations, and the fact that spending for education of all types constitutes such a large share of a state's budget, this may explain why state education managers see themselves as relatively less efficacious in shaping budgetary allocations, broader policies, or the content of rules and regulations.

The technical complexity of the tasks of units with differing functional responsibilities may also play a role here. This may be part of the reason that environmental units have greater impact in various arenas than is true of other units. Sometimes technical complexity may matter only in a particular arena. Thus, units with regulatory responsibilities of varying sorts have especially great impact in determining the content of rules and regulations. It is, of course, the technical complexity of much regulatory decisionmaking that has caused elected officials to delegate substantial authority to promulgate rules or regulations to units with regulatory responsibilities.

Finally, it may be that the differences across units with differing functional responsibilities are spurious. Units with differing responsibilities may differ with respect to other factors that affect the impact that they have in various influence arenas.

The Impact of Organizational Location, Unit Size, and Task Emphasis

Various other factors in addition to a unit's programmatic obligations may affect its level of influence in various arenas. In discussing the work of Svara and Burke I suggested that where managers and administrative units are located in the administrative hierarchy ought to affect the relative balance between "politics" and "administration" in their operations. Lower level managers or units whose influence may be filtered through several intervening levels of organization above them ought, other things being equal, to see themselves as relatively less influential in "political" realms where budgets are determined or broader policies are decided.

The relative emphasis that managers place on particular dimensions of their jobs may also be related to how much impact they see themselves or their units having. A manager who places greatest emphasis on internal management may see his or her unit as relatively more influential in narrowly administrative realms but relatively less influential in more political realms than one who places greater emphasis on program development.

Finally, the size and scope of a unit's activities may also affect its impact. Units with bigger budgets or more employees may wield more influence in certain arenas—especially perhaps the budgetary arena. A bigger budget and more employees may translate into more employees with technical skills who enhance the "professional clout" of an agency. A larger number of employees—especially perhaps if these employees are organized—may affect the political calculus of elected policymakers. Alternatively, bigger units may attract the attention of other actors with a corresponding reduction in the role the unit itself plays in decisionmaking in particular arenas.

Table 5.3 explores the relationship of organizational place, task emphasis, and unit size with managers' estimates of their own and their units' impact in the six influence arenas.[2] The positive correlations between the organizational

Table 5.3

Correlations Between Selected Factors and Agency Impact in Various Decision/ Action Arenas

Arena[1]	Organizational Place[2]	Unit Size[3]	Internal Management[4]	Program Development[4]
Overall budget level	.16**	.15**(.19**)	.00	.09**
Budgets for specific programs	.17**	.12**(.16**)	-.02	.09**
Broader policy	.15**	.10**(.12**)	-.01	.08**
Content of rules and regulations	.12**	.07* (.09**)	-.04	.09**
Establishing administrative processes	.07*	.08* (.12**)	.01	.09**
Daily administrative operations	.08*	.01 (.05)	-.02	-.01

1. Table entries are Pearson product-moment correlation coefficients. Coefficients significant at the .05 level (two-tailed test) are indicated by a single asterisk while those significant at the .01 level or better are indicated by double asterisks.

2. A positive correlation indicates that the higher the organization place of a respondent, the more impact he or she attributes to his or her unit in a particular influence arena.

3. A positive correlation indicates that managers of larger units attribute greater impact to their units in a particular influence arena. The correlation between the size of a unit's budget and impact is reported first. The parenthetical figure is the correlation between the size of a unit's work force and impact in a particular arena.

4. A positive correlation indicates that managers who placed greater emphasis on this task reported that their unit had greater influence than those who placed less emphasis on this task.

location of a manager and his or her unit and impact are modest but significant. Higher level managers attribute greater influence to their units than do those in lower level units. This is especially so in the budgetary and broader policymaking arenas. Managers of larger units similarly see their units as having greater influence in these more political arenas than do those from smaller units. Relative emphasis on internal management is unrelated to estimated impact, however, even in the case of influence in more narrowly administrative realms. Those managers who place relatively greater emphasis on program development do see their units as having more impact in all arenas save for daily administrative operations, a pattern that makes sense. Reflecting the dominant role that nearly all managers see themselves or their units playing in daily administrative operations, only organizational place is significantly correlated and this correlation is extremely modest.

Earlier an effort was made to explain why the functional responsibilities of agencies might be related to differences in attributed influence. Some of the variation may exist because agencies and managers with certain functional responsibilities may occupy higher organizational positions, or have larger staffs or budgets, or tend to place more emphasis on program development than do agencies or managers with other responsibilities. Analysis of variance indicates

Table 5.4
Stepwise Regression of Unit Size, Organizational Place, Task Emphasis, and Functional Responsibility on Agency Impact in Decision/Action Arenas

Agency Impact on:	Explained Variance (Adjusted R^2)	Significant Predictors of at Least One Percent of Variance[1]	B[2]	Beta[3]	Variance Explained by Predictor
Overall budget level of unit	.057	Unit size (staff)	.233	.186	.040
		Organ. "place"	.126	.121	.013
Budgets for specific agency programs	.062	Unit size (staff)	.190	.156	.027
		Organ. "place"	.134	.132	.018
		Health func.	-.369	-.107	.013
Broader policy changes	.045	Organ. "place"	.095	.098	.017
		Education func.	-.345	-.109	.014
Content of rules and regulations	.022	Organ. "place"	.082	.091	.011
Establish administrative procedures	.027	Unit size (staff)	.114	.126	.017
Daily administrative operations	.014	None			

1. This column lists only those significant predictors (F-value of B significant at .05 level or better) that could also explain at least 1% of the variation in agency impact in a specific arena. The final column of the table indicates the variance accounted for by each of the significant predictors. Since the size of a unit's budget and its work force are highly correlated, the regression for each arena was estimated twice--once using budget size as the indicator of unit size and a second time using size of staff. Staff size is noted as the significant predictor because it explained slightly more variation than did size of budget.

2. This is the unstandardized regression coefficient.

3. This is the standardized regression coefficient.

that significant differences do exist across functional categories in the case of organizational place, unit size, and emphasis on program development. For instance, part of the explanation for the fact that managers in fiscal staff agencies generally see their units as more powerful is because these managers hold higher level positions, head larger units, and place greater emphasis on program development than is true of respondents in units with functional responsibilities such as education.

The relative impact of these several variables on the impact of administrative units in particular influence arenas can be better specified using multiple regression techniques. The results of this analysis are summarized in Table 5.4.

Only the location of managers and their units in the administrative hierarchy and the size of those units emerged as consistent predictors of differences in influence. Organizational location was a significant predictor in the case of four arenas—overall budget level, budgets for specific programs, broader policy, and the content of rules and regulations. Unit size emerged as a statistically significant predictor in the case of the first three of these arenas as well as in the establishing of administrative procedures. The regression analysis also indicates that most of the apparent differences in the impact of agencies with differing functional responsibilities are spurious. The responsibility of a unit matters only in the case of impact on budgets for specific agency programs—where managers in health agencies saw their units as less influential—and in the case of impact on broader policy—where education units saw themselves as less influential. None of the regression models can account for more than 6% of variation in managers' attributions of impact. Explanatory power was particularly weak for the rules and regulations, administrative procedures, and daily operations arenas. This is so, in part, because there is little variation in agency impact in these arenas to explain.

CONCLUSION

This chapter has focused on state managers' views of the role they or their units play in several differing arenas as one important element of the state administrative influence matrix. Not surprisingly, these managers perceived their units or themselves to have great impact in more narrowly administrative realms. This finding is consistent with the finding that most of them spend much of their time on internal management tasks. While their role was seen as less significant in more clearly political realms, those surveyed said their units were significantly involved in these realms as well. Hence, as Svara, Burke, and others have argued, the findings suggest that the politics-administration distinction makes sense as a continuum rather than a dichotomy.

Some variation in estimated impact was evident, and was attributable in part to factors such as the functional responsibilities of particular units, the size of units, or their organizational location. But the most important message of this chapter is the consensus that exists among state managers regarding the role that they and their administrative units play in various arenas. Despite important differences in the characteristics of the 10 states in this study, and in the programmatic tasks and other characteristics of individual units, state administrators and administrative units consistently emerge as important policyshapers.

That state administrators consider themselves and their units to be important actors in the making of decisions in areas where we have traditionally expected elected officials to hold sway is no doubt disquieting to many. But in this chapter administrative influence has been considered in isolation. State managers and agencies are but one element, albeit an apparently important one, in a much more complex matrix of influence. Chapters 6, 7, and 8 place administrative influence in the context of this more complex matrix.

NOTES

1. For a more extended discussion of the difficulties in conceptualizing administrative responsiveness, see Saltzstein (1985).

2. In Chapter 3 it was noted that unit size as measured by the log of its budget and the log of number of employees were strongly correlated. Neither was highly correlated

with organizational place. The correlations between internal management emphasis and budget and staff size are − .01 and .04, respectively, while the correlations between program development task emphasis and budget and staff size are .26 and .25, respectively. The correlation between organizational place and internal management emphasis is − .10, while that between place and emphasis on program development is .11. Higher level managers were slightly less likely to emphasize management and slightly more likely to stress program development than were lower level managers.

Chapter 6

Too Important to Leave to Bureaucrats: Significant Others in the Conduct of State Management

INTRODUCTION

Just as state agencies and managers may feel compelled to become involved in the making of decisions in more broadly political arenas, so, too, may various "significant others" consider the conduct of state administration to be too important to leave solely in the hands of bureaucrats. These actors are even more likely to be active in the broader political arenas in which administrators also seek to exert influence. This chapter continues our exploration of the influence matrix of state management by examining the impact of actors other than the agency itself in the six arenas identified in Chapter 5. The fact that administrators sometimes blame "thems" external to their agencies for particular management difficulties suggests, albeit negatively, that these other actors often constitute important components of this matrix.

The list of actors who interact with state agencies, many of whom may be among those that Emmert (1986) defines as "strategic constituencies" of administrative agencies, is long. It includes major state elected or appointed officials or institutions, most especially governors and their staffs, legislatures, and the state courts. Other state administrative units may be concerned about and influence events in a given agency. Staff units such as budget and personnel offices may be closely tied to the governor. A line unit may find its fate to be intertwined with that of other line units.

The influence matrix also has important intergovernmental elements. State agencies interact with local governments as well as the federal government. Finally, nongovernmental actors and institutions such as political parties, organized interest groups, professional associations, employee unions, the media, and the clients of an agency may constitute strategically important elements of the influence matrix.

Elements of the influence matrix of state administration have been investigated by other scholars. Some have focused on several influence arenas across all 50 states but for only a small set of actors (Hebert, Brudney, and Wright, 1983; Brudney and Hebert, 1987). Others have explored the impact of a larger set of actors in a comparative setting but only for agencies with particular functional responsibilities or only for a single arena of influence or activity. An example of the former is Gormley's (1983) excellent 12-state study of state public utility regulation. An example of the latter is Miller's (1987) 50-state study examining the impact of the governor, legislature, state courts, clientele, citizens, agency employees, professional associations, and the agency itself, but only upon the "major policy decisions of the agency."

No previous study examines the impact of a wide range of official and unofficial actors in several influence arenas across a range of agencies with varying functional responsibilities in a number of states. This chapter supplements the previous chapter's insights on the impact of administrators' units in more broadly political as well as more narrowly administrative realms with an analysis of the impact of 15 nonagency actors in the same influence arenas. These include governors and their staffs, legislatures, state courts, the Congress and federal agencies, federal courts, state budget offices, state personnel units, other state administrative agencies, organized interest groups, agency clients, professional associations, employee associations or unions, local governments, political parties, and the communications media. Examining the impact of these actors, with particular attention being paid to the variation in their influence across several discrete arenas, makes it possible to assess the validity of competing models of the roles of administrators and nonadministrators in both policymaking and administration.

The next section presents findings on the relative impact of these various actors in each of the six arenas. An examination of the interrelationships between the influence of various nonadministrative actors follows. Also of interest are the relationships between the influence of nonagency actors and that of a given unit itself. In particular, are influence relationships between actors of the zero-sum variety? This discussion is followed by an effort to account for variation in actor impact in terms of the independent variables used in Chapter 5 such as agency size, a respondent's organizational "place," and the functional responsibilities of his or her unit, along with certain actor-specific variables. The relationships between the perceived influence of various actors and the severity of management problems related to these actors' activities are then explored. The chapter concludes with a discussion of the implications of the findings for the validity of Svara's (1985) model of the role of administrative and nonadministrative actors in the politico-administrative process.

THE IMPACT OF SIGNIFICANT OTHERS

The findings presented in Chapter 5 indicate that a simplistic politics-administration dichotomy is untenable because administrators are important participants not only in more narrowly administrative arenas but in more broadly political ones as well. To some at least, this might suggest an undemocratic nightmare of insulated, professional administrators calling the shots not only in daily administration but also regarding matters over which we have traditionally wanted elected officials to exercise sovereignty.

The findings on the impact of other actors in various influence arenas in these 10 states that are summarized in Table 6.1 suggest that such a view is as wrong as believing that state bureaucrats and bureaucracies leave policymaking entirely in the hands of elected officials while passively awaiting their marching orders. The state administrative influence context is both complex and variable. While substantially involved in more broadly political realms, state agencies face stiff competition from a host of other actors. Moreover, while they are the dominant actors in more narrowly administrative arenas, it is also clear that state agencies share sovereignty over administrative affairs with various strategic constituents.

Before proceeding to discuss the impact of particular nonagency actors in detail, another point deserves emphasis. Administrative units have significant impact across arenas, but such impact is always greatest in more narrowly administrative realms and rather steadily declines as one moves into more broadly political realms. Conversely, while various nonagency actors exert at least some influence in administrative arenas, their influence is nearly always significantly less than it is in the budgeting or broader policy arenas. In short, administrators are not just policymakers by another name nor are nonagency actors administrators by other names. It makes sense to make a distinction between policymaking and administration so long as this is done in terms of a continuum rather than a sharp cleavage.

Since discussing the impact of more than a dozen actors across six influence arenas in a straightforward fashion is difficult, some metaphors drawn from baseball may facilitate discussion. Among nonagency actors there are a few who might be termed "major league stars." These are actors who not only wield substantial influence in political arenas but also have significant, although lower, impact upon administrative affairs. Chief among such stars—with mean impact in the "moderate" to "great" range in political realms and "some" to "moderate" impact in more narrowly administrative realms—are state legislatures, governors and their staffs, and state budget offices—units closely attuned to gubernatorial concerns in most states. It should be noted that agencies themselves qualify as stars by this definition.

"Journeymen" constitute a second group of players. Like the stars, they are regulars. That is, they have at least some impact across all arenas. Such impact is lower than that wielded by stars, however. The data suggest that the nonagency actors falling into this category include federal agencies and the Congress, interest groups, and an agency's clientele. Other state administrative agencies, the state personnel office, and the state courts, while generally less influential than the first three journeymen, might also be so classified.

Table 6.1
Impact of Nonagency Actors Upon Decisions Affecting or Actions of 10 State Bureaucracies

Influence Actors	Determination of Overall Budget Levels			Budget Levels for Specific Programs			Major Policy/Program Changes		
	Mean Impact[1]	Range[2]	Eta[3]	Mean Impact	Range	Eta	Mean Impact	Range	Eta
The agency itself	2.8	(2.5-3.0)	.13	2.9	(2.6-3.0)	.11	3.1	(2.9-3.2)	.09
Governor and staff	2.7	(2.2-3.3)	.25*	2.6	(2.2-3.2)	.21*	2.5	(1.8-2.9)	.30*
State legislature	3.2	(2.9-3.5)	.18*	3.1	(2.9-3.4)	.14	2.8	(2.4-3.1)	.18*
State courts	1.0	(0.6-1.2)	.12	0.7	(0.3-0.9)	.16	1.2	(0.9-1.4)	.16
Federal agy./Congress	1.6	(1.4-2.9)	.12	1.5	(1.4-1.8)	.10	1.6	(1.4-2.0)	.10
Federal courts	0.8	(0.5-1.1)	.12	0.7	(0.3-0.9)	.12	1.0	(0.7-1.1)	.07
State budget office	2.9	(2.2-3.5)	.29*	2.8	(2.1-3.4)	.27*	1.0	(1.6-2.1)	.27*
State personnel office	1.3	(0.6-1.8)	.26*	1.0	(0.4-1.6)	.27*	1.0	(0.4-1.4)	.24*
Other state agencies	1.0	(0.8-1.3)	.16	0.9	(0.6-1.2)	.15	0.9	(0.8-1.1)	.08
Local governments	0.8	(0.5-1.0)	.17*	0.7	(0.5-1.0)	.21*	0.8	(0.5-1.0)	.17
Professional assoc.	0.7	(0.5-0.9)	.14	0.7	(0.4-0.8)	.13	0.8	(0.5-1.0)	.13
Agency clientele	1.2	(1.0-1.4)	.12	1.2	(0.9-1.4)	.14	1.4	(1.2-1.6)	.13
State employee unions	0.8	(0.5-1.3)	.36*	0.7	(9.2-1.1)	.33*	0.6	(0.3-1.0)	.32*
Political parties	0.7	(0.4-1.1)	.19*	0.6	(0.4-0.9)	.16	0.6	(0.4-0.9)	.15
Comm. media	0.9	(0.7-1.3)	.14	0.8	(0.7-1.1)	.12	0.9	(0.8-1.1)	.11
Interest groups	1.3	(0.9-1.4)	.15	1.3	(1.0-1.6)	.18	1.4	(1.1-1.6)	.15

Influence Actors	Content of Rules and Regulations			Establish Administrative Procedures			Daily Administrative Operations		
	Mean Impact	Range	Eta	Mean Impact	Range	Eta	Mean Impact	Range	Eta
The agency itself	3.3	(3.1-3.4)	.10	3.5	(3.2-3.7)	.15	3.7	(3.6-3.8)	.07
Governor and staff	1.7	(1.3-2.0)	.22*	1.5	(1.3-2.3)	.25*	1.1	(0.9-1.4)	.20*
State legislature	2.2	(2.0-2.5)	.15	1.7	(1.5-2.2)	.18*	1.2	(0.9-1.4)	.12
State courts	1.4	(1.1-1.5)	.16	0.9	(0.7-1.2)	.12	0.7	(0.4-0.8)	.10
Federal agy./Congress	1.4	(1.3-1.6)	.10	1.1	(0.9-1.3)	.13	1.1	(0.9-1.3)	.12
Federal courts	1.1	(0.9-1.2)	.08	0.7	(0.5-0.9)	.13	0.6	(0.5-0.8)	.09
State budget office	1.0	(0.8-1.5)	.18*	1.4	(1.0-2.1)	.29*	1.4	(1.0-2.1)	.29*
State personnel office	0.8	(0.4-1.1)	.17*	1.4	(0.6-1.7)	.28*	1.3	(0.4-1.5)	.30*
Other state agencies	1.1	(0.8-1.6)	.26*	1.1	(0.9-1.4)	.18*	1.0	(0.9-1.2)	.12
Local governments	0.8	(0.4-1.0)	.20*	0.6	(0.4-0.7)	.13	0.8	(0.4-0.9)	.17
Professional assoc.	0.9	(0.5-1.1)	.17*	0.6	(0.3-0.7)	.15	0.6	(0.3-0.8)	.14
Agency clientele	1.4	(1.1-1.7)	.16	1.1	(0.8-1.3)	.12	1.6	(1.3-1.8)	.12
State employee unions	0.6	(0.8-0.9)	.28*	0.7	(0.2-1.1)	.40*	0.7	(0.3-1.2)	.42*
Political parties	0.4	(0.2-0.6)	.15	0.3	(0.1-0.4)	.15	0.3	(0.2-0.5)	.15
Comm. media	0.7	(0.6-0.9)	.11	0.5	(0.4-0.7)	.10	0.8	(0.7-1.1)	.13
Interest groups	1.4	(1.2-1.7)	.18*	1.0	(0.7-1.2)	.15	1.1	(0.8-1.4)	.17*

1. Mean attributed impact for an actor on a given decision or action arena based on the responses of managers in all 10 states. Response options were (0) no impact, (1) some impact, (2) moderate impact, (3) great impact, (4) very great impact. Depending on the actor or the decision/action arena, the number of respondents ranged between 780 and 821.

2. Table entry is the range in state means for given actors.

3. Eta is a measure of the strength of association between two variables. When squared it indicates the proportion of total variability in the dependent variable (the impact of a specific actor in a particular decision or action arena) that is explained by knowing the values of the independent variable (the state). An asterisk denotes a statistically significant coefficient (.01 level).

Finally, those actors with limited influence even in the most broadly political realms might be termed "minor league" players. They include the federal courts, local governments, professional associations, state employee organizations, the communications media and political parties.

Only about half of the nonagency actors exert substantial influence across several arenas. Seven of the fifteen nonagency actors rank among the five most influential actors in at least three arenas. These are the state legislature, governor, budget office, federal agencies/Congress, agency clients, interest groups, and the state personnel office. Only three actors—the legislature, the governor, and the state budget office—rank among the five most influential actors in five of the six arenas. Only the state legislature ranks among the five most influential actors in every influence arena. Of the seven actors ranking among the five most influential in at least three arenas, five are either elected state officials or administrative actors. In this sense, state government "insiders" dominate the influence matrix of state management.

Although the impact of most actors declines as one moves from decision-making on budgets or broader policy to more strictly administrative realms, the impact of certain actors is especially great in a particular arena. This appears to reflect the unique nature of that actor's resources, role, or other characteristics. Thus, the state budget office has especially great impact on spending decisions. Because the impact of the state personnel office is relatively constant across influence arenas, it emerges as one of the more important actors so far as the establishment of administrative procedures and daily operations is concerned. The impact of an agency's clientele peaks in daily administrative operations, presumably because it is with these clients that a unit's employees interact on a daily basis. The result is that those an agency serves rank first in impact among the nonagency actors. The impact of both state and federal courts is greatest in shaping agency rules and regulations. This likely reflects the continuing "judicializing" of this process in the states. Returning to the imagery of baseball, the specialized influence patterns for budget offices, agency clientele, and the courts bring to mind those players whose skills are such that they are designated hitters or utility infielders.

INFLUENCE INTERRELATIONSHIPS AMONG NONAGENCY ACTORS

Having sketched the broad contours of the influence matrix, we next explore interrelationships among the influence of various nonagency actors. Do levels of clientele influence vary directly with levels of interest group influence? Does legislative influence decline in absolute terms when that of the governor increases? Moreover, how does the influence of the agency itself vary as the influence of other actors grows or shrinks? Of particular interest is whether zero-sum relationships exist. Is greater influence for one actor, in absolute terms, associated with a decline in the influence of another? Alternatively, does the influence matrix simply become more complex? Do managers of some agencies perceive all actors to have more impact than do managers of other agencies? Is there simply an increase in the total "amount" of influence being exerted?

Cheryl Miller (1987) explored the perceptions of agency heads in all 50 states concerning the policy influence of eight actors: legislators, governor, agency employees, clientele, state courts, professional associations, citizens-at-large, as well as the agency head himself. Her findings disclosed an "absence of zero-sum gains and losses in differences in influence among all eight policy actors" (p. 242). While the intercorrelations were low to moderate, all but four were positive. Only in the case of the perceived influence of legislators and the agency itself was there a small but significant negative correlation ($-.07$) indicative of a competitive, zero-sum relationship.

My analysis supports a conclusion similar to Miller's. Across the six influence arenas, out of 625 possible intercorrelations among the 15 nonagency actors, only *two significant negative* correlations emerged.[1] Instead of a situation in which the reported impact of one actor rises while another's declines, managers more commonly report the influence of all actors to be greater or less than do others. Significant *positive* correlations existed in 94% of the cases. Some 26% of these positive correlations were .30 or greater, while 9% were .40 or above. Zero-sum relationships between various nonagency actors are clearly the exception.

Substantial positive influence linkages are more common among certain actors than others, however—something that factor analysis of these influence interrelationships makes clear (see Table 6.2). Four influence complexes emerge that persist across the six arenas and that together, depending on the arena in question, capture 50% to 60% of the variance. A "nongovernmental/political actors" factor captures one-quarter or more of the variance in each arena. The perceived influence of local governments, professional associations, agency clients, parties, the communications media, and organized interests all load heavily on this factor in every arena save for shaping agency rules and regulations, where parties fail to load heavily. State employee unions load on this factor in the case of determining overall budget levels, while the federal government loads on this factor in the case of determining budgets for specific programs.

A second factor, one that might be labeled "judicial/federal actors," accounts for 7% to 11% of variation, depending upon the arena. In each of the six arenas, substantial loadings exist for state courts, the federal courts, and federal agencies/Congress. State administrative actors such as the personnel office, other line agencies, and the budget office, as well as state employee unions, load on a third factor. Finally, the governor and state legislature both loaded heavily on a fourth factor, joined by the budget office in the case of budgetary and broader policymaking, and the state courts in the determination of agency rules and regulations.

The factor structures are relatively simple. Most actors load heavily on similar factors across arenas. Exceptions include state employee unions and the budget office. State employee union impact loads on the "nonstate/unofficial actor" factor in the case of determination of overall budgets but on the "state administrative actors/unions" factor in the other arenas. The state budget office, logically enough given its mission and close link to the governor, loads heavily on the "state elected officials" factor for budgetary and broader policy decisionmaking, but on the "state administrative actors/unions" factor in the remaining three arenas.

The simplicity of the factor structure is also evident in that only two actors load on more than one factor in a given arena. There are few negative loadings on any factor and those that exist are small. This is further evidence of the absence of zero-sum influence dynamics among various nonagency actors in the environment of state agencies.[2]

A final question regarding influence interrelationships concerns those that exist between the perceived influence of the agency itself and the 15 nonagency actors. While uncommon, zero-sum relationships are somewhat more evident here than in the case of the interrelationships among nonagency actors alone. Significant negative correlations—albeit not strong ones—existed between agency influence and political party influence on budgets for specific programs ($r = -.12$), major policy changes ($r = -.18$), and the content of rules and regulations ($r = -.13$). This may be testimony to the continuing tension between partisanship and administrative neutrality that has often driven administrative reform. The consequences of the passing of managerial "unilateralism" that occurred with the emergence of public employee unions may be attested to by the negative correlations between union impact and agency impact in determining the content of rules and regulations ($r = -.08$) and the course of daily operations ($r = -.07$). Correlations significant at at least the .05 level existed between agency impact and the impact of eight other actors. Of these eight, four had a negative sign, those between agency impact on the content of rules and regulations and the impact in this area of federal agencies and the Congress ($-.07$), the state personnel office ($-.08$), state employee unions ($-.08$), and political parties ($-.13$).

Positive correlations between agency impact and the impact of nonagency actors are most common with actors outside of state government such as professional associations, local governments, and, especially, interest groups and the clientele of an agency. Positive correlations between agency clientele impact and the impact of the agency itself exist for all six arenas, ranging from .09 for establishing administrative procedures, to .20 for content of rules and regulations. Significant positive correlations between interest group and agency impact exist for all but the administrative procedures and daily operations arenas, and range from .08 to .12. These correlations suggest the existence of administrative "constituencies" that may reinforce an agency's voice in various influence arenas—a possibility that is explored in Chapter 8.

Because the correlations are small, one should not speculate too boldly. In

Table 6.2
Oblique Factor Structure of Nonagency Actor Influence Across Six Arenas

Factor and Actor Loadings on Factor	Determination of Overall Budget Levels	Budget Levels for Specific Programs	Major Policy/ Program Changes
Factor 1: Nonstate and Unofficial Actors			
Eigenvalues/Percent of Variance Explained [1]	4.26 (28%)	4.22 (28%)	4.20 (27%)
Actors Loading on This Factor [2]:			
Local Government	.543	.530	.460
Professional Associations	.727	.669	.658
Clientele	.649	.683	.738
Political Parties	.543	.428	.485
Media of Communication	.693	.667	.637
Interest Groups	.770	.792	.774
State Employee Unions	.487	------	------
Federal Agencies/ Congress	------	.405	------
Factor 2: State Administrative Actors/Unions			
Eigenvalue/Percent of Variance Explained	1.05 (7%)	1.21 (8%)	1.72 (12%)
Actors Loading on This Factor:			
Personnel Office	.826	.824	.834
Budget Office	-------	------	.504
Other State Agencies	.764	.581	.615
State Employee Unions	-------	.489	.644
Factor 3: Judicial/Federal Actors			
Eigenvalue/Percent of Variance Explained	1.66 (11%)	1.68 (11%)	1.41 (9%)
Actors Loading on This Factor			
State Courts	.668	.778	.661
Federal Courts	.813	.853	.861
Federal Agencies/Congress	.658	.515	.693
Factor 4: State Elected Officials			
Eigenvalue/Percent of Variance Explained	1.40 (9%)	1.28 (9%)	1.16 (8%)
Actors Loading on This Factor:			
Governor	.710	.812	.821
Legislature	.784	.826	.838
Budget Office	.720	.674	.526

Table 6.2 (Continued)

Factor and Actor Loadings on Factor	Content of Rules and Regulations	Establish Admin. Procedures	Daily Operations
Factor 1: Nonstate and Unofficial Actors			
Eigenvalue/Percent of Variance Explained	4.24 (29%)	4.93 (33%)	4.91 (33%)
Actors Loading on This Factor:			
Local Governments	.551	.562	.496
Professional Associations	.658	.715	.664
Clientele	.782	.727	.709
Political Parties	------	.531	.428
Media of Communication	.552	.642	.639
Interest Groups	.827	.788	.796
Factor 2: State Administrative Actors/Unions			
Eigenvalue/Percent of Variance Explained	1.93 (13%)	1.48 (10%)	1.51 (10%)
Actors Loading on This Factor:			
Personnel Office	.834	.884	.859
Budget Office	.642	.678	.692
Other State Agencies	.578	.551	.631
State Employee Unions	.664	.594	.570
Factor 3: Judicial/Federal Actors			
Eigenvalue/Percent of Variance Explained	1.16 (8%)	1.39 (9%)	1.14 (8%)
Actors Loading on This Factor:			
State Courts	.471	.582	.600
Federal Courts	.853	.865	.866
Federal Agencies/Congress	.836	.752	.754
Factor 4: State Elected Officials			
Eigenvalue/Percent of Variance Explained	1.28 (9%)	1.06 (7%)	1.31 (9%)
Actors Loading on This Factor:			
Governor	.803	.834	.820
Legislature	.863	.838	.829
State Courts	.478	-------	------

1. From unrotated solution. Because it was anticipated that these factors would overlap to some extent, an oblique rotation was used to obtain a final solution.

2. Only factor loadings above .400 are reported.

general, the impact that managers attribute to their units in various arenas seems unrelated to variation in the impact attributed to other actors active in these same arenas. Factor analysis makes the independence of the influence of the agency itself across arenas even more apparent. The factor structure that emerged when the influence of the agency itself, as well as that of the 15 nonagency actors, is focused on was quite similar to that detailed above for the 15 nonagency actors alone. The major change—and this was true for every influence arena except the determination of agency procedures and structures—was the emergence of an additional factor on which, with few exceptions, *only* the agency itself loaded, suggesting the independence of agency impact from that of other actors.

SOURCES OF VARIATION IN THE INFLUENCE OF NONAGENCY ACTORS

It is possible to generalize to some extent about the relative impact of nonagency actors. But considerable variation also exists in the impact of particular actors. It has been noted that actor impact varies across arenas. Moreover, even within an arena considerable variation in impact is evident, as a glance back at Table 6.1 makes clear.[3] Significant interstate variation exists in every arena for the impact of governors and their staffs, state budget and personnel offices, and state employee unions, and in several arenas for the influence of state legislatures, local governments, and interest groups. Such variation may stem from differences that distinguish one state from another, such as formal gubernatorial powers, extent of legislative professionalization, or the presence or absence of collective bargaining by state employees. The impact of particular "state" variables will be explored in subsequent chapters.

Variation in nonagency actor influence is also a function of agency-specific variables. The fact that variability in the influence of many actors is not related to the "state" supports this assertion, as does the finding that variation in the influence of various nonagency actors is nearly as great, if not greater, within particular states as it is across the entire 10-state sample.[4] Using state court impact as an example, the overall coefficient of variation of .58 compares to within-state coefficients ranging from .47 to .63.

Actor Impact and the Functional Responsibilities of State Agencies

The interest of a nonagency actor in an agency and, hence, that actor's impact, may be piqued by what an agency's programmatic task is. In Chapter 5 we saw that significant, albeit quite modest, relationships existed between estimates of the impact of the agency itself and an agency's functional responsibilities in the case of four of the influence arenas. The impact of many nonagency actors in most arenas is also significantly related to the functional

Table 6.3

Relationship Between Nonagency Actor Influence and the Functional Responsibilities of Agencies

Influence Actor[1]	Determination of Overall Budget Levels	Budget Levels for Specific Programs	Major Policy/ Programs Changes	Content of Rules and Regulations	Establish Administrative Procedures	Daily Operations
Governor and staff	N.S.	N.S.	.23	N.S.	N.S.	N.S.
State legislature	.18	N.S.	N.S.	N.S.	N.S.	N.S.
State courts	.25(4)	.23(4)	.22(4)	.21(3)	.24(3)	.27(6)
Federal agencies/Congress	.58(10)	.59(10)	.55(9)	.48(8)	.47(9)	.48(9)
Federal courts	.31(8)	.30(6)	.28(7)	.31(6)	.30(4)	.28(6)
State budget office	.22(3)	.23(2)	.19(3)	.19(3)	N.S.	.18(6)
State personnel office	N.S.	N.S.	N.S.	.24(1)	N.S.	N.S.
Other state agencies	.18(3)	.19(1)	.19(1)	.21(1)	.19(2)	.22(2)
Local governments	.24(5)	.25(5)	.28(7)	.23(3)	.18(5)	.25(4)
Professional associations	.19(3)	.25(2)	.24(4)	.28(5)	.17(5)	.23(2)
Agency clientele	.22(3)	.21(1)	.22(2)	.22(2)	.20(3)	.22(2)
State employee unions	.21(3)	.19(4)	.24(5)	.29(4)	.22(3)	.22(2)
Political parties	N.S.	N.S.	N.S.	N.S.	N.S.	N.S.
Communications media	.22(3)	.23(2)	N.S.	.20(6)	.20(5)	N.S.
Interest groups	.27(4)	.29(4)	.30(2)	.28(3)	.23(3)	.22(3)

1. Table entries are eta coefficients measuring the strength of the relationship between the impact of a nonagency actor or a particular administrative unit in a particular arena and the functional responsibility of that unit. All coefficients are significant at the .01 level except where indicated by N.S. Figures in parentheses are the number of states in which a significant relationship (F-test, .01 level) existed between the impact of an actor and the functional responsibilities of managers' units.

responsibilities of responding administrative units (Table 6.3). Moreover, the eta statistics indicate that these relationships are generally stronger than those that exist between the impact of the agency itself and its functional responsibilities.

The functional responsibility of a unit is often more strongly related to the impact of a particular actor in a specific arena. Subsequent chapters will examine these relationships for governors, legislatures, interest groups, and agency clients. The actors focused on here are those whose impact varies most sharply across agencies with differing functional responsibilities and/or those whose impact will not be examined in greater depth in subsequent chapters.

The supreme courts of the four states studied by Frank (1978) most often reversed state agency actions in the public safety, health, social welfare, and utility regulation areas. Federal court decisions have often forced states to increase funding for and modify the operations of correctional institutions as well as facilities for the mentally ill or developmentally disabled. They have also affected the provision of public assistance and social services to the poor (Cooper, 1988; Diver, 1979; Gormley, 1989a, esp. pp. 136–137 and 145–147; Harriman and Straussman, 1983; Straussman, 1986). Nearly one-third of the agency heads in an eight-state study (Hale, 1979) reported that their agency had been required to alter existing programs or initiate new programs in response to federal court decisions. Among the states that Hale focused on were two that are included in my study—California and Texas. Of the California agency heads surveyed, 52% reported having to alter or initiate programs, while in Texas 39% claimed that this was the case. Hale found that federal court impact was particularly great in the case of agencies with criminal justice/corrections, education, human services, and energy/environmental responsibilities, with 40% or more of the respondents from these agencies reporting programmatic changes prompted by federal court decisions.

Federal or state court impact upon the state agencies focused on in this study generally varies by functional responsibility in ways that are consistent with previous research. Thus, administrators in criminal justice agencies report greater state and federal court impact than do administrators in agencies with other programmatic obligations. Indeed, administrators of criminal justice units rank state courts fourth as a source of influence on broader policy—behind the governor, legislature, and the budget office—and second as a source of influence in shaping rules and regulations and administrative procedures, trailing only the legislature.

Agencies with regulatory responsibilities also report greater state court, although not federal court, impact in the determination of broader policies and the shaping of rules and regulations. Administrators of such agencies rank state courts relatively low, so far as impact on budgetary affairs, establishing administrative procedures, and daily operations is concerned, however. Units with social services/income security responsibilities similarly report relatively higher levels of both state and federal court impact. The federal courts rank among the most important actors for such agencies in all six influence arenas, while state courts are relatively more influential for such units in the case of impact on overall budget levels, establishing administrative procedures, and daily operations.

In contrast, units with economic development, environmental protection, and education responsibilities generally report their state's judiciary to be a relatively less significant source of influence in most arenas. The federal courts are generally less significant actors in the case of units with economic development, regulatory, and staff responsibilities. Moreover, in contrast to Hale's findings, the 10-state data do not indicate that the federal courts have particularly great impact upon units with environmental responsibilities. Across all such agencies in the 10 states, the proportion of administrators attributing great or very great impact to the federal courts was only about 10% for each of the six influence arenas.

Variation in nonagency actor impact as a function of the programmatic responsibilities of agencies is also evident in the case of local government influence. Health and transportation managers report local governments to be more influential than do other managers. The activities of such units may be intertwined with those of counterpart units at the county and municipal levels. Professional associations are seen as having greatest impact by administrators of units with education and health responsibilities. This may reflect the variety of organized professions active in these program areas such as teachers, physicians, public health nurses, and the like.

Administrators of units with staff responsibilities report limited impact for most of these actors. The exceptions are those actors—such as ''other state administrative agencies''—who are themselves part of the state administrative apparatus. Agencies with major programmatic missions such as criminal justice, natural resources, and health consider media impact on their affairs to be especially great. The media's fascination with crime may explain why agencies with criminal justice responsibilities see it as having more impact than do administrators of other agencies.

The Impact of Other Agency Characteristics

Functional differences may mask other differences affecting the relative impact of certain actors. For instance, greater union impact on criminal justice and transportation agencies may exist because their work forces are more highly organized. The impact of federal actors may vary across units with differing functional responsibilities because federal funding is greater in certain programmatic areas than others.

In Chapter 5 we saw that the impact of an agency itself was conditioned to some extent by its size or its location in the state administrative hierarchy. The impact of various nonagency actors may also be related to an agency's size or its organizational ''place.'' Agencies with more employees, or bigger budgets, may be viewed as more important and may attract more attention from various external actors. The media may focus on larger agencies or those at the top of the bureaucratic pyramid. Higher level units may be more vulnerable to intervention by elected officials.

The influence of some nonagency actors is positively related to agency size. This is most clearly so in budgetary arenas. While nonagency actor impact and unit size are often positively related, the correlations are generally small. The only correlations greater than .20 are those between the size of a unit's budget and the impact of federal agencies and the Congress as well as local governments on overall budget levels, between budget size and the impact of these two actors on budgets for specific programs, and those between either the number of employees in a unit or the size of its budget and the impact of state employee unions across all six influence arenas.

Although higher level managers tend to attribute more impact to their units in various arenas than do lower level managers, there is little difference among higher and lower level managers in the influence they attribute to nonagency actors. Significant correlations existed for particular arenas between organizational place and the impact of only three or four of the nonagency actors and none of the correlations were larger than +.13. The relationship between federal agency/congressional impact and organizational location was negative rather than positive. Lower level managers saw this actor to be more influential than did higher level managers.

Even the modest relationships between agency size or organizational place and actor influence may be spurious. In my sample, units with income security/ social services, transportation, criminal justice, and health responsibilities are substantially larger than those with education or economic development responsibilities. The organizational place of respondents also varies significantly across functional categories.[5]

To better specify the explanatory power of agency size, organizational place, and functional responsibility, the impact of the nonagency actors in each of the six arenas was regressed on these three independent variables. The resulting models could account for at least 5% of the variation in the impact of only a few nonagency actors, however (see Table 6.4); 5% or more of the variation in the impact of state courts, federal courts, local governments, and state employee unions can be accounted for across several arenas.

Functional responsibility most often emerges as a significant predictor. In the case of state court impact, criminal justice and income security units stand out. The same pattern holds for federal court impact. That the courts should matter more for components of the criminal justice system is hardly surprising. The special nature of the relationship between criminal justice units and the judiciary is also evident from the fact that having criminal justice responsibilities is rarely a significant predictor of variation in the impact of any other nonagency actor.

The greater impact of the federal courts on income security units may result in part from court rulings concerning eligibility for services, client rights, and the like. But, as will be discussed below, the greater impact of the federal courts may also reflect the greater dependence of agencies with social services/ income security responsibilities on federal aid.

The relevance of functional responsiblity is evident in other ways from the regression analyses. The fact that a unit having regulatory responsibilities is often *negatively* related to the impact of one or the other of the nonagency actors of interest here may be testimony to the success of efforts to insulate regulatory units from external influence. The negative relationship between a unit having regulatory responsibilities and federal court impact may largely be spurious, however. In contrast to agencies with income security responsibilities, those with regulatory responsibilities are not heavily dependent on federal funding. Hence, federal court impact may be minimized.

The negative relationship between a unit having regulatory duties and the influence exerted on it by local governments may exist because such units do not rely heavily on local governments in discharging those duties. The contrast here is with units having health responsibilities that often rely on county and municipal health departments in implementing programs and otherwise interact with them.

Significant variation in the impact of professional associations is evident for

Table 6.4

Summary of Most Powerful Models Predicting Impact of Various Nonagency Actors (Stepwise Regression Using Organizational Size, Organizational "Place" and Functional Responsibility of Unit as Predictors)

Nonagency Actor and Arena of Influence[1]	Explained Variance (Adjusted R^2)	Predictors Accounting for at least One Percent of Variance[2]	B[3]	Beta[4]	Percent Variance Explained by Predictor
State Court Impact On:					
Overall budget level	.067	Criminal justice func.	.836	.207	.040
		Income security func.	.501	.145	.024
Budgets for specific programs	.050	Criminal justice func.	.747	.224	.046
Daily operations	.076	Criminal justice func.	.712	.228	.056
		Unit size (staff)	.096	.088	.011
Federal Court Impact On:					
Overall budget level	.094	Income security func.	.760	.238	.055
		Criminal justice func.	.468	.126	.020
		Regulatory func.	-.275	-.086	.012
Budget for specific programs	.094	Income security func.	.642	.221	.043
		Unit size (staff)	.156	.130	.021
		Regulatory func.	-.251	-.084	.016
Determination of broader policy	.086	Income security func.	.699	.222	.051
		Criminal justice func.	.454	.123	.020
		Organizational "place"	-.119	-.109	.011
Content of rules and regulations	.094	Income security func.	.735	.233	.056
		Criminal justice func.	.467	.127	.021
		Unit size (staff)	.169	.131.	.012
		Organizational "place"	-.110	-.102	.010
Establishing administrative procedures	.109	Income security func.	.643	.243	.048
		Criminal justice func.	.568	.186	.037
		Unit size (staff)	.154	.144	.015
		Education func.	.357	.119	.013
Daily operations	.103	Criminal justice func.	.661	.224	.056
		Income security func.	.628	.248	.053
		Unit size (staff)	.158	.153	.015

Table 6.4 (Continued)

Nonagency Actor and Arena of Influence	Explained Variance (Adjusted R^2)	Predictors Accounting for at least One Percent of Variance	B	Beta	Percent Variance Explained by Predictor
State Employee Union Impact On:					
Overall budget level	.091	Unit size (staff)	.297	.281	.068
		Organizational "place"	-.115	-.131	.016
Budgets for specific programs	.073	Unit size (staff)	.260	.250	.050
		Organizational "place"	-.122	-.140	.018
Determination of broader policy	.094	Unit size (staff)	.224	.230	.057
		Organizational "place"	-.100	-.122	.018
		Criminal justice func.	.293	.106	.014
Content of rules and regulations	.100	Unit size (staff)	.202	.203	.045
		Criminal justice func.	.512	.180	.026
		Organizational "place"	-.101	-.121	.014
		Nonfiscal staff func.	.407	.110	.010
		Transportation func.	.307	.107	.011
Establishing administrative procedures	.102	Unit size (staff)	.294	.292	.075
		Organizational "place"	-.132	-.155	.024
Daily operations	.095	Unit size (staff)	.271	.262	.062
		Organizational "place"	-.123	-.142	.021
Local Government Impact on:					
Overall budget level	.069	Regulatory func.	-.537	-.206	.043
		Unit size (staff)	.157	.146	.019
		Income security func.	-.281	-.108	.011
Budgets for specific programs	.086	Unit size (staff)	.193	.183	.042
		Regulatory func	-.460	-.176	.025
Determination of broader policy	.075	Regulatory func.	-.419	-.166	.035
		Health func.	.389	.134	.022
Daily operations	.068	Regulatory func.	-.393	-.145	.034
		Health func.	.507	.162	.026

Table 6.4 (Continued)

Nonagency Actor and Arena of Influence	Explained Variance (Adjusted R^2)	Predictors Accounting for at least One Percent of Variance	B	Beta	Percent Variance Explained by Predictor
Professional Assns. Impact On:					
Budgets for specific programs	.050	Health func.	.458	.171	.029
		Education func.	.456	.174	.024
Content of rules and regulations	.065	Health func.	.578	.190	.027
		Education func.	.575	.194	.022
		Regulatory func.	.322	.119	.011
		Fiscal staff func.	.355	.102	.010
State Personnel Agency Impact On:					
Determination of broader policy	.052	Criminal justice func.	.370	.111	.022
		Regulatory func.	-.378	-.127	.016
		Unit size (staff)	.127	.107	.012

1. Included in this table are only those regression models that could account for at least 5% of the variation in the impact of a nonagency actor in a particular arena of influence. The independent variables entered, using stepwise methods, were organizational size, organizational "place," and the functional responsibility of a unit. Since, as previously noted, the size of a unit's budget and the size of its staff are highly correlated, the regressions for the impact of each of the nonagency actors focused on in this chapter were estimated twice, once using budget size with the other independent variables and a second time using staff size instead of budget size. Whenever staff size emerged as a significant predictor so did budget size. But size of staff consistently had slightly greater explanatory power. Organizational "place" was calculated from a question that asked each manager how many levels in his or her agency were above his or her unit. Since for an agency head the number of higher levels is zero, one (1) was added to the number of levels reported. This sum was then subtracted from 10. Hence, the higher a manager and his or her unit is in the administrative hierarchy, the higher the organization "place" score. Scores on this variable ranged from 2 to 9.

2. This column lists only those significant predictors (F value of B significant at .05 level or better) that could also explain at least 1% of the variation in the impact of a particular nonagency actor. The final column of the table indicates the precise amount of variance accounted for by each of these predictors.

3. This is the unstandardized regression coefficient.

4. This is the standardized regression coefficient.

two arenas, with functional responsibility the only factor that can account for at least 1% of the variance in impact. The strongest positive relationships are those between professional associations' impact and a unit having health or education responsibilities. These relationships almost certainly reflect the existence of numerous, well-organized professional groups such as teachers, school administrators, doctors, and other health professionals as well as organizations representing local school boards or medical facilities. Interestingly, only the impact of professional associations is *positively* related to the fact that a unit has regulatory obligations. Perhaps this is so because units with these responsibilities include those charged with licensing members of particular professions and monitoring their conduct.

Consistent with the correlational analysis, unit size and the organizational location of managers and their units rarely emerged as significant predictors of variation in the impact of the nonagency actors focused on here. Moreover, the relationships that did emerge may be due largely to the influence of variables not included in the models. The positive relationship between number of employees and federal court impact may reflect the fact that larger units happen to be those that are also more dependent on federal funding. That unit size and organizational place are significant predictors of variation in the influence of state employee unions may reflect correlations between these variables and extent of collective bargaining. These possibilities will now be examined.

Some Actor-Specific Predictors of Impact

The inability of the unit-specific variables of size, organizational location, and, to a lesser extent, functional responsibility to explain much of the variation in the impact of most nonagency actors suggests that characteristics unique to particular actors, along with various other agency-specific characteristics, must be examined. Chapter 7 explores the ability of other factors to account for variation in the impact of the governor and the legislature, while Chapter 8 focuses on interest groups and agency clientele. Here I will illustrate this important point with several examples.

The size of a unit's work force, as an indicator of unit size, emerged as a consistent predictor of variation in the impact of state employee unions on decisions affecting or actions taken by particular state agencies. Since unions represent employees, staff size is a relevant variable conditioning union impact whereas it is not so in the case of many other actors.

Staff size may be a significant predictor for another reason. In Chapter 3 we saw that variation in the severity of certain ''union'' problems was positively related to the extent of collective bargaining by state employees. Significant positive relationships similarly exist between the impact of state employee unions in various influence arenas and the proportion of state employees who collectively bargain. Correlations between the proportion of state employees who collectively bargain and estimates of union impact were .33 in the case of impact on overall budget level, .30 for impact on budgets for specific programs and broader policy changes, .25 for impact on the content of rules and regulations, .37 for impact on administrative procedures, and .39 for impact of unions on daily operations.[6]

The responding units in those states in which collective bargaining is most extensive also tend to have more employees. The correlations between the number of employees of a unit and extent of collective bargaining is .14. Hence, at least some of the impact of unit size is due to the fact that larger units are found in states in which collective bargaining is more widespread.[7]

A properly specified model of state employee union impact must include a measure of extent of collective bargaining. When the percentage of state employees engaged in collective bargaining is entered into the regression model for union impact, the proportion of variance accounted for by the model rises sharply. This is evident if one compares the appropriate panel of Table 6.4 with the regression results summarized in Table 6.5. For most arenas, the variance in union impact that can be accounted for doubles, with extent of collective bargaining replacing unit size as the most powerful predictor. Depending upon arena, extent of collective bargaining can account for between 7% and 15% of the variation in union impact. Unit size continues to be a significant predictor of variation in union impact, but its explanatory power is substantially reduced. Organizational place is no longer a significant predictor of union impact. The explanation for this is that states in which collective bargaining is widespread tend to be states in which the average organizational location of respondents was lower (i.e., California, New York, Michigan).

Variation in the impact of the state personnel office also illustrates the predictive power of an actor-specific variable. In Chapter 3 we saw that extent of civil service coverage could account for some of the variation in the severity of various personnel-related problems. Extent of civil service coverage is also positively associated with the impact that state personnel offices exert on the activities of state administrative agencies. Significant correlations exist for determination of overall budget level (+ .10), budgets for specific unit programs (+ .13), determination of broader policy (+ .12), content of rules and regulations (+ .11), the nature of agency administrative procedures (+ .18), and daily operations (+ .21).

When the regression model of personnel agency impact is reestimated using extent of civil service coverage along with the three other independent variables, the explanatory power of the model increases. The respecified models can account for 5% or more of the variation in the impact of the personnel agency on the content of rules and regulations, the nature of administrative procedures, and the course of daily operations. Civil service coverage can explain at least 1% of the variance in personnel agency impact in all but the broader policy arena. It accounts for more than 3% of the variation in personnel agency impact on administrative procedures and nearly 5% of the variance in personnel agency impact on daily operations. The size of a unit's staff can

Table 6.5

Models of State Employee Union Impact (Regressed on Organizational Size, Organizational Place, Functional Responsibility, and Extent of Collective Bargaining by State Employees)

State Employee Union Impact on:	Explained Variance (Adjusted R^2)	Predictors Accounting for at Least One Percent of Variance[1]	B [2]	Beta [3]	Percent Variance Explained by Predictor
Overall budget level	.177	Collective bargaining [4]	.007	.313	.120
		Unit size (staff)	.224	.212	.048
Budgets for specific programs	.139	Collective bargaining	.006	.277	.090
		Unit size (staff)	.192	.185	.038
Determination of broader policy	.155	Collective bargaining	.006	.275	.089
		Unit size (staff)	.168	.172	.041
		Regulatory func.	-.269	-.112	.010
		Criminal justice func.	.285	.103	.014
Content of rules and regulations	.148	Collective bargaining	.005	.239	.069
		Criminal justice func.	.450	.159	.032
		Unit size (budget)	.135	.136	.024
		Regulatory func.	-.237	-.094	.011
Establishing administrative procedures	.210	Collective bargaining	.007	.349	.142
		Unit size (staff)	.222	.221	.052
Daily operations	.201	Collective bargaining	.008	.361	.153
		Unit size (staff)	.189	.182	.040

1. Significant predictors (F value of B sign. .05 level or better) that could also explain at least 1% of variance in impact of state unions. The precise amount of variance explained by each predictor is listed in the last column.

2. Unstandardized regression coefficient

3. Standardized regression coefficient

4. Percent of state employees engaged in collective bargaining

account for 1% or more of variation only in the content of rules and regulations, administrative procedures, and daily operations arenas.

The best example of the explanatory power of an actor-specific variable involves the relationship between the proportion of a unit's budget coming from federal sources and the influence that certain federal government actors wield in state administrative affairs. Some have questioned whether the federal government gains much leverage over state or local administration as a result of the fact that federal dollars come to agencies with various conditions attached (Altenstetter and Bjorkman, 1976; Friedman and Dunbar, 1971; Hale and Palley, 1981; Ingram, 1977; Murphy, 1973; Rosenthal, 1980; Thomas, 1976). Others argue, however, that the federal piper is often able to call the state or local government tune (Wright, 1978; Derthick, 1970; Clynch, 1976; Elling, 1985; Elling and Schottenfels, 1980).

At least in the 10 states focused on here, dependence on federal dollars is strongly related to the impact that the Congress/federal administrative agencies wield over various aspects of state administration. The correlations between the impact of this federal actor complex and the proportion of federal funds in a state administrative unit's budget range from .69 for impact on the the overall budget level for a unit, and .62 for budget levels for specific programs, to .55 for impact on daily administrative operations. Among units that depend upon the federal government for four-fifths or more of their budget, 79% see "federal agencies/Congress" as having "great impact" or "very great impact." This compares to 14% of the administrators of units who receive less than one-tenth of their budget from federal sources. While 47% of those who receive four-fifths or more of their budget from federal sources attribute great or very great impact upon daily operations to federal agencies/Congress, this is true of just 5% of the managers of units who receive less than one-tenth of their funding from federal sources.[8] Even moderate dependency on federal funding is associated with substantial federal agency/congressional influence. Thus, among the managers of units that depend upon federal sources for 20% to 40% of their budgets (N = 94), 40% attribute great impact to these federal actors in the two budgetary arenas and 29% attribute great impct to federal agencies/Congress in determining broader policies.

Earlier in this chapter we saw that federal impact varied as a consequence of the functional responsibilities of state administrative units. But units with varying functional responsibilities differ in their reliance upon federal funding. At one extreme, units with staff responsibilities, criminal justice, and regulatory responsibilities rely on federal sources for less than 10% of their budgets. At the other extreme, health units depend upon federal sources for 28% of their revenues, while those with education and income security responsibilities depend upon federal sources for an average of 38% and 67% of their budgets, respectively.[9]

Multiple regression analysis permits us to sort out the impact of functional responsibility, dependence upon federal funding, and other factors for the impact of federal agencies and the Congress on state agency decisions and activities. Multivariate models of federal agency/congressional impact that included the share of a unit's budget coming from federal sources along with the organizational location of a unit, the size of a unit's budget, and its functional responsibilities can account for 50% of the variance in federal influence on overall unit budget levels. The amount of variance explained by a similar model for the other five influence arenas ranges from 48% for budgets for specific unit programs, and 42% for impact on broader policies, to 32% for federal impact in each of the other three influence arenas. In every case, the lion's share of the variance is accounted for by federal funding. The proportion of total variance in federal agency/congressional impact explained by federal funding ranges from 44% in the case of overall budget levels, and 40% for impact on budgets for specific programs, to 36% for impact on broader policy, and 29% in the case of each of the other three arenas.

Functional responsibility emerges as a significant predictor in the multivariate model, but it rarely accounts for more than a few percent of the variance in federal impact. Thus, agencies with regulatory responsibilities report somewhat less federal impact on budgets for specific programs, but this accounts for less than 2% of variance. Similarly, agencies with environmental, income, or transportation responsibilities report greater federal impact on broader policy. Together, however, these variables account for less than 4% of the variance in federal agency/congressional impact.[10]

Since fiscal devices, and particularly categoric grants, are a primary means by which federal administrative or legislative influence is exercised, the linkage between federal funding and the impact of these actors on state administrative affairs is to be expected. To some extent the impact of the federal courts on the affairs of state agencies should also depend upon levels of federal funding, since the linkages to federal administrative or legislative actors that result from agency participation in federal grant programs may require the federal courts to resolve disputes concerning grant conditions and state agency adherence to them. But the impact of the federal judiciary should be less clearly tied to state agency dependence on federal funding, since it can pass judgment on the actions of subnational administrators even when an agency receives no federal funds. Hence, while we would expect positive correlations to exist between extent of federal funding and the impact that state administrators attribute to the federal courts, these correlations should be weaker than those that exist between federal funding and the impact of the federal agencies and the Congress.

This is indeed the case. Across the six influence arenas, the correlations between extent of federal funding and federal court impact range from a low of .20 (Pearson's r, p = .001), in each of the two budgetary arenas, to .27 in the case of the rules and regulations arena. The limited relevance of federal funding for federal court impact is exemplified best in the case of criminal justice units. Units with such responsibilities generally attribute more influence to the federal courts than do those with other responsibilities. Yet criminal justice units receive, on average, only about 3% of their revenues from federal sources.

Whereas multivariate analysis of determinants of federal agency/congressional impact highlighted the importance of federal funding as a source of that impact, multivariate analysis of determinants of federal court impact on state administrative affairs highlights the insignificance of such funding. Across the six influence arenas, a model that includes the proportion of federal funds in a unit's budget, the size of a unit's budget, the organizational location of a unit, and the functional responsibilities of a unit, can account for only between 8% and 13% of the variance in the impact of the federal courts. To be sure, extent of federal funding emerges as a significant predictor of federal court impact in five of the six arenas, one capable of explaining between 1% (overall budget level) and 7% (impact on rules and regulations) of the variance. But the functional responsibility of a state administrative unit is often as significant as federal funding, if not more significant. In the case of federal court impact on budgets for specific programs, whether a unit has income security responsibilities is positively associated with federal court impact and can account for roughly 4% of the variance, while the fact that a unit has regulatory responsibilities is negatively associated with federal court impact and can account for approximately 1% of the variance. In five of the six influence arenas (the exception is impact on budgets for specific programs), the fact that a unit has criminal justice responsibilities is positively associated with federal court impact and accounts for 2–5% of the variation in the impact of this federal actor.

To summarize this portion of the chapter, multivariate analysis suggests that the impact of various nonagency actors bears some relationship to the functional responsibility of an administrative unit. Functional responsibility is a more consistent predictor of variation in the impact of particular nonagency actors than it is of variation in the impact of the agency itself. On the other hand, unit size and organizational place are less strongly and consistently related to variation in nonagency actor influence than to variation in the impact of the agency itself.

Functional responsibility could account for variation in the impact of only a few nonagency actors, however, and for a relatively small amount of variation even in those cases. When models of union impact were respecified using extent of collective bargaining as an independent variable, and models of personnel office impact were respecified using extent of civil service coverage, explanatory power increased. Models of federal administrative agency/congressional impact that included administrative dependence upon federal dollars were particularly powerful.

These findings suggest the necessity of identifying appropriate agency-specific as well as actor-specific variables if one hopes to be able to account for much of the variation in the impact of particular nonagency actors on state administrative units. While the 10–state survey provides information on only a few such predictors, several additional ones are used in subsequent chapters of the book in an effort to account for variation in the impact of particular nonagency actors on the course of state administration.

NONAGENCY ACTOR IMPACT AND MANAGEMENT PROBLEMS

The picture painted in this chapter suggests that state administrative units are far from autonomous. Numerous nonagency actors exert moderate influence upon a number of the major decision arenas affecting state agencies and in more narrowly administrative realms as well. A smaller number of actors, most notably state elected officials, have moderate to great impact in all but the most narrowly administrative arenas.

The density or complexity of influence in administrative decision and action arenas may, however, exact a price in administrative performance. The analysis in prior chapters did not suggest that an "if only" management outlook, which causes managers to attribute managerial difficulties to the efforts, well-meaning or not, of nonagency actors to exert influence upon their affairs, was common among the managers in these 10 states. Still, important trade-offs between efforts to assure administrative accountability and the ability of bureaucracies to execute their responsibilities effectively may exist. The nature of these trade-offs can be explored via an examination of the relationships that exist between the impact of various nonagency actors and the severity of certain management problems. The focus is again on those actors whose influence will not receive more extended examination in either Chapter 7 or Chapter 8.

In Chapter 3 we saw that the severity of various personnel-related problems was related to the extent of civil service coverage and collective bargaining in the 10 states, while the severity of various problems stemming from agency relationships with federal actors was positively associated with the extent to which a state administrative unit depended on the federal government for its funding. In the preceding section of this chapter we noted that personnel office impact was related to extent of civil service coverage and that the impact of federal actors was correlated with agency dependence on federal dollars. Hence, it should come as no surprise that personnel office impact is positively correlated with various personnel problems while federal influence is associated with various federal government-related impediments to effective management.

In the case of personnel office impact, positive correlations of the magnitude of .15 or so exist between such impact on daily administrative operations, and difficulties rewarding outstanding performance, problems disciplining or dismissing employees, and filling vacancies or retaining key staff. The severity of problems created by civil service procedures for hiring employees was also positively correlated with personnel office impact on daily administrative operations ($r = .25$) and in establishing of agency administrative procedures ($r = .20$).

We have seen that extent of federal funding is positively associated with the severity of various "federal government" management problems, mostly related to the dynamics of federal grants-in-aid and was also strongly associated with levels of federal administrative agency/congressional impact on agency affairs (although not nearly so strongly associated with variation in the impact of the federal courts on state administrative affairs). Hence, it is hardly surprising that positive relationships also exist between the influence attributed to the federal government and the severity of these problems.

Depending upon the arena of influence, the correlations between federal agency/congressional impact and complaints about the strings attached to federal grants range from .33 to .42. Correlations between federal impact and problems stemming from paperwork and delay in federal programs range between .29 and .40, while those between federal impact and unpredictability of federal grant

levels range from .35 to .51. Complaints about federal matching funds requirements and the impact of these federal actors on various aspects of agency operations are also positively correlated, and range from .13 to .27. Almost without exception the severity of these problems is most strongly correlated with
estimates of federal administrative/congressional impact on overall budget levels for a unit or budgets for specific programs. Thus, the correlations between
estimates of federal impact on the overall budget level for a unit and complaints
about grant "strings," funding predictability, delay, and matching funds are
.42, .49, .36, and .27, respectively. That this is so is hardly surprising given
that issues of revenue availability are central to budgetary deliberations.

Several other examples illustrate how the impact of particular actors may
exact a cost in terms of state management effectiveness, at least as effectiveness is defined by state managers themselves. In Chapter 3 we saw that the
extent of collective bargaining in a state was positively associated with the
severity of several "union" problems. Even stronger positive correlations existed between the severity of collective bargaining-related problems and the
influence of state employee unions. Across arenas, correlations ranging from
.27 to .43 existed between union influence and bargaining on "inappropriate
matters such as program planning" and in constraining the ability of managers
to direct subordinates.

The impact of the budget office in determining overall budget levels, and on
daily operations, is modestly correlated (r = .20) with the severity of the problem of insufficient appropriations. Given the inclination of budget offices to
trim agency requests, and the tendency of state legislatures to rely on budget
office recommendations, a more powerful voice for the budget office may translate
into lower appropriations for agencies. A positive correlation of similar magnitude exists between budget office impact on an agency's overall budget level
and legislative expansion of programs without additional funding. Interestingly,
legislative impact is unrelated to the severity of either of these problems. The
problem of excessive restrictions on expenditures is also positively correlated
with budget office impact on both daily operations (r = .24) and establishing
agency procedures (r = .24), as well as with personnel office impact on daily
operations (r = .21).

Two final examples of the trade-offs between nonagency actor influence and
effective management involve political parties and the courts. Political parties
are among the least significant nonagency actors. But where party impact is
greater (as in Indiana), so are problems of patronage hiring practices. For the
entire sample, across the six arenas, correlations of .20 to .27 exist between
the impact of political parties and such practices. Finally, managerial complaints about having to cope with court-mandated levels of service are moderately correlated with the influence exerted by both federal and state courts. The
correlation of federal court impact with the problem of court-mandated service
levels ranges from .30 to .38 across the six arenas. In the case of the state

courts, this problem is correlated with estimated court impact on overall agency budget levels (r = .23), on budgets for specific programs (r = .28), and on daily agency operations (r = .22).

These relationships, along with others to be explored in subsequent chapters, suggest some of the costs of increased bureaucratic accountability for administrative effectiveness. Nonetheless, except perhaps for the correlations between union impact and certain problems, between federal agency/congressional impact and various grant-related problems, and between federal court impact and the problem of mandated service levels, the relationships between the impact of nonagency actors and various management problems are modest. This suggests that the price to be paid in decreased administrative performance for greater accountability may be an acceptable one.

CONCLUSION

In this chapter and in Chapter 5 an effort has been made to specify some of the dimensions of the role of state administrative agencies in the state political process and the interaction of these agencies with a range of nonagency actors. The picture that emerges provides little support for the politics/administration dichotomy simplistically understood.

Although variation exists as a function of a unit's size, its organizational "place," its programmatic responsibilities, along with other factors, the managers surveyed believed that their units exerted considerable influence not only in more narrowly administrative realms but also in the political arenas in which broader policy is determined and spending is approved. The technical and other resources of state administrative agencies are one source of their influence in broader policy and budgetmaking. Equally important is the fact that the consequences of the decisions made in these arenas for the ability of agencies to execute their administrative obligations are such that state managers do not feel they can sit on the sidelines while elected officials and other political actors deliberate on them. Any wall that may once have separated the making of policy from its execution in these states has clearly been breached from the administrative side.

At the same time, a host of nonagency actors, both inside and outside of state government, exert moderate to great impact in both the budgeting and policymaking arenas, although variation in such influence is evident as a consequence of the functional responsibilities of state agencies, in particular, as well as various agency or actor-specific factors. Governors and their staffs, the budget office and the state legislature are particularly influential, with federal government actors, interest groups, and agency clientele also being quite important. The impact of nonagency actors generally declines as one moves into more narrowly administrative realms such as establishing procedures and structures or conducting daily operations. Many nonagency actors exert a modicum of influence even in these arenas, however. Indeed, some actors—the state personnel office and the clientele of an agency are the best examples—have as much or more impact in more narrowly administrative realms as in more political ones. State agencies clearly share sovereignty over administrative affairs with various nonagency actors. The politics/administration wall has also been breached from the political side.

All of this is not to say, however, that administrators are simply policymakers by another name nor that the settings associated with what traditionally has been called administration are merely another venue for the play of political influence typical of the legislature or the governor's office. The influence of agency actors is greatest—both in absolute terms and in comparison to that of other actors—in more narrowly administrative realms, while it is both absolutely and relatively less in determining spending levels or broader policy. The opposite pattern is evident in the case of nearly all of the nonagency actors.

James Svara (1985, p. 228), after examining and rejecting a variety of alternative models of the relationship between city councils and city managers, concludes that the most accurate description of this interaction is "mission-management separation with shared responsibility for policy and administration." As Figure 6.1 indicates, councils dominate questions of *mission* (purpose, scope of services, tax level, constitutional issues) while, at the other end of the continuum, city managers (and, by extension, administrative agencies) dominate in matters of *management*—those actions taken to support policy and administrative functions including controlling and utilizing the human, material, and informational resources of the organization to best advantage as well as the specific techniques used in generating services. Although a council is involved to some extent even in this sphere, it rarely "interferes with details of management" (p. 227). As one moves from the sphere of management to *administration* and then to *policy,* the role of administrators wanes while that of the council waxes. But even in the policy dimension administrators perform important tasks, including making recommendations on decisions and formulating budgets.

Two recent studies of state policymaking boards provide support for Svara's continuum model. Henry and Harms (1987) report that the vast majority of 66 appointed boards in Virginia concentrated their activities at the mission and policy end of the continuum. A study based on the perceptions of members of the Wisconsin Natural Resources Board who had served over the past 20 years concludes that "the Wisconsin Natural Resources Board, a body with a high degree of statutory authority, operates primarily at the mission/policy end of the decision continuum" (Thomas, 1990, p. 449).

Assessing the congruence of the 10-state findings with the model that Svara outlines is difficult because the 10-state study focuses on numerous nonagency actors both inside and outside of state government instead of only the legislature. The next chapter assesses the validity of Svara's perspective in terms of the impact of governors and legislatures specifically. Furthermore, the "arenas" of influence in my study do not precisely correspond to Svara's four

Figure 6.1

Mission-Management Separation with Shared Responsibility for Policy and Administration on the Part of City Council and City Manager

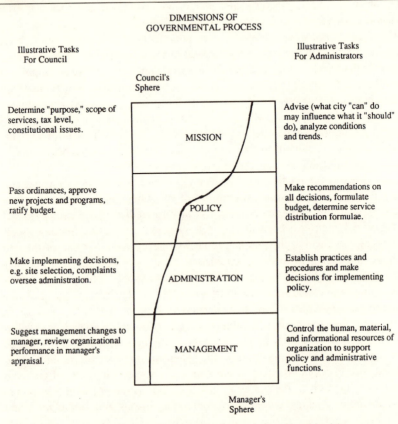

DIMENSIONS OF
GOVERNMENTAL PROCESS

Illustrative Tasks
For Council

Illustrative Tasks
For Administrators

Council's
Sphere

Determine "purpose," scope of
services, tax level,
constitutional issues.

MISSION

Advise (what city "can" do
may influence what it "should"
do), analyze conditions
and trends.

Pass ordinances, approve
new projects and programs,
ratify budget.

POLICY

Make recommendations on
all decisions, formulate
budget, determine service
distribution formulae.

Make implementing decisions,
e.g. site selection, complaints
oversee administration.

ADMINISTRATION

Establish practices and
procedures and make
decisions for implementing
policy.

Suggest management changes to
manager, review organizational
performance in manager's
appraisal.

MANAGEMENT

Control the human, material,
and informational resources of
organization to support
policy and administrative
functions.

Manager's
Sphere

(The curved line suggests the divisions between the council's and the city
manager's spheres of activity, with the council to the left and the city manager to the right of the line.)

Source: Svara (1985, p. 228).

"dimensions of the governmental process." The dimension he labels *policy* would encompass the two budgetary arenas as well as determination of broader policy. *Administration* would appear to correspond to determination of the content of rules and regulations and establishing administrative procedures and structures, while *management* is roughly equivalent to the arena I have identified as "daily operations." In this study no arena corresponds to what Svara terms *mission*.

These caveats aside, my findings are consistent with the division suggested by Svara. Nonagency actors, with the possible exception of agency clients and other state administrative agencies, nearly always exert greatest influence upon policy. Their influence declines for administration and declines even more for management. Conversely, the impact of the agency itself increases as one moves from realms of policy to administration and then to management. While all of the actors—whether an agency itself or the various nonagency actors both within and outside of state government—have a voice in most arenas, meaningful distinctions can be drawn regarding the breadth or significance of that involvement.[11] Administrators are not simply politicians by another name nor are the settings associated with what has traditionally been called administration just another venue for the play of political influence that typifies legislative chambers or governors' offices.

One question raised by these patterns of influence is the desirability of a host of nonagency actors having significant influence in narrowly administrative realms. Those obsessed with the threat that hordes of unelected bureaucrats supposedly pose to democratic government ought to take some comfort from my findings, although they might wish that administrators had even less autonomy in these realms than they apparently do. Leaving aside for now the question of who ought to be involved in articulating the "public interest" in an increasingly complicated world, several other issues suggest themselves.

One issue is what are the consequences for administrative effectiveness when a host of nonagency actors have some influence on the ongoing efforts of an agency to execute its administrative responsibilities? The discussion in the preceding section of this chapter highlighted some of the potential costs of the influence of personnel offices, budget offices, federal administrative agencies and the Congress, political parties, and the courts. Administrative effectiveness may also be adversely affected by the range and number of actors who are involved. In seeking to satisfy various competing sovereigns, or to pursue competing objectives simultaneously, an agency may temporize or it may pursue lowest common denominator courses of action unlikely to displease any of them. The ironic result of the efforts of differing actors to get state agencies to do certain things may be a decrease in the ability of agencies to do anything! Struggles for control over administration by competing sovereigns may reinforce preexisting bureaucratic tendencies to play it safe. Gormley (1986a) argues that the result of intense battles for custody of state bureaucracies has not been administrative paralysis so much as "routinized responsiveness to any and all external stimuli. When a bureaucracy's circuits become overloaded, reflective behavior becomes impossible and reflexive behavior becomes inevitable" (p. 6; see also Gormley, 1989a, 1989b).[12]

The evidence presented in this chapter does not permit us to determine the "influence energy" that courses through the circuits of the administrative units in the 10 states. But the problem of "influence overload" should be borne in mind as we focus in the next two chapters on several nonagency actors who are especially important elements of the influence matrix of state administration.

NOTES

1. These correlations, like all the other correlations reported in this chapter, are—unless otherwise noted—Pearson product-moment correlation coefficients, significant at the .05 level or better, two-tailed test.

2. Factor analyses of nonagency actor influence relationships were also conducted for each of the states. Factor structures similar to those that emerged for the entire sample also emerged in individual states. The major difference was that various unofficial or outside political actors loaded on more than one factor in some states. An "elected state officials" factor on which both the governor and the legislature loaded heavily was not always evident in individual states.

3. Coefficients of variation greater than .30 are considered to be substantial. For the influence of nonagency actors in the two budgetary arenas, these exceed .40 except in the case of the governor, legislature, and budget office, for whom they are .30 or less. For determination of broader policy, the coefficient of variation exceeds .40 for every actor except the governor and legislature. In the other three arenas, the coefficients exceed .40 for all of the nonagency actors with but one exception—legislative impact on the content of rules and regulations.

4. Even when a significant "state effect" is evident, this is frequently due to the distinctiveness of just one or two states. The Scheffe multiple comparison of means test indicated that significant differences in impact for particular actors rarely existed between a large number of *pairs* of states.

5. State differences in organizational complexity may also confound the measure of organizational "place." A state with a more highly integrated bureaucratic apparatus will have fewer high-level managers than one with a more fragmented bureaucratic establishment containing a larger number of separate agencies. To control for this possibility, correlational analysis was also conducted within each state. Significant correlations between organizational place and the impact of a given nonagency actor in any arena almost never emerged in 3 of the 10 states. Significant positive correlations existed between a respondents' organizational levels and their estimates of the impact of five or more actors only in South Dakota, and then for just two arenas.

6. Some influence is attributed to "state employee associations/unions" even in Arizona, Texas, Indiana, and Tennessee, where true collective bargaining by such organizations is prohibited. I suspect that this is so because employee organizations can exert influence even when not permitted to collectively bargain. They may influence state administrative affairs via informal discussions with agency heads as well as through lobbying directed at the legislature or the governor. But in these states, while 15% to 25% of managers see such organizations as having at least some impact, virtually none see them as having great or very great impact.

7. If the proportion of employees collectively bargaining in individual units were known, I believe this and other correlations with extent of collective bargaining would be even stronger.

8. Relationships between federal funding and federal agency/congressional impact persist in individual states. Statistically significant correlations (p = .01, one-tailed test) exist between federal funding and attributions of federal agency/congressional impact in every state save for Tennessee, where the correlation of funding with impact upon administrative procedures/structures is not significant at the .01 level. In the case of impact

on overall budget levels for a unit, the correlations ranged from a low of .62 in Tennessee to .77 in Arizona and Indiana. For impact on budgets for specific unit programs, the correlations with extent of federal funding ranged from a low of .53 in Tennessee to .80 in Indiana. For impact on daily operations, the correlations ranged from lows of .41 in Tennessee and .45 in Michigan and Texas, to .68 in Delaware.

9. Within functional categories, significant (.05 level, one-tailed test) positive correlations between extent of federal funding and federal agency/congressional impact generally persist. The only exceptions are insignificant positive correlations between federal funding and federal influence upon rules and regulations, administrative procedures, and daily operations, in the case of criminal justice units; insignificant positive correlations in the case of federal impact on regulations and daily operations in the case of nonfiscal staff units; and an insignificant positive correlation between federal funding and federal administrative/legislative impact on administrative procedures in the case of state transportation units. But the strength of the positive correlations does vary depending upon functional area. The correlations between federal administrative/legislative impact on overall budget levels and federal funding range from a low of .20 in the case of criminal justice units, to .67 in the case of units with environmental responsibilities. In the case of federal administrative/legislative impact on broader policy decisions and federal funding, the correlations ranged from .31 and .32 for units with criminal justice and transportation responsibilities, respectively, to .57 and .59 for those with environmental or economic development obligations. The most consistently strong correlations between federal funding and federal administrative/legislative impact exist in the case of units with environmental, economic development, income security, and education responsiblities.

10. It has been noted that agency size, as measured by size of budget, was positively correlated with federal administrative agency/congressional impact. This relationship is apparently not simply a reflection of the fact that units with larger budgets are also more dependent on federal dollars, since it persists in the multivariate model. The size of a unit's budget is positively related to federal impact on overall budget levels, budgets for specific programs, and broader policy. Indeed, it is the next most powerful predictor after extent of federal funding itself. In none of these cases does it account for even as much as 3% of the variance in federal agency/congressional impact, however. When the log of the size of a unit's work force is substituted for the log of its budget as the indicator of organizational size, the structure of the models does not change. Size as measured by number of employees has slightly less explanatory power than does size as measured by budget. What generally occurs is that the explanatory power of federal funding increases by a percent or two along with a similar increase in total variance explained by the model.

11. It should be noted that the nature of the council's and manager's spheres of influence across the four dimensions of the governmental process that Svara identifies in his model are those considered to be the " 'average' division among the five cities" he studied, or those that "can be regarded as 'typical' " (p. 227). He also indicates that the "size of the spheres is not based on absolute values at this stage in the development of the model, but rather is intended to be suggestive of tendencies in council-manager relations" (p. 227). In his article he goes on to identify variations on the basic model in each of his five study cities and abstracts out four "deviations" from the typical division as outlined in Figure 6.1. A "partial test" of Svara's model focusing

on council-manager cities in Michigan (Browne, 1985) suggests that possible deviations may be even more extreme than Svara recognizes.

12. Another possibility is that the multiplicity of actors seeking to influence the affairs of state agencies provides maneuverability for administrators as they play these actors off against one another.

Chapter 7

Governors, Legislators, and State Management

INTRODUCTION

The preceding chapter's examination of the impact of various nonagency actors on decisions affecting, or the conduct of the operations of, state administrative agencies disclosed that the governor and state legislature were typically the most important of these actors. This chapter explores the impact of these two actors in depth and builds on prior research exploring the role of governors and legislatures in the state administrative process.

A second objective of this chapter is to identify some of the consequences for effective management that flow from the exercise of gubernatorial or legislative influence. Most of the literature on the relationships that exist between elected executives or legislators, on the one hand, and career civil servants, on the other, has tended to stress the tensions inherent in these relationships. As D. L. Dresang (1991, pp. 34–35) has observed,

the antipathy between politicians and civil servants is commonplace and worldwide. A profession, almost by definition, typically seeks autonomy and a status that commands deference. The mixing in a common arena of a political official pursuing the mandates of the ballot box and a professional expecting to dominate in the policymaking process is bound to generate conflict and distrust. There are likely to be frustrations, too, because the politician and the professional need each other.

As the exploration of "if-only" management in Chapter 2 suggested, governors and legislators loom large among the "thems" that may be seen by state managers as complicating their lives.

DIMENSIONS OF GUBERNATORIAL AND LEGISLATIVE INFLUENCE

Table 7.1 contains information on gubernatorial and legislative impact on state administration that extends beyond that presented in Chapter 6. The table helps convey several important points. First, although both governors and legislators are influential, the legislature generally has greater impact. The mean impact of the legislature on budgetary matters exceeds that of the governor in 9 states; in 7 of 10 states in the broader policy arena, and in 9 of 10 states so far as shaping the content of agency rules and regulations is concerned.

The governor's weaker hand in shaping broader policies is evident in some findings presented in Chapter 5 (see Table 5.3). Of the state administrators surveyed, 40% said *none* of the legislation affecting them originated with governors or their staffs. In contrast, only 15% said none of the legislation affecting them originated with the legislature.

A second point is that the legislature's influence advantage erodes as one moves from budgetary and broader policy realms to more narrowly administrative ones. Indeed, in half of the states, the governor is either slightly more influential, or as influential, as the legislature in establishing administrative procedures/structures and shaping daily operations. While not exerting as much impact as the legislature in more "political" dimensions of administration, gubernatorial influence holds up better as one moves into more narrowly administrative arenas.

The picture of legislative and gubernatorial influence in state administration that emerges from the data is similar to that painted by other scholars. Agency, legislative, and gubernatorial budget staff in five western states interviewed by Duncombe and Kinney (1986) ranked the legislature as more significant in determining appropriations increases for state agencies than the governor and executive budget staff. In a replication of Sharkansky's earlier (1968) study of determinants of agency budget success, Thompson (1987, p. 775) finds evidence in an 18-state study that "the role of the governor vis-a-vis the legislature in general fund budget decisions is not as dominant as before. Undoubtedly governors still play an important, if not paramount, role in short-term budget decisions. But legislatures, especially in terms of budget expansion, appear to be taking a more affirmative role."

In her 50-state survey of state agency heads, Miller (1987) reports that the governor is seen as exerting slightly less influence than the state legislature. Another 50-state study based on the views of agency heads (Abney and Lauth, 1986b) found that only 38% of these state managers chose the governor as the most influential of seven actors in terms of influence on "departmental programs and objectives." This compared to 43% who ranked the legislature as the most influential.

A longitudinal perspective is provided by the surveys Deil Wright and his associates have conducted since 1964. In these surveys, agency heads were asked whether the governor or the legislature exercised greater control and oversight over the affairs of their agencies. Save for 1964, the proportion who said the governor exercised greater control exceeded the proportion who said the legislature did so. However, "the size of the plurality of agency heads who name the governor peaked in 1974. State legislatures (and legislators) are apparently reasserting themselves in the 1980s" (Haas and Wright, 1987, p. 274).

Table 7.1

Gubernatorial, Legislative, Budget Office, and Agency Impact Across Arenas, by State

	AZ	CA	DE	IN	MI	NY	SD	TN	TX	VT	Overall
					Determining Overall Agency Budget Level						
Governor/staff[1]	2.7	2.8	2.8	2.6	2.6	3.1	3.3	2.6	2.2	2.8	2.7 (.25*)[2]
Legislature	3.5	3.3	3.2	3.1	3.2	3.0	2.9	3.2	3.4	2.9	3.2 (.18*)
Budget office	2.8	2.7	2.8	3.3	2.9	3.5	3.0	2.8	2.9	2.2	2.9 (.29*)
Agency itself	2.8	2.9	2.5	2.8	2.8	2.7	2.5	2.8	3.0	3.0	2.8 (.13)
Gov./legis. diff.[3]	-0.8	-0.5	-0.4	-0.5	-0.6	-0.1	0.4	-0.6	-1.2	-0.1	-0.5
Gov./agy. diff.	-0.1	-0.1	0.3	-0.2	-0.2	0.4	0.8	-0.2	-0.8	-0.2	-0.1
Legis./agy. diff.	0.7	0.4	0.7	0.3	0.4	0.3	0.4	0.4	0.4	-0.1	0.4
					Budget Levels for Specific Agency Programs						
Governor/staff	2.6	2.6	2.6	2.4	2.5	2.9	3.2	2.6	2.2	2.7	2.6 (.21*)
Legislature	3.4	3.2	3.0	2.9	3.1	3.0	3.1	3.1	3.4	3.0	3.1 (.14)
Budget office	2.5	2.7	2.5	2.9	2.9	3.4	3.0	2.6	2.7	2.1	2.8 (.27*)
Agency itself	2.5	2.9	2.6	2.8	2.8	2.9	2.6	2.8	3.0	3.0	2.9 (.11)
Gov./legis. diff.	-0.8	-0.6	-0.4	-0.5	-0.6	-0.1	0.1	-0.5	-1.2	-0.3	-0.5
Gov./agy. diff.	0.1	-0.3	0.9	-0.4	-0.3	0.0	0.6	-0.2	-0.8	-0.3	-0.3
Legis./agy. diff.	0.9	0.3	0.4	0.1	0.3	0.1	0.5	0.3	0.4	0.0	0.2
					Broader Policy/Program Changes						
Governor/staff	2.6	2.8	2.5	2.5	2.1	2.9	2.9	2.2	1.8.	2.5	2.5 (.30*)
Legislature	2.9	3.1	2.5	2.6	2.7	2.9	2.7	2.4	2.9	2.6	2.8 (.18*)
Budget office	1.8	1.9	1.6	2.1	2.0	2.8	2.1	2.7	1.8	1.6	2.0 (.27*)
Agency itself	3.1	3.1	2.9	3.1	3.1	3.1	2.9	3.1	3.2	3.1	3.1 (.09)
Gov./legis. diff.	-0.3	-0.3	0.0	-0.1	-0.6	0.0	0.2	-0.2	-1.1	-0.1	-0.3
Gov./agy. diff.	-0.5	-0.3	-0.4	-0.6	-1.0	-0.2	0.0	-0.9	-1.4	-0.6	-0.6
Legis./agy. diff.	-0.2	0.0	-0.4	-0.5	-0.4	-0.2	-0.2	-0.7	-0.3	-0.5	-0.3
					Content of Rules and Regulations						
Governor/staff	1.7	1.8	1.6	2.0	1.5	2.0	1.9	1.4	1.3	1.9	1.7 (.22*)
Legislature	2.1	2.3	2.0	2.0	2.5	2.2	2.1	2.3	2.3	2.3	2.2 (.15)
Budget office	0.8	1.1	0.9	1.0	0.9	1.5	0.9	0.9	1.0	1.0	1.0 (.18*)
Agency itself	3.2	3.2	3.3	3.2	3.3	3.4	3.1	3.2	3.4	3.2	3.3 (.10)
Gov./legis. diff.	-0.4	-0.5	-0.4	0.0	-1.0	-0.2	0.2	-0.9	-1.0	-0.4	-0.5
Gov./agy. diff.	-1.5	-1.4	-1.7	-1.2	-1.8	-1.4	-1.2	-1.8	-2.1	-1.3	-1.6
Legis./agy. diff	-1.1	-0.9	-1.3	-1.2	-0.8	-1.2	-1.0	-0.9	-1.1	-0.9	-1.1

Table 7.1 (Continued)

	AZ	CA	DE	IN	MI	NY	SD	TN	TX	VT	Overall
				Establish Administrative Procedures and Structures							
Governor/staff	1.3	1.5	1.5	1.9	1.3	1.6	2.3	1.4	1.4	1.5	1.5 (.25*)
Legislature	1.6	1.7	1.5	1.5	1.7	1.5	2.1	1.8	2.0	1.6	1.7 (.15)
Budget office	1.0	1.5	1.2	1.8	1.3	2.1	1.4	1.4	1.2	1.0	1.4 (.29*)
Agency itself	3.4	3.5	3.4	3.7	3.5	3.6	3.2	3.5	3.5	3.4	3.5 (.15*)
Gov./legis. diff.	-0.3	-0.2	0.0	04.	-0.4	0.1	0.2	-0.4	-0.6	-0.1	-0.2
Gov./agy. diff.	-2.1	-2.0	-1.9	-1.8	-2.2	-2.0	-0.9	-2.1	-2.1	-1.9	-2.0
Legis./agy. diff.	-1.8	-1.8	-1.9	-2.2	-1.8	-2.1	-1.1	-1.7	-1.5	-1.8	-1.8
				Daily Administrative Operations							
Governor/staff	1.3	1.0	1.2	1.4	1.0	1.2	1.4	0.9	0.9	0.9	1.1 (.20*)
Legislature	1.2	1.3	1.3	1.1	1.3	1.2	1.1	1.1	1.4	0.9	1.2 (.12)
Budget office	1.2	1.4	1.1	1.8	1.4	2.1	1.1	1.3	0.9	0.9	1.4 (.29*)
Agency itself	3.6	3.6	3.7	3.7	3.7	3.7	3.6	3.6	3.7	3.8	3.7 (.07)
Gov./legis. diff.	0.1	-0.3	-0.1	0.3	-0.3	0.0	0.3	-0.2	-0.5	0.0	-0.1
Gov./agy. diff.	-2.3	-2.6	-2.5	-2.3	-2.7	-2.5	-2.2	-2.7	-2.8	-2.9	-2.6
Legis./agy. diff.	-2.4	-2.3	-2.4	-2.6	-2.4	-2.5	-2.5	-2.5	-2.3	-2.9	-2.5

1. The entry for each actor is the mean impact of that actor in a particular state or overall where 0 = no impact, 1 = some impact, 2 = moderate impact, 3 = great impact, and 4 = very great impact.

2. The parenthetical figure is the value of eta, a measure of the strength of association between two variables. When squared it indicates the proportion of total variability in the dependent variable (the impact of a specific actor in a particular decision or action arena) that is explained by knowing the values of the independent variable (the state). An asterisk denotes that the value of eta is significant at the .01 level.

3. The values in the final three rows of each panel of the table are the differences between the impact of one actor versus another. A positive entry indicates that the first-named actor in the pair has more impact than the last-named.

Several scholars have assessed gubernatorial and legislative impact in terms of specific arenas similar to those focused on in this book. Drawing on Wright's 1978 50-state survey, Dometrius (1979) found that the legislature was considered to have "high influence" more often than the governor so far as determination of the total agency budget and specific program budgets was concerned. The governor was, however, more often highly influential in the making of "major agency policies" and on decisions affecting agency rules and regulations. Brudney and Hebert (1987), relying on the same data as Dometrius, constructed an additive scale of actor influence across the four arenas of influence. As measured by this scale, legislative and gubernatorial influence were comparable—a mean score of 9.3 for the legislature and 9.2 for the governor. The Dometrius and Brudney and Hebert studies are most similar to mine in how influence is assessed in particular arenas. The less consistent legislative advantage that they find may reflect the fact that they examined all 50 states rather than only 10.

A third point to be made about the balance between gubernatorial and legislative power is that judgments about the former must take into account the role of the state budget office. Responsibility for development of an executive budget has increasingly been centralized in state budget offices that are closely aligned with the governor. These offices typically have policy development and management improvement responsibilities as well. Across the 10 states in this study, the budget office is a close staff aid to the governor in every state except Texas. At the time of the survey, Texas developed its state budget using a joint legislative-administrative committee (ACIR, 1985).

While not a simple additive relationship, the influence of the budget office does augment the governor's power in most states. If this is so, the governor's hand in these 10 states is as strong as that of the legislature, especially in budgetary affairs. Moreover, the budget office often has more influence than any other nonagency actor on an agency's daily operations. This finding, combined with the evidence that the governor alone often exerts influence equal to or greater than that of the legislature in this arena in many states, suggests chief executives may play a more significant role in more narrowly administrative realms than often supposed.

Another bit of evidence from the survey provides support for the argument that governors are the influence equals of state legislatures. The respondents were asked to indicate whose preferences they would follow if what the governor wanted their unit to do conflicted with what the legislature desired. Overall, 60% said they would side with the governor either all of the time (34%) or most of the time (26%). Only 16% said they would side with the legislature all or most of the time. The remaining one-quarter hedged by saying "sometimes the governor but sometimes the legislature."

The data from the 10–state survey can be combined with Svara's model of the four dimensions of the governmental process to map the relative roles of the governor, legislature, and state agencies themselves. Figure 7.1 constitutes a tentative effort to do so. The absence of indicators in my study of actor influence on what Svara terms "mission" means I can only speculate regarding the division between spheres for this dimension. Nonetheless, the curve defining spheres for the other three dimensions seems consistent with data presented in Table 7.1. Reflecting some evidence that legislative influence exceeds that of the governor, the curve marking the limits of legislative influence across particular dimensions is slightly to the right of that marking the limits of gubernatorial influence. Although the contours of the curves are similar, the gubernatorial curve exhibits a less sharp "dogleg" as one moves from management to administration. This reflects the erosion of the legislature's advantage over the governor in the arena of daily operations. The significant role of state agencies as "policyshapers" stressed in Chapter 5 is evident from the fact that the curve for both the governor's and the legislature's influence is near, or to the left of, the midpoint for every dimension except "mission."

PATTERNS OF VARIATION IN GUBERNATORIAL AND LEGISLATIVE INFLUENCE

The tabular and graphic analysis just presented has value in an effort to generalize about the impact of governors and legislatures. The research on the

Figure 7.1

A Profile of Agency, Gubernatorial, and Legislative Roles Across Four Dimensions of Governmental Process in 10 American States

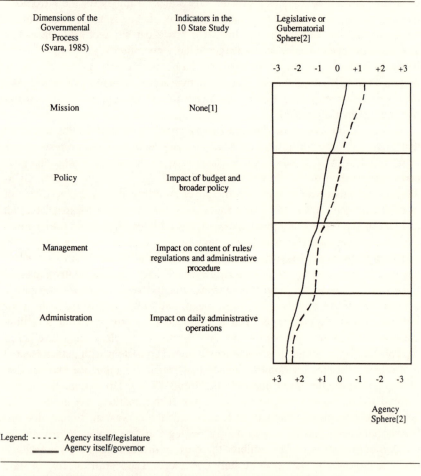

Dimensions of the Governmental Process (Svara, 1985)	Indicators in the 10 State Study	Legislative or Gubernatorial Sphere[2]
		-3 -2 -1 0 +1 +2 +3
Mission	None[1]	
Policy	Impact of budget and broader policy	
Management	Impact on content of rules/ regulations and administrative procedure	
Administration	Impact on daily administrative operations	
		+3 +2 +1 0 -1 -2 -3
		Agency Sphere[2]

Legend: - - - - - Agency itself/legislature
              ——— Agency itself/governor

1. Extrapolated in light of impact of given actors in the six influence arenas for which data exist.

2. At midpoint, the influence of each actor in a given dyad is equal. When the administrative agency impact in a given dimension exceeds that of the governor (or legislature), the boundary moves to the left of the midpoint. When the impact of the governor (or the legislature) exceeds that of the agency itself, the boundary lies somewhere to the right of the midpoint.

influence dynamics of state administration cited above tends to favor generalization across agencies and states. Generalization is important to enhanced understanding. But our zeal to generalize ought to be tempered. James Svara, after having depicted the typical or ideal model of what he terms "missionmanagement separation with shared responsibility for policy and administration" (see Figure 6.1), discusses several deviations from this ideal-type that emerged in the five cities he studied, or that might exist in other communities (see especially, Svara, 1985, pp. 228–230). The preceding two chapters have explored some of the variation across states in the influence of the agency itself or that of selected nonagency actors. Nonagency actor impact was especially variable.

The eta statistics reported in Table 7.1 suggest it is easier to generalize about legislative than gubernatorial impact. Significant interstate variation in legislative influence exists only for its impact on overall budget levels and making broader policy and program changes. The impact of the governor, as well as the governor's close ally the budget office, exhibits greater interstate variability. Significant etas exist for these actors in each of the six arenas. Although the coefficients of variation reported for the governor, the budget office, and the legislature are quite substantial, especially for the rules and regulations, administrative procedures and structures, and daily operations arenas, they are less substantial than those that exist for other less powerful nonagency actors.

Data on the origins of legislation affecting their agencies, and on whose side administrators would take in a situation of conflict, further illustrate the variability that exists. Although governors' offices are not seen as major sources of legislation affecting agencies in any of the states, the mean proportion of bills originated in them varies from 5% or less in Arizona, California, Delaware, Indiana, Michigan, and Texas, to 10% in New York and 17% in South Dakota. Similarly, while the legislature plays a major role in shaping an agency's policy agenda in every state, the proportion of legislation originating with it ranges from 15% in South Dakota to 30% or more in California, Michigan, New York, and Vermont. The proportion of administrators asserting that they would side with the governor "all of the time" was 40% or greater in Arizona, California, Indiana, New York, and Tennessee. It was, however, only 23% in Michigan and a scant 11% in Texas.

Although other research exhibits a penchant for generalization, closer examination of the findings of those studies discloses substantial variation as well, especially in the case of gubernatorial influence. In a two-state study using an instrument to assess impact very similar to that used in the present study, Elling (1980a) found that gubernatorial impact on broader policy and on daily operations exceeded that of the legislature in Kentucky but not in Minnesota. Miller (1987) reports coefficients of variation for gubernatorial and legislative influence similar in magnitude to those found to exist in this study. In Duncombe and Kinney's (1986) five-state study, the proportion of budget officials who perceived the governor and the executive budget staff to have "major" impact on appropriations ranged from just 18% in Idaho and 22% in Washington, to 62% in Nevada and 85% in California. Attributions of legislative influence varied from 35% among budget officials in Washington to 85% in Idaho. Abney and Lauth (1986b) report that the proportion of state agency heads ranking the governor as the most influential political actor ranged from none in South Carolina and Colorado to 91% in Maryland. Figures from their study for the 10 states focused on in the present study are: New York (69%), California (60%), Tennessee (43%), Vermont (38%), Indiana (35%), Michigan (27%), Delaware (20%), South Dakota (17%), Texas (15%), and Arizona (14%). Finally, in the study most like my own, Brudney and Hebert (1987) report great variance in gubernatorial influence along with substantial, although less pronounced, variation in legislative influence.

GUBERNATORIAL AND LEGISLATIVE INFLUENCE: RESOURCES AND CONSTRAINTS

This part of the chapter considers various factors that modify the influence that governors and state legislatures exert over state administrative agencies and their affairs. The formal constitutional or statutory powers that governors and legislatures possess may well condition their influence. In the postwar period the formal power resources of both governors and legislatures have been enhanced. One impetus for this was a desire to assure effective "overhead" control of state bureaucracies.

Efforts to strengthen the governorship generally preceded efforts to enhance the capabilities of state legislatures. The "quest for executive leadership" (Kaufman, 1956) extends at least as far back as the 1920s. The budgetary powers of governors were strengthened and their role in filling high-level administrative posts was expanded by making more of these officials subject to gubernatorial appointment (Roberts, 1988). Changes making it easier for governors to restructure state bureaucracies have also been made (ACIR, 1985). Centralization of various staff functions within departments of administration, and expansion of governors' immediate staffs, were also seen as facilitating their ability to keep tabs on administrative activities. Finally, four-year gubernatorial terms have become the norm and limits on reelection have been relaxed. By 1982, governors served four-year terms with no restrictions on reelection in 18 states. They could serve two consecutive four-year terms in 24 states.

Although efforts to enhance the formal tools of gubernatorial influence have occurred in all of the states, significant variation remains. This is evident in the 10 study states (see Table 7.2). Across the nation, governors remain weakest in two areas that should bear most directly on their duties as "chief bureaucrat." One is their ability to appoint high-level administrators. The other is their "organizational power." The appointment and organizational powers of the governors in the 10 states run the gamut from very weak to very strong.

Table 7.2

Characteristics of the Office of Governor and the Legislature in Study States

Formal Powers of Governors[1]	AZ	CA	DE	IN	MI	NY	SD	TN	TX	VT
Tenure potential	5	5	4	4	5	5	4	4	5	2
Appointive power	3	5	4	5	2	5	3	4	1	4
Budgetmaking power	5	5	5	5	5	5	5	5	1	4
Organization power	3	3	4	2	5	4	5	3	1	3
Veto power	5	5	5	1	5	5	5	4	3	2
Combined index	21	22	21	16	22	24	22	20	11	16
F.A.I.I.R Criteria[2]										
Functionality	11	1	43	44	15	4	23	30	45	19
Accountability	47	3	48	38	22	13	12	44	36	20
Informed	38	2	47	41	9	1	15	11	43	34
Independent	17	3	38	43	12	8	16	9	45	42
Representative	50	2	29	20	3	1	37	26	17	47
Overall ranking	43	1	48	40	8	2	17	26	38	37

Sources: The source for information on gubernatorial power resources is Beyle (1983). The source for the F.A.I.I.R. criteria is Citizens Conference on State Legislatures (1971). The table of rankings is on pp. 52-53.

1. The higher the number the greater or more extensive the formal power of the governor. See Appendix 2 for the operational definition of each of the formal powers and the combined index.

2. The lower the ranking, the higher the score of a legislature on a dimension. Thus, the California legislature ranks as the most "functional" legislature in the nation. The overall ranking is the average of the ranks of a given state legislature across the five separate F.A.I.I.R dimensions. See Appendix 2 for the operational definition of each of the dimensions.

Efforts to enhance the ability of state legislatures to discharge their responsibilities have proceeded more slowly and unevenly. Moreover, such efforts have not necessarily sought to enhance the legislature's role in the conduct of state administration except insofar as that might be related to its ability to deliberate on public policy and the governor's budget.

The best effort to define the qualities central to improved legislative performance—despite the fact that it is nearly two decades old—is that of the Citizens Conference on State Legislatures (CCSL) (1971). The CCSL called these its F.A.I.I.R criteria. A capable or high-quality legislature is one that is functional, accountable, informed, independent, and representative. The CCSL calculated the ranking of each of the 50 state legislatures on each of these criteria as well as an overall ranking based on all five. Since these rankings were published, changes along the lines suggested by the CCSL and others have continued to occur. A recent study asserts:

Today's legislatures in general are more functional, accountable, independent, and representative, and are equipped with greater information handling capacity than their predecessors, if the F.A.I.I.R. recommendations are used as a standard. Of the 73 recommendations proposed by the Citizens Conference, 30 can not be assessed because of lack of information. Among the remaining 43, little or no change was reported on five. State legislatures changed significantly, however, in regard to the remaining 38. In most instances, an overwhelming majority of the states now follow the recommendations (ACIR, 1985, p. 123).

Alas, this update does not permit us to assign scores to individual legislatures. Hence, as have other scholars, I report, and will later use as independent variables, the rankings on the F.A.I.I.R. criteria assigned to these legislatures a decade prior to the time of my survey. I do so with the caveat that all of the legislatures would score higher today on the indicators and that the gap between the most and least capable legislatures is narrower today than 20 years ago. The rankings of the 10 study state legislatures on each of the five criteria, and an overall ranking based on a legislature's score on all five, are indicated in Table 7.2

Improvements in state legislative capabilities were one reason that many of them engaged in more extensive administrative oversight activities in the 1970s. Changes relating to a legislature's "information handling" capacity, its "functionality," and its "independence" are especially relevant. These included such things as longer and more frequent sessions, better use of the interim when the legislature is not in session, creation of specialized oversight committees, and expansion in professional staffing, especially for standing committees, as well as for fiscal review, postaudit, and program evaluation units (Elling, 1984).

Increased emphasis on oversight also reflected growing public and legislative distrust of state bureaucracies. It also reflected the continuing growth in the size and responsibilities of the state administrative apparatus. New tools designed to bring supposedly "runaway" state agencies to heel such as sunset laws emerged, along with more widespread use of existing tools such as legislative review and/or veto of proposed administrative rules and regulations (Common Cause, 1982; Craft, 1977; Drury, 1977; Elling, 1980c; Ethridge, 1984; Hamm and Robertson, 1981; Johnson, 1983; Kearney, 1990; Renfrow, West, and Houston, 1986; Renfrow and Houston, 1987).

Possibilities for oversight of a more individualistic nature that may repay significant political benefits existed through state legislators' handling of constituency "casework" (Elling, 1979, 1980b). Casework handling was stimulated by the expansion of staffing for individual legislators among other changes.

These developments certainly impacted the states in this study. Michigan has one of the oldest and most powerful arrangements for legislative review and veto of proposed agency rules. Tennessee and South Dakota have similar arrangements, although at the time of this study no specific provisions for legislative review of administrative rules existed in California, Delaware, and Indiana (Benson, 1986; Ethridge, 1981, 1984; Renfrow, West, and Houston, 1986; Renfrow and Houston, 1987; Jones, 1982). As of 1982, sunset laws covering all agencies existed in Arizona, Indiana, Tennessee, and Texas, with coverage for regulatory units only in Delaware and Vermont (Common Cause, 1982; Kearney, 1990).

Changes in the intensity of legislative oversight are apparent in administrators' responses to one of the survey questions. Overall, 58% reported that the legislature in their state was placing increased emphasis on overseeing the activities of administrative agencies, while just 3% felt it was placing less emphasis on oversight. At least half reported greater emphasis on oversight in every state except South Dakota.

Existing research suggests that the changes just discussed affect the influence that the governor and the state legislature wield in the administrative process. This is clearest in the case of gubernatorial influence. Dometrius (1979) found that a governor's appointment authority was most strongly correlated across influence arenas with administrators' perceptions of his or her influence (r = .21 to .37). The governor's budget authority was also significantly, if more modestly, correlated with gubernatorial influence on budget decisions. The extent of a governor's veto power was rarely related to his or her influence, however, while the governor's "reelection" ability was correlated (r = .10) only with influence on budgets and major policy changes.

Two thirds of Abney and Lauth's (1986a) agency respondents considered the budget authority that governors possessed to be a significant factor underlying their influence, while only 30% cited appointing power. In a study of Georgia appropriations decisionmaking, Lauth (1984) found that strong budgetary powers resulted in significant gubernatorial influence over agencies even when the heads of those agencies were not gubernatorial appointees. Using Dometrius' measures of formal gubernatorial power, Brudney and Hebert (1987) found that these powers were a significant predictor of gubernatorial impact summed across four arenas when entered into a multiple regression model. The governor's appointment power was an especially powerful predictor.

Comparative research on the consequences of reform for the legislature's impact on administrative affairs is less common. When samples of agency heads and legislators in Kentucky and Minnesota were asked to estimate the impact of the legislature on administrative affairs, the Minnesota legislature, ranked 10th in the CCSL ratings, had significantly greater impact than did the Kentucky legislature, ranked 31st in the CCSL ratings, so far as impact on agency organizational structure, financial resources, overall program priorities, daily operations, and developing proposals for new programs were concerned (Elling, 1980c). In their 50-state study, however, Brudney and Hebert (1987) found that the relationship between their measure of legislative professionalism and legislative impact on agency affairs, while positive, was not strong.

Gubernatorial Powers and Impact in the 10 Study States

Based on the views of administrators in the 10 study states, it is evident that formally more powerful governors have greater impact on administrative actions and decisions (see Table 7.3). The overall measure of power resources is most strongly correlated with gubernatorial impact on an agency's budget and making broader policy decisions affecting it. But the appointment and budgetmaking authority that governors possess have an equally strong effect. A governor's organizational authority is significantly correlated with impact on budget issues. The strength of a governor's veto is much less strongly or consistently correlated with increased gubernatorial influence, however, while tenure potential is either unrelated or negatively related to gubernatorial impact. Various formal powers matter least for influence in more narrowly administrative realms.

While the correlations between gubernatorial resources and impact are not large, examination of the influence of governors whose power resources are at the extremes indicates that formal powers do matter. Among the states in the sample only Texas does not grant its governor substantial authority to develop the state budget. In Texas only 40% of managers attributed great or very great impact (hereafter referred to as "great impact" in the discussion) to the governor on overall budget levels. In the other nine states the proportion reporting great impact ranged from 62% in Indiana to 87% in South Dakota.

A Michigan governor has more limited appointive powers than does a governor in California. In California 62% of the managers saw the governor as having great influence on making major policy decisions affecting their agencies, while in Michigan just 37% reported this level of impact. Only in Texas did the governor have less impact on major agency policy decisions than in Michigan.

Since the survey asked administrators how they had been selected for their positions, we possess an alternative, agency-specific measure of a governor's ability to determine higher level administrative staffing.[1] Across all 10 states, the correlation between estimates of gubernatorial influence and method of selection ranged from .15 (for impact on regulations and on daily operations) to .23 (for impact on broader policymaking). Positive correlations of similar magnitude existed within individual states.[2] These findings on the significance of the governor's ability to influence administrative staffing on gubernatorial impact mirror those of other studies (Brudney and Hebert, 1987; Dometrius, 1979, 1981; Hebert, Brudney, and Wright, 1983; Wright, 1967). According to Abney and Lauth (1986b), 57% of administrators appointed by the governor reported gubernatorial influence to be greater than that of the legislature, as opposed to only 25% of those appointed by a board without the governor's consent, and just 16% of popularly elected administrative officials. In my study, gubernatorial influence was lowest for agencies headed by board-selected administrators rather than elected officials. Legislative influence exceeded gubernatorial influence not only in the case of units headed by managers selected in these two ways, but also in the case of managers selected via civil service procedures or appointed by other administrators. Only administrators directly appointed by the governor, with or without legislative confirmation, reported that gubernatorial influence exceeded legislative influence. The greatest variation in gubernatorial impact across managers selected in differing ways occurred for impact on major policy decisions affecting agencies. While just one-third of the elected or board-selected managers said the governor had great impact in this arena,

Table 7.3

Correlations Between Gubernatorial and Legislative Powers/Resources and Actor Impact on Administrative Influence Arenas

	Determination of Overall Budget Levels		Budget Levels for Specific Specific Programs		Major Policy/Program Changes	
	Gov. Impact	Leg. Impact	Gov. Impact	Leg. Impact	Gov. Impact	Leg. Impact
Gubernatorial Power[1]						
Tenure	-.06*[2]	.07*	-.04	.06	-.08**	.04
Appointment	.15***	-.06*	.07*	-.06*	.24**	.03
Budgetmaking	.17***	-.09**	.11***	-.08**	.21***	-.03
Organization	.11**	-.10**	.12**	-.06	.03	-.08*
Veto	.06*	-.04*	.08**	-.01	-.02	-.08*
Total Gov. Power	.16***	-.10**	.14***	-.07*	.14***	-.06*
Legislative Power[1]						
Functionality	.13***	-.02	.09**	.01	.19***	.11***
Accountability	.12***	-.06*	.09**	-.01	.17***	.11***
Informed	.09**	-.10**	.10**	-.06*	.03	-.06*
Independent	.12***	-.02	.09**	.00	.16***	.07*
Representative	-.01	.00	-.04	-.02	.01	.07*
Overall Index	.10**	-.04	.07*	-.01	.13***	.09**

	Content of Rules and Regulations		Establish Administrative Procedures		Daily Administrative Operations	
	Gov. Impact	Leg. Impact	Gov. Impact	Leg. Impact	Gov. Impact	Leg. Impact
Gubernatorial Power						
Tenure	-.06	.05	-.07*	.00	.01	.07**
Appointment	.16***	-.07*	.06*	-.10**	.06	-.06*
Budgetmaking	.13***	-.08	.05	-.09**	.07*	-.06*
Organization	.01	.04	.04	.01	.04	-.01
Veto	-.04	.01	-.01	.01	.04	.01
Total Gov. Power	.08*	-.01	.04	-.06	.08	-.03
Legislative Power						
Functionality	.09**	.06	-.04	-.04	-.03	-.01
Accountability	.10**	.06	.05	.02	-.03	-.01
Informed	.03	.05	.03	.00	.01	-.04
Independent	.05	.06*	-.03	-.01	-.03	.00
Representative	.01	.08**	-.06*	-.03	-.07*	.04
Overall Index	.06*	.08*	.00	.00	-.04	.01

1. See Appendix 2 for definition of gubernatorial or legislative powers.

2. Table entries are Pearson's product-moment correlation coefficients. * = significant at .05 level, two-tailed; ** = significant .01 level; *** = significant .001 level or better.

Table 7.4

Correlation of Gubernatorial or Legislative Powers with Selected Manifestations of Influence

	Proportion of Legislation Affecting Agency Originating From:				Side With Legislature When in Conflict With Governor[3]
	Gov.	Legis.	Interest Groups	Agency	
Gubernatorial Power[1]					
Tenure	.00	-.02	.03	.00	.09**
Appointment	.06	.03	.00	-.04	-.26***
Budgetmaking	.09**	.00	-.06	.01	-.32***
Organization	.16***	-.05	-.16***	.09**	-.09**
Veto	.13***	-.06*	-.18***	.11***	.00
Total Gov. Power	.17***	-.04	-.16***	.07*	-.21***
Legislative Power[2]					
Functionality	.03	.08**	.07*	-.12***	-.18***
Accountability	.04	.06	.09**	-.13***	-.11**
Informed	.15***	-.03	-.13***	.06	-.09**
Independent	.06	.04	.07*	-.11**	-.18***
Representative	-.01	.10**	.12***	-.16***	-.02
Overall Index	.05	.06	.09**	-.14***	-.13***

1. See Appendix 2 for definition of indicators of gubernatorial or legislative power.

2. * = Pearson's r is significant at .05 level, two-tailed; **= significant .01 level; *** = significant .001 level or better.

3. Responses to this questionnaire coded so that 1 = "governor all of the time" and 5 = "legislature all of the time." Hence, for the correlations with gubernatorial powers, a <u>negative</u> correlation indicates that administrators more often side with the governor in states in which the governor has greater powers. For the correlations with legislative power, a <u>positive</u> correlation indicates that administrators are more likely to side with the legislature in states with more powerful legislatures.

approximately three-quarters of the gubernatorial appointees reported great gubernatorial impact.

The utility of a governor's formal power resources is also evident from Table 7.4. Those with stronger formal powers are the source of a larger portion of legislation affecting particular agencies. When the legislature and the governor disagreed, administrators were more likely to side with a governor who possessed stronger appointment, budgetary, organizational, and overall power resources. Texas again stands out in comparison with the other nine states. Only 17% of the Texas respondents indicated they would side with the governor all or most of the time in a case of gubernatorial-legislative conflict as compared to more than 70% in New York and South Dakota.

The value of formal gubernatorial powers is also evident from their effect on legislative influence in particular arenas (See Table 7.3). There is some tendency for administrators in states with formally more powerful governors to report less legislative influence. Note, as well, that the proportion of bills originating in the legislature and from interest groups, although not agencies themselves, declines. More powerful governors are somewhat better able to control the content of agency policy agendas.

Legislative Capabilities and Impact in the 10 Study States

Levels of legislative capability or quality are less consistently related to differences in legislative influence than are differences in the formal powers of governors and gubernatorial impact (see Table 7.3). Indeed, depending upon the indicator examined, *more capable* legislatures often exert *less influence.* Legislative capability is most clearly associated with enhanced impact on major policy decisions affecting an agency. Both the overall index of capability, and all of the individual dimensions except for "informedness," are positively correlated with legislative influence in this arena. The overall index and several individual dimensions are also modestly but positively correlated with legislative impact on the content of rules and regulations. More functional and representative legislatures also tend to be the source of more of the legislation affecting an agency (see Table 7.4). While the governor is no less important a source of legislation in a state with a more capable legislature, the proportion of bills originated with the agency itself tends to be lower. Reform appears to make a legislature less dependent on agencies themselves in the development of policies relevant to those agencies.

Table 7.4 also indicates, however, that administrators in states with more capable legislatures are actually *less* likely to side with the legislature when situations of gubernatorial-legislative disagreement exist. Although the correlation is not presented in Table 7.4, a significant positive correlation of .07 exists between the proportion of managers reporting that the legislature in their state is placing greater emphasis on oversight and the "independence" of the legislature. Since one of the elements of "independence" is the ability of a legislature to "oversee and evaluate the programs and expenditures which it has authorized" (CCSL, 1971, p. 121), such a correlation would be expected. It contrasts, however, with the findings of J. A. Thompson (1986). Although he found that the overall measure of legislative capability was positively correlated with oversight activity relating to state unemployment compensation programs, this was not so for the independence dimension.[3]

The absence of strong positive relationships between legislative capability or quality and legislative influence is not entirely surprising. Using a measure of overall legislative capability similar to that used here, Brudney and Hebert (1987) report only a small and statistically insignificant relationship between it and legislative influence across four influence arenas. The limits of the CCSL indicators, and their datedness, have already been noted. States ranked low on the F.A.I.I.R. criteria in the early 1970s likely improved more substantially over the following decade than did those that were already high on these criteria in the earlier period. Hence, differences among the legislatures of the 10 states in their capabilities are likely narrower than the data in Table 7.2 suggest. Moreover, states having more powerful governors often have institutionally more capable legislatures as well. In my sample, while the overall indexes of gubernatorial power and legislative capability are only modestly correlated ($r = .16$), certain of the individual F.A.I.I.R. dimensions are highly correlated with the overall measure of gubernatorial power or with specific powers. Thus, the rank of a state's legislature on the "informed" dimension is strongly correlated with its score on gubernatorial tenure potential (.36), organizational authority (.82), and veto authority (.66). The correlation between the governor's appointment power—the most significant power resource of a governor according to this and other analyses—and a state's overall legislative capability rank is .46.

The relationships between the formal capabilities of governors or legislatures and their influence on state bureaucracies may be attenuated because such capabilities must be exploited if they are to make a difference. The potential for influence inherent in appointing high-level state administrators could be squandered if a governor pays little attention to the policy or administrative priorities of these appointees. The stronger correlations between gubernatorial powers and impact than between legislative capabilities and impact may reflect a greater gubernatorial than legislative willingness or skill in exploiting those resources. As a collective body, the legislature may find it difficult to realize its power potential. This is a question that I will address shortly. Governors may try harder precisely because the inherent powers of legislative bodies are so great. Every legislature has the power of the purse, regardless of how often it chooses to follow the recommendations of others concerning its exercise of those powers. Every legislature possesses the ultimate authority over agencies and their programs. The abolition of an agency or the transferring of its programs is rare. But it does occur. Governors can propose a course of action affecting an agency, but the legislature disposes. Facing an institution of such potential, governors may be especially motivated to exploit the power resources at their disposal.

In concluding this section, a final point deserves emphasis. Strong governors often are found in states with strong legislatures. This fact may reflect the existence of a social, economic, and political environment in a state that demands that the capabilities of both institutions be strengthened. As a result, the fact that the governor or the legislature of one state possesses greater powers than the governor or legislature of another state does not mean that, within the context of a given state, a formally more powerful governor or legislature is, in fact, more powerful.

The gubernatorial-legislative influence differentials in Table 7.1 illustrate this. The governors of California and Michigan are both relatively powerful in formal terms, but the legislatures of those two states rank as the first and eighth most capable in the nation. The result is a larger influence deficit for the governors of these two states than in most of the other states. Indeed, in competition with the legislature for influence over state administrative affairs, California and Michigan governors are worse off than is the formally much weaker Vermont governor, who, however, confronts an institutionally less capable legislature. Texas presents another example. Its institutionally weak legislature is seen by administrators in that state to be quite powerful in part because the Texas governor is even less well supplied with power resources.

Beyond Formal Powers: Other Determinants of Gubernatorial and Legislative Impact

Even in the case of governors, the correlations between formal powers and influence are modest. Hence, gubernatorial as well as legislative influence on administrative affairs must be a function of other factors. More extensive formal powers may create a greater potential for influence, but a governor or a legislature may fail to fully exploit that potential. To be sure, even in the absence of their exercise, the formal powers possessed by a governor or legislature have an anticipated reactions effect. Managers may do certain things, or refrain from doing them, because they know that the governor or the legislature can punish them for their actions or for their failures to act. Nevertheless, high levels of influence likely depend upon active use of available power resources.

Effective use of power resources would seem to require some direct contact between administrative agencies and governors or legislatures. If formal power resources are limited, interaction that takes the form of efforts at persuasion is even more crucial. Even when formal powers are extensive, and even when, as in the case of governors, administrators are at least nominally their subordinates, influence may still hinge on the power to persuade (Neustadt, 1960). Hence, the intensity and quality of the interaction between governors or legislatures and administrative agencies may not only enhance the potential for influence inherent in formal powers but constitute a source of power in its own right.

Legislatures and governors have many things to do, however, and seeking to influence the course of events in particular state bureaucracies may not rank high among them. It may be true, as Sabato (1983) argues, that contemporary governors are more "managerially minded" than in the past. In the late 1970s governors in 16 states reported spending more time on "managing state government"—an average of 27%—than on any other task (Beyle, 1978). Still, the conclusions of a participant-observation study of 14 states conducted in the 1960s likely remain valid today: "A substantial segment of the state bureaucracy operates without much contact with or influence by the governor. . . . Governors do not have great concern for day-to-day operating problems of coordination and administration in any part of the bureaucracy" (Wyner, 1968, p. 203).

In the 10 study states, administrators reported widely varying levels of interaction with governors and their staffs. The proportion reporting "frequent" or "very frequent" interaction (hereafter referred to simply as "frequent" interaction) averaged 26%, and ranged from 12% in California and 19% in New York to 36% in South Dakota and 45% in Tennessee. There is evidence that frequency of interaction and gubernatorial influence are positively related. Correlations ranging from .09 for the content of regulations arena to .20 for the daily operations arena existed between gubernatorial influence and intensity of interaction. Those managers who interacted more intensely with the governor were also somewhat more likely to side with the governor in a conflict with the legislature.

These findings are consistent with those that emerged from a 50-state survey of agency heads (Hebert and Brudney, 1988). Those surveyed ranked the amount of interest that the governor had in their agencies second only to the governor's budget authority as a source of influence over their units. Moreover, the correlations between administrators' estimates of gubernatorial influence and extent of gubernatorial interest—defined as amount of agency legislation originating with the governor, "policy initiatives" from the governor, and "new ideas" from the governor—were .25, .30, and .41, respectively. The correlations between gubernatorial impact and the extent of direct contact with the governor or the governor's staff were .19 and .22, respectively.

Interaction appears to enhance gubernatorial influence independently of the formal powers that governors possess. The partial correlation between intensity of interaction and gubernatorial impact controlling for the overall formal powers of governors ranges from .08 to .20 across the six arenas of influence.[4] Interestingly, interaction matters most for levels of gubernatorial influence over daily operations. Governors seem to be able to shape the course of ongoing agency administration if they work at it.

Factors Affecting Gubernatorial Interaction

Because interaction with administrative agencies has an independent effect on gubernatorial influence, it becomes important to identify the correlates of that interaction. Various factors may prompt gubernatorial interaction with state agencies. Martha Weinberg (1977) argues that governors balance the need to devote some attention to administrative affairs with the demands of other duties by practicing "crisis management." They pay most attention to agencies with the greatest potential for the occurrence of problems that will be politically damaging or those in which a crisis has occurred.

This perspective leads Weinberg to develop a typology of agencies because "different kinds of agencies demand different kinds of management" (p. 66). Several different types of agencies demand constant gubernatorial scrutiny. One type includes those agencies in which a crisis—if it occurred—"would be so spectacular or in which the cost of a malfunction would be so high that the governor under no circumstances could afford not to attempt to anticipate it" (p. 67). In Massachusetts, Weinberg argues, Governor Francis Sargent focused on the Departments of Public Welfare and Corrections for this reason. A second type of agency requiring sustained attention is one with a large budget or work force. A third is one whose programs involve such well-organized interests that a problem would prompt an outcry from some important constituency or constituencies.

According to Weinberg, governors also pay closer attention to those agencies that implement policies of special interest in light of their personal, political, or programmatic priorities. Which agencies these might be is, of course, highly idiosyncratic. In his 14–state study, Wyner (1968) notes how governors were sometimes interested in certain departments "just because." He notes one governor who was an active outdoorsman and was, as a consequence, especially interested in his state's Department of Wildlife and Conservation.

Agencies that do not fall into the categories just discussed—and this may be a majority of agencies—will, Weinberg argues, receive little gubernatorial scrutiny unless a specific, unanticipated crisis emerges. An example from one of the study states occurred as the Michigan Department of Agriculture (MDA) sought to deal with a 1973 incident in which a highly toxic fire retardant (PBB) was erroneously mixed into cattle feed that was subsequently distributed to farmers across the state. This had dire consequences not only for cattle but also for Michigan residents, as the highly toxic chemical entered the food chain. Some of the anger of farmers over this disaster was directed at Governor William Milliken—despite the fact that the director of the MDA was appointed by a commission whose members, while gubernatorial appointees, served staggered, four-year terms (Coyer and Schwerin, 1981). Although the governor was re-elected in 1978, "voting increased sharply in those counties for which PBB was most salient and the larger turnout went against the incumbent governor" (p. 716). In response to the perceived failure of the MDA to deal effectively with the problem, and the political fallout this generated for him, the governor sought to bring the MDA under closer control: "Milliken made it known after the 1978 election that he would use his two 1979 appointments to the Agriculture Commission to change MDA policy, starting with the replacement of B. Dale Ball as Director. Ball resigned before he could be fired" (p. 719).

Finally, in every state and in every administration, there are agencies that governors deal with in a very limited way if at all. Agencies receive such treatment for somewhat contradictory reasons. On the one hand, a governor may not devote time and energy to an agency because it is generally performing along the lines that the governor prefers. Alternatively, governors may leave certain agencies alone because they lack the resources necessary to affect the course of events in those units anyway. Given efforts to insulate certain functions from direct gubernatorial control, governors may go out of their way to make it clear to the public that they lack influence over a particular function. Such a strategy of studied neglect may give a governor a degree of "deniability" if a crisis does occur. Governors are also likely to ignore agencies that perform highly technical tasks; those that serve easily identifiable, discrete, or specialized goals; or otherwise seem to have little crisis-generating potential

(Weinberg, 1977, p. 69). Interestingly, Weinberg notes that most Massachusetts governors have assumed that the Department of Agriculture presents little potential for a damaging crisis. Governor Milliken's experience with the Michigan Department of Agriculture in the 1970s suggests how difficult it may be for a governor to estimate the crisis-generating probabilities of agencies.

Research by other scholars as well as some of the findings of the present study provide support for the arguments of Weinberg. The relatively limited amount of interaction between agency administrators and governors in the 10 study states has been noted. Haas and Wright (1987) report that agencies interacted less often with the governor or the governor's staff than with personnel from other agencies, clientele groups, or citizens. Although perhaps an extreme example, a 1989 address by Michigan Governor Blanchard to that state's elected Board of Education represented only the second time in history that a Michigan governor had met with the board (*Michigan Education Report,* 1989).

My data do not permit me to say if it is crises that prompted more intense gubernatorial interaction with particular agencies. But administrators were asked whether they believed governors paid attention to what was happening in state agencies only when a crisis that threatened to have serious political or other consequences for them occurred. Nearly two-thirds agreed or strongly agreed that this was so. Those interacting less often with the governor were slightly more likely to agree that their state's governor was primarily a crisis manager ($r = -.21$).

If governors pay attention to agency affairs only when things go wrong, a less successful agency might be expected to report more intense interaction with the governor. There is no evidence that this is so in the 10 study states, however, based on the correlation between responses to a question asking administrators how successful their units had been in achieving their goals and the reported extent of gubernatorial interaction. Part of the problem here is that virtually no managers said that their units had been "less than successful."

Managers were also asked about the general orientation of the governor toward their unit and its programs. Only 5% considered the governor to be "consistently unsupportive or unsympathetic," while 52% felt the governor was "consistently supportive" and 45% felt the governor's orientation was "highly variable—sometimes supportive or sympathetic, sometimes unsupportive or unsympathetic." Considerable interstate variation existed, particularly in the proportion of managers reporting the governor's orientation to be consistently supportive as opposed to highly variable. While more than 70% of the Tennessee and Vermont respondents said the governor was consistently supportive of their units, only about 40% of the respondents in California, New York, and South Dakota said this was so.

Although a more negative gubernatorial orientation might be expected to prompt greater gubernatorial involvement in agency affairs, this was not the case in the 10 study states. Administrators of units who reported *more* favorable gubernatorial attitudes reported *more* intense interaction ($r = .15$). One explanation for this relationship is that "familiarity breeds support." Increased gubernatorial interaction—whatever may have initially prompted it—may, over time, increase a governor's appreciation of the accomplishments of a unit, the quality of its staff, and the challenges it confronts.

Another interpretation is that governors interact most intensely with units over which they exercise greatest control, and it is these agencies whose policies are easiest for governors to support because they are highly congruent with their own priorities. This suggests a link between the management priorities of governors and their ability to exert influence. Weinberg contends that governors ignore units that they lack the resources or authority to control, even when they are dissatisfied with how those units are performing. Both Wyner (1968) and Abney and Lauth (1986a) report that governors interact more actively with units headed by persons they have appointed.

Only a modest correlation (r = .11) existed between the extent to which administrators owed their positions to the governor and extent of interaction in the 10 study states. Just over half (55%) of the respondents appointed by the governor without legislative confirmation reported frequent interaction. The proportion reporting frequent interaction among those who were board-appointed, had secured their positions via civil service procedures, or were appointed by an agency head, was roughly 25%. Even among gubernatorial appointees who had been confirmed by the legislature, only 35% reported frequent interaction with the governor. Moreover, in support of the second interpretation advanced above, a positive relationship of .15 exists between how administrators secured their positions and gubernatorial support. Approximately two-thirds of direct gubernatorial appointees felt the governor was consistently supportive of their endeavors. This was true of only about half of the respondents who secured their positions in other ways. It remains the case, however, that governors interact more intensely with agencies whose programs they support, even when method of selection is taken into consideration (partial correlation = .13).

Units and managers higher up the administrative hierarchy may also interact more frequently with governors and their staffs. Organizational place is moderately correlated (r = .18) with interaction. Of those managers who reported directly to the governor, 40% interacted with him frequently as compared to 20% of those two levels below the governor.

Higher level administrative positions are often filled in a different manner than are lower level positions, however. But a partial correlation between interaction and organizational place of .17 exists when method of selection is taken into account. Among respondents appointed by a board, 37% of those at the top of the organizational pyramid reported frequent interaction with the governor as opposed to just 15% of those several levels lower. Some 55% of those appointed by the governor without legislative consent situated at the highest organizational level (i.e. agency heads) report frequent interaction, but only 40% of the direct gubernatorial appointees two levels below interact frequently with the governor. Regardless of their organizational location, respondents covered by civil service reported especially low levels of interaction. To be sure, there are few managers with civil service status at the highest levels of state management. Still, just 29% of these managers report frequent gubernatorial interaction. While 70% of the 300–plus respondents with civil service status are in units two to four levels below the governor, less than 20% of these managers report frequent gubernatorial interaction. To the extent that interaction increases gubernatorial influence, civil service status for key administrators reduces such interaction. Whether or not this is desirable is, of course, the subject of continuing debate among scholars of public administration and political science as well as political leaders and citizens.

A number of scholars have suggested that the functional responsibilities of an agency, or its size, may affect not only the intensity of gubernatorial interaction but impact as well. Weinberg's (1977) observations on this point have already been discussed. Wyner (1968) found a consistent pattern in the 14 states he studied for the attention of governors to be concentrated on four departments: economic development, highways, education, and public welfare. Hebert et al. (1983) found that governors exerted more influence on staff than line units. Staff units are often especially close to governors and perform functions such as budgeting or planning that are considered central to the ability of governors to achieve their goals. This same study also found that governors had greater impact on "major" agencies—measured by size of agency budget and number of employees—than upon "minor" ones. In a related study, Brudney and Hebert (1987) found evidence that governors had less impact on "economic" agencies and those with criminal justice responsibilities.

In the 10 state study, agency size was only weakly, if positively, associated with levels of gubernatorial interaction. The correlation between the number of employees in a unit and interaction was a statistically insignificant .05, while a modest, significant positive correlation (r = .07) existed between the size of a unit's budget and interaction.

The relationship between the functional responsibilities of agencies and levels of gubernatorial interaction is murky. While there is some evidence of differences in interaction, a modest eta of .15 emerges when analysis of variance is conducted. Across all 10 states, governors interacted more frequently with economic development, environmental, education, and criminal justice units than with transportation, natural resources, and regulatory units. Respondents from staff units, whether they had fiscal or nonfiscal responsibilities, reported intermediate levels of interaction, contrary to the arguments of some scholars. One-third or more of the managers of units with economic development, environmental, and educational responsibilities reported frequent interaction with the governor, while less than one-fifth of managers of units with regulatory or transportation functions reported frequent interaction.

Similar patterns of differential interaction with units having certain functional responsibilities emerged in individual states. The responsibilities of units ranking among the top four in gubernatorial interaction in five or more states were education (five states), environmental protection (five states), criminal justice (six states), and economic development (seven states). Ranking among the four functional categories with *lowest* levels of gubernatorial interaction in five or more states were transportation (seven states), natural resources (six states), health (five states) and fiscal staff (five states).

Wyner's (1968) conclusion about the big four so far as gubernatorial attention is concerned is borne out by my data in the case of economic development and education units but not public welfare or transportation units. I suspect a major reason for the differing findings is that the 1980s was a very different political era than the late 1960s. If one reflects on the issues that dominated political debate in many states at the time my study was conducted, they often involved problems that economic development, environmental, education, and criminal justice units had some responsibility to address. A lack of gubernatorial interest in units with income assistance/public welfare responsibilities in the 1980s may reflect a similar shift in the political saliency of this issue as compared to the Great Society era during which Wyner wrote.

To better sort out the determinants of gubernatorial interaction with state administrative agencies, multiple regression analysis was conducted. A model that included unit size, organizational location, gubernatorial orientation, and how an administrator was selected could account for less than 10% of the variation in gubernatorial interaction.[5] The only variables that could account for more than 1% of the variance apiece were organizational location and gubernatorial orientation. When the model was separately estimated for individual states, few of the variables were significant predictors in more than a few states. As compared to the overall model, the functional responsibility of a unit more often emerged as a significant predictor and was the most powerful single predictor in seven states.

In sum, while gubernatorial interaction with state agencies affects gubernatorial impact, substantial variation in the intensity of such interaction exists and accounting for such variation is difficult. This fact buttresses the arguments of Weinberg, Wyner, and others that such interaction is heavily dependent on the particular priorities, interests, and managerial styles of governors.

Patterns of Legislative-Administrative Interaction

Legislative impact may exceed gubernatorial impact because the legislature interacts more intensely with state agencies. Some 35% of the respondents reported frequent or very frequent communication with those legislative committees having jurisdiction over their unit's programs, while only 11% reported that they never communicated with those committees. Frequent communication with the committees that reviewed and acted upon their budget requests was also reported by 35% of the managers, while only 18% said they never communicated directly with these committees. Levels of communication with the two types of committees are strongly correlated (r = .64). Significant interstate differences in intensity of communication existed only in the case of program committees. Just 22% of South Dakota managers and 27% of Delaware managers reported frequent communication as compared to 45% of the Michigan respondents.

As was true for gubernatorial interaction and gubernatorial impact, frequency of contact with legislative committees is positively correlated with legislative impact. Significant correlations exist between program committee communication and legislative impact in all of the influence arenas save for determination of administrative procedures, with these correlations ranging from .10 to .17. The correlations between communication with budget committees and legislative impact on overall agency budget levels and on specific programs were .18 and .21, respectively. Significant correlations existed for the other four arenas as well.

Legislative committees tend to be less supportive of units' goals than are governors. Approximately 25% of the administrators said program committees were consistently supportive of or sympathetic with their unit's efforts and programmatic requests. Asked about the "general orientation and actions of appropriations or budget committees toward their budget requests," 28% said these committees were consistently supportive or sympathetic and generally approved budget requests with few changes. This compares to more than 50% who felt that the governor was positively oriented toward their activities and programs.

Agency-legislative interaction may be affected by a number of factors. The literature on legislative oversight has featured a debate over what stimulates more extensive or effective oversight. One view is that it is institutional capabilities or resources that are of primary importance. It is argued that the ability of a legislature to engage in oversight is limited by such things as session limits, limits on the use of interims, staffing inadequacies, diffusion of oversight responsibilities within the legislature, and committee structure (Elling, 1984). An alternative view holds that the best explanation for variation in oversight of administrative agencies lies within legislators themselves. Oversight is a function of the interest that legislators have in its performance and the incentives, particularly of an electoral variety, for engaging in it. Adequate resources will not stimulate efforts to oversee or influence administrative agencies unless the personal, political, career, or policy rewards for a legislator doing so are greater than those to be secured from an investment of time and energy in other legislative activities (on this debate see Rosenthal, 1981; and Rockman, 1985).

Although the validity of the preceding arguments can not be completely tested with the data at hand, it is possible to examine whether institutionally more capable legislatures interact more intensely with state agencies. Earlier I noted that more "independent" legislatures were somewhat more likely to stress oversight. But levels of interaction between legislative committees and state administrative units are unrelated to various indicators of legislative capability or quality. The only significant relationship is a modest positive correlation

($r = .07$) between the "representativeness" of a legislature and reported levels of communication between administrative units and program committees.

Legislative interaction is unrelated to some of the factors that were related to gubernatorial interaction, while it is related to others that were not associated with variation in administrative-gubernatorial contact. The operational indicator of method of administrator selection is constructed in such a way that a higher score indicates an administrator who is presumably "closer" to the governor. Since this variable was positively associated with gubernatorial interaction, we would expect that it would be negatively correlated with intensity of legislative interaction. In fact, the correlation between method of selection and frequency of communication with program committees is .06 and that with communication with budget committees is .11. Sixty percent of administrators appointed by the governor but confirmed by the legislature report frequent communication with both types of committees. Managers who were appointed by a board reported more intense interaction with the legislature than did those selected in ways other than by gubernatorial appointment. Just under 50% of board-selected managers reported frequent communication with both types of committees, while only 24% of the managers covered by civil service reported frequent communication with program committees, and only 15% communicated frequently with budget committees.

Differences in how managers reach their positions may be intertwined with differences in the organizational location of the units that they head. As it turns out, organizational location is much more strongly correlated with legislative than gubernatorial interaction. The zero-order correlation between organizational place and frequency of communication with program committees is .36 and that between place and communication with budget committees is .39. Wyner (1985) has argued that higher level administrators are less subject to gubernatorial influence because they have more numerous contacts with other significant political actors. The correlations between organizational location and committee interaction in this study support Wyner's contention.

In contrast to the findings for agency-gubernatorial interaction, no clear relationship existed between the orientation of a committee toward a unit and frequency of communication. The correlation between program committee orientation and interaction was .05 ($p = .06$) while that between budget committee orientation and interaction was .06 ($p = .04$)

Finally—and also in contrast to the patterns for gubernatorial interaction—communication with budget and program committees was not strongly related to the functional responsibility of an agency. The lowest levels of communication existed with environmental and education units, with 25% or less of the managers of these units reporting frequent communication with program or budget committees. The most intense interaction existed between fiscal staff units and program committees, with 46% reporting frequent communication, although intensity of communication with budget committees was not especially great. Criminal justice units also reported higher levels of communication with program and budget committees, while economic development managers reported frequency of communication with budget committees equal to that for criminal justice units.

On the one hand, the data suggest that gubernatorial and legislative interaction with agencies with differing functional responsibilities are inversely related. Governors tended to interact most intensely with education and environmental agencies, the units with whom legislative committees seem to interact least. Legislative committees reported relatively higher levels of interaction with regulatory agencies—agencies that reported quite low levels of gubernatorial interaction. On the other hand, criminal justice and economic development units tended to report higher than average levels of interaction with both the governor and legislative committees.

When multiple regression analysis is used to sort through relationships between various factors and administrative communication with legislative committees, it happens that relatively more of the variation can be accounted for than in the case of gubernatorial interaction. This may be additional evidence that gubernatorial involvement is more dependent on the personal predilections or priorities of particular governors whereas, because it is a collective body, the legislature's interaction with state agencies is more highly routinized.

Consistent with the correlational analysis, the location of a unit in the organizational hierarchy is the strongest predictor of interaction with legislative committees. Organizational location accounts for 12% of the variance in communication with program committees, while the size of a unit's budget accounts for an additional 5% of variance. Although how administrators secured their positions is a third significant predictor of communication with program committees, it can account for only 1% of the variation. Organizational location accounts for 14% of the variance in communication with budget committees while the size of a unit's budget accounts for another 6%. Neither method of selection nor any other variable emerges as a significant predictor of frequency of communication with legislative budget committees.[6]

A MULTIVARIATE MODEL OF DETERMINANTS OF GUBERNATORIAL IMPACT ON STATE ADMINISTRATION

We have seen that both the formal powers possessed by governors and the intensity of their interaction with individual agencies are positively correlated with gubernatorial influence. This section of the chapter extends the correlational analysis using multiple regression techniques to estimate best-fitting models of the determinants of gubernatorial impact upon various decisions affecting or the actions of state administrative units. The independent variables used to explain gubernatorial impact include those discussed in the preceding sections such as intensity of gubernatorial interaction, the orientation of the governor toward a unit, the size of a unit's budget, the organizational "place" of a unit, and the method used to select a manager. Also included are indicators of the formal powers of the governor and legislative capabilities as well as dummy variables representing the functional responsibilities of units. Colinearity between certain variables required that they not be entered together. When these variables emerged as significant predictors, the variable with the strongest theoretical link to gubernatorial impact was used.[7]

Table 7.5 summarizes the results of this analysis. Few variables emerge as significant predictors and even these have modest explanatory power. The best-fitting models account for about 14% of the variance in gubernatorial impact on the broader policies affecting a unit, but only 6–7% of the variance in gubernatorial impact on unit budgets, and 5% or less of the variation in the impact of the governor on a unit's rules and regulations, structures and procedures, and daily operations.

The most consistent predictor of gubernatorial impact is how administrators reached their positions, with those owing their positions most directly to the governor reporting greater gubernatorial influence. Method of selection is the most powerful predictor in every influence arena except daily operations. Even this predictor can account for no more than 5% of the variance in gubernatorial impact, however. Although the level of interaction between a governor and a unit emerges as a significant predictor in the case of four arenas and such interaction is especially important in the case of the impact that a governor is seen as having on daily operations, interaction typically accounts for only about 1% or so of the variance.

One or another of the other formal powers that governors possess emerges as a significant predictor in four arenas. The formal budgetary authority of a governor is associated with an increase in impact on overall budget levels, in particular, as well as on broader policies and the content of rules and regulations. A governor's formal organizational power is linked to greater impact on budgets for specific unit programs.

The functional responsibilities of a unit affected gubernatorial impact primarily in budgetary and policy arenas. Agencies with environmental responsibilities reported greater gubernatorial impact in these two arenas, while those with transportation responsibilities tended to report greater gubernatorial impact on broader policies. In no case, however, could functional responsibility account for much more than a percent of so of the variance in gubernatorial impact.

Finally, the quality of a state's legislature was unrelated to gubernatorial influence over agencies, except that legislative "functionality" was related to determination of major agency policies. But this relationship was positive not negative. In states with legislatures that have longer and more frequent sessions, more staff support, and more adequate facilities—all of which ought to enhance legislative influence in the policymaking process—governors seem to have somewhat greater power than is true in states with less "functional" legislatures.

This seeming anomaly is, however, consistent with the evidence that those

Table 7.5
Multivariate Models of Gubernatorial Impact on State Administrative Affairs

Arena of Influence[1]	Explained Variance (Adjusted R^2)	Predictors Accounting for at Least One Percent of Variance [2]	B[3]	Beta [4]	Variance Explained by Predictor
Impact on overall budget level of unit	.077	Method of selection	.152	.175	.030
		Gov. budget power	.140	.157	.024
		Gov. interaction	.160	.112	.012
Impact on budgets for specific unit programs	.062	Method of selection	.213	.170	.032
		Gov. organization power	.103	.130	.017
		Environmental func.	.435	.100	.010
Governor's impact on broader policies	.142	Method of selection	.230	.233	.054
		Legis. "functionality"	.010	.192	.037
		Gov. interaction	.188	.128	.016
		Transportation func.	.508	.122	.015
		Environmental func.	.535	.115	.013
		Gov. budget power	.115	.119	.010
Impact on content of rules and regulations	.037	Method of selection	.157	.147	.022
		Gov. budget power	.099	.113	.013
Impact on administrative structures and procedures	.049	Method of selection	.159	.161	.026
		Gov. interaction	.196	.121	.015
Impact on daily operations	.053	Gov. interaction	.233	.200	.040
		Method of selection	.111	.125	.015

1. Using stepwise regression techniques, various independent variables were used in an effort to account for variation in gubernatorial influence in particular arenas. These included the various formal powers of the governor noted in Table 7.2, with the exception that my own indicator of method of selection was substituted for Beyle's indicator of appointment power. Also entered into the model were the various indicators of legislative capability outlined in Table 7.2. The extent of gubernatorial interaction with a unit and the governor's orientation toward a unit were also used. Finally, the size of a unit, its functional responsibility, and its organizational "place" were used as predictors.

2. The regression equations of each of the arenas of influence were significant (Prob. of F, .001 or better). The table lists only those predictors that were significant (Prob. of F, .05 level) and that could account for a minimum of 1% of the variance in the impact of the governor in a particular arena. The final column of the table indicates the precise amount of variance accounted for by each of these predictors.

3. This is the unstandardized regression coefficient.

4. This is the standardized regression coefficient.

states that have strengthened their governors are often the same ones that have enhanced the capabilities of their legislatures. Indeed, the indicator of the "informedness" of a state legislature was highly correlated with the aggregate measure of gubernatorial formal powers as well as with the veto and organizational powers possessed by the governor. The formal budget power of the governor was colinear with the "independence" of the legislature. As a result it is impossible to determine the independent contributions of these differing indicators to gubernatorial impact. If both a legislative indicator and an indicator of the formal powers of the governor proved to be significant predictors when each was separately entered into the regression analysis, the indicator of formal gubernatorial power was included in the equation. This occurred in the model for gubernatorial impact on the budgets for specific unit programs. Organizational power emerged as a significant predictor; as did the "informedness" of the legislature when it was substituted for organizational power, a variable with which it is colinear. The same was true for the measure of legislative independence and the governor's formal budget power in this arena of influence.

The limited predictive power of the regression models is due to a number of factors, including the fact that I rely on administrators' estimates of gubernatorial influence.[8] Still, my success in accounting for variation in gubernatorial influence on state agency affairs in 10 states is comparable to that of scholars with a 50-state database who also rely on administrative judgments of gubernatorial influence. Using a measure of gubernatorial impact averaged across several arenas of influence similar to mine, and a set of independent variables that included some that are similar to those used in this study, Brudney and Hebert (1987) were able to account for approximately 20% of the variation in gubernatorial impact. Using variables that include the formal powers of the governor, various agency characteristics, and how an agency head was selected, among others, Hebert, Brudney, and Wright (1983) could account for 15% of the variation in gubernatorial impact, measured as in the Brudney and Hebert study.

Consistency with past research is evident as well in the predictive power of particular variables. Brudney and Hebert (1987) found the formal powers of a governor along with the influence of the governor in the selection of an agency head to be among the top two or three predictors in the set of a dozen or so variables included in their analysis. In the Hebert, Brudney, and Wright analysis, the index of formal gubernatorial power they used was among the most powerful predictors of gubernatorial influence, as was the nature of the appointment process and the fact that an administrator reported directly to the governor.

It is important to stress that the best predictors of gubernatorial influence are those that are subject to manipulation. Governors who interact more intensely with an agency have somewhat more influence. This seems to be especially true for gubernatorial influence on the day-to-day operations of a unit. If governors are indeed crisis managers, and if crises necessitate at least temporary involvement in the details of agency operation, my findings suggest that increased efforts to interact with agencies can enhance gubernatorial influence. A quarter of a century ago, in speaking of presidential relations with federal bureau chiefs, David Brown (1966) argued that it was not the unwillingness of administrators to follow presidential dictates that limited presidential influence so much as their lack of awareness of what presidential wishes regarding their unit and its operations are. Brown argued that presidents needed to do a much better job of communicating their preferences to the middle and lower levels of the federal bureaucracy where most of the work gets done. More recently, Durning (1986, p. 77) used the metaphor of an "internal campaign" to describe the efforts of governors to "influence the attitudes and beliefs of their employees." He went on to assert that those at the bottom of a state's administrative hierarchy, upon whose actions much of the success of any governor depends, will make the right decisions "if the internal campaign convinces them that the governor's values and priorities should guide their actions" (p. 81; see also Cole, 1989). Increased gubernatorial interaction may enhance gubernatorial influence because it reduces administrators' doubts about what a governor expects of them.

My findings, like those of other scholars, also indicate that the formal powers of governors—whether reflected in the processes used to staff state agencies, determine their budgets, or reorganize them—matter. These formal powers can be strengthened if an increase in gubernatorial influence is desired. At the same time, it is evident that formal powers are not the sole key to gubernatorial influence and that effective gubernatorial leadership may be possible even when formal powers are relatively limited (Brough, 1987).

A MULTIVARIATE MODEL OF DETERMINANTS OF LEGISLATIVE IMPACT ON STATE ADMINISTRATION

It is even more difficult to account for variation in legislative impact on state administration than for variation in gubernatorial impact. As Table 7.6 indicates, even as little as 5% of variance can be explained only in the two budgetary arenas. Method of selection was not a significant predictor. More so than was true of gubernatorial interaction with administrative units, frequency of communication between program or budget committees was a consistently significant predictor of variation in legislative impact.[9]

Although legislative capabilities were not related to variation in gubernatorial impact, certain formal powers possessed by governors were negatively associated with legislative impact in the case of budgetary decisions and the legislature's impact in determining broader agency policies. The capabilities of state legislatures themselves failed to emerge as significant predictors of legislative impact, except that more functional legislatures exerted somewhat greater influence in broader policymaking.[10]

This inability to explain much of the variation in legislative impact stems in part from the fact that such impact varies relatively little across agencies. The predictive power of formal legislative capabilities may also be limited because the indicators of these capabilities are dated. Their explanatory impotence also provides support for the argument that legislative influence is more a function of the will to oversee administrative operations than of the adequacy of the means to do so.

Substantial explanatory power may also be difficult to achieve without more detailed information on the political dynamics of particular states. One example will serve to make this point. Earlier it was noted that Michigan has one of the best developed arrangements for legislative review and possible veto of proposed agency rules. This may be why nearly 60% of Michigan administrators

Table 7.6

Multivariate Models of Legislative Impact on State Administrative Affairs

Arena of Influence[1]	Explained Variance (Adjusted R^2)	Predictors Accounting for at Least One Percent of Variance[2]	B[3]	Beta[4]	Variance Explained by Predictor
Overall budget level of unit	.060	Interact/budget comm.	.207	.182	.033
		Income security func.	-.346	-.123	.015
		Total powers of gov.	-.024	-.099	.010
Budgets for specific unit programs	.058	Interact/budget comm.	.260	.210	.044
Determining broader policies affecting unit	.040	Interact/prog. comm.	.181	.137	.019
		Gov. organization power	-.077	-.112	.013
		Legis. "functionality"	.088	.108	.012
Content of rules and regulations	.021	Natural resources func.	.327	.100	.010
Establishing unit structure and procedures	.017	None			
Daily operations	.042	Interact/budget comm.	.242	.207	.042

1. The independent variables used in the stepwise regressions were the same as those used to predict gubernatorial impact (see note 1 of Table 7.5) with the following exceptions. Interaction with the governor was replaced by interaction with program and budget committees, and legislative committee orientation toward a unit replaced gubernatorial orientation toward it. Emphasis on legislative oversight was also added as a predictor. The equations for legislative impact in particular arenas were all significant (Prob. of F, .01 level or better).

2. The table lists only those predictors that were significant (F-test) at the .05 level or better and that could account for at least 1% of the variation in legislative impact in a particular arena. The final column of the table indicates the precise percentage of variance accounted for by each of these predictors.

3. Unstandardized regression coefficient.

4. Standardized regression coefficient.

saw the legislature as exerting great or very great impact on the content of rules and regulations, while the average for the other nine states was 39%.

In any event, I am hardly alone in having limited success in accounting for variation in legislative impact on state administrative affairs. In their 50-state study, Brudney and Hebert (1987) are able to account for only 5% of variation in legislative influence, using a model that includes a dozen independent variables. In their analysis as in mine, how administrators reached their positions was unrelated to variation in legislative influence, while extent of legislative professionalism was only modestly related to increased influence.

MANAGEMENT PROBLEMS, MANAGEMENT TECHNIQUES, AND GUBERNATORIAL AND LEGISLATIVE IMPACT

This section of the chapter places the discussion of the influence of the legislature and the governor on state administrative agencies in the context of the examination of impediments to effective management and the utilization and

efficacy of various strategies for improving the performance of state agencies
that was the focus of Chapters 2, 3, and 4. To this point, the question of
whether or not the levels of gubernatorial and legislative impact that exist in
the 10 study states are "appropriate" has not been addressed. Some level of
influence by elected officials on the actions of nonelected administrators is essential in democratic polities. The desirability of such influence must, however,
be balanced against the costs for administrative efficiency and effectiveness that
may result from the efforts of legislators and governors to influence administrative affairs. Several scholars have lamented the lack of attention to the consequences of legislative oversight and have questioned the common, if implicit,
assumption that "more oversight is better than less" (Bowers, 1989, p. 218;
see also Aberbach, 1979, and Rockman, 1985). Since my data indicate that
fairly substantial levels of both gubernatorial and legislative influence on various decisions affecting or actions of state administrative units already exist,
increasing such influence may be counterproductive. Insight into the consequences of legislative and gubernatorial influence can be gained by reexamining
the severity of certain management "problems" first considered in Chapter 2.

Legislatures as Impediments to Effective Management

Various impediments to "effective management" that can be said to involve
the legislature in some way are listed in Table 7.7. Only a few of these problems are viewed as serious by more than one manager in four. Two are budgetary in nature—an alleged tendency for the legislature to expand responsibilities but not provide agencies with sufficient additional dollars to carry out
those expanded responsibilities, and appropriations that are inadequate. The
other major legislatively related problem is the complexity of the process for
promulgating rules and regulations. While not a situation for which the legislature is solely to blame, state legislative enthusiasm for adding or strengthening rule review or veto provisions to administrative procedure acts often makes
the process more complex and time consuming. Michigan has the largest percentage of managers (45%) who consider the complexity of the rulemaking
process to be a serious problem, and Michigan has a well-established process
for legislative review and possible disapproval of proposed rules. In South Dakota and New York, two states that do not provide for legislative veto, less
than 20% felt the complexity of the rulemaking process was a problem.

Relatively few managers see the other "legislative" problems as severe,
however. Consistent with the findings on levels of legislative influence in daily
operations, only one manager in ten believed that "legislative meddling in purely
administrative matters" seriously impeded effective management. Few managers considered accommodating requests or intervention by legislators on behalf of constituents to be a serious problem. This may be so because administrators believe that handling such requests has important political and other
benefits for their agencies (Elling, 1979, 1980b; Abney and Lauth, 1986a).

Table 7.7

Correlations Between Legislature-Related Management Problems and Committee Interaction and Orientation

Legislature-Related Problem	Percent of Managers Viewing Problem as Serious[1]	Correlation of Problems With:			
		Communication with Program (Budget) Committee[2]		Orientation of Program (Budget) Toward Unit Committee[3]	
Insufficient budgetary support	45%	.05	(.04)	-.21*	(-.33*)
Legis. expansion of unit programs without commensurate appropriations increases	41	.16*	(.07*)	-.16*	(-.25*)
Complex and lengthy process for rule promulgation	40	.09*	(.07*)	-.10*	(-.06)
Excessive restrictions on expenditure of appropriations	23	.08*	(.08*)	-.20*	(-.24*)
Adoption of programs difficult to implement effectively	17	.13*	(.09)	-.20*	(-.15*)
Insufficient legis. interest in unit	16	-.08	(-.02)	-.25*	(-.30*)
Specific legislative language limiting discretion needed to effectively implement programs	12	.11*	(.09*)	-.15*	(-.15*)
Legislative meddling in purely administrative matters	11	.25*	(.17*)	-.20*	(-.13*)
Vague legislative intent	10	.03	(.04)	-.13*	(-.11*)
Legislator inquiries regarding actions affecting constituents	5	.12	(.08*)	-.16*	(-.11*)

1. Table entry is percentage of managers considering given problem to be a "serious" or "very serious" hindrance to the efficient and effective administration of the programmatic responsibilities of their units.

2. Asterisk indicates Pearson's r significant at .05 level. Correlations in parentheses are between management problem and <u>interaction</u> with budget committees.

3. Asterisk indicates Pearson's r significant at .05 level. Correlations in parentheses are between management problem and <u>orientation</u> of budget committees.

Since interaction was related to legislative impact, it may be that the perceived severity of legislative problems may also be related to the intensity of interaction with legislative committees. Table 7.7 indicates this is indeed the case. Frequency of communication with program committees is most strongly correlated with complaints about inappropriate legislative meddling, about the legislature's tendency to expand programs without sufficient revenues, the adoption of hard-to-implement programs, having to accommodate legislators' inquiries on behalf of constituents, and specific language limiting administrative discretion. The correlations between the perceived severity of these problems and interaction with budget committees are similar, although generally smaller, than those between problem severity and interaction with program committees.

The positive correlations between complaints about legislative efforts to limit discretion, and between limitations placed on the expenditure of appropriations, and committee interaction, mirror the findings of Abney and Lauth (1986b). They report that administrative discretion in expending appropriations was most circumscribed for those agencies whose heads more often testified before legislative committees.

The smallest correlations between interaction with either type of committee and legislative "problems" existed for complaints about vague or ambiguous legislative intent, inadequate budgets, and a lack of legislative interest. The need to use general language to build legislative majorities may be such that clarity of legislative intent is a problem even when high levels of communication between agencies and the legislature exist. There may be no significant correlation between complaints about inadequate budgets and intensity of committee communication because low budget levels primarily reflect factors constraining revenue availability. While the correlations between committee communication and an agency feeling ignored by the legislature were not significant, they did have the expected negative sign.

The orientation of legislative committees toward particular units has been shown to bear little relationship to committee interaction or the impact of the legislature on them. But the relationships between the orientation of program and budget committees toward units and perceptions of the severity of certain "legislative" problems indicate that committee orientation matters. Administrators who consider program committees to be consistently supportive of their unit and its programs are less likely to complain about various problems (see Table 7.7). Nor are these relationships a product of the fact that managers in certain states may encounter a generally more positive or negative legislature. With few exceptions, the same relationship between a less positive committee orientation and more severe problems exists for individual states.[11]

A more hostile relationship with budget committees is similarly related to more severe "legislative" problems. The relationships are even stronger for fiscal problems such as inadequate budgets, limits on expenditure of appropriations, and the tendency for the legislature to expand programs without additional resources. Again, this relationship between budget committee orientation and problems is consistent across the states.[12] Unhappy committees are inclined to make fewer resources available to a unit and to place limits on the use of those resources that are provided.

It is difficult to make sense of the negative relationships between committee orientation and various other "legislative" problems, however. Why should administrators confronting more hostile committees report both more meddling *and* a lack of legislative interest in their units? Perhaps the explanation is that the committees exhibit the wrong kind of interest—unfriendly as opposed to friendly. Or perhaps an agency that has, for reasons that may include programmatic failure, lack of adequate leadership, and a fragmented clientele, failed to establish a positive relationship with key legislative actors may view all that the legislature does negatively.

Despite the fact that variation in legislative capacity was only weakly related to variation in legislative impact upon state administration, the existence of a more capable legislature may exacerbate certain legislatively related management impediments while it reduces the severity of others. Better informed, more independent, or more functional legislatures may be more "meddlesome" and may more actively seek to limit administrative discretion. More professional legislatures may legislate more effectively so that vague legislative intent or the adoption of hard-to-implement programs is less of a problem. Changes that expand legislative staffing may permit more extensive casework-handling by legislators and increase managerial complaints about the burden of responding to such inquiries. On the other hand, professionalization may have little to do with problems of low budgets or adding programs with too few additional dollars, since these problems stem from state fiscal circumstances more than anything else.

No significant relationships existed between the placing of "excessive" restrictions on how agencies could expend their appropriations and various legislative capabilities. Nor were more professionalized legislatures seen as more likely to create administrative problems by including "specific language in legislation limiting discretion necessary to effectively implement programs." Bureaucratic critics who believe that abuse of administrative discretion is a problem, and that more capable legislatures will be able to influence the course of policy implementation by more precisely specifying legislative intent, can take little comfort in this finding. Nor can they take comfort in the absence of significant relationships between the various indicators of legislative quality and managers' perceptions of legislative vagueness as a problem. The existence of a more capable legislature is, however, associated with greater administrative concern over the complexity and length of the rule promulgation process. Correlations between the severity of this problem and various indicators of legislative capability ranged from .08 for the overall indicator, to .11 for legislative independence, and .12 with functionality. It may be that more capable legislatures seek to limit administrative discretion by involving themselves more directly in rulemaking through the type of procedure used in Michigan—a state with a highly functional and independent legislature.

Administrators in states with more capable legislatures actually complained more, not less, about the passage of legislation that was difficult to implement. Correlations ranging from .11 to .15 existed between the overall indicator of legislative quality and each of the individual indicators, except for "informedness," and the proportion of managers who saw this as an impediment to effective management. Legislators in more capable legislatures may be more confident of their ability to address public problems. But the solutions to these problems may be administratively more complex.

The data provide little support for concerns that legislative reform will stimulate undesirably high levels of legislative intrusion into more narrowly administrative realms. In addition to the earlier noted findings that efforts to control how appropriations are expended, or to otherwise limit administrative discretion, are no more of a problem in states with more capable legislatures; only small, albeit positive, correlations of .07 exist between complaints about legislative "meddling in purely administrative affairs" and the fact that a legislature is more functional or more independent. Recall that legislative independence was also modestly and positively correlated with an increased emphasis on oversight. One manifestation of this may be increased legislative involvement in daily operations. Providing additional support for this hypothesis is the finding that overall legislative capability, and all of the individual dimensions of capability except "informedness," are negatively correlated with administrative complaints that the legislature ignores them, with correlations ranging from $-.09$ to $-.16$. In addition, when the legislature is more capable, greater administrative concern exists over the complexity of the process required for agencies to promulgate rules and regulations. At the same time, administrators in states with more capable legislatures are not more likely to complain about having to handle legislators' inquiries concerning agency actions affecting their constituents. Indeed, the only significant correlation that emerges is a negative one ($-.12$) between perceptions of casework-handling as a problem and a legislature being informed. In short, the findings suggest that hopes as well as fears concerning the consequences of enhanced legislative capacity for administrative performance are exaggerated.

The level of influence that the legislature exerts over an agency is much more clearly related to differences in administrators' perceptions of the severity of various legislature-related impediments to effective management than are differences in legislative capability. Significant positive correlations existed between legislative impact in various arenas and the severity of most of the problems. Managers who report greatest legislative impact on daily operations are more likely to see casework-handling as a problem ($r = .13$). This suggests that casework is an important way for legislators to become involved in the daily affairs of an agency. Complaints about legislative "meddling" in purely administrative matters were also most strongly correlated with legislative impact on daily operations ($r = .13$) Administrators were slightly more likely to complain that the legislature expands their unit's responsibilities without sufficient additional funding when it had greater impact on the determination of overall agency budgets ($r = .08$) and on broader agency policies ($r = .09$). A legislature that has more impact on the overall budget level for a unit is also more likely to be said to approve inadequate budgets ($r = .07$). The exerting of greater influence by the legislature in various arenas is also associated with more complaints about limits on how budgeted funds can be expended, about the complexity of the rules process, legislative limits on agency discretion, and the adoption of programs that are difficult to implement.

While we would expect that complaints about being ignored by the legislature would decline as legislative influence grows, no significant negative correlations emerged. Finally, legislatures that legislate in more specific terms ought to exert greater influence. Hence, when legislative influence is greater, complaints about legislative vagueness as a problem ought to be less common. But the expected negative relationships did not emerge. Indeed, significant positive correlations, albeit modest ones, existed between the severity of legislative vagueness as a management problem and the legislature's impact on rules and regulations (r = .07), unit procedures (r = .06), and daily operations (r = .06). As noted above, the need to use vague language to construct legislative majorities may outweigh the attractiveness of more specific language as a way for the legislature to shape the administration of programs.

Governors and Management Problems

Given the limited role of governors in more narrowly administrative realms, it is hardly surprising that only 5% of managers considered "gubernatorial meddling in purely administrative matters" to be a serious impediment to effective management. Nor—given limited gubernatorial interaction with most administrative units and the fact that many managers believe gubernatorial interaction with their units occurs only when something goes seriously wrong—is it surprising that more of them (13%) considered "insufficient gubernatorial interest in agency programs and operations" to be a problem.

In contrast to the legislative pattern, no significant positive correlation exists between complaints about gubernatorial meddling and intensity of interaction with the governor (r = .02). This may be so because managers prefer gubernatorial to legislative influence (Haas and Wright, 1987; Miller, 1987). In a two-state study, Elling (1980a) found that three times as many Minnesota administrators, and nearly twice as many Kentucky administrators, felt that legislative interference made it harder for them to do an effective job as said that this was true of gubernatorial interference. This suggests that administrators are more sensitive or resistant to legislative involvement in daily administrative affairs and may explain why the proportion of managers complaining about legislative meddling is more than twice as great as those who consider such meddling by governors to be a serious problem. It may also be why an increase in gubernatorial interaction is significantly correlated with a decline in complaints about a lack of gubernatorial interest in their unit (r = −.07) while this was not true of complaints about a lack of legislative interest and legislative interaction. Recall, as well, that legislative committees were less supportive of state administrative units. Increased interaction is less desirable if what prompts it is dissatisfaction with a unit's performance, something that is more likely in the case of the legislature than the governor.[13]

As in the case of the legislature, the governor's orientation toward a unit is strongly and negatively correlated with managers' complaints about being ignored by the governor (r = −.49) as well as with complaints about the gubernatorial "meddling" in purely administrative matters (r = −.34). Units toward which the governor is favorably disposed may benefit from greater gubernatorial interest at the same time that such increased interest is not expressed as involvement in more narrowly administrative matters. Differently put, the governor may be seen as interested in the sense that he or she supports what an agency is doing. Since this is so, the governor sees no need to become actively involved in daily administrative operations.

Moreover, and despite the fact that the governor's orientation toward a unit is only modestly correlated (.22) with the orientation of program or budget committees, gubernatorial orientation is negatively related to various "legislative" problems that might also stem to some extent from gubernatorial actions. The less supportive a governor is of a unit, the more likely managers are to complain about programs being expanded without sufficient additional funding (r = −.16), that the rulemaking process is too complex (r = −.14), that excessive limits are placed on how appropriations can be expended (r = −.24), that statutory language too narrowly limits administrative discretion (r = −.13), and that budgets are too low (r = −.27). Governors who believe that particular agencies are not doing what they should be doing may seek to reorient them using one or more of the above strategies.

Formal gubernatorial powers and gubernatorial impact are less consistently related to managers' complaints about various problems. Managers in states with formally more powerful governors are actually somewhat *more* likely to complain about a lack of gubernatorial interest in their unit (r = .07). That larger states with more complex bureaucracies tend to have more powerful governors may explain why this is so. The only significant relationship between formal powers and complaints about inappropriate gubernatorial "meddling" is a small negative (r = −.07) correlation with the governor's tenure potential.

On the other hand, using the measure of method of selection that has been among the most consistent predictors of differences in gubernatorial influence on state agencies, it is the case that complaints about being ignored by the governor are rarer among those managers who owe their positions to the governor most directly (r = −.08). But the correlation represents only a difference between the 9% of managers appointed by the governor, with or without legislative consent, who complain about being ignored, and the 13% of agency-head-appointed, and the 14% of classified civil servants, who considered insufficient gubernatorial interest to be a serious impediment to effective management of their units.

Inadequate budgets, a complex rulemaking process, and excessive limits on the expenditure of unit appropriations may be problems for which governors as well as legislators are responsible. While no significant correlations existed between various formal powers of governors and the complexity of the rulemaking process, complaints about low budgets were more common among managers in states whose governors have stronger appointment powers (r = .07), stronger budgetmaking powers (.10), or were more powerful overall (.11). A stronger hand in staffing the state bureaucracy and in constructing the state budget may make it easier for a governor to restrain agency spending. Stronger appointment powers are also modestly correlated with complaints about limits on the expenditure of appropriations (r = .06), although neither formal budget powers nor overall powers are significantly related.

Turning from formal gubernatorial powers to estimates of actual influence, we see that increased gubernatorial influence is positively associated with complaints about inappropriate gubernatorial meddling in administrative matters. Although gubernatorial impact in all arenas is positively associated with meddling, the correlations are especially strong with gubernatorial impact on regulations (r = .12), administrative procedures and processes (r = .15), and daily operations (r = .12).

Complaints about a lack of gubernatorial interest might be expected to decrease as gubernatorial influence increases. However, no significant correlations emerged between this situation and gubernatorial influence, although the correlations had the right sign in the case of gubernatorial influence in five of the arenas. Complaints about an excessively complex rule promulgation process were also somewhat more common from managers who see the governor as having a greater ability to shape budgets for specific programs (r = .07) and to shape agency procedures (r = .06). Complaints about restrictions on the expenditure of appropriated funds were slightly more common from managers who perceived greater gubernatorial impact on daily operations.

Regression analysis confirms as well as clarifies the implications of the analysis of correlates of "legislative" and "gubernatorial" management problems. The orientation of key committees toward a unit is the most powerful predictor of complaints about a lack of legislative attention, inadequate budgets, the expansion of programs without sufficient additional funds, legislative language limiting discretion, and handling casework, accounting for 2% to 11% of variation in the severity of these problems. In all instances, the coefficients are negative. All of these problems are seen to be more severe when legislative committees are less supportive. Committee orientation is among the significant predictors in the case of all other "legislative" problems, except for complaints about the complexity of the rule promulgation process.

Intensity of committee interaction is a significant predictor in the case of five problems: adoption of hard-to-implement programs, complexity of the rulemaking process, expansion of programs without commensurate appropriations increases, handling casework, and, most strongly, complaints about legislative meddling, where it accounts for 6% of the variation. One or another legislative capability was a significant predictor only of adoption of hard-to-implement programs (where functionality could account for 2% of variation) and handling casework (where "informedness" could account for 1% of variation). Legislative influence emerged as a significant predictor only in the case of the 1% of variance in the severity of casework-handling and legislative meddling explained by legislative impact on daily operations.

The governor's orientation toward a unit was the only significant predictor of complaints about a lack of gubernatorial interest. When the governor is hostile, a lack of attention is not the problem. Indeed, orientation can account for 24% of variation in complaints about insufficient gubernatorial interest. Here is further evidence of a crisis-driven management style. Gubernatorial orientation also explains 11% of variation in complaints about excessive meddling. Managers who report more positive interaction complain about meddling less.

"Meddling" in administrative affairs is also more common when the governor has more impact on administrative procedures, with this factor accounting for 2% of variation. Gubernatorial orientation is the most powerful predictor of complaints about excessive limits on the expenditure of appropriations, accounting for 6% of variation, and of the adoption of hard-to-implement programs, accounting for 5% of the variance. Orientation is also among the significant predictors of complaints about inadequate budgets, the expansion of programs without sufficient additional funding, the limiting of administrative discretion, and the complexity of the rulemaking process. In all cases the relationship is negative. Agencies toward whom the governor is less favorably disposed report these problems to be more serious.

To summarize, circumstances whose existence may plausibly be attributed in whole or in part to the actions of the legislature or the governor sometimes constitute serious impediments to effective management. Variation in the severity of these problems is sometimes related to the formal powers or capabilities of a state legislature, to the formal powers of the governor, or to the influence of either actor on agency affairs.

Are these management situations truly "problems," however? Even if we grant that these situations do impede effective management, most managers consider few of them to be serious. Moreover, differences in the severity of these problems as a function of formal gubernatorial powers and influence, or of legislative capabilities and influence, are not great. Strengthening the ability of legislatures or governors to influence administrative units does not seem to be exacting an unreasonable toll on administrative effectiveness in these 10 states.

GOVERNORS, LEGISLATURES, AND STATE MANAGEMENT IMPROVEMENT

William Gormley (1989b) has argued persuasively that governors and legislatures ought to eschew *coercive* means of increasing their influence in the administrative process in favor of *catalytic* controls. The former, represented by legislative vetoes, executive orders, and other "solution-forcing statutes" (p. 13), are designed to severely limit bureaucratic options. Catalytic controls, in contrast, encourage considerable bureaucratic discretion but seek to influence administrative decisionmaking by expanding the range of issues and alternatives that administrators consider in discharging their responsibilities. Gormley argues that catalytic controls foster bureaucratic flexibility and innovation, while the imposition of coercive controls risks formalism, legalism, and micromanagement. Nevertheless, coercive-type controls continue to attract the interest of governors and legislators.

In Chapter 4 we saw that state managers were least sanguine about those strategies for "improving" the operation of their units that reduced their autonomy. A number of the management "improvement" strategies first discussed in Chapter 4 have the likely effect of increasing the influence of the legislature or the governor. Legislative influence may be increased by sunset laws that provide for the termination of programs or agencies at specified intervals unless the legislature acts to retain them; by legislative review and/or veto of proposed agency rules; and through the activities of a legislative postauditor. On the other hand, legislative influence is presumably reduced when agencies receive appropriations as a lump sum absent line-item appropriations detail, or when an agency can reprogram budgeted funds.

Gubernatorial influence ought to increase if agency heads are subject to appointment by the governor, if reorganization has occurred, if the governor possesses the authority to undertake reorganization subject only to legislative veto within a short period, and if a career executive system or "senior executive service" exists. Both legislative and gubernatorial influence may increase if fewer middle and upper level managers are covered by civil service. The use of zero-base budgeting methods may also increase the influence of the governor as well as the legislature.

Considerable variation exists in the extent to which units have been affected by one or another of these practices. Most widely used were reorganization (with 69% of managers reporting that it had been been used in or affected their units), gubernatorial appointment of high level managers (49%), zero-base budgeting (46%), legislative postaudit (45%), legislative review or veto of proposed rules (42%), and use of sunset laws (41%). Less commonly used in a particular state or affecting a given unit were provisions permitting agencies to reprogram funds (29%), a "rollback" of civil service coverage (26%), lump-sum appropriations (25%), career executive systems (20%), the expansion of civil service coverage (9%), and the governor possessing greater authority to undertake reorganization (7%). Those "improvements" likely to enhance either legislative or gubernatorial influence are much more common than are those that would reduce the impact of these actors.

While administrators are often uncertain about the benefits for agency management of those techniques that increase gubernatorial influence, they are especially unenthusiastic about those that increase legislative influence.[14] Consistent with other scholarship, it appears that if an increase in control must occur, administrators prefer that it involve the governor rather than the legislature.

Among those who were familiar with a particular practice—regardless of whether it was actually used in or affected their unit—51% felt that legislative review/veto of agency rules had negative effects for management effectiveness while only 34% felt it had positive effects (the remaining respondents felt it would not affect agency performance one way or the other). Negative assessments of efficacy outweighed positive assessments in the case of reducing civil service coverage as well, with only 41% believing this would have a positive effect. On the other hand, only half felt that expanding civil service coverage was a good idea either. The proportion viewing this as a bad idea (35%) ranked third among the techniques.

More than half of the respondents believed sunset laws, giving the governor more power to undertake reorganization, expanding the governor's ability to appoint administrators, and zero-base budgeting to have positive effects for agency performance, although approximately a third of those familiar with any one of these felt it had negative effects.

State managers were more enthusiastic about the impact of a legislative post-auditor (62% positive, 19% negative) and reorganization (75% positive, 22% negative). The former, of course, only involves the legislature in post hoc review of agency operations. Managers were also quite enthusiastic about career executive systems (77% positive, 12% negative). Although such systems may increase gubernatorial control, they may also provide important opportunities for upward mobility and enhanced salaries. Finally, these managers were certain of the benefits of lump-sum appropriations and possessing the authority to redirect funds within their budgets. As many as 80% saw the former as having positive effects for agency operations while 86% saw the latter as having positive effects.

Regardless of what managers think of them, legislators or governors advocate various of the practices under consideration here at least in part because they believe these practices will enhance their ability to influence administrative affairs. It appears from the data, however, that only some of these strategies increase legislative or gubernatorial influence.

Governors are most clearly strengthened by an increase in the number of administrators subject to their appointment. This finding is consistent with evidence that the best predictor of gubernatorial impact is how administrators secure their positions. Only 30% of those who saw the governor as having no impact on overall budget levels reported the existence of efforts to expand the governor's powers of appointment, and this was true for just 41% of those who reported that the governor had only "some impact" on broader policy. But 52% of those reporting moderate impact, 62% of those reporting great impact, and 73% of those reporting very great impact on broader policy had experienced such an expansion in the appointment authority of the governor.

Often the impact of various strategies for enhancing gubernatorial influence was most evident at the extremes. Only 19% of managers who said the governor had no impact on budget levels for specific programs reported the existence of efforts to reduce civil service coverage for middle and upper level managers. But among those managers who said that the governor had even "some" impact, 34% said efforts along these lines had occurred. This proportion was nearly as great as the percentage of managers reporting very great gubernatorial impact who said their unit had been affected by such efforts (40%). Similar patterns existed for reorganization, zero-base budgeting systems, and career executive arrangements. Only 56% of managers who said the governor had no impact on overall budget levels had been affected by reorganization efforts as compared to more than 70% of the managers reporting greater gubernatorial impact.

Sometimes the use of a particular method only enhanced gubernatorial influence in a single arena. Although there was some evidence that managers subject to greater gubernatorial impact had been affected by efforts to reduce civil service coverage, the differences were especially sharp for influence on daily operations. Only 26% of those who said the governor had no impact on daily operations reported the existence of efforts to roll back civil service, as did 35% of those who reported only some gubernatorial impact. In contrast, 67% of the managers who accorded the governor very great impact upon daily operations were in units that had been affected by such efforts.

Only some of the techniques presumably designed to increase legislative influence clearly did so. As was true of techniques to increase gubernatorial impact, the effect of such techniques was most visible at the extremes. Thus, 30% of managers who said the legislature had no impact on overall budget levels reported the existence of legislative rule review or veto provisions, as opposed to 50% or more of those perceiving greater legislative impact. As might be expected, the impact of the legislative veto was clearest for the determination of the content of rules and regulations. Only 28% of those units reporting no legislative impact in this arena said legislative review or veto of rules affected their unit. This compares to nearly 50% of the managers who reported great or very great legislative impact on the content of rules and regulations.

Efforts to reduce civil service coverage and to budget using zero-base methods were both associated with increased legislative influence, although the effects were most visible at the extremes and primarily for specific arenas. Only 18% of the managers who said the legislature had no impact on overall budget levels reported the existence of ZBB. This compares to 44% of those who reported moderate legislative influence, and more than 50% of those experiencing great or very great impact. As was true for gubernatorial impact, a rollback in civil service coverage most enhanced legislative impact on daily operations. Approximately 33% of the managers who reported either no or only some legislative impact on daily operations were in states or units that had experienced such efforts as compared to 60% of the managers who reported very great legislative influence upon daily operations.

The existence of sunset laws did little to enhance legislative influence. In several arenas, the proportion of managers reporting that their units were affected by sunset laws was lower for managers reporting greater legislative influence.[15] Administrative enthusiasm for being able to reprogram budgeted funds may be due in part to the fact that the possession of this authority is associated with a decrease in legislative control over the agency in budgetary matters. Of those who said the legislature had no impact on the budgets for specific unit programs, 58% possessed the authority to reprogram funds, as did 55% of those who felt the legislature had only some impact. Among managers reporting legislative influence to be great or very great, however, only about 40% possessed this authority. The fact that agencies received lump-sum appropriations was not, however, similarly related to variation in the legislature's say in budgetary affairs.

In short, some of the management techniques presumed to increase the ability of the governor or the legislature to influence administrative affairs appear to have that effect. This may be why managers are unenthusiastic about them. State managers tend to believe that good management is enhanced to the extent that the influence of external political actors is reduced. On the other hand, and consistent with the argument in Chapter 2 that an "if-only" style of management is not the norm, many managers see even those approaches that enhance the influence of legislatures or governors in state management to have beneficial effects. Thus, 33% of them believed legislative review or veto of proposed rules or regulations had positive effects. More than 40% saw efforts to roll back civil service as having positive effects, while nearly 60% viewed an expansion in the appointment power of the governor favorably. Together with the fact that administrators did not see most problems that might be attributed to the actions of the legislature or governor to be especially serious impediments to effective management, their relatively sanguine view of the consequences of these strategies for improving management would seem to indicate acceptance of the legitimacy of the influence that these two actors wield. Efforts to expand legislative influence tend to be viewed less favorably than those that benefit the governor, however. Perhaps this is because governors are generally more favorably inclined toward state administrative units than are legislatures. It may also reflect the fact that legislatures already exert more influence than governors in most cases.

CONCLUSION

This chapter has focused on the role of governors and legislatures in the conduct of state administration. Consistent with the findings of other scholars, in the 10 study states the legislature generally seems to exert more influence in the administrative process than does the governor. The data presented in the chapter permitted us to extend the work of James Svara (1985). His analysis of the role of city councils versus city managers across four dimensions of the governmental process portrayed a picture of "mission-management separation with shared responsibility for policy and administration." The patterns of influence for both governors and legislatures in the 10 states across the six influence arenas—particularly the fact that the impact of each declined steadily and substantially as one moved from more broadly political budgetary or policymaking realms to more narrowly administrative realms—supports the validity of Svara's model (see Figure 7.1).

But variation in gubernatorial and legislative influence was also evident. One factor here involves differences in the formal powers possessed by governors. Governors with stronger formal powers—particularly appointive and budget powers—are more influential. But formal powers are not the entire story. Differences in the formal powers of governors explain relatively little variance. Differences among legislatures in their capabilities explained even less.

In the case of both governors and legislatures, intensity of interaction with administrative units made a difference. A governor, especially one with strong formal powers, willing to make the effort to influence administrative affairs should be able to overcome the influence advantage of the legislature. But legislative impact is also positively correlated with legislative interaction with administrative units, and the intensity of such interaction is generally greater than the intensity of gubernatorial interaction.

Precisely what promotes greater interaction is unclear, however. In the case of governors at least, the data provide some support for Weinberg's (1977) contention that gubernatorial interaction is prompted by the emergence of "crises" in the administration of particular programs or the operations of particular agencies. Waiting for crises is a high-risk management strategy. But it appears that even governors with strong formal powers often embrace it as they seek to function effectively as chief executives.

The existence of substantial legislative and gubernatorial influence on the course of state administration suggests that concerns about "runaway" state bureaucracies are exaggerated. But it raises others. The ability of governors and legislatures to influence aspects of the administrative process must be balanced against the costs for administrative efficiency and effectiveness that may flow from their involvement in administrative affairs. The severity of various legislature-related management problems was slightly greater in the case of units that interacted more intensely with legislative committees or over which the legislature generally exerted greater influence. But the correlations were modest. There was even less evidence that various management problems were related to intensity of gubernatorial interaction or impact. Nor did it appear that enhancing the formal powers or capabilities of governors or legislatures led to more serious problems.

State managers were not wildly enthusiastic about management "improvements" that promised to enhance gubernatorial control. They were even less enthusiastic about those likely to enhance legislative influence. Consistent with the arguments of William Gormley, the administrators I surveyed were particularly concerned about the negative consequences of "coercive" controls such as legislative review and/or veto of proposed rules and regulations.

At the same time, these managers often saw some benefit in even the most coercive of management "improvements." Combined with evidence that various legislature-related or governor-related management problems were rarely viewed as terribly severe, this suggests that substantial levels of legislative and gubernatorial influence on the administrative process can exist without exacting too high a price so far as state administrative efficiency and effectiveness are concerned. A major reason for this is that such influence tends to be confined to more broadly political realms.

Governors and legislatures are important external influences on the decisions affecting and actions taken by state agencies. But there are other important actors as well. Interest groups and agency clients are among them. Their role in state administration is the subject of Chapter 8.

NOTES

1. Discrete methods of appointment or selection were combined and ordered to produce a six-point scale similar to one used by Hebert, Brudney, and Wright (1983). The coding was such that a higher score indicated greater gubernatorial involvement in the selection process. The methods of selection, coding, and number of managers selected via each method are: (1) directly elected, 10; (2) appointed by a board or commission, 99; (3) selected and holding office under civil service procedures, 316; (4) appointed by the head of an agency, 269; (5) appointed by the governor with legislative confirmation required, 55; (6) appointed by the governor with appointment not subject to legislative confirmation, 63. Excluded from the coding were 34 managers who were selected in ways other than those indicated, such as appointed by the governor but serving a fixed term longer than the governor; or appointment by the governor to a position in the classified service. The board-appointed category included 23 managers appointed by a board with the governor's consent.

2. Unless otherwise noted, the correlations reported in the text are Pearson's r, significant at the .05 level or better, two-tailed test.

3. No significant correlations existed between increased legislative interest in oversight and the other indicators of legislative capability.

4. The positive impact of interaction on influence remains when controls for variation in specific gubernatorial powers are imposed. The tendency for administrators who interact more intensely with the governor to side with the governor in a conflict with the legislature also persists when controls for formal powers are imposed.

5. Because they were highly correlated, the number of employees in a unit and the size of its budget were separately entered as predictors. The variable with the greatest explanatory power is noted.

6. Within states, significant predictors of interaction with program committees emerge in all ten with the variance accounted from these predictors ranging from 6% in Tennessee to 31% in Arizona and Delaware. The organizational location of an administrator's unit was a significant predictor in seven states, accounting for between 11% and

23% of variance in interaction with program committees. The size of a unit's budget was a significant predictor in nine states, accounting for from 2% to 14% percent of variance. Together, organizational location and size of budget accounted for between 14% and 31% of the variance in 6 of the 10 states.

In the case of communication with budget committees, organizational location is a significant predictor in every state and is the most powerful predictor in eight states, while size of a unit's budget is a significant predictor in eight states and most powerful in South Dakota and Texas.

7. Each independent variable was regressed against the other independent variables to test for colinearity. Colinearity was evident in the case of certain indicators of formal gubernatorial powers with others, certain indicators of legislative capability with others, and between certain indicators of gubernatorial formal powers and certain indicators of legislative capability.

8. Given the limited predictive power of the models of determinants of gubernatorial impact, it is hardly surprising that the models that emerge when analysis is conducted for individual state samples differ from those for the sample as a whole. This point can be illustrated in the case of the arena for which I could account for the greatest proportion of the variance: broader policy. While no significant predictors of gubernatorial impact on the determination of broader policy emerged in either Vermont or Delaware, 41% of the variance could be accounted for in Arizona. Method of selection was a significant predictor in four states as was gubernatorial interaction. The functional responsibility of a unit emerged as a significant predictor in five states with units with income assistance responsibilities reporting less gubernatorial impact in two states and those with education responsibilities reporting lower gubernatorial impact in two.

9. Because of the substantial correlation between frequency of communication with program committees and frequency of communication with budget committees, indicators of both were not entered simultaneously. The indicator with greatest predictive power was used.

10. Oversight emphasis emerged as a statistically significant predictor only of increased legislative impact in determining administrative procedures and structures. This is not noted in Table 7.6 because it could explain less than 1% of variance.

11. Significant negative correlations between the orientation of program committees and the severity of problems existed in nine states and ranged from $-.11$ in California and $-.17$ in Texas to $-.36$ in South Dakota and $-.41$ in Arizona.

12. Significant negative correlations between budget committee orientation toward a unit and budget problems existed in each of the 10 states and ranged from $-.16$ in New York to $-.41$ in Arizona, $-.45$ in Texas, and $-.49$ in Indiana.

13. The correlation between gubernatorial interaction and orientation is .15 (p = .000), while that between program committee interaction and program committee orientation is only .05 (p = .06), and that between budget committee interaction and program committee orientation is .06 (p = .04).

14. As was true of managerial assessments of other techniques, there was a tendency for managers who had actually been affected by these techniques to be more positive about their effects. This was most evident in the case of an expansion of civil service coverage, expanding gubernatorial appointment power, a career executive service, reorganization, and, especially, zero-base budgeting. Those directly affected by practices likely to increase legislative influence were not typically more positive about their effects, however.

15. A study of the sunset experience of Tennessee (Lyons and Freeman, 1984) found that legislators believed that the existence of sunset provisions had increased their influence. Thus, 67% felt that sunset provisions had made agencies more conscious of legislative authority. But legislatures in other states have apparently come to less sanguine conclusions about the efficacy of the sunset process. Since 1983, 12 states have suspended or repealed their sunset review process (Kearney, 1990). None of the study states with sunset provisions at the time of the survey had taken such action, however.

Chapter 8

The "Public" Dimensions of the State Administrative Influence Matrix: State Agency Interaction with Interest Groups and Clients

INTRODUCTION

Since state agencies engage in activities that directly affect a state's citizens, these citizens have a stake in how the agencies discharge their responsibilities. For most, the reality of bureaucracy is manifested in their interaction with various "street level" bureaucrats. Both citizens and agencies are affected by these "public encounters" (Goodsell, 1981). When citizen or other societal interests are represented in a more organized fashion, the consequences for agency operations—both negative and positive—may be even greater. This chapter examines state administrative agency interaction with the "public." It begins with a brief discussion of the impact of several actors that constitute elements of an agency's public. This discussion extends that presented in Chapter 6. The interaction between state administrative agencies and organized interest groups, the purposes and character of such interaction, and sources of variation in such interaction are then focused upon. This is followed by efforts to identify some of the predictors of variation in interest group impact upon state administrative affairs and a discussion of the costs and benefits of such impact for state administration. The latter portion of the chapter focuses on state administrative interaction with clients.

The importance of interest groups in state politics is widely acknowledged and has received considerable scholarly attention. While the significance of administrative agency interaction with interest groups has also been recognized, it has received much less scholarly attention. Yet, as noted by Harmon Zeigler (1983, p. 123),

it is quite important to understand that estimates of group strength are usually based upon their role in the legislature, while the expansion of state government services has increased the role of administration. . . . The upshot of these developments is that it is no longer adequate to consider interest groups solely as they relate to legislatures, rather we need to know something about their participation in proposal development and other administrative activities.

Indeed this is so, but Zeigler himself devotes but a few paragraphs to administrative-interest group interaction and presents no comparative data on such interaction. More recently, an otherwise excellent examination of interest groups in state politics (Thomas and Hrebenar, 1990) includes virtually no discussion whatsoever of the relationships between interest groups and state agencies. And this in the face of a 1980 survey (Walker, 1991) of interest groups in which 80% of the respondents indicated that administrative lobbying was important or very important for the work of their organization, while 78% reported that legislative lobbying was of such importance.

A limited literature exploring the impact of organized groups on state administration has, however, begun to emerge. Studies by Wright and Light (1977), Miller (1987), and Brudney and Hebert (1987) examine the impact of interest groups, as well as that of other "public" components of a state agency's environment such as professional associations or clients, in one or more arenas of influence across all 50 states. William Gormley's (1983) multistate study of the dynamics of public utility regulation is another noteworthy addition to the relevant literature. A more recent effort by Gormley (1989b) features considerable discussion of efforts to restructure interaction between state agencies and organized groups, clients, and the general public (see especially, Chapter 3). The most important exception to the neglect of interest group-state administrative dynamics is Abney and Lauth's recent 50-state study (1986b), which explores the "contents and consequences of exchanges between state government department heads and interest groups." One goal of my 10-state study is to test as well as extend the conclusions of the Abney and Lauth work.

SOME PERSPECTIVE ON THE ROLE OF THE "PUBLIC" IN STATE ADMINISTRATION

The data presented in Chapter 6 (see Table 6.1) suggest that the public in its various guises exerts moderate impact on the making of decisions relevant to the fortunes of state agencies as well as on how those agencies discharge their responsibilities. In that chapter I classified interest groups—in the parlance of baseball—as "journeymen"—that is, as among those actors that have at least some impact across all arenas but whose impact is less than that wielded by "stars" such as governors or legislatures. Still, interest groups are among the five most influential actors in budgetary decisionmaking and are tied with three other actors for fourth rank so far as influencing the content of rules and regulations is concerned. Interest group impact is also relatively constant across states, varying significantly only in the case of impact on rules and regulations and daily administrative operations (see Tables 6.1 and 8.1).

Another component of the public dimension of an agency's environment—

Table 8.1

Interest Group, Professional Association, and Clientele Impact Across Influence Arenas, by State

	AZ	CA	DE	IN	MI	NY	SD	TN	TX	VT	Overall [2]
				Determining Overall Agency Budget Level							
Interest groups[1]	1.3	1.4	1.2	1.3	1.3	1.3	1.1	1.1	1.2	0.9	1.3 (.15)
Professional assoc.	0.8	0.7	0.6	0.9	0.8	0.6	0.6	0.6	0.8	0.5	0.7 (.14)
Clientele	1.3	1.4	1.3	1.1	1.3	1.1	1.1	1.0	1.2	1.0	1.2 (.12)
				Budget Level for Specific Agency Programs							
Interest groups	1.4	1.6	1.2	1.1	1.4	1.2	1.0	1.0	1.3	1.1	1.3 (.18)
Professional assoc.	0.8	0.6	0.6	0.8	0.8	0.6	0.7	0.5	0.8	0.4	0.7 (.13)
Clientele	1.2	1.4	1.2	1.0	1.2	1.2	0.9	1.0	1.2	1.0	1.2 (.14)
				Broader Policy/Program Changes							
Interest groups	1.4	1.6	1.3	1.2	1.6	1.3	1.1	1.4	1.5	1.1	1.4 (.15)
Professional assoc.	0.9	0.8	0.8	0.9	0.9	0.8	0.8	0.7	1.0	0.5	0.8 (.13)
Clientele	1.4	1.4	1.4	1.3	1.6	1.4	1.2	1.2	1.5	1.3	1.4 (.13)
				Content of Rules and Regulations							
Interest groups	1.4	1.7	1.4	1.3	1.6	1.4	1.2	1.2	1.4	1.2	1.4 (.18*)
Professional assoc.	1.0	0.8	0.9	1.0	1.1	0.9	0.8	0.7	1.0	0.5	0.9 (.17*)
Clientele	1.5	1.5	1.4	1.3	1.7	1.5	2.2	2.1	2.6	2.3	1.4 (.16)
				Establish Administrative Procedures and Structures							
Interest groups	0.9	1.2	1.0	0.9	1.1	1.0	0.8	0.7	0.9	0.8	1.0 (.15)
Professional assoc.	0.5	0.5	0.6	0.7	0.7	0.6	0.6	0.4	0.6	0.3	0.6 (.15)
Clientele	1.1	1.1	1.1	1.3	1.2	1.1	1.1	0.8	1.0	1.0	1.1 (.12)
				Daily Administrative Operations							
Interest groups	1.2	1.4	1.0	1.0	1.2	1.1	1.0	0.9	1.1	0.8	1.1 (.17*)
Professional assoc.	0.7	0.6	0.6	0.6	0.8	0.6	0.7	0.5	0.7	0.3	0.6 (.14)
Clientele	1.5	1.7	1.4	1.5	1.8	1.6	1.6	1.6	1.3	1.6	1.6 (.12)

1. The entry for each actor is the mean impact of that actor in a particular state or overall. Response options were: (0) no impact, (1) some impact, (2) moderate impact, (3) great impact, and (4) very great impact. Variation in the number of responding administrators across influence arenas, or actors is as follows: Overall: 790-817; Arizona: 61-63; California: 142-148; Delaware: 67-70; Indiana: 68-70; Michigan: 116-123; New York: 103-109; South Dakota: 60-62; Tennessee: 54-56; Texas: 70-86; Vermont: 33-34.

2. The parenthetical figure is the value of eta. When squared, it indicates the proportion of total variability in the dependent variable (the impact of a specific actor in a particular decision arena) that is explained by knowing the value of the independent variable (the state). An asterisk indicates eta is significant at the .01 level.

professional associations—exerts less influence than do interest groups. In Chapter 6 such organizations were classified as a "minor league" influence player. Significant interstate variation in the impact of this actor exists only for impact on the content of rules and regulations.

The influence of the clients of an administrative unit is—like that of organized interest groups—of the "journeyman" variety. The mean impact of the clientele of an agency (Table 6.1) is nearly identical to that of interest groups in five arenas and exceeds group impact in the case of daily administrative operations.

The impact attributed by state administrators to these public elements of an agency's influence environment is generally consistent with that found to exist by other scholars. On a 12-point scale, Brudney and Hebert (1987) found the impact of professional associations to average only 3.0, well behind that of the governor (9.2), the legislature (9.3), and clientele groups (4.9). Miller (1987) found that professional association impact ranked next to lowest across eight actors and was only slightly greater than that wielded by "citizens-at-large." In Miller's study, agency clientele—although seen to exert less influence than the agency head, legislature, governor, or agency employees—had a mean impact of 2.6 on a four-point scale. Abney and Lauth (1986b) found interest group impact to be relatively modest, with just 29% of the department heads they surveyed across the 50 states ranking interest groups as among the top three actors in impact on "agency programs and objectives." In relative terms, the impact of this actor trailed that of the legislature, governor, federal administrative agencies, the Congress, and the president.

Several difficulties exist in assessing the impact of various elements of the public dimension of a state administrative agency's influence environment. The first pertains primarily to assessing the impact of groups and, to a lesser extent, that of professional associations. Given the normatively ambiguous status of interest groups in American politics, and the opprobrium associated with being a "captured" administrative agency, one would expect managers to underestimate the influence of these two actors. Since it is presumably more acceptable for agencies to respond to clients, some interest group impact may be captured in administrators' estimates of clientele influence. "Professional association" may also be a more acceptable term than interest group.

This first point is related to a second. Although interest groups, professional associations, and the clients of an agency are conceptually distinct, overlap in influence estimates is likely among the three. Interest groups may represent clients of an agency but not all groups do so. Nor is it the case that all clients have the benefit of organized group representation. Professional associations often function much like interest groups and they may sometimes represent the concerns of clients.[1]

The substantial correlations that exist in the influence of these three elements of an agency's public are evidence of overlap in influence. In Chapter 6, factor analysis disclosed that these three actors loaded on the same "nongovernmental political actors'' factor. At the same time, while the impact exerted by these three external actors may overlap, they are not surrogates for one another. Evidence to support this assertion comes not only from the fact that the influence intercorrelations are far from perfect but also from variation in impact across arenas.[2] For instance, while in nearly every case the impact of nonadministrative actors is least on daily operations, clientele impact peaks in this arena (see Tables 6.1 and 8.1). This likely reflects that fact that, even if clients matter in no other way, their presence is a fundamental fact of life for the daily operations of state administrative agencies. In this arena, state administrators view clients as having an impact that is exceeded only by the agency itself. In contrast, interest group impact relative to that of other actors is greatest in determining the content of agency rules or regulations, where groups are tied for third rank.

A final difficulty in sorting out the impact of various elements of the public dimension of administrative agencies' environments is that such impact may be indirectly manifested. It may be wrapped up with the influence attributed to various elected officials or institutions, in particular the governor and the legislature. The influence of interest groups on administrative affairs may come via lobbying aimed at the decisions these actors make concerning agency affairs. The existence of legislative veto arrangements or sunset laws may—as noted in Chapter 7—present opportunities for organized interest groups to affect legislative decisions regarding administrative issues. Clients may influence agency affairs as legislators engage in constituency service and casework. When state agency heads were asked by Abney and Lauth (1986a) which route—the legislature, the governor, or ties with their agency itself—offered groups the best opportunity to influence policy, 49% rated influence with the legislature as most important, while just 44% ranked close ties with the agency first, and just 11% considered influence with the governor to be of greatest importance. Hence, some of the influence that the administrators in the 10-state study attributed to the legislature may be a manifestation of interest group influence.

In interpreting the nature and magnitude of the influence wielded by various elements of an administrative agency's ''public,'' it is well to keep the preceding caveats in mind. Still, the data at hand provide important insight into the interaction between state agencies and these public elements of their environment, and the consequences for state administration that result.

INTEREST GROUP-ADMINISTRATIVE AGENCY INTERACTION PATTERNS

As reported in Chapter 5, the administrators I surveyed reported that they devoted most of their time to internal management of their units or to working with fellow administrators or political officials in the development of broader agency policy and new programs. Also receiving considerable emphasis, however, was ''working with clientele or other nongovernmental groups in determining their interest and needs, and explaining, promoting, and implementing agency programs.'' Some 13% of the respondents said they spent more time on this function than any other, while 23% ranked it second. Moreover, when asked how much emphasis they preferred to place on this task, 20% gave it top priority and 27% ranked it second in preferred emphasis. Dealing with interest groups and clientele is an important part of the role conceptions and the world of these state managers.

Whatever else accounts for relatively limited interest group impact on state administrative affairs, it is certainly not a lack of interaction between groups and agencies. Overall, two-thirds of the administrators I surveyed reported that interest groups contacted their unit either frequently or very frequently (hereafter referred to as ''frequent'' interaction). The proportion reporting frequent group-initiated contacts ranged from 56% in Vermont to 75% in Michigan. Administrators reported only slightly lower levels of contacts with groups that had been initiated by their agencies. A high frequency of such unit-initiated contacts was indicated by 55%, with the proportion varying from 44% in Vermont to 62% in California. These data indicate that most units interact more intensely with interest groups than with either the governor or the legislature.

The moderate impact of groups on state administration despite high levels of interaction indicates that interaction does not automatically translate into influence. Intensity of interaction is, however, positively correlated with interest group influence. Depending upon the arena of influence, the correlations between frequency of group-initiated contacts and administrative perceptions of group impact range between .27 and .31 (all significant, p = .000, one-tailed test). Comparable correlations between group impact and the frequency of unit-initiated contacts with groups ranged from .20—for group impact on the content of rules and regulations—to .29—for group impact on budget decisions.

We might expect interest group impact to be greatest, and also most pernicious so far as the broader public interest is concerned, when intense group-initiated interaction occurs in the absence of a comparable level of unit-initiated contacts with groups. Conversely, we might expect group impact to be lower when contacts of both types are limited as well as when contacts of both types are extensive. When unit-initiated contacts are common but group-initiated contacts are not, group influence should be especially limited.

Symmetrical patterns of agency-interest group interaction are the norm. Almost half of the administrators reported high levels of both group and unit-initiated contacts (the ''mutually active'' pattern), while one quarter reported low levels of both types of contacts (the ''mutually inactive'' pattern).[3] If one is concerned about excessive interest group impact on administrative affairs, it may be good news that a ''besieged agency'' pattern—in which group-initiated contact is great while agency-initiated contact is not—occurs only 20% of the time. Finally, a situation in which unit-initiated interaction is intense but levels of group-initiated contact are not (the ''agency active'' pattern) occurs just 9% of the time.[4]

Variation in interest group impact across patterns of interaction is significant (eta statistics of .25 to .30, significant at the .000 level) and is as hypothesized with one exception. Regardless of the arena of influence considered, interest group impact is generally least when neither groups nor the administrative unit are active in seeking to influence one another. When an agency is active but groups are not, interest group impact is also low—although not quite so low as when neither the unit nor groups are active. Interest group impact is greater still in the ''besieged agency'' setting in which groups frequently contact units but units less often initiate contacts with groups. Thus, to take the broad policy arena as an example, the mean impact of groups in the ''mutually inactive'' situation is 0.9 as compared to 1.3 in the ''agency active'' case and 1.4 in the ''besieged'' case.

Group influence is greatest when both group and agency-initiated contacts are most intense. This is somewhat surprising since unit-initiated contacts might be expected to balance group-initiated contacts. One explanation for this finding is that those units exhibiting this pattern are vulnerable to interest groups because of other characteristics that have not been taken into account, such as their functional responsibilities. Alternatively, intense symmetrical interaction may enhance the power of both actors as an agency relies on interest group allies for support in dealing with the governor, the legislature, or other elements of its influence environment.

An agency may pay a price for such support by granting groups a greater voice in agency matters, however. Indeed, in every influence arena the difference between the impact of the agency itself and that of interest groups is smallest when a mutually active pattern of interaction exists. Moreover, in all but the two budgetary arenas, the pattern is for the agency's influence advantage to decline as one moves from the mutually inactive interaction pattern to that in which only the agency is highly active, that in which an agency is ''besieged'' by active interest groups, and, finally, to the mutually active situation. For example, the mean influence difference between agency impact and interest group impact on the content of agency rules and regulations declines from 2.1 units when neither agency nor interest groups are active, to 1.7 units when both are equally active. This suggests that, while an agency that takes the initiative in contacting groups enhances its own influence to some extent, when groups are also active any gain in agency influence is more than offset by an increase in the influence that groups exert.

OBJECTIVES OF AGENCY AND GROUP-INITIATED CONTACTS

The purposes that prompt interest group-administrative agency interaction provide additional insight into the nature and significance of that interaction. What do groups seek to gain as a result of their contacts? How do agencies seek to use interest groups? The top half of Table 8.2 summarizes administra-

Table 8.2

Purpose of Interest Group-Initiated Contacts with State Administrative Units, and of Unit-Initiated Contacts with Groups

	Percent of Administrators Indicating Contacts for a Given Purpose Are "Frequent" or "Very Frequent"										
	Overall	AZ	CA	DE	IN	MI	NY	SD	TN	TX	VT
Purpose of Interest Group-Initiated Contacts with Administrative Units [1]											
Secure information on programs	60%	46%	66%	54%	58%	64%	65%	59%	61%	63%	42%
Influence rules and regulations	42	49	51	29	32	53	48	33	34	44	33
Support/influence unit's legislative programs	37	37	43	24	29	40	37	31	35	49	30
Affect allocation/level of services for group members	35	32	44	30	31	39	39	31	25	32	21
Complain about unit's performance	22	18	24	21	18	26	29	25	24	17	12
Seek to obtain new unit programs	18	16	19	14	16	20	24	9	16	22	15
Support/influence unit's budget prop.	17	20	23	7	19	17	18	8	18	22	9
Seek to influence personnel decisions	9	5	15	7	13	10	9	6	4	9	9
Purpose of Unit-Initiated Contacts with Interest Groups [2]											
Solicit group input on proposed regulations	46%	46%	47%	47%	39%	52%	43%	37%	43%	49%	53%
Gain information on effects of unit's programs	42	40	49	40	36	47	41	36	38	44	37
Build support for unit's legislative program	39	39	44	39	29	44	38	33	44	35	34
Determine groups' policy preferences	39	32	50	32	28	54	37	30	37	34	54
Secure technical information for decisions	35	30	35	40	35	38	30	40	33	37	22
Solicit group support with federal officials	8	6	9	6	5	12	15	5	6	2	9
Solicit group support with governor	7	6	9	4	10	8	10	6	4	7	3
Solicit group input in filling staff vacancies	4	2	5	6	6	4	3	6	6	2	6

1. Depending upon the purpose that prompts a group-initiated contact, the number of responding administrators varies as follows: Overall: 826-831, Arizona: 65; California: 142-143; Delaware: 70-71; Indiana: 71-72; Michigan: 123, New York: 110-111; South Dakota: 64; Tennessee: 56-57; Texas: 86-88; Vermont: 33.

2. Depending upon the purpose that prompts a unit-initiated contact, the number of responding administrators varies as follows: Overall: 819-824; Arizona: 64-65; California: 139-142; Delaware: 70-71; Indiana: 72; Michigan: 123; New York: 109-110; South Dakota: 63-64; Tennessee: 54-55; Texas: 85-86; Vermont: 32.

tors' judgments on the purposes of group-initiated contacts with their units. The most common reason that groups contact administrative agencies is to secure information about the programs that an agency implements. This is so in 9 of the 10 states. Next most common are contacts likely to shape existing or future agency programs—seeking to affect the content of existing or proposed agency rules or regulations and providing support for and seeking to influence the legislative agendas of agencies. There is relative stability in the frequency of contacts of this sort across the 10 states.

The extent to which groups seek to shape the legislative agendas of state agencies is also evident from the fact that an average of just over one-fifth of the legislation affecting a unit was said by administrators to have originated with organized groups. Of the managers surveyed, 20% said that at least two-fifths originated with groups and 17% said that half or more was group-originated.

Rounding out the top four objectives of interest group-initiated contacts are those involving the allocation or level of services or benefits received by those represented by particular groups. Contacts for this purpose ranked third or fourth most frequent in 8 of the 10 states. Group contacts that register complaints about the performance of an agency, that seek to support or influence its budget, that seek to obtain new programs, or that represent attempts to influence agency personnel actions are much less common.

If one views group-initiated contacts in terms of a dichotomy between those likely to have broader policy consequences and those with a more narrowly administrative—and often particularistic—thrust, a mixed picture emerges. Neither type of contact predominates among either the four most or least frequent objectives. Overall, contacts likely to have broader policy implications ranked third, sixth, and seventh (seeking to support or influence legislation, seeking to support or influence budget requests, and seeking to obtain new programs). If one considers efforts to influence the promulgation of rules and regulations to be a policy-oriented contact, the ranks are second, third, sixth, and seventh. It appears, therefore, that interest group-initiated contacts in the 10 study states are often aimed at facilitating the utilization of agency services by those that a group represents (information-seeking contacts), at improving service delivery to those affected by an agency's programs via complaints, or at modifying existing patterns or levels of services provided to group members.[5]

Comparison of the data in the lower portion of Table 8.2 with that in the upper portion suggests that the purposes that prompt state agencies to contact groups evidence considerable symmetry with those that prompt groups to contact state agencies. Administrators report a high proportion of group-initiated contacts designed to elicit information on agency programs along with a high proportion of agency-initiated contacts seeking information on the effects of programs. They also report a high frequency of interest group contacts aimed at influencing rules and regulations and—perhaps a stimulus of the former—numerous contacts by their units designed to elicit group input on rules and regulations. Administrators report a high frequency of group-initiated contacts aimed at influencing or supporting a unit's policy agenda, together with a high frequency of unit-initiated contacts designed to generate such support. Finally, administrators report both a low frequency of group-initiated contacts aimed at influencing agency personnel decisions and of unit-initiated contacts with interest groups on such matters. Evidence of symmetry in the objectives of group-initiated and unit-initiated contacts in this study is consistent with the findings of Abney and Lauth.

State administrative reliance on interest groups is evident in yet another way. Of those surveyed, 58% indicated that they had advisory committees attached to their units that were composed of members of clientele groups or organized interest groups. Across the states in the study the percentage reporting the existence of advisory committees ranged from 44% in Vermont to 72% in Michigan. Moreover, 62% said their unit relied on organized groups for aid in implementing their programs. In short, the integration of groups and their perspectives into state agency deliberations and operations is substantial.[6]

OTHER PARAMETERS OF STATE AGENCY-INTEREST GROUP INTERACTION

The consequences for state management as well as the public interest that flow from high levels of interaction between state agencies and interest groups may be conditioned by other aspects of such interaction. One important parameter of this interaction is its affective quality. Another is the number of groups with which agencies interact.

Each administrator was asked to characterize the orientation of the major interest groups that interacted with his or her unit toward that unit's programs and goals. Only 5% characterized this orientation as "consistently unsupportive," while 25% characterized it as "consistently supportive." While support is more common than opposition, neither consistent group opposition nor support of agency programs is the norm. Rather, the orientation of major interest groups toward agency programs was described by 70% as being "highly variable—some are supportive, others are unsupportive."[7] The affective quality of administrative-group interaction is similar to that which characterizes administrative interaction with legislative committees—depicted as "highly variable" by around 70% of state managers and as "consistently supportive" by 25% percent. It is less positive than than which characterizes the orientation of governors toward state agencies—an orientation described as consistently supportive by 52% of the respondents.

Most units interacted with a fairly large number of groups. Overall, 46% of the 836 administrators who responded to the question indicated that seven or more groups paid "close attention" to their unit's programs and operations while 25% said that four to six groups paid close attention. Except in Vermont, in no state did less than 33% of the respondents report that seven or more groups paid close attention to the affairs of their unit.

Notions of "countervailing power" in interest group theory are premised on the belief that, while public officials are subject to pressure from a large number of groups, these groups represent diverse perspectives. When this is so, officials are not only supposed to hear all sides of an issue, but ought also to be able to play groups off against one another. The findings on the affective quality of state agency-interest group interaction and regarding the number of groups with which these agencies interact suggest that a situation of countervailing power may often exist in these states.

This conclusion is reinforced by evidence that intensity of agency-group interaction is positively related to the number of groups involved in the process.

Thus, 79% of those agencies that reported very frequent group-initiated contacts also reported that seven or more groups paid close attention to their activities. This compares to only 17% of those reporting "occasional" interaction.[8]

There is also evidence that more intense interest group-initiated contact with state agencies does not make hearts grow fonder. While 26% of the administrators who reported only occasional group-initiated contact with their unit characterized such interaction as consistently supportive, this was true of just 21% of those who reported very frequent group-initiated contact. The proportion who perceived consistently unsupportive relationships increased from less than 4% to more than 9%.

In contrast, intensity of agency-initiated contact with groups was positively related to the affective quality of such interaction. Thus, among those who reported only occasional unit-initiated contact with groups, 23% reported consistently supportive relationships, while such relationships existed 32% of the time for units that frequently contacted groups. This pattern suggests one of two possibilities. An agency that seizes the initiative in interacting with groups may be able to shape the attitudes of groups toward itself. Alternatively, an agency may be more aggressive when it perceives a more favorable climate to exist among the groups interested in its programs.

So far as variation in the affective quality of interaction across the four basic patterns of group-agency interaction is concerned, major differences occur only for the "besieged agency" and "agency active" patterns. This is so because perceptions of affective quality are shaped by who initiates contact. In the besieged agency case, 11% of the managers reported consistently unsupportive group orientations and only 19% reported consistently supportive ones. When the agency dominates interaction, only 4% of the managers report consistently hostile group orientations, while 29% perceive a consistently benign interest group milieu. These findings are consistent with those of Abney and Lauth (1986b), who report that administrators perceive more negative consequences for administrative performance stemming from interest group involvement in administrative affairs when interest groups dominate the interaction relationship but are more likely to perceive such involvement to have positive consequences when their agency dominates interaction.[9]

The existence of diverse objectives among the groups with whom administrative agencies interact, particularly when agency-group interaction is intense, is evidenced by yet another fact. One of the potential impediments to effective management about which administrators were queried was "interest group opposition to agency programs." Overall, 16% of state managers saw this to be a serious or very serious impediment to effective agency performance, while 36% felt it was no problem at all, and 47% percent said it was only a minor problem. But the proportion considering group opposition to be a serious problem rises sharply as the intensity of group-initiated contact increases. Among administrators reporting only occasional group-initiated contacts, only 6% report group opposition to agency programs to be a serious problem. Among those who report very frequent group-initiated contacts, 34% considered group opposition to be a serious impediment. If we treat the frequency of contact responses as interval level data, the correlation (Pearson's r, one-tailed test, p = .000) between frequency of group-initiated contacts and the severity of group opposition as a management impediment is .30.[10]

Interest group opposition is also more often seen to be a problem by administrators of units that interact with a larger number of groups. Group opposition is a serious problem in the eyes of 10% of managers who report that three or fewer groups pay close attention to their unit, while it is perceived to be a serious problem by 18% of those who interact with between four and six different groups and by 21% of those who reported that seven or more groups pay close attention to the affairs of their unit.

While none of the foregoing relationships are terribly strong, the direction of the relationships are consistent with countervailing power arguments. In conjunction with the findings regarding intensity of interaction and affective quality, they suggest that a countervailing group context may be quite common in the 10 study states.

To summarize this portion of the chapter, the state administrators I surveyed reported relatively intense interaction with organized interest groups. Nearly half of the time a high level of group-initiated contacts with state administrative units is matched by a high level of unit-initiated contacts with groups. Most units also interact with a relatively large number of groups. While consistently hostile relationships with groups are not common, neither are consistently supportive ones. Variability in the affective quality of group-administrative interaction is the norm. Affective quality varies as a function of intensity of contacts and as a function of the number of groups with whom units interact. While the data suggest the existence of "countervailing power" dynamics among groups involved with state administration, examination of the purposes served by group or unit-initiated contacts suggests that both parties derive substantial benefits from their interaction.

SOURCES OF VARIATION IN ADMINISTRATIVE-INTEREST GROUP INTERACTION

While fairly intensive interaction between state administrative agencies and organized interest groups is the norm, variation in interaction does exist. Some understanding of possible predictors of such interaction is important given that estimates of interest group impact have been shown to be positively correlated with levels of both group and agency-initiated contacts. This portion of the chapter explores some of the factors that may account for differences in the intensity of interaction between organized groups and state administrative units.

Group-Agency Interaction and Functional Responsibility

Because interest groups are "policy-preoccupied," the nature of the programs that particular state agencies administer may well be related to levels of interaction between groups and agencies. The linkage of agency purpose to interest group interaction and impact has been suggested by a number of scholars (Rourke, 1984; Gruber, 1987; Freidman, Klein, and Romani, 1966; Abney and Lauth, 1986b; Brudney and Hebert, 1987; Meier, 1987, esp. Ch. 4; J. Q. Wilson, 1973, 1989, esp. Ch. 4). Agencies that bestow tangible benefits on citizens, those that provide—in Lowi's words (1964)—"distributive benefits," should experience higher levels of group-initiated contacts. Agencies established to address the needs of well defined groups—so-called clientele agencies such as departments of veterans affairs or agriculture—may experience especially intense interaction with groups, whether initiated by clientele groups or by the unit itself (Rourke, 1976). Highway or transportation departments that contract extensively with private firms for the provision of services may also be the targets of more group contacts (Friedman et al., 1966).

Some of the gravest concerns about interest group influence have involved agencies with regulatory responsibilities. The vision of the "captured" regulatory agency implies intense, group-initiated interaction, if not unit-initiated interaction. On the other hand, administrative staff agencies whose focus tends to be inward on aspects of state government ought to evidence less intense interaction with organized groups. Finally, units with custodial care functions and "captive clientele," such as departments of corrections and those that operate facilities for the mentally ill, should interact less intensely with groups, in part because their clients lack the socioeconomic or other resources associated with political mobilization.

The relationship between the functional responsibility of a unit and levels of both interest group-initiated contact with a unit and unit-initiated contact with groups is explored in Table 8.3. While significant variation in group-initiated contact exists, the explanatory power of functional responsibility is not great (eta = .19, F- test, significant, .001 level).

As hypothesized, levels of group-initiated contacts are lowest for units with fiscal or nonfiscal staff functions as well as for those with criminal justice responsibilities. In contrast, units with regulatory responsibilities experience some of the highest levels of group-inititated contacts. Included in this category are units with banking, consumer protection, food and drug, insurance, securities, and public utility regulatory duties as well as those that engage in occupational licensing. The highest levels of group-initiated interaction exist for units with natural resources, and environmental protection and energy responsibilities. Intense interaction with natural resource units likely reflects the fact that this category includes clientele units such as agriculture and fish and game. The environmental protection category includes units with regulatory responsibilities relating to air and water quality as well as solid waste management.

Table 8.3

Variation in Intensity of Group and Unit-Initiated Interaction by Functional Responsibilty of State Administrative Units

Functional Responsibility	Intensity of Group-Initiated Contact with Unit	Intensity of Unit-Initiated Contact with Group	Interaction Differential
Criminal justice	1.71 (10) [1]	1.56 (9)	.15 [2]
Economic development	1.75 (9)	1.68 (5)	.13
Education	1.87 (7)	1.78 (2)	.09
Environmental/energy	2.02 (2)	1.64 (6)	.38
Health	1.84 (5.5)	1.73 (4)	.11
Income security/social services	1.97 (3)	1.75 (3)	.22
Natural resources	2.09 (1)	1.96 (1)	.13
Regulatory	1.94 (4)	1.62 (7)	.32
Staff-fiscal	1.64 (11)	1.34 (11)	.30
Staff-nonfiscal	1.76 (8)	1.55 (10)	.21
Transportation	1.84 (5.5)	1.60 (8)	.24
	Eta = .19	Eta = .19	Eta = .15
	F - test,	F - test,	F - test,
	sig.: .001	sig.: .002	sig.: .002

1. Table entry is the mean frequency of group-initiated or unit-initiated contact where: (0) Never, (1) Occasionally, (2) Frequently, (3) Very frequently. The figure in parentheses is the rank of mean interaction for units with a particular functional responsibility as compared to those with other responsibilities.

2. This is the difference between mean group-initiated interaction and mean unit-initiated interaction. A positive value indicates mean group-initiated interaction exceeds mean unit-initiated interaction.

It is unlikely that the poor are well represented among the groups that frequently initiate contact with units in the income security/social services category, which includes public assistance programs. But the elderly may well be since this category includes units with aging policy management responsibilities. Since state social service agencies frequently contract for services, interaction initiated by organizations representing providers may be important.

Patterns of unit-initiated contact with groups across differing functional categories roughly parallel those for group-initiated contacts. The most aggressive units are those with natural resources, education, and income security responsibilities. The least aggressive are those with fiscal or nonfiscal staff functions and those in the criminal justice area.

Patterns of unit-initiated contacts with groups do not completely parallel patterns for group-initiated contacts, however, as the third column of Table 8.3 makes clear. In every functional category, group-initiated contact is more intense than agency-initiated contact. But this difference is especially pronounced for units with regulatory responsibilities of the environmental or economic sort. Unit aggressiveness relative to that of groups is greatest for units with education, health, economic, and natural resources responsibilities.

Differences in the balance between intensity of group and unit-initiated contacts that reflect a unit's functional responsibilities are made more clear if the frequency with which the four interaction patterns identified earlier occurs is examined. The proportion of units that exhibit the "mutually inactive" pattern ranges from just 14% of units with natural resources responsibilities to 39% of the units with fiscal staff responsibilities. Consistent with earlier arguments, criminal justice and economic development units, as well as those with both fiscal or nonfiscal staff responsibilties, most often manifest the "mutually inactive" pattern. Units that engage in economic regulation are also quite likely to exhibit this pattern (30%). This may be evidence of the success of efforts to insulate the operations of such units from external influence.

The proportion of units that exhibit the "besieged" interaction pattern ranges from 14% to 26% across functional categories. Units with fiscal staff, income security, and transportation duties are most likely to come under siege from highly active interest groups. Units with economic development, nonfiscal staff, and health responsibilities are least likely to come under "siege" from highly active interest groups.

As noted earlier, the most common interaction pattern across the units was the "mutually active" one, with 46% of the units exhibiting this pattern. This is also the case when units are classified according to their functional responsibilities, save for the fact that fewer fiscal staff units exhibit this pattern (26%) than exhibit the mutually inactive pattern (39%). Natural resource units—many with well-defined clientele—are especially likely to display a mutually active interaction pattern (64%). Approximately 50% of the units with environmental, income security, education, health, and economic development responsibilities display this pattern. In contrast, only 40% of transportation units and 37% of criminal justice units exhibit this pattern.

Although they operationalized interaction differently than I did, Abney and Lauth (1986b) found that interaction patterns varied according to the functional responsibilities of agencies in ways that mirror my findings. Thus, those departments with staff functions were most likely to display the "mutual independence" pattern that is analogous to my "mutually inactive" pattern. Consistent with the findings of the 10-state study, Abney and Lauth found such a pattern to be uncommmon among natural resources, income security, and education units.

Abney and Lauth found that the "interest group active" pattern often emerged for units with transportation functions—just as units with similar tasks in my study were more likely to display the analogous "besieged agency" pattern. Education departments were especially likely to display an "administrator active" pattern, just as education units in my study were more likely to display the "agency active" pattern. Finally, "mutually dependent" interaction was especially common for environmental protection and natural resources departments but was especially rare for law, administration, and revenue departments. These patterns mirror those for agencies of this type and the analogous "mutually active" pattern in the 10-state study.

Variation across units with differing functional responsibilities is evident, as well, in the number of groups that pay attention to particular units and in the orientation of these groups toward units. Units with economic development responsibilities experience the most favorable interest group milieu with 42% reporting consistently supportive groups. One reason for this is surely that such units, in an effort to stimulate investment, often bestow tax benefits or provide other incentives to entrepreneurs. Although they interact at relatively low levels with groups, 41% of managers of units with nonfiscal staff functions consider the groups with which they do interact to be friendly. Some 30% of managers of units with regulatory responsibilities perceive interest groups to be supportive. This figure might be taken as evidence of some degree of capture of those units by the interests that they are charged with regulating. It also may be testimony to the fact that some "regulation," of occupations, for instance, is of the protective or promotional variety.

Roughly 25% of units with education, health, natural resources, environmental, and transportation responsibilities report consistently supportive interest groups. Units with criminal justice, income security, and fiscal staff responsibilities report the least favorable contexts, with the proportion reporting consistently supportive interest groups being 21%, 18%, and 16%, respectively. Neither criminal justice nor income security units have high status, well-organized constituencies. Especially in the 1980s, fiscal units were involved in cutting state budgets and may have been the targets of groups opposed to such cuts.

The proportion of managers who reported that seven or more groups interacted with their units ranged from 32% among those in economic development units, and 41% of those with nonfiscal staff functions, to more than 50% of those with fiscal staff, environmental, and natural resources responsibilities. That economic development and nonfiscal staff units experience a favorable but less complex interest group milieu is evidence of the negative relationship between affective orientation and complexity noted earlier in the chapter.

Other Possible Predictors of Interaction Intensity

Beyond the functional obligations of administrative agencies, interaction intensity may be related to various characteristics of state administrative agencies. Other things being equal, it might be expected that higher level units, those headed by elected officials or by political appointees whose fortunes are closely tied to elected officials, and those that have larger budgets might experience higher levels of interaction. Interaction intensity may also be higher when the affective tone of the relationships between groups and agencies is more supportive.

There was weak evidence that higher level units experienced more group-initiated contacts ($r = .11$, $p = .001$) and also initiated more contacts with groups ($r = .10$, $p = .002$). There was also weak evidence that units headed by elected or gubernatorially appointed managers experienced higher levels of both group and unit-initiated contacts than did those headed by classified civil servants, although the analysis of variance statistics were not significant at the .05 level.

Larger agencies may be the focus of greater interest group attention. This may be so, in part, because they administer a wider range of programs that affect the lives of more state citizens. The bivariate correlation between frequency of group-initiated contact and the size of a unit's budget was .16 (p = .001). Because larger units may have a wider variety of programmatic responsibilities, they may also initiate more contacts with groups. The correlation between the size of a unit's budget and frequency of unit-initiated contacts was .13 (p = .001).

The intensity of group-initiated contacts did not vary significantly as a function of the affective quality of the group-agency relationship. But agencies that enjoyed a more supportive group milieu were more likely to initiate contacts with groups (analysis of variance indicates that this relationship is significant at the .01 level [F-test] and that the eta statistic is .12).

Multivariate Models of State Agency-Interest Group Interaction

While significant bivariate relationships sometimes existed between the functional responsibilities of a state administrative unit, its location in a state's organizational hierarchy, its size, how its manager was selected, and the affective orientation of groups toward it, on the one hand, and group interaction intensity, on the other, multivariate analysis that controls for relationships between these independent variables indicates that none has great explanatory power.[11] A regression model into which dummy variables for functional responsibilities and method of selection were entered, along with measures of group affective orientation, the organizational place of a responding manager's unit, and the size of a unit, could account for only about 4% of the variance in frequency of interest group-initiated contacts. The significant predictors that emerged (with the direction of their relationship to frequency of group-initiated contact noted in parentheses) were the size of a unit (+), the fact that it had fiscal staff responsibilities (−), the fact that it had natural resources responsibilities (+), the fact that the responding administrator was appointed by a board (+), and the affective orientation of groups toward the unit—a more hostile milieu is associated with *more* intense interest group-initiated interaction. Only unit size could account for more than 1% of the variance in levels of group-initiated interaction, however.

Nor can a multivariate model explain much of the variation in levels of agency-initiated contact with interest groups. Larger units—those with natural resources responsibilities, those reporting more positive affective orientations on the part of groups, and those headed by gubernatorial appointees—are all slightly more likely to report higher levels of unit-initiated contacts with groups, while those with fiscal responsibilities report lower levels of unit-initiated contact. Only size of unit, having natural resources responsibilities, and affective orientation can account for even 1% of the variance in levels of unit-initiated contacts, however.

In sum, while interest group impact is positively related to the extent of administrative-interest group interaction, various agency characteristics are only weakly related to variation in the intensity of such interaction. The functional responsibility of a unit and its size can explain only a small amount of variation.[12]

The fact that interest group-administrative interaction is fairly intense for all the units in the study is one reason that the variables at hand have only limited explanatory power. It may also be that what best accounts for variation in levels of interest group interaction with state administrative agencies—and especially levels of group-initiated contact—are various characteristics of those groups. Unfortunately, my questionnnaire generated no information on these characteristics save for their managers' views of the general orientation of groups toward the programs of particular units.

EXPLORING DETERMINANTS OF INTEREST GROUP INFLUENCE UPON STATE ADMINISTRATION

Intensity of interaction between interest groups and state administrative units is positively associated with the impact of those groups on administrative affairs. But interaction does not automatically equal influence. Hence, this section of the chapter explores some of the other determinants of interest group impact upon state agencies. It concludes with the development of a multivariate model that includes various other predictors in addition to intensity of interaction.

Functional Responsibility and Group Impact

Over and above any relationship that exists between the functional obligations of a state administrative unit and the intensity of its interaction with interest groups, these obligations may condition how receptive or how vulnerable to interest group pressures various units happen to be. The literature is replete with references to the closer ties that exist between groups and agencies with one set of programmatic responsibilities as opposed to others (see, among others, Peters, 1984; Rourke, 1984; Meier, 1987). Brudney and Hebert (1987) found that the influence of both clientele groups and professional associations varied depending upon the functional role of a state agency. Thus, clientele groups had significantly greater impact on "human resources" (i.e., income security and social services) agencies as well as on those with natural resources/transportation and economic development and regulation responsibilities. Although the impact of professional associations was less variable, they, too, had significantly greater impact on units with human resources and criminal justice responsibilities, and less impact on those with staff, natural resources/transportation, or economic development and regulation duties.

In the 10 states, interest group impact varied significantly across all six of the influence arenas as a consequence of differences in the functional responsibilities of those units (see Tables 6.5 and 6.6). Units with health, natural resources, education, and social services/income security responsibilities consistently reported greater group impact across arenas, while those with staff responsibilities reported lowest impact. Consistent with the literature on regulation, agencies with regulatory responsibilities report relatively high levels of group impact on the content of rules and regulations, although regulatory units rank near the bottom in the case of other influence arenas. Units with health, natural resources, and environmental responsibilities also may rank higher in terms of group impact because their missions include various regulatory tasks. Economic development units may be subject to greater group influence because their role often includes allocating incentives to potential entrepreneurs. Units with criminal justice responsibilities report much lower levels of interest group impact. This may be a reflection of the truly "captive" nature of their clientele and the fact that few groups represent those clients.

Organizational Characteristics, Method of Selection, and Interest Group Impact

Interest groups' impact on state administrative affairs may be conditioned by various organizational characteristics as well as by how managers have secured their positions. We have seen that organization size, as measured by the size of a unit's budget, was modestly related to intensity of agency interaction with interest groups. To the extent that it may be harder for external actors to monitor the activities of larger administrative units, all nonadministrative actors in the political environment, including organized groups, may exert less influence on larger units. Brudney and Hebert (1987), following the argument of Meier (1979), assert that "major state agencies enjoy a degree of protection from outside influences" (p. 196). They suggest that "larger size makes possible the development of specialization and the acquisition of expert knowledge useful to agencies in protecting themselves from their environments" (p. 196). In their 50-state analysis, the heads of "major agencies" (as measured by size of staff as well as size of budget) reported lower levels of impact by both professional associations and clientele groups than did managers of smaller units.

In the 10 states in this study, agency size—as measured by the log of an agency's budget—was positively related to interest group impact, with significant correlations (p = .05 level or better, two-tailed test) ranging from .08 for group impact on daily operations to .16 for impact on agency budgets. These relationships have the opposite sign, however, from those found to exist for clientele and professional association impact in the Hebert and Brudney study. One explanation for this difference in findings, given that I have not taken any confounding variables into account, may lie in the link of agency size to inter-action and the link of interaction to impact noted earlier. Another explanation may be differences in how organizational size was operationally defined in the two studies. Rather than assign a score to each agency based on number of employees or size of budget as I did, Abney and Lauth classified the largest 18 "agency types" as major and the others as minor. My measure of agency size would seem superior.

While it is a mistake to assume that lower levels of an organization are automatically closer to the "grass roots" than are higher levels, it may be that interest group influence is more often felt by lower level than higher level units. One reason that this may be so is because the countervailing influence of the governor may be less strong in the case of lower level than higher level units.

At least in the 10 states focused on in this study, however, where a unit is located within the larger administrative hierarchy is unrelated to the amount of influence that interest groups exert on it. No significant simple correlations emerged between the organizational location of a respondent's unit and the influence they attributed to interest groups in any of the six influence arenas.

While variation in group-agency interaction is only weakly related to how the head of an administrative unit is selected, it may be that the process by which managers secure or retain their positions is independently related to the impact that groups are seen to exert. In their 50-state study, Brudney and He-bert (1987) suggest that clientele groups might have more impact on popularly elected administrators while civil service selection and job security may aug-ment the impact of professional associations. Their multivariate analysis of de-terminants of impact disclosed that elected as well as board-appointed agency heads attributed significantly greater impact to clientele groups than did those administrators that were appointed by the governor or were in the classified civil service. On the other hand, method of selection bore no relationship to variation in the influence of professional associations.

The bivariate relationship that exists between interest group impact and method of selection in my data contradicts the findings of Hebert and Brudney. No significant difference existed in group impact in any of the six influence arenas across five different methods of selection (elected, board appointed, classified service, agency-head appointed, and gubernatorial appointment). The small number of elected administrators in the sample consistently reported the *lowest* levels of interest group impact, while the highest levels of impact were reported for those units whose head had been appointed by a higher level administrator, was a gubernatorial appointee, or was in the classified service.

Characteristics of Agency-Interest Group Interaction and Differences in Interest Group Impact

In addition to interaction intensity itself, other aspects of the relationships that exist between interest groups and state administrative agencies may condition the impact of such groups. The orientation of groups toward a unit and its program might affect group influence. On the one hand, interest group influence may be enhanced when the relationships between groups and a given agency are positive in tone, while an agency may resist influence efforts on the part of groups that are unsupportive of existing agency priorities.[13] On the other hand, the true test of an interest group's clout may be its ability to get a unit to do something that the unit itself opposes.

As it turns out, analysis of the relationship between the orientation of groups toward a unit and the influence of those groups on agency affairs provides precious little support for either line of argument. State administrative agencies report group influence to be about the same regardless of whether most of the groups with which they interact are generally supportive or unsupportive of existing agency programs and priorities.

Earlier in the chapter I argued that data on both the intensity and affective quality of interest group-agency interaction suggested conditions consistent with a "countervailing power" situation. When agencies experienced more intense interest group-initiated contacts they were somewhat more likely to report variable or unsupportive relationships with those groups. Moreover, an increase in the number of groups exerting influence on an agency was modestly related to the affective nature of group-agency interaction, with the affective environment being less positive when a unit interacted with more groups.

We have just seen, however, that affective orientation is unrelated to variation in interest group influence. Although the existence of a countervailing power situation may subject a unit to the petitions of groups representing a somewhat wider variety of views, this does not generally reduce the impact that those groups are seen to have. In other words, conflict among groups does not seem to provide an opportunity for an agency to reduce the influence that groups exert in toto, perhaps as it seeks to play one group off against another. The benefit—for the agency as well as for the broader public interest—may simply be that an agency must take a wider range of views into account.

As previously indicated, most of the administrators surveyed wished that more time could be devoted to interacting with interest groups and clientele. This increased interaction could be positively related to a manager's views on either the legitimacy or the functionality of such interaction. The bivariate relationships between preferred emphasis on group/clientele interaction and group impact provide some support for this hypothesis. The correlations between emphasis on this managerial function and group impact are positive and significant for all six influence arenas, although none is larger than .11.

Advisory Groups and Interest Group Impact

Nearly 60% of the responding units indicated the existence of one or more advisory committees composed of members of clientele or interest groups. On the one hand, such bodies may provide a vehicle that various groups can exploit as they seek to influence agency policy or operations. On the other hand, such committees may be passive bodies that create the illusion of participation in agency affairs while their real function is to legitimize courses of action that agencies have already settled upon.

At least in these 10 states advisory bodies are an instrument that enhances the influence of groups in the state administrative process. The mean impact on overall budgets, budgets for specific programs, and broader agency policies attributed to groups by administrators of units with advisory bodies is 1.5, 1.5, and 1.6, respectively. Comparable levels of impact for these three influence arenas in the case of units lacking such bodies are 1.0, 1.0, and 1.1, respectively. Influence means are significantly different in the case of all six influence arenas, with etas ranging from .18 to .26.

The existence of advisory committees may, however, be associated with enhanced interest group impact because those units that interact most extensively with interest groups are more likely also to report the existence of advisory bodies. Thus, only 42% of those who report only occasional interest group-initiated contact with their units report the existence of advisory committees as compared to more than two-thirds of those units that experience frequent or very frequent interaction.

Federal Funding and Interest Group Impact

In Chapter 6 we saw that agency dependence upon federal funding sources was strongly correlated with the influence that federal government actors are seen to exert on state administrative affairs. Hebert and Brudney (1987) speculated that because federal funding makes an agency less dependent on the regular state appropriations process, it may reduce the impact of various actors in an agency's influence environment—including the governor and the legislature as well as clientele groups and professional associations—on an agency. Indeed, their subsequent multivariate analysis of determinants of actor influence disclosed that the influence of clientele groups and professional associations decreased as the proportion of federal funds in agency budgets increased.

In the 10 states focused on here, however, federal funding is not associated with a decrease in interest group impact. The simple correlation between extent of federal funding and interest group impact is positive rather than negative. The resulting correlations are significant ($p = .05$) in the case of group impact on overall budget levels (.14), budgets for specific programs (.15), broader policy (.11), and the content of rules and regulations (.06).

Interaction with Other Actors and Interest Group Impact

Interest group impact on state agencies may also be conditioned by the relationships that exist between other elements in the influence environment of those agencies. To the extent that the governor and the legislature have preferences that differ from those of key interest groups, group influence may be tempered. The involvement of the governor may be especially significant as a counterweight to narrower group concerns given the governor's broader, state-wide political constituency.

On the other hand, interest groups may be able to enhance their influence upon state agencies by working through other actors, most especially the legislature. In their 50-state study, Abney and Lauth (1986a) found that administrators believed interest groups were more likely to be able to influence those policies of concern to themselves and a particular agency if those groups focused their efforts on the state legislature as opposed to the governor or individual administrative agencies. But Abney and Lauth (1986b) also found that intensity of agency interaction with the governor or the legislature conditioned the strength of the relationship between intensity of group-agency interaction and the perceived influence of interest groups. The correlation between group-agency interaction and administrators' perceptions of group impact was only .06 overall. But this correlation increased to .18 in cases of low levels of agency-gubernatorial interaction and to .20 when low levels of agency-legislative interaction existed. Thus "high interaction between departments and groups does not itself mean interest group domination of a department. If domination is to occur, it is more likely to happen when administrative oversight by the legislative body is weak or where the governor is not a vigorous chief administrative officer" (p. 100).

Given the relationship just noted, it is significant that Abney and Lauth also found that interest group interaction with agencies was rather strongly correlated with intensity of gubernatorial interaction with agencies (r = .42) and with intensity of legislative interaction with state agencies (r = .38). In my 10 state database, the correlations between frequency of group-initiated contacts with agencies and intensity of interaction with legislative program committees or with legislative budget committees are .37 and .29, respectively. The correlations between levels of agency-initiated contact with groups and interaction with these two types of legislative committees are .32 and .24, respectively.

The correlations between group-agency and gubernatorial-agency interaction are much lower than those that Abney and Lauth found, however. The correlation between intensity of group-initiated contacts with agencies and intensity of agency-gubernatorial interaction was only .15 (p = .000) while that between intensity of agency-initiated contacts with groups and intensity of agency-gubernatorial interaction was only .13 (p = .000).

Abney and Lauth's finding that the influence-enhancing impact of group-agency interaction is reduced when agencies interact more intensely with the governor finds some support in the 10-state data. The correlation between frequency of group-initiated contacts with agencies and interest group impact is lower for agencies that report a higher level of gubernatorial interaction in the case of four of six influence arenas. The moderating effect of gubernatorial involvement is especially evident in budgetary and broader policy realms. For those agencies that report low levels of interaction with the governor ("no" or only "occasional" interaction) the correlations between group-initiated inter- action and group impact are .29, .29, and .34 for the overall budget, budgets for specific programs, and broader policy arenas, respectively. The correlations for the same three arenas in the case of those units that report high levels of interaction with the governor ("frequent" or "very frequent" contact) are .22, .18, and .23, respectively.[14]

The 10-state data provide considerably less support, however, for the asser- tion that more intense *administrative-legislative* interaction *weakens* the link between interest group-agency interaction and interest group influence. Using interaction with legislative committees that have responsibility for a unit's pro- grams as an indicator, it is the case that the correlation between frequency of group-initiated contacts with an agency and group impact is *stronger* rather than weaker in five of the six arenas when agency-legislative interaction is more intense. A similar picture emerges when frequency of interaction with those legislative committees that have responsibility for agency budgets is used as the indicator of administrative-legislative interaction. In this case, differ- ences are particularly sharp in the two budgetary arenas as well as for the determination of broader policies affecting an agency. Thus, the leverage over administrative affairs that flows from the level of interaction between interest groups and administrative agencies is enhanced when agencies also interact intensely with key legislative actors.[15]

This difference from the findings of Abney and Lauth is understandable in light of another finding of their 50-state study, however. As noted, the admin- istrators they surveyed felt that the legislature represented the most favorable environment for interest groups seeking to influence those policies that partic- ular agencies implement. The fairly strong positive correlations between inten- sity of interest group-agency and legislative-agency interaction can be inter- preted as evidence that groups often pursue a two-pronged strategy. Efforts to directly influence agency actions are supplemented by efforts to convince key legislative actors to take actions with respect to agency programs, budgets, or operations that these groups desire.

A Multivariate Model of Interest Group Influence in State Management

To more precisely specify the determinants of interest group influence upon state administrative affairs, a multivariate model comprised of the variables discussed in the last few pages was estimated. Among the predictor variables were the functional responsibility of a unit, the size and organizational location of a unit, how the head of the unit was selected, and a unit's dependence on federal funding. Other variables included intensity of interest group interaction with a unit (variously measured as discussed below), the affective quality of that interaction, whether or not a unit had advisory groups, and an administrator's preferred emphasis on working with clientele groups or other nongovernmental actors. Finally, the model included indicators of the intensity of administrative unit interaction with the governor and key legislative actors.

Models into which all of the predictors were entered, and which used frequency of group-initiated contacts with administrative agencies as the sole indicator of agency-group interaction, could account for between 11% and 15% of the variation in interest group impact depending upon the arena of influence. Interestingly, the explanatory power of the models for these 10 states is nearly identical to the explanatory power of the multivariate model of determinants of clientele group impact estimated by Brudney and Hebert (1987) from their 50-state database.

In five of the six arenas, frequency of group-initiated contacts with agencies is the most powerful predictor of group impact, capable of accounting for between 7% and 9% of total variance. The second most powerful predictor is another indicator of agency-group interaction—the presence or absence of advisory committees. When such committees exist, group impact is enhanced. The existence of such committees is especially strongly related to an increase in interest group impact on the content of rules and regulations, where it can account for approximately 7% of the variance. In the case of the other arenas it can account for between 2% and 4% of the variance.

The only other variable that could consistently account for even so much as 1% of the variance in group impact was the functional responsibility of a unit. Agencies with health policy responsibilities reported greater group impact upon overall budget levels, budgets for specific agency programs, broader policy, and establishing administrative procedures than did units with other responsibilities. This finding is consistent with those of Friedman, Klein, and Romani (1966), who concluded that public health officials relied upon interest groups and professional organizations to a greater extent in the initiation of policy and were "particularly cognizant of the importance of the participation of voluntary organizations and the medical professions" (p. 203). Health officials also displayed a "very great propensity to seek information from professional sources and a substantial tendency to seek information from interest groups" (p. 205).

Units with natural resources responsibilities also reported greater group impact upon budgets for specific programs, broader policy, and administrative procedures. Units with fiscal staff responsibilities report lower group impact in the two budgetary arenas while criminal justice and transportation units both report lower group impact upon the content of rules and regulations.

Following Hebert and Brudney, extent of federal funding was among the predictors entered in the original equations. Dependence on federal funding was positively associated with group impact on budgets for specific agency programs and on broader policy. In no case, however, did it explain more than 1% of the variance. Moreover, extent of federal funding is quite strongly related to functional responsibility. Indeed, if federal funding is regressed on functional responsibility, the latter can account for 40% of the variance in federal funding. Hence, the models were reestimated using federal funding but not functional responsibility, and using functional responsibility but not federal funding. Models that included federal funding were less powerful than those that included functional responsibility. In the interests of parsimony, and because I believe the theoretical grounds for including functional responsibility are much stronger than those for including federal funding, the latter variable was not used in subsequent analyses.

Contrary to the arguments and evidence of Abney and Lauth (1986b), in my sample increased interaction with the governor or with the legislature *did not* moderate the impact of interest groups on state administrative affairs. One possible reason for this difference is that this study focuses on 10 as opposed to all 50 states. Another is that interest group impact is measured somewhat differently in this study from how Abney and Lauth measured it in their study.[16]

As noted earlier in the chapter, considerable symmetry exists in intensity of group-initiated contact with units and unit-initiated contact with groups. When intensity of unit-initiated contact with groups was used as a predictor in place of frequency of group-initiated contact, the resulting multivariate models differed little from those that emerged when intensity of group-initiated contact was used. But the explanatory power of unit-initiated contact is generally less. Since the two types of interaction are not so strongly related as to be colinear, the interest group impact models were reestimated using indicators of both group and unit-initiated contact. So doing increased the explanatory power of the model slightly (see Table 8.4), particularly in the case of group impact on broader agency policy, rules and regulations, and daily operations. Intensity of agency-initiated contact with groups accounts for at least 1% of the variance in four of the six arenas. Interestingly, intensity of group-initiated contacts is no longer a significant predictor of group impact on overall agency budget levels and can account for scarcely 1% of the variance in impact so far as budgets for specific programs are concerned. This is an arena where intensity of unit-initiated contact with groups is the most important predictor, accounting for more than 8% of the variance. Intensity of group-initiated contact with agencies remains the most powerful predictor of group impact on broader policy, establishing of administrative procedures, and the conduct of daily operations, however.

One way to make sense of these patterns is to assume that agencies contact groups in order to build support for agency budget requests. While such unit-initiated contact is associated with increased interest group impact, it is "influence" that is consistent with agency budgetary priorities. In the case of the other arenas, agencies may feel they have more to lose than gain from mobilizing interest groups. Hence, group impact is more often a reflection of group-initiated influence efforts.

To summarize, intensity of interaction between organized interest groups and state administrators—whether manifested in group-initiated contacts, agency-initiated contacts, or institutionalized in the form of advisory committees—can

Table 8.4

Multivariate Models of Interest Group Impact on State Administrative Affairs (Using Both Group and Agency-Initiated Interaction as Predictors)

Interest Group Impact on:	Explained Variance (Adjusted R^2)	Significant Predictors of at Least One Percent of Variance[1]	B[2]	Beta[3]	Variance Explained by Predictor
Overall budget level of unit	.16	Unit contacts groups	.188	.155	.08
		Fiscal function	-.587	-.154	.03
		Advisory committee	.236	.123	.03
		Unit size (budget)	.083	.084	.01
Budget for specific unit programs	.15	Unit contacts groups	.209	.153	.08
		Advisory committee	.221	.103	.03
		Fiscal function	-.531	-.125	.02
		Groups contact unit	.189	.134	.01
Broader policy changes	.15	Groups contact unit	.297	.221	.09
		Health function	.555	.165	.03
		Advisory committee	.208	.101	.01
		Unit contacts groups	.136	.104	.01
Content of rules and regulations	.14	Advisory committee	.442	.207	.06
		Groups contact unit	.259	.183	.03
		Nat. resources function	.477	.151	.01
		Heath function	.496	.142	.01
		Regulatory function	.383	.121	.01
Establish administrative procedures	.14	Groups contact unit	.351	.281	.09
		Advisory committee	.192	.101	.02
		Health function	.361	.115	.01
		Natural resources func.	.261	.093	.01
Daily administrative operations	.12	Groups contact unit	.245	.192	.08
		Unit contacts group	.171	.138	.02
		Advisory committee	.186	.096	.01

1. This column lists only those significant predictors (F - value of B significant at .05 level or better) that could also explain at least 1% of the variation in interest group impact in a specific arena. The final column of the table indicates the variance accounted for by each of the significant predictors, rounded to a whole percent.

2. This is the unstandardized regression coefficient.

3. This is the standardized regression coefficient.

explain about one-tenth of the variance in interest group impact in the 10 study states. Agency characteristics, while not completely insignificant, are much less important, as is interaction between administrative agencies and either the governor or the legislature.[17]

Consideration of the nature of the multivariate models of interest group impact within particular states suggests that one should be cautious in asserting the explanatory power of a number of the variables that emerged as significant predictors in the overall models. On the one hand, a larger proportion of the variance in interest group impact can often be explained when models are estimated for individual states than was so of the overall models of interest impact in particular arenas.[18] For instance, more than 20% of the variance in interest group impact on broader policy was accounted for in the equations that were estimated for Arizona, California, Delaware, Michigan, Texas, and Vermont.

But the structures of the single state models rarely mirrored that for interest group impact across the 10 states. For example, while at least 20% of the variance in interest group impact on overall agency spending levels can be accounted for in six states, the most powerful predictor in the overall model—frequency of agency-initiated contact with groups—was a significant predictor in just three states. The presence of an advisory committee, the second most powerful predictor of interest group impact in the overall model, emerged as a significant predictor in just four states.

One explanation for the differences between the overall model and the individual state models of determinants of interest group impact is that a specific variable that has particularly great impact in a single state may distort the overall model if that state happens to include a large percentage of the total number of respondents in the database. Thus, the fact that a unit had health policy responsibilities could explain 2% of the variation in interest group impact on overall agency policies. While having health responsibilities is a significant positive predictor only in California and New York, these two state samples contain the largest number of respondents.

A second explanation is that individual states constitute unique political contexts, as least insofar as interest group influence on state administration is concerned. In their 50-state study, Abney and Lauth (1986b) argue that "political cultural" differences affect the perceived legitimacy of interest group activities and, in turn, affect the intensity of the exchanges between agencies and groups. They go on to present some evidence in support of this assertion (p. 100). Without buying into "political culture" as an explanation, it is surely true that a variety of state-specific factors on which I do not possess information may well condition the relationships that exist between organized groups and state administrative agencies.

Information is available, however, on a few potentially important differences among the states that might affect the role that interest groups play in state administrative affairs. One of these relates to characteristics of a state's legislature—its "capacity" or "professionalism." The other relates to the formal powers possessed by the governor of a state. In Chapter 7 we saw that legislative characteristics could account for little of the variation in legislative impact upon state administrative agencies. Gubernatorial power resources were more strongly related to variation in gubernatorial impact upon state administration, however.

Differences in legislative capacity or gubernatorial power can account for virtually none of the interstate variation in interest group impact upon state administration, however. Neither the summary indicator of legislative "capacity" nor of gubernatorial power were significantly related to differences in administrators' estimates of interest group influence in various arenas. Nor were more specific indicators of gubernatorial power significantly related to variation in interest group influence. As for specific indicators of legislative capacity, administrators in states with more "representative" legislatures reported lower interest group impact on the shape of rules and regulations while interest group influence on daily operations was less in states with more "functional" legislatures. But neither relationship was strong enough to explain even as much as 1% of the variance in interest group influence.

Specific state practices may create particular opportunities for interest groups to influence matters of concern to administrative agencies. One of the best examples is processes that provide for legislative review and/or veto of proposed agency rules and regulations. More than 75% of the respondents in Michigan said that their unit was affected by such a process, as did approximately 60% of the administrators in Texas and South Dakota. This was true of less than 20% of the Indiana respondents (see Table 4.5). The mean impact of interest groups on the content of rules and regulations was 2.3 in the case of units not subject to legislative review or veto procedures, while it was 2.6 for those subject to such procedures. Only 30% of those who said that groups had no impact on the content of rules and regulations were required to submit proposed rules or regulations for review. This compares to 40% of those reporting "some impact" and more than 50% of those reporting "moderate" or greater interest group impact. To the extent that a state's legislature requires some or all administrative units to submit proposed rules or regulations to it for review and possible veto, it expands interest group clout as well.

REFLECTIONS ON THE CONSEQUENCES OF INTEREST GROUP INFLUENCE IN STATE ADMINISTRATION

Precisely how much group influence on state administrative affairs is desirable is not clear. On the one hand, agencies benefit from their contacts with groups. Groups may provide feedback on the severity of the problems an agency is charged with ameliorating or on the relative success of particular programs in ameliorating those problems. To the extent that agency contacts with groups increase client awareness of existing programs, the public interest is also advanced. The ability of interest groups to influence spending for agency programs, as well as the administration of those programs, might also be seen as an important means by which the concerns of those likely to be affected by the programs make known to policymakers and administrators what their concerns are.

On the other hand, lobbying efforts in support of the maintenance or expansion of existing programs or on behalf of new programs might be viewed as dysfunctional. Critics charge that the result is unnecessary spending and the persistence of ineffective programs or agencies. At the extreme, the interaction of administrative agencies with interest groups, combined with the involvement of key legislative actors, may come to constitute a "policy subsystem," "subgovernment," or "iron triangle" that dominates not only policy imple-mentation, but policy formulation and adoption as well. In the regulatory arena, agencies charged with regulatory responsibilities may become the "captives" of the very interest they are supposed to regulate. Writing 25 years ago, Grant McConnell (1966) was extremely pessimistic about the perverse consequences of interest group influence in the state administrative process: "the machinery of state government has made an extensive accommodation to the demands of particular groups. . . . this accommodation has amounted to a parcelling out of public authority to private groups" (p. 189).

Others are more concerned about the ability of an administrative agency to structure interest group interaction so as to benefit itself. Here the concern is not "captured" agencies so much as "captured" groups. The specter of "cor-poratism" or "neocorporatism" is raised by some (Chubb, 1983). This section of the chapter explores both possibilities.

Considerable symmetry between the purposes that prompt interest groups to contact state agencies and those that motivate agencies to initiate contacts with groups suggests the value that each has for the other. This might be taken as evidence that a group-administrative linkage exists that excludes others. An excessively close relationship between organized groups and administrative agencies also may be evidenced by the frequent existence of advisory commit-tees composed of members of clientele or organized interest groups in the 10 study states. The existence of such committees was a significant predictor of greater interest group impact upon agency affairs.

Over against this evidence of possibly excessive interest group impact is other evidence that suggests that the role of organized groups in the state ad-ministrative process is not excessive. Administrators themselves do not report organized group impact to be especially great. One might doubt the validity of such estimates given various pressures to understate the role of groups. But my findings are consistent with those of other studies that rely upon administrator judgments, most notably those of Abney and Lauth (1986b) and Brudney and Hebert (1987).

Moreover, while intensity of group-initiated interaction is a significant pre-dictor of greater interest group impact, it was not a terribly powerful one. Certainly the appointed as opposed to elected status of most state administrators limits the effectiveness of many of the influence resources that groups can bring to bear on state administrative agencies. Robert Fried (1976, pp. 336–337) suggests why interest group influence attempts may often generate little return:

Administrators often resent an attempt by a group to exercise "pressure." In their re-sponsiveness to groups, administrators are bound by their official role, which requires some impartiality and attention to the public interest. Administrators may, because of conscience, professional honor, or prudence, refuse to listen to demands involving ille-gal or improper action. Moreover, administrators are de facto interest groups of their own, with distinctive interests to protect, advance, and defend. Even with their financial resources, interest groups are no better able than any other public actor in the political process to shake the inertial tendencies of public bureaucracies.

More recently, James Q. Wilson (1989, p. 88) has observed that

government agencies are not billiard balls driven hither and yon by the impact of forces and interests. When bureaucrats are free to change a course of action their choice will reflect the full array of incentives operating on them: some will reflect the need to manage a workload; others will reflect the expectations of workplace peers and professional colleagues elsewhere; still others may reflect their own convictions. And some will reflect the needs of clients; that is, those people or groups that are affected disproportionately by the actions of the agency.

In their 50-state study, Abney and Lauth (1986b) found that "when the exchanges (between groups and departments) became skewed, and a department receives more requests than it makes, the result is likely to be more negative for the department than if it were in a symmetrical relationship with interest groups" (p. 90). The proportion of respondents who felt that the effect of group interaction was to "distort departmental priorities" was 21% for those respondents in a "mutual dependence" relationship as opposed to 29% when interest groups were actively contacting an agency but the agency initiated little interaction with groups (the equivalent of the "besieged agency" interaction pattern in the 10–state study). Only 13% of the respondents in a mutually dependent relationship felt that group influence discouraged impartiality of rule application in comparison to 20% of those in the "interest group-active" setting. Findings from my 10-state study on the severity of interest group opposition to agency programs as a problem stemming from variation in agency-group interaction patterns are consistent with the findings of Abney and Lauth. Among administrators whose units were involved in a "mutually active" relationships with interests groups, 21% considered group opposition to their unit's programs to be a serious problem. But this is true of 25% of respondents from "besieged" agencies.

Given the foregoing, what must be stressed is that in nearly half of the cases in these 10 states intense group-initiated interaction was matched by equally intense levels of unit-initiated interaction. A pattern of interaction "skewed" in favor of interest groups, on the other hand, occurred less than 20% of the time.

Adverse consequences for the public interest stemming from interest group involvement in administrative affairs are also more likely if administrative units interact with a narrow range of groups that speak with one voice. Rourke (1976, p. 55) contends that the "heterogeneity of an administrative agency's group support" is extremely important in "determining its freedom of action." If this is so, then it is significant that in the 10 study states most administrative units interacted with a fairly substantial number of groups. Moreover, while hostile relationships with groups were not common, neither were consistently supportive ones. Last, group-agency comity is less likely when high levels of group-initiated contacts occur, and when the number of groups with which an agency interacts is greater.

Group opposition to agency programs is another indicator of conflict between interest groups and administrative agencies. The negative impact of greater complexity in the group-administrative milieu for the affective quality of that relationship is evident from the fact that more than 33% of those managers who reported very frequent group-initiated contacts considered interest group opposition to be a serious problem. This was true of only 16% of those who reported only "frequent" contacts and just 6% of those who experienced occasional interest group-initiated contacts. Respondents from units that interacted with seven or more groups were more than twice as likely to consider group opposition to be a serious impediment to effective management as were those in units that interacted with three groups or less.

Most of the administrative units in the 10 study states appear to manifest relationships with groups that are consistent with J. Q. Wilson's (1989) description of an "interest group agency." Such an agency is "neither the tool nor the victim of an outside interest" because it is the object of "offsetting pressures from rival interest groups" (p. 78). These competing forces will, again in Wilson's words, "hold the agency erect." Although most state administrative agencies may exist in such an environment, this is not to say that groups do not sometimes constitute a problem for them or that interaction with other political actors will necessarily be uncomplicated. Regarding the political life of such agencies, Wilson (1989, p. 81) observes that

agencies confronting interest-group politics might seem to have an easy time of it: with their environment split among contending groups they can pick and choose how they define their tasks, secure in the knowledge that somebody out there is likely to be their ally. But in fact it is not so easy. For one thing, anything they do will be criticized by somebody and, like most people, bureaucrats don't enjoy criticism. For another, their political superiors in the executive branch and the [legislature] will tilt, depending on the political winds, first toward one interest group and then toward another. Under these circumstances it will be hard to know what one is supposed to do; things that were once rewarded now are penalized, and vice versa.

Evidence of the complicated life of an "interest-group" agency can be found in the fact that one-fifth of the managers of units who described the orientation of the groups with which their units interacted to be highly variable, reported interest group opposition to their unit's programs to be a serious impediment to effective management. While group opposition to their agencies' efforts seems to seriously complicate the lives of many state managers, this is a different issue from concerns that groups and agencies are too often locked in loving embrace. Such opposition may be the price to be paid for the fact that three-fourths of the units in these 10 states experience a group milieu characteristic of interest group agencies. On balance, however, a state bureaucracy filled with numerous interest group agencies would seem preferable, from both the point of view of managers and of the average citizen and taxpayer, to one filled with numerous "captured" agencies.

Although this has been of relatively less concern to observers, at least some are concerned about the possibility that administrative agencies may dominate the groups with which they interact. It is argued that agencies may be able to structure or organize group support in ways that may benefit those agencies but not necessarily the broader public interest. Here the problem is "captured" groups rather than "captured" agencies. Chubb (1983) has raised the specter of "neocorporatism" in the interaction between federal administrative agencies and organized interests when, "through 'advisory' incorporation, selective cooperation, 'biased' ground rules for participation, and outright cooptation, the administration structures group-access and influence as assuredly as does any so-called corporatist system." Hence, "the bureaucracy is not a passive recipient of group demands, but rather it actively encourages, impedes, and otherwise manipulates group participation" (p. 13; see also Peters, 1984, pp. 151–153).

In the 10 states focused on here, interest group impact is quite modest. Perhaps this is so because agencies dominate or manipulate groups. State agencies clearly "use" groups to achieve various purposes. Advisory bodies consisting of interest group representatives among others are common, and administrators' comments on the role played by such bodies suggest that agencies often use them as vehicles for mobilizing political support, or for communicating the "agency line" to group members. I also found that the orientation of interest groups toward particular agencies was most consistently supportive when the frequency of agency-initiated contacts with those groups was most intense.

Still, it is difficult to conclude that the nature of interest group-agency interaction in these 10 states can fairly be characterized as "corporatist" or "neocorporatist." Graham Wilson (1981) contends that "corporatist" tendencies are much less likely to characterize administrative-interest group relationships in the United States than in Europe because American interest groups are rather badly equipped to provide administrative agencies with the two primary resources that agencies seek. One of these is detailed information of a technical nature needed by an agency to make decisions. Wilson's analysis suggests that interest groups typically "have had little of a technical nature to tell bureaucrats that they did not know already" (p. 126). Moreover, because interests have been divided into competing groups, the bureaucracy has not been able to depend upon groups to supply the necessary "consents" to policies—guarantees that the groups in question can live with a given policy.

Just as evidence of affectively variable group milieus that include numerous groups would seem to argue against the validity of the "captured agency" model, so, too, does it argue against the validity of the "neocorporatist" view.

The orientation of groups toward a unit's programs is most positive when a unit dominates the exchanges between it and various groups. But such a "besieged groups" pattern emerged only about 10% of the time. Even then, the percentage of respondents reporting a "consistently supportive" group environment is at most 10% greater than for other interaction patterns. This 10% difference may be testimony to the limits of a state agency's ability to construct a supportive group constituency. As Peters (1984, p. 153) observes, "in general, corporatism is of limited importance for understanding how government manages its relationships with interest groups" because "the pressures that almost all developed economies confront have made interest groups less cooperative with government and less willing to be coopted."

Data on group opposition to unit programs as an impediment to agency performance suggests that proactive state administrative units experience some success in structuring group interaction. Only 11% of the administrators of units that exhibit the "agency active" pattern report group opposition to be a serious problem. This compares to 25% of the managers of the "besieged" agencies (group-active pattern) and 21% of those in the "mutually active" situation. But again, less than 1 agency in 10 exhibits a pattern where agency contact with groups is pronounced but contacts initiated by groups are infrequent.

If "captured groups" exist in the 10 states, we would expect that the correlation between interest group impact in a particular influence arena and agency impact in the same arena ought to be more strongly positive when agencies dominate the interaction between themselves and organized groups. The logic is that group allies enhance a unit's ability to have its way vis-a-vis other actors. As discussed earlier in the chapter, modest positive correlations ranging from .08 to .12 existed between agency impact and interest group impact on overall budget levels, budgets for specific unit programs, broader policies, and the content of rules and regulations. When the intensity of unit-initiated interaction with groups far exceeds the frequency of group-initiated interaction with the unit, stronger positive correlations existed between group and unit impact on establishing administrative procedures ($r = .19$, $p = .06$) and on daily operations ($r = .10$, $p = .22$) than was true overall. This might be interpreted as indicating that a compliant set of interest groups facilitates execution of more narrowly administrative tasks by a unit itself. There is also a stronger positive correlation between agency impact and interest group impact on broader policy ($r = .16$, $p = .09$) when the agency dominates interaction. The link between agency and interest impact is no stronger when the agency dominates interaction with groups in the case of the other three arenas, however.

In summary, in these 10 states it is possible to discern evidence of both "captured agencies" and "captured groups." Neither model adequately describes the dominant reality of state administrative-interest group interaction, however. The broader public in these states is presumably better off because this is so.

STATE ADMINISTRATIVE AGENCIES AND THEIR CLIENTELE: A SECOND FACE OF THE "PUBLIC"

The performance of public bureaucracies often depends upon how well they deal with their clients, those individuals or groups that often are—in a fundamental sense—why these organizations exist.[19] Standards of bureaucratic performance often focus on how successful an agency is in getting its clients to take advantage of particular services or benefits, or in regulating or modifying their behavior.

One of the supposed virtues of bureaucracies is that they treat similar cases similarly. Once a client has satisfied established criteria for receiving services, the ideal bureaucrat, drawing upon his or her professional expertise, proceeds to provide those services while ignoring irrelevant factors such as a client's social status, ethnicity, gender, political connections, or the like. This optimistic view of the admnistrative-client interface is challenged by those who argue that a bureaucracy's emphasis on reliability and consistency causes administrative officials to overemphasize the importance of formal rules. "Going by the book" becomes an end in itself so that the bureaucrat "never forgets a single rule binding his actions and, hence, is unable to assist many of his clients" (Merton, 1940). The bureaucratic norm of equal treatment also gets perverted as bureaucrats treat all clients in an equally nasty, unhelpful fashion.

The question is whether administrator-client relations are fairly characterized in this way. Certainly many of the administrative horror stories so popular with the mass media portray situations where client needs seem to be among the very last things that administrative agencies care about. On the other hand, in this study, only 4% of those administrators surveyed thought there was a serious problem with clients being treated inappropriately by agency employees, although another 39% felt that this was at least a minor problem. This finding might be dismissed as little more than a self-serving misperception of reality by these administrators were it not for the fact that it is consistent with other research that relies on the views of citizens who have actually dealt with particular public agencies, or with assessments of records of agency dealings with clients. A number of these studies were discussed in Chapter 2.

The ability of public organizations to meet the needs of citizens is hampered by much more than bureaucrats with bad attitudes, however. Administrative offices may be inaccessible, especially for those who must rely on public transportation, and hours of operation may be inconvenient. Clients with little education may find application forms or procedures difficult to understand. The remedies for these barriers to clientele service, along with a number of others, often lie in the hands of the political sovereigns of state bureaucracies. Resources adequate to meet clientele demand are a problem for many agencies. Recall that 40% of the managers saw insufficient appropriations and legislative expansion of programs without sufficient additional funding to be serious impediments to effective performance. Program success may also depend upon whether citizens are aware of the existence of a program in the first place, and of the criteria that must be satisfied to be eligible for program benefits. A study of 11 Canadian and American public agencies at all levels of government found that administrators believed that there was "widespread constituency ignorance of agency programs" (Friedman et al., 1966; see also Nelson, 1980, and Prottas, 1981). In the 10–state study, 10% of the managers surveyed saw inadequate publicity on their units' programs, or on the eligibility criteria for these programs, as seriously impeding the performance of their units. Another 37% felt that this was at least a minor problem.

Clients impact upon administrative agencies in ways other than by simply availing themselves of agency programs. Under the best of circumstances, clients can provide useful information on the effectiveness of current programs that can be used to fine tune the operation of those programs. Demands for existing services, or for services that are not currently being provided, provide insight into the extent to which various needs are being met. Administrators may be able to use such information to make the case for expanded funding for existing programs or for the establishment of new ones.

The service orientation of agencies, combined with the critical nature of the client-agency nexus for organizational success, is surely one reason that administrators generally seem to accept, if not always warmly welcome, increased clientele impact on agency affairs. When Gruber (1987, p. 94) asked administrators in three agencies in one city—"Who do you think has a right to a say about what goes on in your department?"—she found that the most commonly cited outside groups "were those affected by decisions (clients, parents, tenants)." A more extensive survey of New Jersey municipal administrators (Greene, 1982) found that these administrators preferred citizen contacts to those from elected officials. They also stated that they responded more favorably to contacts from citizens than from elected officials. One reason was that they believed citizens/clients provided more accurate information about service delivery problems. Finally, in her 50-state study, Miller (1987) compared administrators' estimates of the actual influence of various actors to the amount of influence that these administrators preferred these various actors to have. Agency clients, along with "citizens at large," were among the three actors whose influence these administrators most wanted to see increased.

Whatever may be the context of agency-client interaction, and its consequences for agency operations in the 10 study states, it is the case that the clientele of an agency typically had at least a moderate amount of impact across the six influence arenas.[20]

In contrast to the pattern for nearly every other nonagency actor, those served by an agency are seen to have their greatest impact on the daily operations of an agency. Nearly half of those surveyed felt that clients had moderate or greater influence in this arena. Agency clientele are the most significant nonagency actors in this area with interest groups ranking sixth. The impact attributed to clientele surely reflects the fact that contact between administrative employees and clients occurs most regularly as programs are carried out on a day-to-day basis. It reflects another factor as well. In her single-city study, Gruber (1987) found that citizen contacts with municipal agencies were highly "particularistic" in content, involving specific, service-related problems, rather than concerned with broader policy. Particularistic contacts should logically most affect daily administrative routines.

Although not influencing the nature of administrative procedures or structures quite as much as daily operations, agency clients rank as the fifth most powerful nonagency actor with nearly 30% of the respondents seeing them as at least moderately influential. Again, the clients of a unit exert more influence than do organized groups.

Clientele impact is not limited to more narrowly administrative realms, however. Those served by a unit are estimated to average somewhere between "small" and "moderate" impact in determining overall budget levels for a unit as well as on spending levels for specific unit programs, in determining broader policies affecting a unit, and shaping rules and regulations. Indeed, clientele impact equals or is only slightly less than that attributed to interest groups in all but the broader policy arenas. If the influence attributed to clientele in a given arena is subtracted from the influence attributed to organized groups in the same arena, the mean influence differentials (with a negative sign indicating that clientele influence exceeds interest group influence) for the six arenas are:

Determining the overall budget level for a unit	.06
Determining budgets for specific unit programs	.11
Making major agency policy or program changes	.53
Determining the content of rules and regulations	.00
Establishing administrative procedures/structures	− .14
Conducting daily administrative operations	− .47

Considerable variation in clientele impact exists across the agencies, however, with coefficients of variation ranging from .44 to .49 across the six influence arenas. We would expect that agencies with differing functional missions might experience different relationships with their clientele, just as they experienced differing relationships with organized interest groups. This is indeed so, as significant differences in clientele impact exist across functional categories for all six arenas. Units with natural resources responsibilities reported greatest clientele impact across the six arenas, while those with education responsibilities also ranked high in clientele impact. On the other hand, units with transportation functions generally reported less clientele impact, as did units with fiscal staff responsibilities. Those directly affected by the latter type of units are, of course, not private groups or individuals so much as other state agencies. On the other hand, units with nonfiscal staff responsibilities such as personnel agencies tend to report among the highest levels of clientele impact despite the fact that their primary clientele is other units of state government.

Since we have seen that interest group impact and clientele impact are correlated, and that interest group impact also varies by the functional responsibility of a unit, it is unsurprising that clientele impact also varies as a consequence of differences in the programmatic responsibilities of agencies.[21] But functional responsibility is not related to clientele influence in quite the same fashion as was interest group impact. Units with natural resources responsibilities reported higher than average levels of both interest group and clientele group impact, while fiscal staff units reported lower than average levels of impact, on the part of both actors. But, while health units rank high in reported interest group impact, they rank low in clientele impact. Nonfiscal staff units, on the other hand, report fairly limited interest group impact upon their affairs while reporting relatively high levels of clientele impact.

One implication of these findings is that there is a sharper division, a lower degree of overlap, between those who are organized to exert influence upon an agency and those whom an agency supposedly serves in the case of units with certain responsibilities than others. In some cases this may reflect the fact that the clients of certain agencies are less completely mobilized. It might also reflect the fact that those whom an agency may rely upon for service delivery via contractual arrangements are more highly organized than are the consumers of those services.

Variation in the overlap between interest group and clientele impact as a consequence of the functional responsibility of a unit becomes clearer if we examine the strength of the correlations between interest group and clientele impact for agencies with differing functional missions. Perhaps the best example of this bifurcation comes in the case of criminal justice units. The correlations between client impact and interest group impact are .22 or smaller for all of the arenas except daily operations. Recall that comparable correlations for the entire sample across the six arenas ranged from .47 to .59. If we look at the mean difference in impact attributed to each actor in particular arenas, criminal justice units consistently report either a smaller than average influence advantage for interest groups, or a larger than average influence advantage for clients. Given the fact that many of the clients of criminal justice agencies are incarcerated, what this pattern really highlights is the impotence of those interest groups concerned with criminal justice programs.

In contrast to the criminal justice situation, the correlations between interest group impact and clientele impact for agencies with natural resources and environmental responsibilities are stronger than average. The same is true to a lesser extent for education units. For natural resources units, these correlations ranged from .53 to .71; for environmental units they ranged from .44 to .86; for education units the range was .52 to .60. In the case of these functions, clients may be more fully integrated into the interest group structure of a state.

A final vantage point from which to view state administrative agency interaction with clientele is provided by data on the use of various management "improvements" and managers' judgments as to the efficacy of these improvements. Among the techniques, practices, and strategies concerning which I sought the views of state managers were a few that might be seen as expanding clientele influence on agency affairs. These include the use of citizen committees, open meeting ("sunshine") requirements, and freedom of information (FOI) requirements. A few others might be seen as vehicles for enhancing the quality of service that agencies provide. These include an ombudsman office to whom citizens may resort if they feel they have been unfairly treated, as well as systematic efforts by agencies to secure information from clients about agency program operations. Access to services might also be enhanced if units were open for business in the evenings and/or on Saturdays.

Consistent with the data on the existence of advisory groups that was reported earlier in the chapter, 58% of the managers surveyed said that a citizen advisory committee of some sort existed that provided their unit with input, while 62% reported that sunshine provisions applied to their unit, and 78% said that their units were affected by freedom of information provisions. A high 90% or more of the respondents were familiar with each of these strategies or practices.

The managers in the 10 states were quite sanguine about the consequences of citizen committees and "sunshine" provisions. Of those familiar with citizen committees, 80% thought their consequences for agency performance were generally positive, while just under 70% were positive about sunshine provisions. This may be evidence of something of a clientele orientation among these state managers. Only 43% saw freedom of information requirements as enhancing agency performance, however. This proportion is only slightly lower than the proportion of state agency officials responsible for responding to FOI requests surveyed by Klemanski and Maschke (forthcoming) who felt that such laws had improved state government. One explanation for the difference in managers' views on the first two techniques as compared to those regarding FOI provisions is that FOI provisions do not so much benefit the typical individual client seeking information concerning the grounds for agency actions that are considered to be unjust, as they do business and other organized interests. (Regarding the beneficiaries of the Federal Freedom of Information Act, see *Public Administration Review,* 1986, pp. 603–639.) In this regard, it may be significant that those who had actual experience with the effects of citizen committees and open meeting provisions were more sanguine about them than were those who had no direct experience with them, while the opposite was true in the case of FOI provisions.

The managers I surveyed were less familiar with ombudsmen offices (71% familiar), surveys of clientele to ascertain either the relative need for or satisfaction with services (78% familiar), or the utility of evening or Saturday hours of operation (63% familiar); than they were with the practices discussed in the preceding paragraph. They were also less likely to have had direct experience with these three as opposed to citizen committees, sunshine provisions, or FOI provisions. Only 13% had direct experience with an ombudsman office and only 14% had experience with evening or weekend hours. More than 33% claimed to have used clientele surveys, however.

Nearly 90% of those familiar with clientele surveys thought they were likely to have positive consequences for the operation of their units, as did 75% of those familiar with ombudsman offices. While neither is particularly widely used, those who had direct experience with either of the two were even more positive. Overall, only 64% of those familiar with evening/Saturday hours felt that the effects for agency operations would be positive, despite the fact that extending hours presumably makes it easier for clients to secure services. This may reflect managerial concerns about staffing needs or staff resistance to a move away from the traditional workday or workweek. On the other hand, among the small percentage of managers who had more direct experience with such hours of operation, the proportion who saw them as having positive effects on agency effectiveness was 74%. Among those lacking direct experience with this practice only 54% believed its effects to be positive.

To the extent that citizen committees, sunshine provisions, an ombudsman, or clientele surveys make it easier for clients to communicate their concerns or make state agencies more sensitive to their needs, the impact attributed to clientele should be enhanced. In general this is the case, although the relationships are not terribly strong. Units that reported the use of citizen committees had greater clientele impact across five of the six influence arenas, with eta statistics ranging from .07 to .12. The presence of an ombudsman is associated with a significant increase in clientele influence on the determination of spending for specific agency programs, determination of broader policy, and the content of rules and regulations. Units whose decisionmaking processes are open to greater public scrutiny under the terms of open meeting provisions report somewhat greater clientele impact on broader policy and the content of rules and regulations. These findings are broadly consistent with those of Gormley concerning the effects of public hearings for environmental policymaking and an ombudsman for the quality of long-term health care for the elderly (Gormley, 1986b; see also Gormley, 1989b, pp. 74–77 and 82–85).

Agencies that seek feedback on the needs of clients or on their experiences with agency programs report somewhat greater clientele impact on overall agency spending, spending for specific agency programs, the shape of broader policy, and, in particular, daily operations. Agencies that systematically survey those whom they currently serve, or those whom they might potentially serve, may find information so gained to be useful in deciding how to allocate money among existing programs. They may also use such information to convince the governor or the legislature of the need for more money or new programs. Such information is likely to be especially useful in fine-tuning the ongoing operations of a unit.

CONCLUSION

This chapter has explored some of the "public" dimensions of the state administrative influence matrix, with a particular focus on the impact of organized interest groups and those served by state administrative agencies. Both are significant elements in this matrix, although neither actor exerts as much influence as the state legislature or the governor.

Many of the managers reported high levels of group-initiated contacts with their units. Such interaction did not necessarily translate into influence, however. One reason for this is that most agencies interact with a substantial number of groups and these groups typically disagree over agency programs or operations. Another reason is that agencies are not passive objects of interest group influence efforts. Rather, a substantial proportion of the units in these 10 states report frequent unit-initiated contact with groups.

The picture of interest group impact that emerges from this study is consistent with previous comparative analyses of state administrative dynamics. Moreover, it is not a picture of interest group domination and "captured" agencies. At the same time, although units often initiate contact with organized groups, and clearly make use of interest groups in the pursuit of their objectives, the data do not provide much support for a "corporatist" or "neocorporatist" view of group-administrative agency influence dynamics.

In this chapter I have paid little attention to interstate differences in interest group impact. This was so because significant variation existed only for group impact on the content of rules and regulation and on daily operations, and here the differences were not great. I make this point because studies of interest group influence upon the state legislative process generally assert the existence of significant differences across states.[22] One explanation for this discrepancy may be that, across the nation, state bureaucracies are more similar to one another than are state legislatures. This may be a reflection of the fact that elements of bureaucratic professionalization, such as civil service systems, that serve to insulate state managers from interest groups have diffused more generally than have changes associated with legislative professionalization.

The 10-state survey provided less insight into clientele impact on state administration than into interest group impact. One reason was the possibility that the influence of one overlaps with estimates of the impact of the other. Still, I argued that administrators do not view the two as synonymous. Often those most directly affected by an agency were seen to have greater impact on agency affairs than were organized groups. This was especially so in more narrowly administrative realms. The managers I surveyed were also favorably disposed to arrangements likely to enhance client impact on agency decisionmaking such as citizen committees, more open agency deliberations, and an ombudsman. They also believed that efforts to survey clients regarding their experiences with, and judgments concerning the adequacy of, agency programs had important benefits in terms of agency performance. Since this is so, it is encouraging that at least a third of those surveyed claimed to have actually had the benefit of such surveys in their units.

NOTES

1. The universe of influence actors ignores the impact of the general public, what Miller (1987) calls "citizens-at-large." Here my focus is on more highly attentive or active publics that have a greater stake in what a given agency does. State employee associations or unions might also be considered to be interest groups, and at least some of these organizations view their role as similar to that of professional associations. Indeed, in speaking of professional associations in their 50–state study, Brudney and Hebert (1987) assert that they represent "some or possibly many of their employees." While possessing data on the impact of employee associations, I have chosen not to explore this impact in this chapter. One reason is that, as discussed in Chapter 6, employee unions usually loaded on a different factor than did interest groups, professional associations, and clients. Generally, their influence was associated with that wielded by state personnel and budget offices and other line agencies, suggesting much more of an "insider" role for them. Moreover, unlike the elements of an agency's public that I choose to focus on, the significance of employee associations or unions is substantial only in those states in which collective bargaining is well established.

2. The zero-order correlations between administrative estimates of interest group impact and professional association impact range from .39 for the broad policy arena to .49 for influence on overall budget levels. Comparable correlations between interest group and clientele impact range from .47 in the determination of spending levels for specific programs to .59 for influence on the content of agency rules and regulations. The correlations between clientele and professional association impact range from .36 in the daily operations arena to .42 in the case of influence on overall budget levels.

3. "High" levels of group or unit-initiated interaction were defined as existing when either type of contact was said by respondents to occur "frequently" or "very frequently." "Low" interaction existed if respondents indicated that contacts of either sort never occurred or occurred only occasionally.

4. These findings on patterns of administrative agency-interest group interaction are broadly consistent with those of Abney and Lauth in their recent 50–state study (1986b). They explore the need of interest groups for "resources" controlled by administrative agencies, along with the need of administrative units for "resources" that groups can provide. They then analyze the resulting "exchange patterns." Their "mutual dependence" pattern (high group need for agency resources and correspondingly high agency need for group resources), seemingly analogous to the "mutually active" pattern in my schema, existed in 35% of the cases. "Mutual independence" occurred 39% of the time. This pattern, although analogous to the "mutually inactive" pattern in my schema, was less common than was the "mutually inactive" pattern in the 10 state study. An "administrator active" pattern emerged 12% of the time, a proportion only slightly larger than that of cases falling into the analogous "agency active" pattern in my study. Finally, Abney and Lauth report that 15% of the cases fell into the "interest group active" category. This compares to the 20% of cases that fell into the analogous "besieged agency" category in the 10 study states.

5. The 10-state findings on the purposes that prompt group contacts with administrative agencies are similar to those that Abney and Lauth (1986b) uncovered in their 50-state study. They found the most common "departmental resources" sought by interest groups to be, in decreasing order of significance: obtaining information on departmental programs, seeking to affect departmental regulations, seeking to influence the department's legislative program, obtaining new departmental programs, registering complaints about service delivery, gaining support for their legislative priorities, influencing a department's proposed budget, and seeking the department's support for the group in its dealing with federal agencies. The rank order of the first four of these resources is identical to that for the comparable purposes of group-initiated contacts in the 10-state study.

6. Administrators' responses to an open-ended survey question regarding the involvement of interest groups in agency affairs are consistent with the findings on the purposes of both group and agency-initiated contacts that emerge from the close-ended questions. Thus, among the 523 responses to this question, 21% related to how agencies rely upon groups in implementing agency programs. Of this number, more than half (57) noted how groups were used to disseminate information to their members and others regarding new agency programs or changes in existing programs. Some 16% of those responding noted that groups were involved in the policy formulation process or were at least asked to review and comment upon proposed changes in agency policies, rules and regulations, or procedures. Group involvement in lobbying the legislature or other state decisionmakers regarding agency programs or budget requests was mentioned by 18% of the respondents.

7. The proportion of administrators who described the orientation of groups toward their unit to be consistently unsupportive ranges from 2% in Texas to 13% in Vermont. The proportion who described the orientation of groups toward their unit to be consistently supportive ranged from 16% in Vermont and 17% in Delaware to 34% in Arizona and Indiana. The proportion characterizing the orientation of groups toward their unit as highly variable ranged from 59% in Indiana to 76% in New York.

8. Frequency of unit-initiated contacts is also positively associated with number of groups interested in a unit's affairs although less strongly. Thus, only 29% of the managers who reported only occasional unit-initiated contacts with groups said that seven or more groups paid attention to their unit's activities. This compares to 71% of the managers of units that very frequently initiated contacts with groups.

9. An increase in the number of groups involved in influencing agency affairs is weakly associated with a less favorable group milieu. Among the administrators who reported that three or fewer groups paid close attention to their affairs, 32% reported supportive relations. But this was true of just 22% of the respondents whose units interacted with four or more groups.

10. The relationship between frequency of agency-initiated interaction and perceptions of interest group opposition as a management problem is less strong; the bivariate correlation is .13 ($p = .000$, one-tailed).

11. Analysis of variance indicates that agencies with differing functional responsibilities differ significantly in the size of their budgets with the eta statistic for these two variables being .40. But they do not appear to be so closely related that they can not be entered simultaneously in the same regression model. Variation in the size of unit budgets within functional categories is substantial.

12. Multivariate models of group or agency-initiated contact were also estimated for

each of the state samples. While there is little consistency across states in the structure of these models, the results suggest that the predictive power of unit size may be linked to functional responsibility and may also reflect the fact that more populous states, whose units tend to have larger budgets, also tend to be among the states in which more intense group-agency interaction occurs. The size of a unit's budget can account for even as little as 1% of the variance in group-initiated interaction in just four states. One or another of the dummy variables representing functional responsibilities can account for 3% or more of the variance in interest group-initiated contacts in every state but Texas and Vermont. What these functional responsibilities are varies considerably, however. Functional responsibility emerges as an even more consistent predictor of variation in levels of agency-initiated contact with groups. Having economic development responsibilities is associated with more intense contacts in three states. Having natural resources responsibilities—a significant predictor in the overall model—is a significant predictor of more intense interaction in three states, accounting for between 2% and 15% of the variance.

13. Precisely what "impact" or "influence" means when groups are seen to be consistently supportive of a unit and its programs is unclear. In such a situation groups may be "demanding" precisely what the agency is inclined to do.

14. For all six arenas the correlations between agency-initiated interaction and interest group impact are weaker among units that interact more intensely with the governor and his staff. Gubernatorial-agency interaction dampens the significance of agency-initiated interaction for interest group impact on budget levels for specific agency programs and daily operations in particular.

15. The linkages between levels of agency-initiated contacts with groups and interest group impact are also stronger when legislative interaction between agencies and the legislature is more intense.

16. When all variables were entered into the models, gubernatorial interaction emerged as a significant negative predictor of interest group impact on the content of rules and regulations, establishing administrative procedures, and daily operations, but it could account for less than 1% of the variance. Intensity of agency interaction with legislative program committees never achieved statistical significance, nor did intensity of agency interaction with budget committees.

17. When a similar set of variables was used to predict the impact of professional associations on state administration, their explanatory power was even lower. Total explained variance ranged from 3% in the case of determination of overall agency budget levels, to 7% in the case of determination of broader policy and the content of rules and regulations, and 8% in the case of budgets for specific agency programs. In Brudney and Hebert's research (1987), about 8% of the variance in professional association impact could be explained. In my models, as in theirs, the functional focus of a unit most often emerged as a significant predictor, with health or education units reporting greater professional association impact.

18. The significance criteria were relaxed for the single state models so that any variable significant at the .10 level was included.

19. Rourke (1976) makes the important point that the clients of some government agencies are other agencies in their unit of government or in different units of government. This would seem to be more true of federal than state agencies, however, given the federal government's heavy reliance on grant-in-aid arrangements for the accomplishment of federal purposes.

20. The reader is reminded of the substantial correlations between estimates of interest group and clientele influence. The correlations between clientele impact in a particular arena and interest group impact in the same arena range from .47 to .59. When the clientele that an agency serves is substantially represented by organized groups, it may be difficult for administrators to distinguish the impact of the one from the other. But I believe that administrators' estimates of clientele impact are measuring something separate from interest group impact in most cases. Some of the reasons for believing this to be so will become apparent as the discussion in the text proceeds. But one reason worth noting here is that the correlations between intensity of group-initiated contacts with agencies, or of agency-initiated contacts with groups on the one hand, and interest group impact on the other, are much stronger than are the correlations between these two indicators of interest group-agency interaction and estimates of clientele impact. The correlations between interest group impact on overall budget levels and budgets for specific agency programs, and intensity of group-initiated contacts with agencies, are .28 and .27, respectively. The correlations between clientele impact and intensity of group-initiated contacts with agencies for these same two arenas are only .14 and .15, respectively. The correlation between interest group impact on daily operations and intensity of group-initiated contacts is .31. For this same arena the correlation between clientele impact and intensity of group-initiated contact is only .11.

21. The eta statistics, which range from .20 to .22, are slightly smaller than the comparable statistics for interest group impact variation across functional areas.

22. See, for example, Francis (1967), Zeigler (1983), and Morehouse (1981), all of which focus on group impact on the legislative process. In their recent study, Thomas and Hrebenar, (1990, p. 141) seek to ascertain "the extent to which interest groups as a whole influence public policy when compared to other components of the political system, such as political parties, the legislatures, the governor, etc." They imply that they are interested in group impact on all aspects of state government, including administrative agencies. But they also list state agencies as a "type of interest," presumably one that seeks to influence the legislature. Since their subsequent discussion includes few specific references to group efforts to influence administrative agencies, I am inclined to conclude that their findings on interstate differences in group impact apply to impact on the legislative process alone.

Chapter 9

Managing to Manage in the American States?

This book has explored the performance of administrative agencies in 10 American states. The severity of various potential impediments to effective performance has been examined, as has the utility of various possible "solutions" to these problems. The second half of the book examined the role that state administrative agencies play in the broader state political process. An effort was also made to specify the significance of various elements of the "influence matrix" within which the conduct of state management is embedded. These issues have been examined through the eyes of one of the most important participants in state administrative affairs—senior managers.

STATE MANAGEMENT PROBLEMS AND THEIR SOLUTION

The examination of managerial difficulties in Chapters 2 and 3 suggested that certain state agencies and managers faced serious obstacles to the achievement of their objectives. But few seemed overwhelmed by those obstacles. These state agencies "managed to manage" most of the time. Nor was it the case that the managers surveyed generally blamed most of their problems on the actions of, or restrictions imposed by, external actors such as the legislature, the governor, the courts, the federal government, interest groups, or the media. Despite disagreement over what constitutes "good" management, and despite the complex environment for public agencies that results from this disagreement, views that Whorton and Worthley (1981) have dubbed "if-only management" were rare. Administrators in these 10 states tended to strike a balance between blaming circumstances or actions beyond their control for their problems and recognizing that many of the solutions to their problems lie within their own grasp.

Given that state administrative performance is less than ideal, another concern of the study was to examine the utility of various techniques or strategies for enhancing that performance. Efforts to "improve" American public management reflect differential attachment to conflicting values, however. In recognition of this fact, I opted for a very broad definition of what might be considered to constitute a management "improvement." Included were those techniques or strategies whose effects were likely to limit the operational autonomy of state agencies.

The analysis in Chapter 4 indicated that familiarity with various management improvements was quite high among the managers in these 10 states. Thus, 60% or more of the managers were familiar with 42 of the 53 techniques. Actual use of various techniques, or an agency having been made subject to them, was less common, however. Still, 35 of the techniques were used by or affected one-quarter of more of the units.

Familiarity with and use of various "improvements" was conditioned by their likely effects on agency autonomy, however. Strategies likely to limit the operational autonomy of administrative agencies were significantly more widely used than were those that either expanded such autonomy or had little effect on it. Familiarity and use were positively related. In the case of techniques that limited administrative autonomy, however, it would appear that use stimulates familiarity. This is so because autonomy-constraining "improvements" are frequently imposed on agencies by legislatures, governors, or the courts. Hence, state administrators are most likely to use, or be subjected to, those techniques that not they but others are inclined to adopt. Increased use of autonomy-reducing techniques reflects the vigorous struggles for "custody" of state administrative agencies that have occurred in many states (Gormley, 1989a).

A majority of the managers surveyed attributed positive effects for agency operations to all but four techniques, while roughly half of the techniques were positively viewed by three managers in four. Judgments of efficacy were linked to the effects of particular techniques for agency autonomy. Four of the five practices that managers viewed least positively are among those techniques that I classified as autonomy-constraining: the legislative veto, whistleblowing, rolling back civil service coverage, and zero-base budgeting. Autonomy-constraining techniques also constituted 11 of the 20 about which administrators were least enthusiastic. Views on the efficacy of particular improvements were generally positively related to use. Use made managers' hearts grow fonder. This relationship did not, however, hold for techniques whose likely effects were to constrain administrative discretion. Relatively few managers familiar with such techniques considered them to be highly efficacious and actual experience with them dampened enthusiasm even more.

THE INFLUENCE MATRIX OF STATE MANAGEMENT

In the second half of the book, four chapters explored the role of state administrative agencies in state policymaking as well as the relationships of these agencies with various nonagency actors. The analysis in Chapter 5 suggested that state administrative agencies are important "policyshapers" that not only dominate narrowly administrative realms but also have an important voice in the making of broader policy decisions. Any wall that once may have separated the making of policy from its execution in these 10 states has clearly been breached from the administrative side. As suggested by Svara (1985), Burke (1989), and others, the politics-administration distinction makes sense only if viewed as a continuum.

The examination of the nonagency elements of the state administrative influence matrix that was the focus of Chapters 6, 7, and 8 indicated that nonagency actors also consider administration to be too important to leave to administrators. The most important nonagency actors are state legislatures, governors, and state budget offices. Certain federal government actors, interest groups, and agency clients are among the actors that also exert considerable influence, but the influence of these actors tends to be less than that exerted by the legislature, governors, or budget offices. The influence of these actors also tends to be less consistent across influence arenas. The detailed examination of legislative, gubernatorial, interest group, and clientele involvement in state administration in Chapters 7 and 8 further confirms these conclusions. Suffice it to say that the politics-administration wall has also been breached from the nonadministrative side in these 10 states.

Drawing upon and extending the insights of James Svara (1985), I would argue that the most appropriate model of the power relationships between state administrative agencies and various nonadministrative "thems" is that of "mission-management separation with shared responsibility for policy and administration." On the one hand, various nonagency actors, and particularly elected officials such as legislators and governors, dominate questions of *mission*—the broad goals that a jurisdiction sets for itself including the scope of services, the philosophy of taxation and spending, and constitutional issues. At the other end of the continuum, administrative agencies dominate in matters of *management*—those actions that support policy and administrative functions, including controlling and utilizing the human, material, and informational resources of the organization to best advantage and the application of specific techniques for delivering services. As one moves from the sphere of management to *administration*—the specific decisions, regulations, and practices employed to achieve policy objectives—the role of administrative actors remains dominant, but nonadministrative actors play a more important role than they do in the management sphere. The role of elected and other nonagency actors is even more important in the *policy* sphere. This sphere refers to "middle-range policy decisions" (Svara, 1985, p. 225), such as how to spend government revenues, whether to initiate new programs or create new offices, and how to distribute services at what levels within the existing range of services provided. But the role of administrators in making these decisions is also substantial. These relationships in the 10 study states in the specific case of state administrative units, state legislatures, and governors are mapped in Figure 7.1.

The cost of efforts to enhance bureaucratic accountability is a major theme linking the first and second parts of the book. Nonadministrative actors wield considerable power over the affairs of state administrative agencies. "Rogue" bureaucracies rarely existed in the 10 study states. For many readers I am sure that this is good news. But control has its costs, and certain means of bringing public bureaucracies to heel exact more of a cost in terms of administrative performance than do others.

This is also the central theme of William Gormley's recent book, *Taming the Bureaucracy* (1989b). Various of the findings of my study support the arguments of Gormley. Many of the managers I surveyed thought that the involvement of nonadministrative actors in administrative affairs, and the requirements imposed by some of these actors, complicated their unit's efforts to effectively discharge its responsibilities. Especially significant were constraints on how agencies may expend their appropriations and how higher level management may utilize human resources. Constraints on the expenditure of federal dollars, as well as processes to be followed in promulgating rules or regulations, were also perceived to be serious impediments.

As discussed in both Chapters 3 and 7, and reflecting the ability of various nonagency actors, most especially legislatures and governors, to impose their will on state agencies, the most frequently used techniques for "improving" the operations of those agencies are those whose effect is to constrain their autonomy. But it is just such techniques that managers felt had the least positive consequences for the ability of their units to perform.

The toll that may be exacted in administrative effectiveness as a consequence of the influence that nonagency actors wield in administrative affairs is also evident from some of the analyses reported in Chapters 6, 7, and 8. In general, as the influence exerted by a particular actor increased, administrative complaints about impediments to effective management resulting from such involvement grew. Thus, state personnel office impact was positively correlated with various personnel-related impediments, while the extent of federal government influence was associated with the severity of various federal government-related impediments to effective management. Where state employee unions are seen to exert greater impact, various collective-bargaining related problems are more severe. Complaints about excessive restrictions on appropriations are positively correlated with the amount of influence that the state budget office wields in several arenas. Increases in state and federal court impact are positively correlated with managers' complaints about court mandating of service levels. Finally, as discussed in Chapter 7, the level of influence that a legislature exerts over a state agency is positively related to the severity of a number of legislature-related impediments to effective state management. Such problems are more severe in the case of those units whose relationships with key legislative committees are least favorable.

Gormley (1989b) has argued that the major problem with recent attempts to "tame" state and federal bureaucracies has been the penchant for political sovereigns to utilize "coercive" rather than "hortatory" or "catalytic" means of control. Coercive controls, represented by such things as legislative vetoes, executive orders, court rulings, and other "solution-forcing statutes" (p. 13), seek to severely limit administrative choice. Catalytic controls, on the other hand, encourage bureaucratic discretion but seek to influence administrative decisionmaking by expanding the range of issues and alternatives that administrators must consider in discharging their responsibilities. As Gormley puts it,

catalytic controls require the bureaucracy to act but do not predetermine the nature of the bureaucracy's response. They require the bureaucracy to address a problem, but they do not specify a mandatory solution. Catalytic controls are attention-grabbing, action-forcing and energizing. They seek to raise the bureaucracy's consciousness by forcing bureaucrats to take certain ideas, problems, and interests seriously (p. 12).

Examples of catalytic controls include ombudsmen, proxy advocates, environmental impact statements, and agenda-setting statutes such as "the Public Utility Regulatory Policies Act (PURPA), which required state public utility commissions to 'consider and determine' the merits of various rate structure reforms" (p. 12). The category of controls that Gormley labels "hortatory" are "catalytic controls with 'bite,' coercive controls with an 'escape hatch' " (pp. 12–13). Examples of hortatory controls include the use of financial incentives to alter bureaucratic behavior or the possibility of a legislative postaudit.

Many of the management "improvement" strategies that are most widely used in these 10 states—those that I have labeled "autonomy-constraining"—are examples of coercive controls. Such controls often do seem to "work" in the sense of enhancing the influence of a particular actor. Perhaps the best example is the direct relationship between legislative impact and the existence of a process for legislative review or veto of rules or regulations proposed by state agencies.

Gormley argues against excessive reliance on coercive approaches to enhancing bureaucratic responsiveness on the grounds that such approaches exact too great a price so far as administrative efficiency and effectiveness are concerned. In his view, while coercive controls promote speed, coherence, and predictability, they also risk formalism, legalism, and micromanagement. While catalytic controls may not always be strong enough to reorient a bureaucracy, in the best of circumstances they stimulate flexibility, creativity, and imagination. The managers in my study tended to share Gormley's less-than-sanguine views of the effects of coercive controls while they looked more favorably upon those of a catalytic variety such as an ombudsman.

The managers whom I have surveyed for this study believe that a lack of adequate financial and human resources, together with constraints on how these resources can be used, are among the more serious impediments to administrative performance. They also tend to believe that practices that permit a stronger voice for nonagency actors in more narrowly administrative realms often have negative consequences for agency performance. Some readers may be inclined to dismiss these views as predictable in light of the supposedly insatiable desire of public managers and agencies for ever more resources and autonomy. I would argue, however, that those who are sincerely concerned about enhancing the performance of state bureaucracies ought to give considerable weight to these judgments. The involvement of these managers in the day-to-day implementation of state policies means that they are in a particularly good position to see the often negative consequences of budget cuts, staff reductions, or various forms of "micromanagement" by external actors.

The dilemma that confronts those concerned about state administrative performance has been aptly summarized by Gormley (1986a, p. 6):

Without some external pressure, bureaucrats will be less responsive, less efficient, and less innovative than they might otherwise be. However, if external pressure becomes excessive, bureaucrats will be less innovative, responsive, and efficient than they could be. In short, when we think of bureaucracy we need to think of a different ideal type— not a *complaint* bureaucracy that responds dutifully to numerous external stimuli but rather a *well-tempered* bureaucracy forced to respond in some fashion to important problems but free to respond sensibly and creatively.

In our zeal to cure the ills of state bureaucracy, we must be careful not to replace one ailment with an equally serious, albeit different, one.

MODELS OF STATE MANAGEMENT DYNAMICS AND IMPLICATIONS FOR FUTURE RESEARCH

The large number of managers surveyed in this study, combined with the fact that individual state samples were also relatively large, made it possible to test more complex models of the determinants of the various phenomena of interest in the study. On the one hand, while I was able to construct more complex models, their explanatory power was often limited. Sometimes this was so because there was relatively little variation to explain. The 10 states included in the study were selected with an eye to maximizing interstate variation. But whether the focus was on management difficulties, the use and efficacy of management techniques, the role of administrative agencies in the policymaking process, or the impact of external actors on state administrative affairs, the findings often displayed less variation across states than might have been expected. The fact that "state" was often not a significant predictor suggests that the context for state management is more constant across states than often supposed.

The general characteristics of administrative units or managers on which I possessed data, variables such as budget or staff size, location of a manager and his or her unit in a state's administrative hierarchy, and the functional responsibility of a unit, could explain relatively little variation in the severity of management problems or the use of management techniques. Nor could these factors account for much of the variation in the impact of the agency itself, or particular nonagency actors in specific influence arenas.

On the other hand, where I possessed information on variables that were more highly problem-, technique-, arena- or actor-specific, the explanatory power of the multivariate models was often substantial. Thus, variation in the severity of problems that could plausibly be seen as consequences of civil service arrangements were rather strongly and positively correlated with the extent of civil service coverage in particular states. Similarly, variation in the severity of management difficulties relating to state agency relationships with the federal government were strongly and positively correlated with agency dependence on federal funding. The educational level of state managers—and especially whether they had graduate training in public management or not—was quite strongly associated with greater familiarity with various strategies for improving agency performance.

Differences in the functional responsibilities of state agencies were often associated with differences in the impact wielded by one or another external actor on the affairs of those agencies. Thus, units with criminal justice responsibilities stand out in terms of the impact that state courts exert on agency operations. Finally, those governors who possessed more extensive powers exercised more influence in the state administrative process.

The frequently limited explanatory power of the models developed in this study may also reflect the limits of survey-based public management research. I might have been able to construct more powerful models if I had collected information on a more extended set of independent variables. Still, there are very real limits on how much time busy people can be expected to devote to completing a mail survey, even when most of the questions are of a closed-ended variety. Marginal comments by some of my respondents suggested that the questionnaire that I did use severely tested those limits.

One last point is relevant here. As noted, interstate differences in the severity of particular management problems, the use and efficacy of particular management techniques, and the influence of various actors were frequently minor. At the same time, the multivariate models developed to explain variation in particular phenomena often did not hold up well when they were estimated for particular states. Sometimes the absence of significant relationships reflected the smaller number of respondents in individual states. But it also appears to be the case that factors such as agency size, managerial rank, or functional responsibility, to name but a few independent variables, impact differently on particular dependent variables in different states.

All of the foregoing suggest to me that our understanding of the dynamics of state management might best be advanced by more intensive study of a relatively smaller number of state agencies. An excellent model here is Kaufman's (1981) study of a half dozen federal government bureaus. Unfortunately, even if one limits one's focus to a single state, Kaufman's research methods are highly time- and labor-intensive. One approach might be for the members of a research team to focus on only a single administrative unit each while using a common research framework. Since such a design lacks a comparative state dimension, it would be even better if a larger number of scholars examined a similar set of administrative units in several states. The "field network evaluation methodology" that Nathan and Doolittle (1983) adopted in studying the impact of the Reagan administration's budget cuts on states and localities represents a strategy similar to that which I am suggesting.

I hope that this book has expanded our understanding of the dynamics of public management in the American states. I would also hope that it has helped to define an agenda for future research on those dynamics that might employ the more intensive research strategy just suggested.

APPENDIXES

Comparison of State Samples on Selected Characteristics

	AZ	CA	DE	IN	MI	NY	SD	TN	TX	VT	Overall
Number of responding Administrators	68	149	72	73	125	113	64	60	89	34	847
Response rate	50%	40%	40%	37%	47%	40%	34%	38%	38%	35%	40%
Functional Responsibility of Respondents' Units											
Criminal justice	10%	8%	11%	7%	11%	10%	10%	10%	7%	9%	9%
Economic development	9	2	6	7	8	6	0	2	7	6	5
Education	6	4	14	10	8	9	17	13	11	6	9
Environment/energy	15	12	3	4	4	7	3	3	7	3	7
Health	3	11	13	8	12	12	8	13	7	0	9
Income security/soc. ser.	13	10	8	18	13	5	20	17	15	21	13
Natural resources	9	15	15	7	8	15	14	8	10	12	12
Regulatory	16	13	4	15	16	10	3	13	16	12	12
Staff-fiscal	12	6	10	8	7	10	3	10	3	3	7
Staff-nonfiscal	2	6	1	4	13	5	11	5	7	9	5
Transportation	4	11	11	11	8	8	5	5	10	15	9
Other	0	2	3	1	1	4	3	0	1	3	2
Organizational Rank of Respondents											
Top	29%	13%	13%	30%	15%	10%	16%	25%	24%	32%	18%
Second level	46	56	34	56	50	57	54	50	62	41	52
Third level	25	31	53	14	35	33	30	25	14	27	30
Median staff size of respondents' unit	45	150	35	55	100	125	23	112	76	26	80
Percent of Unit Budget Comprised of Federal Funds											
None	46%	52%	34%	44%	40%	47%	40%	42%	46%	44%	44%
More than half	12	15	21	26	19	15	32	22	15	30	19

Operational Definitions of Measures of Gubernatorial Power and Legislative Capability Reported in Table 7.2

GUBERNATORIAL POWER INDICATORS

As noted in the text, the source for the information on gubernatorial power resources is Beyle (1983).

Tenure Potential

Four-year term, no restraint on reelection = 5; four-year term, one reelection permitted = 4; four-year term, no consecutive reelection permitted = 3; two-year term, no restraint on reelection = 2; two year term, one reelection permitted = 1.

Appointive Power

The scores on this power across the 50 states range from a low of 29 in South Carolina to a high of 76 in New York. The score for each state in the table is based on the governor's powers of appointment in a maximum of 46 functions and offices in each state. The score indicates the degree to which the governor can be assured to have sole power over these functions or offices. For each of the functions, the index is scaled according to the governor's power of appointment using the following formula:

$$\text{Index} = \frac{\text{Values of P1} + \text{P2} + \text{P3} \; \ldots \; (100)}{\text{Maximum Values of P1} + \text{P2} + \text{P3} + \; \ldots \; \text{Pn}}$$

where: P = 5 if governor appoints

4 if governor appoints and one house of legislature must confirm

3 if governor appoints and both houses of legislature must confirm

2 if appointed by departmental director with governor's approval or by governor and council

1 if appointed by departmental director, by a board, by legislature or via civil service

0 if elected by popular vote

and: where the subscript indicates the chief administrator for each of the functions and offices in the state.

The resulting appointive power scores were then grouped by Beyle so that a governor with a score of 29 to 40 = 1 point, 41 to 45 = 2 points, 46 to 50 = 3 points, 51 to 60 = 4 points, 61+ = 5 points.

Budgetmaking Power

5 = Governor has full responsibility for developing budget

4 = Governor shares responsibility with a civil servant or an official appointed by someone else

3 = Governor shares responsibility with legislators

2 = Governor shares responsibility with another popularly elected official

1 = Governor shares responsibility with several others with independent sources of strength

Organization Power

This is defined as the "power to create and abolish offices and to assign and reassign purposes and duties to these offices . . . [which] may be used to confer organizational status and give certain programs, purposes, and constituencies higher priority and easier access to others" (Beyle, 1983, p. 199, citing Flentje, 1981). Beyle is less explicit than might be desired regarding how state scores on this power dimension are calculated. The score is based on such factors as whether the governor and lieutenant governor are elected as a team; whether numerous executive authorities have constitutional status; whether the number of dispersed and fragmented state agencies is relatively small, and whether independently elected boards, commissions, and officials abound. The higher the number the greater a governor's organizational power.

Veto Power

5 = Governor possesses item veto and at least a three-fifth legislative vote is required to override

4 = Governor possesses item veto and at least a majority vote to override is required

3 = Item veto plus more than a majority of members of legislature present voting to override is required

2 = Governor does not possess an item veto but a special legislative majority is required to override

1 = No item veto and simple legislative majority to override

0 = Governor has no veto power of any kind

Combined Index

This is the sum of the scores for each of the individual powers. The average score on this combined index across all 50 states is 19. The range is from 10 in South Carolina to 24 in New York.

INDICATORS OF LEGISLATIVE CAPABILITY

Functionality includes measures of legislative use of time such as restrictions on the frequency, length, or agendas of sessions and interim periods as well as techniques for the management of time and the use of presession time. It also assesses the availability of staff for leaders and members, the adequacy of facilities, structural characteristics relating to manageability (size of houses and and standing committee structure), organization and procedures to expedite the flow of work, and provisions for management and coordination.

Accountability assesses the extent to which a legislature in its structure, organization, and procedure is understandable; the extent to which the process is open to view and information about its actions is available; and the extent to which it gives the individual legislator as full an opportunity as possible—consistent with the need to get the work done—to influence the legislature's actions.

Informedness involves the adequacy of time available to conduct necessary business; the number, facilities, and processes for taking testimony by standing committees; the nature of interim activities, staffing for these activities, and reporting and recording those activities; the form and character of bills; professional staff resources for both general and legal research; and the legislature's capabilities for conducting fiscal review.

Legislative *independence* entails control over the frequency and duration of sessions, a legislature's control of its own expenditures and compensation, and its reapportionment. It also involves legislative independence of the executive branch as manifested in access to information and analysis, veto relationships, and budget powers; its capability for effective oversight of executive branch operations; its relative reliance on interest group lobbyists and processes for avoiding or resolving potential conflicts of interest.

Representativeness involves the clarity of the tie between each individual legislator and his or her district, the diversity of the membership of the legislature (involving qualifications for office, compensation, and voting requirements), and a structure and set of procedures that enable individual legislators to act effectively on behalf of their constituents. The latter is reflected in the size and complexity of the legislature, the diffusion and constraints on leadership, access to resources, treatment of the minority party, the clarity of rules of procedures, and provisions for bill reading.

References

Aberbach. J. D. (1979). Changes in congressional oversight. *American Behavioral Scientist, 22* (May–June), 493–515.

Abney, G., & Lauth, T. P. (1986a). Interest group influence in the states: A view of subsystem politics. Paper presented at the 1986 Annual Meeting of the American Political Science Association.

———. (1986b). *The politics of state and city administration.* Albany: State University of New York Press.

Advisory Commission on Intergovernmental Relations (ACIR). (1985). *The question of state government capability.* Washington, DC: Author.

Altenstetter C., & Bjorkman, J. (1976). The rediscovery of federalism: The impact of federal child health programs on Connecticut state health policy formation and service delivery. In C. O. Jones and R. D. Thomas (eds.), *Policymaking in the federal system* (pp. 217–237). Beverly Hills, CA: Sage Publications.

Baird, L. L. (1969). Big school, small school: A critical examination of the hypothesis. *Journal of Educational Psychology, 60,* 253–260.

Baldwin, J. N. (1990). Perceptions of public versus private sector personnel and informal red tape: Their impact on motivation. *American Review of Public Administration, 20,* 7–26.

Barrilleaux, C., Feiock, R., & Crew, R. (1990). Indicators and correlates of administrative quality in the American states. Paper presented at the 1990 Annual Meeting of the American Political Science Association, San Francisco, August 30.

Benson, G. G. (1986). Rational actors and administrative rules: Legislative veto in the State of Michigan, 1972–1984. Ann Arbor: University Microfilms International Dissertation Information Service (facsimile print of microfilm).

Beyle, T. (1978). The governor as chief legislator. *State Government, 51,* 2–10.

———. (1983). Governors. In Virginia Gray, Herbert Jacob, and Kenneth Vines (eds.), *Politics in the American States* (4th ed.) Boston: Little Brown.

Bidwell, C. E., & Kasarda, J. D. (1975). School district organization and student achievement. *American Sociological Review, 40,* 55–70.

Bingham, R. D., Hawkins, B. W., Frendreis, J. P., & LeBlanc, M. P. (1978). *Profes-*

sional associations as intermediaries in transferring technology to city govern-
ments. Milwaukee: University of Wisconsin.

Bowers, J. R. (1989). Agency responsiveness to the legislative oversight of administrative rulemaking: A case study of rules review in the Illinois General Assembly.
American Review of Public Administration, 19, 217–231.

Bowman, A. O'M., & Kearney, R. C. (1986). *The resurgence of the states.* Englewood
Cliffs, NJ: Prentice-Hall.

Bozeman, B., & Straussman, J. D. (1990). *Public management strategies: Guidelines
for managerial effectiveness.* San Francisco: Jossey-Bass.

Brough, R. K. (1987). Strategies for leaders who do not have a lot of power. *Journal
of State Government, 60,* 157–161.

Brown, D. (1966). The President and the bureaus: Time for a renewal of relationships?
Public Administration Review, 26, 174–182.

Brown, K., & Coulter, P. B. (1983). Subjective and objective measures of policy service delivery. *Public Administration Review, 43,* 50–58.

Browne, W. P. (1985). Municipal managers and policy: A partial test of the Svara
dichotomy-duality model. *Public Administration Review, 45,* 620–622.

Brudney, J. L., & Hebert, F. T. (1987). State agencies and their environments: Examining the influence of important external actors. *The Journal of Politics, 49,*
186–206.

Burke, C. G. (1989). Themes from the history of public administration: Rethinking our
past. In J. Rabin, W. B. Hildreth, & G. J. Miller (eds.), *Handbook of public
administration* (pp. 43–103). New York: Marcel Dekker.

Campbell, J. P., Bownas, D. E., Peterson, M. G., & Dunnette, M. D. (eds.). (1974).
*The Measurement of organizational effectiveness: A review of relevant research
and opinion.* San Diego: Navy Personnel Research and Development Center.

Campbell, R., & Bendick, M., Jr. (1977). *A public assistance data book.* Washington,
DC: The Urban Institute.

Chi, K. S. (1988). Privatization and contracting for state services. In *The book of the
states: 1988–89.* Lexington, KY: Council of State Governments.

Christenson, J. A., & Sachs, C. E. (1980). The impact of government size and number
of administrative units on the quality of public services. *Administrative Science
Quarterly, 25,* 89–101.

Chubb, J. E. (1983). *Interest groups and the bureaucracy: The politics of energy.* Stanford, CA: Stanford University Press.

Citizens Conference on State Legislatures (CCSL). (1971). *The sometimes governments:
A critical study of the 50 American legislatures.* Kansas City, MO: Author.

Clynch, E. (1976). The nationalization of block grant spending: An initial determination. *Publius, 6,* 71–80.

Cobb, R. W., & Elder, C. D. (1983). *Participation in American politics: The dynamics
of agenda-building* (2nd ed.). Baltimore: Johns Hopkins University Press.

Cohen, S., & Ingersoll, T. G. (1985). The effect of personnel rules on line managers:
The case of state hazardous waste clean-up organizations. *Public Personnel
Management, 14,* 33–39.

Cole, R. T. (1989). Michigan Governor Blanchard: Managing through messages. *Journal of State Government, 62,* 147–152.

Common Cause. (1982). *The status of sunset in the states: A Common Cause report.*
Washington, DC: Author.

Conant, J. K. (1986). Reorganization and the bottom line. *Public Administration Review, 46,* 48–56.

———. (1988). In the shadow of Wilson and Brownlow: Executive branch reorganization in the states, 1965 to 1987. *Public Administration Review, 48,* 892–902.

———. (1989). The growing importance of state government. In J. L. Perry (ed.), *Handbook of public administration.* San Francisco: Jossey-Bass.

Connolly, T., Conlon, E., & Deutsch, S. (1980). Organizational effectiveness: A multiple-constituency approach. *Academy of Management Review, 5,* 211–217.

Cooper, P. (1988). *Hard judicial choices: Federal district judges and state and local officials.* New York: Oxford University Press.

Coyer, B. W., & Schwerin, D. S. (1981). Bureaucratic regulation and farmer protest in the Michigan PBB contamination case. *Rural Sociology, 46,* 703–723.

Craft, R. (1977). *Legislative follow through: Profiles of oversight in five states.* New Brunswick, NJ: Eagleton Institute of Politics, Rutgers University.

Dalton, D. R., Todor, W. D., Spendolini, M. J., Fielding, G. J., & Porter, L. W. (1980). Organization structure and performance: A critical review. *Academy of Management Review, 5,* 49–64.

Daneke, G. A., & Kolbus-Edwards, P. (1979). Survey research for public administrators. *Public Administration Review, 39* (September/October), 421–426.

DeNicholas, R., & Lutz, C. F. (1979). The New Jersey merit system in transition. *Public Personnel Management, 8,* 1–6.

Derthick, M. (1970). *The influence of federal grants.* Cambridge: Harvard University Press.

Diver, C. (1979). The judge as political broker: Superintending structural change in public institutions. *Virginia Law Review, 65* (February), 43–106.

Dometrius, N. C. (1979). The efficacy of a governor's formal powers. *State Government, 52,* 121–125.

———. (1981). Some consequences of state reform. *State Government, 54,* 93–98.

Downs, G. W., & Larkey, P. D. (1986). *The search for government efficiency.* Philadelphia: Temple University Press.

Dresang, D. L. (1978). Public personnel reform: A summary of state government activity. *Public Personnel Management, 7,* 287–294.

———. (1982). Diffusion of civil service reform: The federal and state governments. *Review of Public Personnel Administration, 2* (2), 35–47.

———. (1991). *Public personnel management and public policy* (2nd edition). New York: Longman.

Drury, J. W. (1977). Sunset laws: A passing fad or a major development? *Midwest Review of Public Administration, 11* (*1*), 61–64.

Duncombe, S., & Kinney, R. (1986). The politics of state appropriation increases. *The Journal of State Government, 59,* 113–123.

Durning, D. (1986). The governor's internal campaign: Managing state government by influencing attitudes and values. *Journal of State Government, 59,* 77–81.

Elling, R. C. (1979). The utility of state legislative casework as a means of oversight. *Legislative Studies Quarterly, 4,* 353–379.

———. (1980a). Contours and determinants of gubernatorial impact upon state administrative agencies: A two state study. Paper presented at the annual meeting of the Southern Political Science Association, Atlanta, November.

———. (1980b). State legislative casework and state administrative performance. *Administration and Society, 12,* 327–356.

———. (1980c). State legislative impact on the state administrative process: Scope and efficacy. Paper presented at the annual meeting of the Midwest Political Science Association, Chicago, April.

———. (1983). State bureaucracies. In V. Gray, H. Jacob, and K. N. Vines (eds.), *Politics in the American states: A comparative analysis* (4th ed.) (pp. 244–283). Boston: Little, Brown.

———. (1984). State legislative influence in the administrative process: Consequences and constraints. *Public Administration Quarterly, 7,* 457–481.

———. (1985). Federal Dollars and Federal Clout in State Administration: A Test of 'Regulatory' and 'Picket Fence' Models of Intergovernmental Relations. Paper presented at the annual meeting of the Midwest Political Science Association, Chicago.

———. (1986). Civil service, collective bargaining and personnel-related impediments to effective state management. *Review of Public Personnel Administration, 6,* 73–93.

———. (1987). Managing the states: Problems and performance. Paper presented at the annual meeting of the American Political Science Association, Chicago.

———. (1988). Federalist tool or Federalist plot: Michigan responds to the Reagan block grants. In P. K. Eisinger and W. Gormley (eds.), *The Midwest response to the new federalism* (pp. 55–96). Madison: University of Wisconsin Press.

———. (1990). Bureaucracy. In V. Gray, H. Jacob, & R. Albritton (eds.), *Politics in the American states: A comparative analysis* (5th ed.) (pp. 287–330). New York: Scott, Foresman/Little, Brown.

Elling, R. C. & Schottenfels, D. (1980). The state administrative influence matrix. Paper presented at the 41st National Conference of the American Society for Public Administration, San Francisco.

Elliot, R. (1985). Personnel professional and state employee perceptions of merit system procedures: What is the level of support? *Review of Public Personnel Administration, 5* (Summer), 26–41.

Emmert, M. A. (1986), Assessing effectiveness: Toward a pragmatic approach for public sector organizations. *State and Local Government Review, 18 (2),* 82–88.

Ethridge, M. E. (1981). Legislative-administrative interaction as "intrusive access": An empirical analysis. *Journal of Politics, 43,* 473–492.

———. (1984). Consequences of legislative review of agency regulations in three U.S. states. *Legislative Studies Quarterly, 9,* 161–178.

Fiedler, F. E., & Gillo, M. W. (1974). Correlates of performance in community colleges. *Journal of Higher Education, 45,* 672–681.

Flentje, H. E. (1981). Governor as manager: A political assessment. *State Government, 54,* 76–81.

Fox, D. (1974). *Politics of city and state bureaucracy.* Pacific Palisades, CA: Goodyear.

Francis, W. (1967). *Legislative issues in the 50 states: A comparative analysis.* Chicago: Rand, McNally.

Frank, S. (1978). State supreme courts and administrative agencies. *State Government, 51,* 119–123.

Frederickson, H. G. (1980). *New public administration*. University: University of Alabama Press.

Freedman, Anne. (1988). Doing battle with the patronage army: Politics, courts and personnel administration in Chicago. *Public Administration Review, 48,* 847–859.

Fried, R. C. (1976). *Performance in American bureaucracy*. Boston: Little, Brown.

Friedman, B., & Dunbar, L. J. (1971). *Grants management in educatuion: Federal impact on state agencies*. Chicago: Public Administration Service.

Friedman, R. S., Klein, B. W., & Romani, J. H. (1966). Administrative agencies and the publics they serve. *Public Administration Review, 26,* 192–204.

Fry, B. R. (1989). Five great issues in the profession of public administration. In. J. Rabin, W. B. Hildreth, & G. J. Miller (eds)., *Handbook of public administration* (pp. 1027–1075). New York: Marcel Dekker.

Fukuhara, R. S. (1977). Productivity improvement in cities. *The municipal yearbook-1977* (pp. 193–200). Washington, DC: International City Management Association.

Garnett, J. L., & Levine, C. H. (1980). State executive branch reorganization: Patterns and perspectives. *Administration and Society, 12,* 227–276.

Glisson, C. A., & Martin, P. Y. (1980). Productivity and efficiency in human service organizations as related to structure, size and age. *Academy of Management Journal, 23,* 21–37.

Gooding, R. Z., & Wagner, J. A. (1985). A meta-analytic review of the relationship between size and performance: The productivity and efficiency of organizations and their subunits. *Administrative Science Quarterly, 30,* 462–481.

Goodsell, C. T. (ed.). (1981). *The public encounter: Where state and citizen meet*. Bloomington: Indiana University Press.

Goodsell, C. T. (1985). *The case for bureaucracy* (2nd ed.). Chatham, NJ: Chatham House.

Gormley, W. T. (1983). *The politics of public utility regulation*. Pittsburgh: University of Pittsburgh Press.

———. (1986a). Muscles and prayers: Bureau-Busting in the 1970s. Paper presented at the 1986 Annual Meeting of the American Political Science Association, Washington, DC, August 28–31.

———. (1986b). The representation revolution: Reforming state regulation through public representation. *Administration and Society, 18,* 179–196.

———. (1989a). Custody battles in state administration. In C. Van Horn (Ed.), *The state of the states*. Washington, DC: CQ Press.

———. (1989b). *Taming the bureaucracy: Muscles, prayers, and other strategies*. Princeton, NJ: Princeton University Press.

Goyder, J. (1985). Face-to-Face interviews and mailed questionnaires: The net difference in response rates. *Public Opinion Quarterly, 49,* 234–252.

Greene, K. R. (1982). Municipal administrators' receptivity to citizens' and elected officials' contacts. *Public Administration Review, 42,* 346–353.

Gruber, J. E. (1987). *Controlling bureaucracies*. Berkeley and Los Angeles: University of California Press.

Haas, P. J., & Wright, D. S. (1987). The changing profile of state administrators. *The Journal of State Government, 60,* 270–278.

Hale, G. F. (1979). Federal courts and the state budgetary process. *Administration and Society, 11,* 357–368.

Hale, G., & Palley, M. L. (1981). *The politics of federal grants.* Washington, DC: Congressional Quarterly Press.

Hamm, K., & Robertson, R. D. (1981). Factors influencing the adoption of new methods of legislative oversight in the U.S. states. *Legislative Studies Quarterly, 6,* 133–150.

Harriman, L., & Straussman, J. (1983). Do judges determine budget decisions? Federal court decisions in prison reform and state spending for corrections. *Public Administration Review, 43,* 343–351.

Hatry, H. P. (1989). Determining the effectiveness of government services. In J. L. Perry (ed.), *Handbook of public administration* (pp. 469–482). San Francisco: Jossey-Bass.

Hebert, F. T., & Brudney, J. L. (1988). Controlling administrative agencies in a changing federal system: Avenues of gubernatorial influence. *American Review of Public Administration, 18,* 135–147.

Hebert, F. T., Brudney, J. L., & Wright, D. S. (1983). Gubernatorial influence and state bureaucracy. *American Politics Quarterly, 11,* 243–264.

Hebert, F. T., & Wright, D. S. (1982). State administrators: How representative? How professional? *State Government, 55,* 22–28.

Henry, G. T., & Harms, S. W. (1987). Board involvement in policy making and administration. *Public Administration Review, 47,* 153–159.

Holzer, M. (1984). Public administration under pressure. In M. Holzer and S. S. Nagel (eds.), *Productivity and public policy* (pp. 71–86). Beverly Hills, CA.: Sage.

Hopkins, A. H. (1980). Perceptions of employment discrimination in the public sector. *Public Administration Review, 40,* 131–137.

Horton, R. D., Lewin, D., & Kuhn, J. (1976). Some impacts of collective bargaining on local government: A diversity thesis. *Administration and Society, 7,* 497–516.

Hyde, A. C. (1991). Productivity management for public sector organizations. In J. S. Ott, A. C. Hyde, & J. M. Shafritz (eds.), *Public management: The essential readings* (pp. 372–388). Chicago: Nelson-Hall.

Ingram, H. (1977). Policy implementation through bargaining: The case of federal grants-in-aid. *Public Policy, 25,* 499–526.

Johnson, S. F. (1983). The legislative veto in the states. *State Government, 56,* 99–102.

Jones, R. (1982). Legislative review of administrative rules: An update. *State Legislative Report—Legislative Management Series, 7* (April), 4.

Katz, D. B., Gutek, B., Kahn, R. L., & Barton, E. (1975). *Bureaucratic encounters: A pilot study in the evaluation of government services.* Ann Arbor, MI: Institute of Social Research.

Kaufman, H. (1956). Emerging conflicts in the doctrines of public administration. *American Political Science Review, 50,* 1057–1073.

———. (1977). *Red Tape: Its origins, uses and abuses.* Washington, DC: The Brookings Institution.

———. (1981). *The administrative behavior of federal bureau chiefs.* Washington, DC: The Brookings Institution.

Kearney, R. C. (1990). Sunset: A survey and analysis of the state experience. *Public Administration Review, 50,* 49–57.

Kimberly, J. R. (1976). Organizational size and the structuralist perspective: A review, critique and proposal. *Administrative Science Quarterly, 21,* 571–597.

Kingdon, J. W. (1984). *Agendas, alternatives, and public policies.* Boston: Little, Brown.

Klemanksi, J. S., & Maschke, K. J. (Forthcoming). Managing freedom of information laws: A survey of state-level departments. *Advances in social science and computers, 3.* Greenwich, CT.: JAI Press.

Lau, A. W., Newman, A. R., & Broedling, L. A. (1980). The nature of managerial work in the public sector. *Public Administration Review, 40,* 513–520.

Lauth, T. P. (1984). Methods of agency head selection and gubernatorial influence over agency appropriations. *Public Administration Quarterly, 7,* 396–409.

Leege, D., & Francis, W. (1974). *Political research: Design, measurement and analysis.* New York: Basic Books.

Lewin, D. (1983). Implications of concession bargaining: Lessons from the public sector. *Monthly Labor Review* (March), 33–35.

Lewin, D., & Horton, R. D. (1975). The impact of collective bargaining on the merit system in government. *The Arbitration Journal, 30,* 199–211.

Loney, T. (1989). Public sector labor relations research: The first generation. *Public Personnel Management, 18,* 162–175.

Lowi, T. (1964). American business, public policy, case studies and political theory. *World Politics, 16,* 677–715.

Lynch, T., & Gabris, G. (1981). Obstacles to effective management. *The Bureaucrat, 10 (1),* 8–14.

Lyons, W., & Freeman, P. K. (1984). Sunset legislation and the legislative process in Tennessee. *Legislative Studies Quarterly, 9,* 151–159.

Mainzer, L. (1973). *Political bureaucracy.* Glenview, IL: Scott, Foresman.

March, J. G., & Olson, J. P. (1983). Organizing political life: What administrative reorganization tells us about governing. *American Political Science Review, 77,* 281–296.

Marini, Frank (ed.). (1971). *Toward a new public administration: The Minnowbrook perspective.* New York: Chandler.

Marsh, J. (1977). Public personnel employees' perceptions of a state merit system. *Public Personnel Management, 6* (March–April), 93–97.

McConnell, G. (1966). *Private power and American democracy.* New York: Alfred A. Knopf.

Meier, K. J. (1979). *Politics and the bureaucracy.* Belmont, CA: Duxbury Press.

———. (1980). Executive reorganization of government: Impact on employment and expenditures. *American Journal of Political Science, 24,* 396–412.

———. (1981). Ode to patronage: A critical analysis of two recent Supreme Court decisions. *Public Administration Review, 41,* 558–563.

———. (1987). *Politics and the bureaucracy: Policymaking in the fourth branch of government* (2nd ed.). Monterey, CA: Brooks/Cole.

Merton, R. (1940). Bureaucratic structure and personality. *Social Forces, 17,* 560–568.

Methe, D. T., & Perry, J. L. (1980). The impacts of collective bargaining on local government services: A review of research. *Public Administration Review, 40,* 359–371.

Michigan Department of Civil Service. (1987). *Public perceptions of state employment in Michigan.* Lansing, MI: Author.

Michigan Education Report. (1989). Blanchard says Michigan schools can lead the nation. (November-December), 1, 3.

Miller, C. (1987). State administrator perceptions of the policy influence of other actors: Is less better? *Public Administration Review, 47,* 239–245.

Morehouse, S. M. (1981). *States politics, parties and policy.* New York: Holt, Rinehart, Winston.

Murphy, J. (1973). The education bureaucracies implement novel policy: The politics of Title I of ESEA, 1965–1972. In A. P. Sindler (ed.) *Policy and politics in America* (pp. 160–198). Boston: Little, Brown.

Nathan, R., and Doolittle, F., and Associates. (1983). *The consequences of cuts: The effects of the Reagan domestic program on state and local government.* Princeton, NJ: Princeton Urban and Regional Research Center.

National Academy of Public Administration. (1983). *Revitalizing federal management.* Washington, DC: Author.

National Association of State Budget Officers. (1975). *The status of productivity measurement in state governments: An initial examination.* Washington, DC: The Urban Institute.

Nelson, B. J. (1980). Helping-seeking from public authorities: Who arrives at the agency door? *Policy Sciences, 12,* 175–192.

———. (1984). *Making an issue of child abuse: Political agenda setting for social problems.* Chicago: University of Chicago Press.

Neustadt, R. (1960). *Presidential power.* New York: Signet.

Nigro, F. A., & Nigro, L. G. (1977). Public sector unionism. In C. Levine (ed.), *Managing human resources* (pp. 141–157). Beverly Hills, CA: Sage.

O'Toole, L. J. (1989). The public administrator's role in setting the policy agenda. In J. L. Perry (ed.), *Handbook of public administration* (pp. 225–236). San Francisco: Jossey-Bass.

Perry, J., & Kraemer, K. (1980). Chief executive support and innovation adoption. *Administration and Society, 12,* 158–177.

Peters, B. G. (1984). *The politics of bureaucracy.* New York: Longman.

Pfeffer, J., & Salancik, G. R. (1978). *The external control of organizations.* New York: Harper and Row.

Pfiffner, J. P. (1983). The challenge of federal management in the 1980s. *Public Administration Quarterly, 7,* 162–182.

———. (1981–82). Management and central controls reconsidered. *The Bureaucrat, 11* (Winter), 13–17.

Poister, T. H., & McGowan, R. P. (1984). The use of management tools in municipal government: A national survey. *Public Administration Review, 44,* 215–223.

Poister, T. H., & Streib, G. (1989). Management tools in municipal government: Trends over the past decade. *Public Administration Review, 49,* 240–248.

Polsby, N. (1984). *Political innovation in America: The politics of policy initiation.* New Haven, CT: Yale University Press.

Porter, L. W., & Von Maanen, J. (1983). Task accomplishment and the management of time. In J. L. Perry and D. L. Kraemer (eds.), *Public management* (pp. 212–224). Palo Alto, CA.: Mayfield.

Prottas, J. M. (1981). The cost of free services: Organizational impediments to access to public services. *Public Administration Review, 41,* 526–534.

Public Administration Review. (1986). Symposium: Toward a government information policy—FOIA at 20. *46,* 603–639.

Rainey, H. G. (1979). Perceptions of incentives in business and government: Implications for civil service reform. *Public Administration Review, 39,* 440–448.

———. (1989). Public management: Recent research on the political context and managerial roles, structures and behaviors. *Journal of Management, 15,* 229–250.

Reese, L., & Ohren, J. (1987). The impact of collective bargaining in four cities: The diversity thesis revisited. *Review of Public Personnel Administration, 8,* 68–81.

Reeves, M. M. (1990). The states as polities: Reformed, reinvigorated, resourceful. *The Annals, 509,* 83–93.

Rehfuss, J. (1989). Maintaining quality and accountability in a period of privatization. In R. E. Cleary, N. L. Henry, and Associates (eds.), *Managing public programs* (pp. 211–230). San Francisco: Jossey-Bass.

Renfrow, P. D., & Houston, D. J. (1987). A comparative analysis of rulemaking provisions in state administrative procedure acts. *Policy Studies Review, 6,* 657–665.

Renfrow, P. D., West, W. F., & Houston, D. J. (1986). Rulemaking provisions in state administrative procedure acts. *Public Administration Quarterly, 9,* 358–381.

Roberts, D. (1988). A new breed of public executive: Top level exempt managers in state government. *Review of Public Personnel Administration, 8,* 20–36.

Robertson, F. D. (1988–89). A way through the woods. *The Bureaucrat, 17* (Winter), 41–43.

Rochefort, D. A., & Boyer, C. A. (1988). Use of public opinion data in public administration: Health care polls. *Public Administration Review, 48,* 649–660.

Rockman, B. A. (1985). Legislative-executive relations and legislative oversight. In G. Loewenberg et al. (eds.), *Handbook of legislative research* (pp. 519–572). Cambridge, MA.: Harvard University Press.

Rosenbloom, D. H. (1983). Public administrative theory and the separation of powers. *Public Administration Review, 43,* 219–227.

———. (1990). What every public personnel manager should know about the Constitution. In S. W. Hays & R. C. Kearney (eds.), *Public personnel administration: Problems and prospects* (pp. 39–56). Englewood Cliffs, NJ.: Prentice-Hall.

Rosenthal, A. (1981). Legislative behavior and legislative oversight. *Legislative Studies Quarterly, 6,* 115–131.

Rosenthal, D. B. (1980). Bargaining analysis in intergovernmental relations. *Publius, 6,* 71–80.

Rourke, F. E. (1976). *Bureaucracy, politics and public policy* (2nd ed.). Boston: Little, Brown.

———. (1984). *Bureaucracy, politics, and public policy* (3rd ed.). Boston: Little, Brown.

Sabato, L. (1983). *Goodbye to good-time Charlie* (2nd ed.). Washington, DC: Congressional Quarterly Press.

Salamon, L. (1981). The goals of reorganization: A framework for analysis. *Administration and Society, 12,* 471–500.

Saltzstein, G. H. (1985). Conceptualizing Bureaucratic Responsiveness. *Administration and Society, 17,* 283–306.

Savas, E. S., & Ginsberg, S. G. (1973). The civil service: A meritless system? *The Public Interest, 32*, 591–604.

Scheirer, M. A. (1978). Program participants' positive perceptions: Psychological conflict of interest in program evaluation. *Evaluation Quarterly, 2*, 53–70.

Schick, A. (1971). *Budget innovations in the states*. Washington, DC: The Brookings Institution.

———. (1979). *Zero-base '80: The status of zero-base budgeting in the states*. Washington, DC: The Urban Institute.

Shafritz, J. M. (1975). *Public personnel management: The heritage of civil service reform*. New York: Praeger.

Shafritz, J. M., Hyde, A. C., & Rosenbloom, D. H. (1981). *Personnel management in government* (2nd ed.). New York: Marcel Dekker.

Sharkansky, I. (1968). Agency requests, gubernatorial support, and budget success in state legislatures. *American Political Science Review, 26:* 1220–1231.

———. (1971). State administrators in the political process. In H. Jacob and K. Vines (eds.), *Politics in the American states* (2nd ed.) (pp. 238–271). Boston: Little, Brown.

Sigelman, L. (1976). The quality of administration: An exploration in the American states. *Administration and Society, 8*, 107–144.

Smyth, D. S. (1982). The relationship between size and performance of mail sorting offices. *Human Relations, 35*, 567–586.

Stahl, O. G. (1983). *Public personnel administration* (8th ed.). New York: Harper and Row.

Stipak, B. (1979). Citizen satisfaction with urban services: Potential misuse as a performance indicator. *Public Administration Review, 39*, 46–52.

———. (1980a). Local governments' use of citizen surveys. *Public Administration Review, 40*, 521–525.

———. (1980b). Using clients to evaluate programs. Paper presented at a symposium, The Public Encounter: Delivering Human Services in the 1980s. Virginia Polytechnic Institute and State University, January 9–11.

Straussman, J. D. (1986). Courts and public purse strings: Have portraits of budgeting missed something? *Public Administration Review, 46*, 345–351.

Svara, J. H. (1985). Dichotomy and duality: Reconceptualizing the relationship between policy and administration in council-manager cities. *Public Administration Review, 45*, 221–232.

Tanimoto, H. S., & Inaba, G. F. (1985). State employee bargaining: Policy and organization. *Monthly Labor Review, 108 (4)*, 51–55.

Thomas, C. L. (1990). The policy/administration continuum: Wisconsin Natural Resources Board decisions. *Public Administration Review, 50*, 446–449.

Thomas, C. S., & Hrebenar, R. J. (1990). Interest groups in the states. In V. Gray, H. Jacob, & R. B. Albritton (eds.), *Politics in the American states* (5th ed.) (pp. 123–158). Glenview, IL: Scott, Foresman/Little, Brown Higher Education.

Thomas, R. (1976). Intergovernmental coordination in the implementation of national air and water pollution policies. In C. O. Jones and R. D. Thomas (eds.), *Policymaking in the federal system* (pp. 129–148). Beverly Hills, CA: Sage publications.

Thompson, J. A. (1986). State legislative reform: Another look, one more time, again. *Polity, 19,* 27–41.

———. (1987). Agency requests, gubernatorial support, and budget success in state legislatures revisited. *The Journal of Politics, 49,* 756–779.

U.S. Congress, Senate Committee on Government Operations (1973). *Confidence and concern: Citizens view American government.* 93rd Congress, 1st session. Washington, DC: U.S. Government Printing Office.

U.S. General Accounting Office. (1980). *Proposed changes in federal matching and maintenance of effort requirements for state and local governments.* GGD-81–7. Washington, DC: Author.

Van Horn, C. E. (1989). The entrepreneurial states. In C. E. Van Horn (ed.), *The state of the states* (pp. 209–221). Washington, DC: CQ Press.

Waldo, D. (1980). *The enterprise of public administration.* Novato, CA: Chandler and Sharp.

Walker, J. L., Jr. (1991) *Mobilizing interest groups in America: Patrons, professions, and movements.* Prepared for publication by J. D. Aberbach, F. R. Baumgartner, T. L. Gais, D. C. King, M. A. Peterson, & K. L. Scheppele. Ann Arbor: The University of Michigan Press.

Washnis, G. (ed.). (1980). *Productivity improvement handbook for state and local government.* New York: John Wiley.

Weick, K. E. (1979). *The social psychology of organizing* (2nd ed.). Reading, MA: Addison-Wesley.

Weinberg, M. W. (1977). *Managing the state.* Cambridge, MA.: MIT Press.

Wellington, H., & Winter, R. (1971). *The unions and the cities.* Washington, DC: The Brookings Institution.

Whorton, J., & Worthley, J. (1981). A perspective on the challenges of public management: Environmental paradox and organizational culture. *Academy of Management Review, 6,* 357–361.

Wilson, G. K. (1981). *Interest groups in the United States.* Oxford: Clarendon Press.

Wilson, J. Q. (1967). The bureaucracy problem. *Public Interest,* No. 6, 3–9.

———. (1973). *Political organizations.* New York: Basic Books.

———. (1989). *Bureaucracy: What government agencies do and why they do it.* New York: Basic Books.

Wright, D. S. (1967). Executive leadership in state administration. *Midwest Journal of Political Science, 11,* 1–26.

———. (1978). *Understanding intergovernmental relations.* North Scituate, MA: Duxbury.

———. (1988). *Understanding intergovernmental relations* (3rd ed.). Pacific Grove, CA: Brooks/Cole.

———. (1990). *Information and introductory materials on ASAP (American State Administrators Project).* Chapel Hill: University of North Carolina (mimeo).

Wright, D. S., & Light, A. (1977). State administrators in the policy process. Paper presented at the 1977 annual meeting of the Southern Political Science Association.

Wright, D. S., Wagner, M., & McAnaw, R. (1977). State administrators: Their changing characteristics. *State Government, 50,* 152–159.

Wyner, A. (1968). Gubernatorial relations with legislators and administrators. *State Government, 41,* 199–203.

———. (1985). The governor as administrator. In J. Rabin and D. Dodd (eds.), *State and local government administration* (pp. 225–244). New York: Marcel Dekker.

Zeigler, H. (1983). Interest groups in the states. In V. Gray, H. Jacob, and K. Vines (eds.), *Politics in the American States* (4th ed.) (pp. 97–131). Boston: Little, Brown.

Index

About the Author

RICHARD C. ELLING is Associate Professor of Political Science at Wayne State University in Detroit where he teaches courses in state politics and policy, public management and bureaucratic politics and has also directed the Graduate Program in Public Administration. A former state budget analyst, Professor Elling has also taught at Wichita State University and the University of Kentucky. In addition to various articles and chapters on issues of state management, his more recently published work includes articles and book chapters on enterprise zones as a state economic development strategy and changing intergovernmental relations in the 1980s.